ACTS OF THE APOSTLES

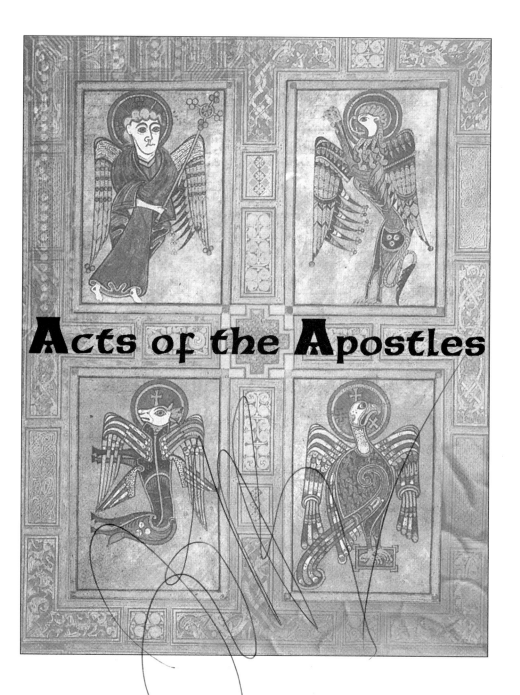

Acts of the Apostles

JOHN F. X. SUNDMAN

MIND OVER MATTER VOL. RED
ROSALITA ASSOCIATES TISBURY

This is a work of fiction. All resemblances to real people and actual events are coincidental.

Rosalita Associates
Greenwood Avenue, Tisbury MA 02568
www.rosalitaassociates.com

Book design by John Hallett, cover design after "The Four Evangelists," from the Book of Kells. Book of Kells copyright © Trinity College, Dublin

Music and lyrics to "The Air" and "El Monte Legion Stadium" are from the album "Uncle Meat" by (Frank Zappa and) The Mothers of Invention.

Music and lyrics to "Pound" and "Andy Fell" are from the album "In a Roman Mood" by Human Sexual Response.

Music and lyrics to "Uh-oh" are from the album "Uh-oh" by Rosenshontz.

The description of Wilder Penfield's work is paraphrased from *Göedel, Escher, Bach*, by Douglas Hofstadter.

Nick and Casey's hack is based upon the article "Diary of a Hacker Break-in" in *Client-Server* magazine.

The phrase "cigarette paper upon which the bumblebees have urinated" is taken from the marvelous poem "Taking a walk with you" by Kenneth Koch.

The character Monty Meekman speaks one sentence that was cribbed verbatim from *A Bend in the River*, by V.S. Naipaul.

Citations from the work of Abraham Maslow and Vannavar Bush are as appear in the text.

ISBN 1-929752-13-X
Printed and bound in the United States of America.
5 4 3 2 1

for Betty Burton, of Boeke Road, Evansville
My N-dimensional isoelectric focusing
Polyacrylamide bride

And for her mother Jo,
Who I hope forgives me the naughty bits

And in memory of her father Gene
Whom I loved

Thus it is clear that the human race has at best a very limited capacity for solving even straightforward social problems. How then is it going to solve the far more difficult and subtle problem of reconciling freedom with technology? Technology presents clear-cut material advantages, whereas freedom is an abstraction that means different things to different people, and its loss is easily obscured by propaganda and fancy talk.

Ted Kaczynsky
"Industrial Society and Its Future"

We have reached an age of cheap complex devices of great reliability; and something is bound to come of it.

Vannevar Bush
"As we may think"

∞ I ∞

BEAST

Chapter 1

Todd Griffith was going to debug Kali or die trying.

Thirty-six strobe lines—an electroencephalogram of the Kali chip's brain waves—danced in parallel from left to right across the four monochrome monitors in his cluttered office. The answer to the riddle lay hidden within them, and he knew that if he looked hard enough he would eventually find it. Unless, of course, he went mad first.

The chip was six months off schedule, and before Kali no chip of Todd's had ever been late by so much as a millisecond. It was the curse of the new guy. It had to be. The original design team of Todd and Casey had met their milestones with monotonous regularity. Then management had stepped in with characteristic stupidity, reassigning Casey to some skunkworks kludge and replacing her with Pavel the Weirdo. For the last nine months, ever since Pavel had taken over as Todd's junior partner, glitches had popped up with distressing frequency. Things that had worked before suddenly stopped working. And although it was tempting to blame Pavel for the bugs, they always turned out to have been there in Todd's logic all along, lying dormant. Week by week Pavel added more capability to the Kali, and week by week this additional logic exposed the weaknesses in Todd's original architecture, as a cantilever added to the tenth floor of a building might expose a flaw in the foundation. Todd, in his arrogance, had built very little debug time into the schedule. And, being a hardware guy, he resolutely eschewed Brooks' famous dictum to "take no small slips." Therefore every new bug meant a new small schedule slip, and every time the schedule slipped management became exponentially more pissed—and Todd's life became exponentially more wretched.

If Casey were still on the project Todd wouldn't be in this mess. If Casey were still on the project, the design would be done by now and some silicon foundry in Texas or Sunnyvale would be cranking out Kalies like jellybeans. Casey would have found work-arounds for the subtle flaws in Todd's logic—she always did. If Todd's specification called for a two microsecond wait-state, Casey's logic would have tolerated any value between one and three. Casey accommodated Todd, subordinated her design goals to his. She reacted instinctively to the feel of his design—as a junior surgeon might address herself to a wound in the scalp so that the senior surgeon could focus his attention on the bullet in the brain.

Pavel wasn't like that. If two microseconds were specified, then Pavel's circuitry demanded two microseconds. Not one, not three, nor even 1.9 or 2.1. Pavel claimed to be a purist when it came to Very Large Scale Integration. Todd thought that 'anal retentive' was a better term.

But he had to give the devil his due. Pavel himself might be an unfriendly, humorless, compulsively orderly and geeky weirdo, but Pavel's designs were magnificent. They were economical of power, heat, real estate, and cycles. They were, in a word, cool, and anybody who knew anything about the aesthetics of VLSI design could see that. Pavel's logic demanded precision, but it paid good dividends. There was no denying that the chip that would ultimately result from the collaboration between Todd and Pavel was going to be vastly more cool than the one originally conceived by Todd and Casey. Therefore it was no good bitching to management about Pavel. Management could clearly see that coolness came from Pavel and schedule slippage came from Todd. Besides, there was no way he could blame an interface bug on the junior designer when his own circuitry didn't meet the spec. So whenever a new bug appeared, Todd owned it. He was not used to owning bugs, and he didn't like it.

As irritating and embarrassing as these bugs had been, they had been relatively easy to diagnose and correct. They were nothing but timing glitches, the kind any smart college kid working on his first chip would be expected to handle. You could find a timing glitch with the silicon equivalent of a flashlight, and you could fix it with the silicon equivalent of string and bubble gum. In the nine months that Pavel had been working on the Kali project, Todd had found and fixed forty-seven such bugs, with an average elapsed time of just four days from the time a report was opened in the bug-track database to the time it was closed. Today, March 28, 1990, only one open bug remained.

But this one was no simple timing glitch, and there was no simple fix for it. It was different from any bug Todd had met in nine years of designing computers for a living. It was a phantom. Irreproducible. Subtle. And fundamentally impossible. Bugtrack number K666. The Beast.

The Kali would run successfully for hundreds of millions—hundreds of *billions*—of cycles, then inexplicably shit the bed, as if deciding that *just this one time* two plus two equaled seventeen, or that just this one time the letter 'x' fell between 'q' and 'r' in the alphabet. Then Kali would resume giving the right answer, failing only once until a power-down and reset, and never, ever repeating the same mistake. It was like that Charles Addams cartoon where a barber holds a mirror to the back of a customer's head to produce an infinite regression of faces in the mirror in front of him, and the seventh face is a monster. The Beast was a monster. It was one true, hairy, son-of-a-bitchin' bug.

Retrospective diagnostics proved that the floating-point section of Kali's Arithmetic Logic Unit was unmistakably, and correctly, executing orders that it had not yet received and that the early arrival of results from the floating point messed up fifteen dependent steps elsewhere in the device. Clairvoyance in an ALU was an intriguing capability, but at this point in his life Todd was much more interested in the prosaic than in the paranormal. Since he didn't really believe that Kali had supernatural powers, he had to wonder if something almost as unexpected was going on.

He was certain that the Beast was caused by a race condition, when electrons on separate paths towards a common logic gate wound up in a dead heat, and the gate could not determine who got there first. When that happened the output from the gate would be unpredictable. Debugging a race condition was usually the most satisfying part of chip design, but chasing the Beast had long ago ceased being fun. How could the *decode* be working correctly if the *fetch* had failed? Unless the laws of the universe had been suspended within the confines of his chip, it simply wasn't possible. And yet it happened. How?

Todd had been hunting the Beast relentlessly for three months now. He hardly ever left the Mill. If he wasn't in the lab huddled over prototype silicon with probes and oscilloscopes he was in his cramped office running simulations and poring over schematics. Other than short exchanges with Pavel, he spoke to virtually nobody. He hadn't answered his phone or e-mail in a month. His food came from Mill vending machines. He slept on the floor of his office. Every third day or so he showered in the locker room, and once a week he went home for a change of clothes, timing his arrival to hours when his house mates would be asleep or at work. Todd didn't want to see anybody. Human companionship was a vague memory, and he wanted to keep it that way.

His office itself bore witness to the frenzy that possessed him: A whiteboard covered with saw-tooth and square-tooth timing diagrams in blue, black and red marker scribbled on top of each other, like a faux Jackson Pollack done by Seymour Cray on acid. A sleeping bag rolled up under a table. Stacks of empty Jolt Cola cans. A wire-wrapped circuit board in the corner collecting dust. Piles of unread memos about schedules and coding practices. Reference catalogues from chip suppliers intermixed with random comic books—*Cheech Wizard* and *The Eternals*. CDs, headphones. On his desk, propped against the window that overlooked the old mill pond, a needlepoint sampler, sewn for him by his sister in cross-stitch:

> Running Round and Round
> In Tiny Circles
> At Very High Speed

And on the wall (its only adornment): a framed two-photo sequence of a
Formula One racing car slamming into the wall at the Montreal Grand Prix. The little figure in the white track-safety volunteer garb slouching out of the path of a flying
tire like Groucho Marx evading bullets in *Duck Soup*— that was Todd. There had
been a time when those mementos had brought a smile, but that time was long gone.
He was aware of one thing only: the deathmatch with his own brainchild, the Beast.

I am Kali, destroyer of worlds. I am become death.

Something like that, wasn't it, that Bobby Oppenheimer supposedly said when
he and his homeboys blew up that first atomic bomb somewhere outside Los
Alamos in the summer of '45? Kali, the Hindu goddess of death and destruction,
patron saint of the Manhattan Project—what a great code name for a chip that now
seemed determined to destroy its creator by cold fusion of his brain cells.

Not that Todd had been thinking of Oppenheimer or atom bombs when he
chose 'Kali' as the project name for this cache-controller. Actually, he had chosen
the name because he thought that particular Hindu goddess had about six elegant
arms (thirty delicate fingers) and two nice breasts, a combination that sort of
appealed to him. If he had known this chip was going to turn out to be such a killer
bitch he would have chosen another name. *Leona*, maybe. Or *Nancy*.

I am Kali, destroyer of worlds. I am become death. . .

Todd stared at the pattern on the dusty screen of monitor 4 and took another
sip from the can in his left hand. His right hand was tapping *one, two, three, four,*
against his left foot's *one, two, three.* Todd didn't know how to think unless he was
drumming, and the harder he was concentrating, the more complex the
polyrhythms became. He absently placed the Jolt Cola on his desk. Now his left
hand began tapping too, adding another level of texture: *one, two, three, four, five;
one, two, three, four, five.*

He had been checking out the strobe lines (all one hundred and twenty-eight
of them, in every permutation) for nearly fifty hours straight and he was prepared
to go another fifty hours. It was a brute force tactic: Stress the chip; find the bug.
Cool it with a hit of Freon. Heat it with a hair drier. *One two three.* Spike the voltage; dim the voltage. *One two three four five.* If Kali wouldn't yield her secret vol-
untarily, he would damn well *torture* it out of her.

Hey, wait. What was that?

It almost looked like a simultaneous hiccough on two lines that didn't touch
each other.

The monitor he was studying was a beat-up old TeleVideo with an interlaced
refresh. Mirages were common when you used that kind of prehistoric jack-leg
equipment. You could get a hiccough interference pattern from the ceiling lights, for
Pete's sake. That was probably all it was, he told himself, an artefact from the ceiling lights. Todd usually subtracted that visual noise from the signal subconsciously,

but maybe in this sleep-deprived buzz-state he had been fooled. His right foot began to tap, doubling the right hand: . . . *two. . . . four. . . . two. . . .four. . .*

Hey. There it was again.

He typed a command on the keyboard to replay the log file. Yes. There it was again: a simultaneous hiccough, ever so tiny, of lines four and eighty-nine. *Gotcha!* He could feel tears welling up in his eyes. Then, as he realized the full meaning of the little hiccough, he shuddered.

"That sneaky worm," Todd said. "I'll kill the little scumpuppy."

From the moment Todd met the Beast he had had an uneasy feeling about deliberate sabotage, but he had always tried to dismiss that feeling as paranoia. Now the hiccough proved his intuition had been right. Line four talking to line eighty-nine was about as innocent as Aldrich Ames talking to the KGB section head. Pavel, Todd's innocent-looking nerdy sidekick, was using one of these lines for double duty. It had taken Todd three months to find the trick, but now that he had it he could hardly believe it. *Son of a bitch!* He got up out of his chair, left his office, got a drink of water from the bubbler, went to the men's room, took a leak, washed his face with ice-cold water and went back to his office to replay the sequence from the log file. The glitch was still there, no mistake. Lines four and eighty-nine. Who would have guessed?

He looked at the wall clock. Nine twelve PM here means six twelve in California. Monty would still be there, probably. Todd picked up the phone and dialed his boss's number.

"Hey, it's me. I found the bug. That little weasel you stuck me with has been yanking my chain. You better get your ass out to Massachusetts, Monty. You better call the police, too, or at least corporate security."

Monty's reaction was entirely predictable.

"Todd, Todd. Slow down, son," he said, with the condescension fairly dripping from his voice. "When was the last time you had any sleep?"

Todd was in no mood for an interrogation.

"Listen, Monty. The BIST is dicking with the refresh. You don't need to know anything else. His logic is reaching clear across an acre of silicon to tickle mine."

"Why would he do that?"

"Why do you think? It's a Trojan Horse."

"You don't know that. It might be accidental."

"Accidental, like Rose Mary Woods accidentally wiping out Nixon's White House tape by holding the erase button with her toe for eighteen minutes. Accident, my ass."

Todd loathed Monty's insipid, patronizing voice. *Todd, Todd, slow down, son.* In truth Todd found Monty only slightly less weasel-like than his co-worker Pavel. But weasel or no weasel, Monty was the boss, so the problem now became his. Todd could imagine Monty sitting in his Menlo Park office, gazing at the Dumbarton Bridge across San Francisco Bay and frantically searching his mental files for a scapegoat for this fiasco. After all, Monty had been the one who insisted on assigning Pavel to work with Todd in the first place. Clearly, as it now turned out, that had been a mistake. But Monty had never admitted a mistake in his life, and the only other logical scapegoat was Todd. Todd was suddenly very happy that he had gone to such lengths to cover his ass.

It didn't matter that Monty was untouchable, that nobody in the entire corporation had the authority, or the balls, to question his judgement. The only thing that mattered was that Monty always required a blood sacrifice when somebody fucked up. That was why Todd was now glad that he had always made backup copies of his work and stored them safely off-site. *When you work with weasels, take care that your flesh does not get ripped.*

After about ten seconds, Monty spoke.

"Okay, I'm coming out to Massachusetts. Don't tell anybody about this until I've looked into it myself. Go home and get some sleep."

"I'm going down to the lab to wring the little jerk's neck first."

"Todd, no. Go home. Please. You found the bug, let me handle Pavel. Go home, okay?"

"Okay," he lied.

So, good: Monty was coming. When would he get here? He might catch the red-eye out of San Francisco tonight and be at the Mill by eight tomorrow morning. Monty might even take the corporate jet to get here sooner. A Trojan Horse in Kali was, after all, a bonafide emergency. Millions of dollars, and Monty's prestige, were riding on the Roadrunner project, and Kali was at the heart of it. Todd's discovery of deliberate sabotage would surely throw a monkey wrench into the whole undertaking. What would happen to it now?

Todd's office was on the seventh floor of building eleven; the Kali lab was one building away—across an elevated walkway — and two floors down. Normally the distance between his office and the lab was a big irritation, but tonight it was just as well. By the time Todd reached the lab he felt less inclined to kill Pavel outright and more inclined to break an arm and a leg and let him die of sepsis. Todd pressed the seven-digit combination to the lock, heard the click and turned the handle. He waited before opening the door long enough for one last attempt at regaining some composure before going inside. As he stood there, his chest heaving from the run, his eyes were drawn to the tenth-generation photocopy of the "hardware debug flowchart" taped to the door:

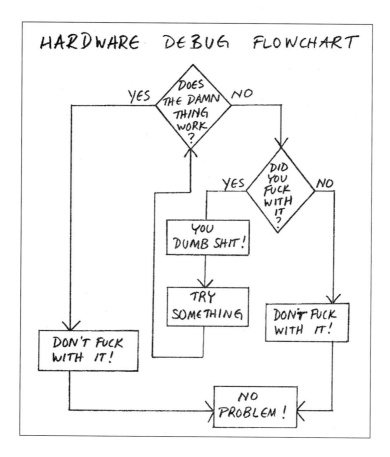

This bogus flowchart with the hopelessly garbled syntax had always made him smile before, but tonight it seemed a very stale joke. He ripped it down, crumpled it and threw it to the floor, imagining himself doing the same thing to pasty-face Pavel: yanking him off his stool and throwing him to the floor, his skin fading into the eggshell white of the linoleum as he gazed up at Todd in terror. Todd threw open the door.

The Kali lab had the feel of a morgue for robots: cold as hell, with dismembered computers on slab-like tables and outlet boxes dangling at the end of fat black power lines that hung like microphones from the ceiling. At the far end of the room, before a massive electron microscope, was an empty stool. Pavel Isaacs was gone.

Todd was across the lab in five quick strides, looking left and right to make sure that the little creep wasn't hiding someplace. No, the room was empty. Fine, let Monty handle Pavel. They deserved each other. Todd turned and walked out of the lab, past the elevators to the stairs. He was ready to bolt down them when it occurred to him that given the situation, it might be prudent to go with a belt and suspenders. He already had the tapes for insurance, but it would probably be smart to confide in somebody, let them know what was going on, just in case. In case what? Todd didn't know. Just in case. The first person he thought of was Casey, but he decided it would be un-cool to lay this problem on her. That would be like going to your wife and whining about your mistress. So whom would he tell? Aubrey, he decided. Nick Aubrey.

Nick was a software boy but he was no pansy. If anybody would watch Todd's back it would be him. In another place and time Todd and Nick, together, had faced sandstorms, malaria, dysentery, and angry people with big knives. Nick Aubrey had balls. There was no way a little office intrigue would phase him. Todd ran back up to his office and dashed off a quick E-mail, using a code that Nick would recognize:

```
Ibu Yagg,
I fear these things.
Bachie M'Bodj
```

A few minutes later he was walking out one of the Mill's thirty-six exits into the crisp and snow-filled night air.

Chapter 2

Nick Aubrey stood atop a drywall partition, his head nearly touching a long fluorescent lamp on the stamped-tin ceiling. With his left hand he steadied himself against a sprinkler pipe; with his right he held a two-pound hammer. He was tired, it was late, yet there was no question of his knocking off: other volunteers would be here tomorrow to continue the transformation he had started, and Nick wasn't going to allow their schedule to slip because he had wimped out. It was grueling, sure, but for a worthy cause—within a few weeks this architecturally charming but long-vacant old building in the blighted downtown of Newcastle, Massachusetts would be home to the Magic Box, a community-run children's museum cum book and toy store.

Strewn about the floor before him were piles of new lumber, some sawhorses, a table saw, a bucket of nails, one sledge and three claw hammers, a pry-bar, heaps of splintered wood and smashed Sheetrock, a paint-splattered floodlamp, an electric saw sitting atop a tangle of bright orange extension cords, and a few cartons—early shipments from orders placed at the Toy Fair a month ago. Until tonight, the bare concrete floor had been covered with depressing blue-grey industrial carpet—cheap to start with, and never cleaned in thirty years of use. Nick had spent the last six hours ripping it up with his bare hands and cutting it into sections with construction-grade razor blades. Strips of the carpet stuck out of two brown plastic garbage cans amid the rubble, making them look like matching muppets with spiky blue-grey industrial hair, Jim Henson doing a variation on a theme by Samuel Beckett. *Nick Aubrey, demolition man. Nick Aubrey, toyseller.* Sometimes this volunteer work beat the hell out of his day job.

He was in full reverie—imagining a life without the Software Architecture Review Committee demanding the impossible, without prima donna programmers to placate— when Bartlett walked in, startling him out of his wits. It was two in the morning.

She was wearing a hooded sweatshirt that was covered with thick wet snow. In her left hand was a large cloth drawstring bag; in her right was a large paper coffee cup. On her back there was a small knapsack. She crossed the room, climbed two rungs up a stepladder and placed the coffee at Nick's feet, then stepped down and walked back to the center of the room.

She put her bag and knapsack on the floor, then threw back the hood of her sweatshirt, revealing black hair pulled into an unruly bun. Some snow fell off the hood onto the floor. Outside, a Newcastle Public Works truck passed, periodically casting yellow light though the translucent sign paper on the windows. Chains clinked loudly and the snowplow rumbled. Bartlett sat cross-legged on the cold floor and withdrew a frosted glass bottle from the knapsack.

"Now tell me what you are doing up there," she said.

"You will remark this ugly wall." Nick touched a partition that ran behind him, towards the rear of the empty store. "I am going to destroy it."

"Do you mind if I watch?"

"I thought with this storm you would be spending the night in Cambridge."

"And miss this cozy scene? The crackling fire, the kettle on the boil? Seems like with you at the Mill all the time and me in my lab we don't hardly have time anymore to take care of everything that needs taking care of."

The woman could say the most provocative things.

"That may change," Nick said.

"How so?"

"Digital MicroSystems has just announced a collaborative research effort with MIT. They've endowed a couple of professorships and given, I don't know, fifty million dollars or so to set up this whole new program. I even had a hint you would be tapped for a lead research position."

"So. Another coupling of industry and academe. I can almost hear the porno music."

"It's big news. I'm surprised you didn't hear about it at MIT."

"The Media Lab selling out to yet another corporate sponsor? That's hardly big news."

"I'm not talking about the Media Lab. I'm talking about physical chemistry, molecular biology."

Bartlett seemed interested in this information but somehow bothered by it.

"Why's a computer company funding a biology department at MIT?" she asked.

"It's not a biology department. It's a new department unto itself: Molecular Computation."

"Define."

"Nanomachines, biological computers, self-modifying software that evolves without human intervention. . ."

"Mixing computer science with life science at the molecular level."

"Their goal is to have a programmable machine to read and write DNA within a decade."

Bartlett drew in her breath, as if someone had just given her bad news about a close relative.

"I don't even want to think about that now."

"Don't think about it, then."

"But I have to think about it. How are you involved?"

"I got an E-mail from the man himself, Montaigne Meekman. He wants to meet with me and talk about having me be the liaison between the Mill and MIT."

"What?"

"I got a mail message today from Monty Meekman about the molecular computation lab."

"Monty Meekman, the monomaniacal billionaire, is personally recruiting you?"

"You'll be even more shocked to hear that he mentioned your work."

"How would Monty Meekman know anything about me?"

"Your work is famous in some circles."

"It's got nothing to do with molecular computation. You don't know anything about molecular computation either, do you?"

"Not really."

"Three thousand people work at the Mill. Why does he want you?"

"I'm a good manager."

"There are lots of good managers at Digital MicroSystems."

"I know software. Some people think I'm pretty brilliant."

"Sure, Nick, you know software. But the Mill is full of software *geniuses.* Why you?"

"Well, thanks for the vote of confidence. Maybe he wants me because I'm the genius who knows how to manage the other geniuses. Why not me?"

Bartlett answered the question by changing the subject.

"If you wind up working for Meekman you'll spend all your time in California. And California will eat your soul."

This was not the response he had expected from her. Nick knew that like many people in Massachusetts, Bartlett had been upset when Digital Data, a Massachusetts institution, had been acquired by Stanford MicroSystems. Their union created Digital MicroSystems, the second largest computer company in the world, with home offices in California's Silicon Valley. Still, Nick was surprised by the vehemence of her reaction to the mention of Monty Meekman, the man said to have engineered the hostile takeover.

"I thought you would be amused by the idea of you and I working together," Nick said.

"Amused, no. Astonished, yes. Why is Meekman hunting you?"

"It's not *that* astonishing. We do work at the same company."

"Wrong. You work there. He plays there."

Nick switched his stance, transferring the bump hammer to the left hand and holding the sprinkler pipe with his right. It occurred to him that this was a rather odd place, time, and posture for this conversation. He should get back to work on the wall, or he should climb down and ravish this beautiful and inscrutable scientist. What he shouldn't do was to keep standing there talking about politics or philosophy or whatever the hell it was that they were talking about.

"That man gives me the creeps," Bartlett added. "Meekman coming to the Mill is like Dracula coming to your castle. I don't like the idea of you working with him."

"What, have you met the man?"

There was an odd hesitancy in Bartlett's answer, Nick thought.

"I know what I've read about him," she said. "That he's brilliant. That he owns thirty percent of Digital MicroSystems, which makes him one of the richest people on the planet. I also know that very few people are willing to talk about him for the record. What exactly does he do at Dijjy-Mike, besides engineer hostile takeovers?"

"Whatever he wants. I don't think he has an official title. He just has a few projects that he personally manages, which always turn out to be revolutionary and enormously profitable. Working on one of his projects is the best thing that can happen to your career."

"So why is nobody willing to talk about it? I've read profiles of him, and they all say the same thing: he's a genius, he's impossibly wealthy, he hand-picks teams of computer scientists that create revolutionary technology, and nobody who's worked for him is willing to talk about it."

"Maybe they respect his desire for privacy."

"Come on, Nick."

"I guess he likes to cultivate an air of mystery."

"People are afraid of him. I don't want you working for him."

"Todd works for him. Todd's not afraid of him."

"Maybe he should be."

Nick's legs were starting to cramp from staying too long in one position.

"Think about it," Bartlett said. "Now that the human genome project is up and running, the structure and function of a new gene gets published to the Internet just about every other day. That in itself is enough to scare me. On top of that, along comes one of the richest and most powerful men on earth, accountable to nobody, who, with a measly fifty-million dollars—about one week's pay, for him— buys the scientific might of MIT, not to mention a great cover story."

"Like you said, nothing new in a prestigious university whoring for a multi-national."

"Yes, but there is something new in the human genome project, and there is something new in programmable machines that can read and write DNA. Not even God has such a machine. *He* still uses restriction enzymes."

"Monty's just keeping up with the Joneses. He is not going to be outdone by Microsoft, and Bill Gates just donated fifty million dollars to endow a nanotechnology program at the University of Washington."

"I rest my case."

Nick looked down at Bartlett. She was not exactly glaring at him, but she was regarding him warily, which was a new and unpleasant experience for him. In the years since he had met Bartlett he had come to know her as his true love and soul mate, yet there were parts of her psyche that he did not know how to reconcile. For all her scientific sophistication, she had an almost Popish belief that some questions were best left unanswered.

"Maybe this isn't the time to talk about it," he said. "Let's drop it."

"Good idea," she said, and some of the concern seemed to lift from her face. "I'm going to try to steer my mind in the direction it was going before I walked in here."

Nick began to pound at the reluctant wall, each blow of the hammer reverberating like a firecracker off the bare walls and concrete floor. Despite the coolness of the room he was soon perspiring, and when he stopped to catch his breath his damp clothes turned cold against his skin.

"While you rest," he heard her saying, "why don't I tell what I was going to tell you when I first walked in here tonight."

Nick's ears were ringing, but her voice sounded as he imagined an angel's would sound to a soul in purgatory.

"I was wondering," she began again, hesitating as she fiddled with the wire on the champagne bottle. "Do you think that if I get this champagne agitated enough, I can make it pop? Do you think I can do that, Nick?"

A trick question?

"I suppose so," he answered, tentatively. It seemed, to his relief, that her foul mood was gone.

She removed the wire and stared at him. "I'll bet I can make it pop without even touching the cork," she said.

Their eyes met for a long time as she sat nearly motionless, slowly caressing, shaking, licking the bottle, rubbing it between her legs, across her breasts, her face perfectly blank, betraying no emotion at all.

"And when it pops, Nick," she said, "I bet it will just spew all over everything."

He went back to his task of dismantling the ugly wall. The champagne went off, eventually, and she took a long first drink from the foaming bottle.

She said, "Would you like to hear what I have been thinking about?"

He was breathing hard and covered with plaster dust. He was thirsty, too, but his coffee had fallen atop the growing pile of debris, and he knew better than to ask her for a sip of champagne.

"Yes, I would love to hear what you were thinking about," he said.

A mouthful of champagne dribbled off her chin onto her sweatshirt, but she made no motion to wipe it dry.

"When I was fifteen I used to like to watch a lifeguard at the pool. The other guards had been there for a couple of years—college kids, I guess— I never paid any attention to them. But in the middle of one summer a new guy came. He was twenty-five years old, and he looked, to me, like a god. And do you know, Nick, when I was fifteen my breasts were already large. I used to swim over to the side of the pool and look up at him, this new god, and as I did I pressed my breasts up against the side of the pool. I was fifteen, I had large breasts, and he was twenty-five, very muscular, and he was high above me as you are above me now. Do you get the picture?"

"Oh, man," he said.

She stood and released her hair from its bun; it was black and reached the middle of her back, cascading around the hood. She took her sweatshirt off, then her bra, and threw them on the table saw. Then she removed her boots and dungarees, and stood naked, save her woolen socks, in the frigid air. Even from this distance he could see the goose bumps all over her skin, but she appeared oblivious to the cold. And still no hint of a smile. *Oh, my God in heaven*, Nick thought.

"Observe," she said. "I am going to place this sleeping bag where it can be watched by people who like to watch."

She bent to pick up the sack that contained her sleeping bag, then stood erect and unfurled it and placed it back on the floor. Her breasts *were* large, he noted, perfectly so. For that matter, everything about her form was perfect—legs, arms, shoulders, tummy: everything. Absolutely perfect. He observed the line of her neck to her shoulders, then regarded her face. Her dark eyes were bright on either side of the nose that he always told her was too tiny for her face, but inexplicably perfect. The shape of her cheekbones hinted Cherokee blood, just as their coloring clearly showed Welsh. When she spoke a dimple appeared in her right cheek, and he glimpsed a gleaming hint of overbite of her top teeth and the nearly imperceptible squiggle in the alignment of her bottom teeth. He felt his entire body flush, and thought he might faint.

"Are you cold, Nick?" she asked, almost as if she had felt the heat pass through him.

"That depends what you mean."

"I'll tell you what I mean. If you were a California boy your ass would be an ice cube by now. And if you were a California boy you wouldn't be here in the first place. People from the land of I-me-mine don't relate to your idealism. A community store, of all things. Now there's an oxymoron only a Puritan could love."

"So I'm a Puritan?"

"You do not desire to eat of the tree."

"What does that make you?"

"We're not talking about me. There's a reason you live here Nick, among the ghosts of an old Massachusetts mill town in the lee of the cold Atlantic. You would be a fish out of water in sunny California, where there are no ghosts because there is no past, only the glorious present and brighter future. You're an anachronism, Nick. That's why you belong here where nothing changes, where money and sex are still private matters."

"Hardly."

"I need a razor blade, Nicholas."

"There are some on the table saw."

She took a step towards it, then gracefully removed her socks, bending each exquisite leg in turn behind her, balancing on the other, like Katrina Witt holding her skate to her derriere. She left the socks on the saw in exchange. She was now completely naked in the forty-degree room.

"It's a blizzard tonight," she said. "The police have asked that nobody drive unless they must. They want to keep the roads clear for emergency vehicles. And yet—" she drew a single-sided blade from the oblong box "—as I came here tonight in all this snow, at one-thirty in the morning, I saw people walking down the street. I saw a man and a woman, arm in arm. And I saw two boys. Now it is two-thirty in the morning. Do you suppose that there are people still about? Do you suppose they're curious about what goes on inside this Magic Box?"

She had walked to the window, and now poised the blade about to cut the paper, a spot about the height of her eyes. She cut. Six inches down. Eight inches across.

"'Coming Soon,' the sign says. "What's coming soon? People want to know."

Six inches up, and eight back: a rectangular hole five feet four inches off the sidewalk level. She tossed the blade to the floor without looking to see where it might land.

"What kind of toys do they got in there anyway?" she said.

"I'm starting to get a little curious myself."

She deftly unzipped the sleeping bag and crawled in, shivering as the cold fabric hit her skin.

"OK," she said. "What do you call that thing in your hand?"

"It's a hammer. A bump hammer."

"Perfect. I want you to take that tool of yours, Nicholas, that bump hammer, and I want you to pound. I want to watch your muscular body above me. I want dust to fly, I want the air thick with your smell. I want you to *pound* and *pound* and *pound*. I want an explosion, and I want it right now. Look into my eyes. Nick, you are my lifeguard. I love you."

"Marry me."

"Alright."

Finally, a smile. A small smile, but he would take it.

"But remember," she said. "You don't work for Montaigne Meekman."

The smile was gone. Her eyes were fixed on his.

"From this moment on, you work for me."

Chapter 3

After eight bottles of beer, one slice of cold pizza and three and a half hours of drumming, Todd Griffith had finally expelled six months of accrued tension. He was stripped down to his boxers (all his other clothes having been taken off an item at a time in syncopated frenzy) and still he perspired as he tapered down his long improvisation with a gentle glissando on the bells. Kali's race condition was finally exorcized. The demon was no more. Todd stood, gloriously alone.

Upon leaving the Mill he had taken a long route home, making what was normally a fifteen minute stroll into a one-hour hike through deepening whiteness. He hadn't noticed when the snow started, but by the time he started his walk home four inches were already on the ground. Along the way he had drummed on his legs a rhythm from *Chunga's Revenge* and tried to guess what would happen next. But before arriving at an answer he had found himself here, home, at the massive Tudor house on Edgell street. Without bothering to remove his boots or shake the snow from his jacket, he walked directly through the mud room at the back door and into the kitchen. There he found his house mates John and Richard finishing the night's dishes. He grunted hello, took a cold slice of pizza and two sixpacks of Bass Ale from the refrigerator and headed for the basement.

"Looks like it's one of those nights," Richard had said, and they had followed him downstairs. As Todd had sat down on the stool behind the massive drum kit, John and Richard took seats on the couch in front of it and placed plugs in their ears. Todd picked up his sticks and kicked the bass pedal, twice.

As he reached over with the drumstick in his left hand to flick the switch to the Fender twin reverb, he invoked the spirit of Zappa by quoting from sacred scripture, the *Uncle Meat* album. Using the words FZ spoke before playing "Louie Louie" on the Royal Albert Hall pipe organ, Todd intoned, in mock solemnity, "They like it loud, you know," and began to play. . .

But that had been hours ago; John and Richard were long gone now, and snow filled the window wells. After noodling on a guitar for a little while Todd realized that he was, at last, sleepy. He was, in fact, utterly exhausted. He put the guitar down and staggered up the stairs to his first floor bedroom. The window was open and there was a pile of snow on the floor. He went over and lifted the sash another inch or two. A gust pushed the curtains up and snow blew into the room. Perfect, he thought. The only thing missing was a beautiful woman, but if one had been there he would have been too tired to notice her. He sat on the edge of his mattress and jotted a few notes in his work diary, then toppled over and pulled the rumpled quilt over his sweaty body.

Some time later, while it was still pitch dark outside and the snow was still coming down hard, the window was pulled up by two gloved hands reaching in from outside. Todd didn't hear a thing. He never noticed the person stepping through the window into the small pile of snow on his bedroom floor, and he stayed oblivious even when the person switched on his bedroom light.

Todd was in REM sleep—dreaming of a little Ansley Dunbar riff from Zappa's white Fillmore album (seven counts on the snare drum racing against four on the high-hat while the bass drum did something totally random) that was somehow associated, in his dream, with the sensation of reading a *Weekly Reader* with his back against the warm barn wall in the summer of 1959—when the bullet pierced his skull.

∞II∞

ANGEL

Chapter 4

Nick Aubrey never would have figured Carl Swirsing for a Mad Antonio's kind of guy. Carl was a California boy—a Porsche-driving, volleyball-playing, market-watching libertarian libertine. So when Carl called Nick up and asked to meet him for a beer, Nick expected him to name some fern bar where they served microbrews to archetypal Silicon Valley yupsters like Carl himself. Mad Antonio's Nut House was no yuppie fern bar. Mad Antonio's was a dark place of pool tables, tattoos, stale beer and TVs that played tapes of Buster Douglas smashing Mike Tyson's face. From a barstool deep within Mad Antonio's there was no way to tell that just outside the door the California sun was shining with a soul-numbing cheerfulness. Nick liked it better here, inside. Maybe that's why Carl had chosen this place. Maybe he knew Nick better than Nick realized.

Nick hardly recognized Carl when he walked through the door. He was wearing clean blue jeans and a faded Stanford sweatshirt—not one of the Armani suits that were Carl's at-work uniform—and Nick was surprised to see how well he seemed to fit in here amid the grungy types. But why should it surprise him? In truth, Nick hardly knew anything about the man. They were from different worlds, Engineering and Marketing, and an unbridgeable gulf was axiomatic.

Nick and Carl had only worked on a few projects together—ad hoc teams to bring customers into the engineering universe: Beta-test focus groups in Stockholm and Toronto, usability walk-throughs in Austin and Hyderabad. On those trips the two men had seldom socialized in the off-hours. Carl was an astonishingly gifted Don Juan, and usually had hooked up with an appropriately beautiful female companion before the second night in any city. Nick, on the other hand, preferred his own company. Sometimes he checked out a cathedral or wandered alone in some funky precinct. More often he found someplace to lift weights, or, failing that, simply went back to his hotel room and read Balzac. Nick and Carl had not even spoken to each other in more than two years. Which made Nick wonder: why had Carl called him? What was up?

"I haven't seen you around much," Nick said as Carl walked over to Nick's spot at the bar. "What've you been up to? Are you still over there in Enterprise Systems Marketing?"

"I left Dijjy-Mike about a year ago. Started my own PR and market-research firm."

Ah. Now Nick had an idea why Carl might have called him.

"You know I'm not going to leak confidential information," Nick said.

"I wouldn't expect you to. You're a very principled fellow."

"Not that I have any information you'd want. I'm kind of in the backwater these days."

"Siberia is more like it," Carl said. "I know. That's why I wanted to talk to you."

An odd response. People like Carl Swirsing trafficked in hot information, and Nick's supply was very cold. Why would cold information be interesting to Carl?

"What is it about my being in Siberia that makes you want to talk to me?" Nick said.

"I've got a strong hunch that you're about to be called back to Moscow and anointed."

"Anointed?"

"By Meekman."

"If you're going to insult me, at least buy me a beer. What makes you say that?"

Carl motioned to the bartender then turned back to Nick.

"Who's your boss now?" he said.

Nick cringed. "Chuckie Johnson," he said, and added, "How art the mighty fallen."

"Johnson's washed up. He'll be history within the month. What are you working on?"

"I thought you didn't want product information."

"Stick to non-confidential information. Don't give me any code names or ship dates."

"It's too embarrassing to even talk about," Nick said.

"Network administration, right? Novell emulation?"

How did Carl know that?

"The project should be canceled," Nick said. "By the time it's ready nobody will want it."

A bartender placed bottles on the bar—Heineken before Nick, Calistoga Water before Carl.

"You're right about that," Carl said. "Code name Docudisk. DOS binaries on a UNIX virtual PC. Ship date forty-three days from today, with an estimated gross margin of 78 percent. It's a well-built crock two years too late."

"OK, so you don't need me to tell you about Docudisk."

"No. How many people are in the group you manage?"

"Seven."

"Six, actually. How many did you manage five years ago?"

"About fifty."

"It was fifty three. Tell me, how would you rate your software engineering skills?"

"Excellent."

"I agree. And your management skills?"

"Excellent."

"I agree with that too. So how come your career's been in a gradual tailspin for the last five years? How come every time you deliver the goods you get assigned to a crappier project and the group you manage gets smaller? Why are you working for a has-been non-entity like Chuckie Johnson? You're good at seeing patterns, Nick. What's the pattern here?"

"You tell me."

"Monty's pulling strings behind the scenes."

"Monty? I don't even work for Monty. I don't know him; I've never even met him."

"You've never met him face to face. But you do know him. You've corresponded with him by e-mail, talked to him on the telephone, even by video conference—"

"—or whatever you call it when he can see me but I can't see him—"

"You and Monty know each other, all right. Not only do you know him, Nick; in fact you're sort of his unacknowledged protégé."

"If you want to look at it that way, I guess I know him," Nick said. "That hardly makes me his protégé."

"He invites you out to dinner once or twice a year, but always stands you up."

"True. How do you know about it?"

"He calls you up when you're not expecting it; he gives you career advice, picks your brain, flatters you, hints that he has a job for you that never quite materializes. . ."

"Now that you mention it."

Now that you mention it. Now that you mention it, Carl had just given a pretty accurate description of Nick's relationship with Montaigne Meekman, the inscrutable billionaire genius. Monty seemed to have taken an interest in Nick, which was flattering. On the other hand, five years of occasional ego-buffing wasn't much reward for what Nick had sacrificed. Because ever since Bartlett moved out, Nick had wondered whether that simple relationship had doomed his marriage. Bartlett had never said why she was leaving, she just left. The first three months of their marriage had conformed to Nick's idea of heaven. But a frost had appeared, years ago, on the day he came back from being stood up by Monty for the first time, and the final freeze, and her moving out, coincided with the last time Nick had spoken with him. Nick could think of racier indiscretions.

"When are you supposed to go back east?" Carl asked.

"Red-eye tonight."

"Have you heard from Monty recently?"

"He sent me an e-mail this morning. Wants to take me for a drive this afternoon, so he says. He's supposed to pick me up from Digital MicroSystems in about two hours. But let's be honest. What are the odds that he'll show up? Probably about as good as the odds that Lucy will let Charley Brown kick the football. To tell you the truth, I'm beginning to wonder if Monty Meekman really exists. I'm starting to think he's a myth, or a software construct like Max Headroom."

Carl reached for his wallet. He took out a hundred dollar bill and put it on the bar in front of Nick. Then he reached into his pocket for a red felt-tipped pen, and made some kind of mark.

"If Monty doesn't show up and offer you a job today, you keep the hundred bucks. Otherwise mail it back to me."

Nick glanced at the bill. It was crisp.

"What's the job going to be?"

"I don't know. But it will come with a lot of cash and stock options. You know about Monty's anointed ones: preposterously wealthy. Fiercely loyal. You're about to join their ranks."

Nick took a long pull from his beer. The bill sat where Carl had left it.

"I don't know what you mean by 'anointed,'" Nick said. "Lots of people have worked on Monty's projects without getting rich, and most of them aren't shy about dissing him."

"Absolutely true. But not his anointed ones. I'm sure you've noticed the difference."

"Oh." Nick suddenly realized what Carl was getting at. "You're talking about the Corporate Fellows. The guys with Lab clearance."

"Precisely. They're the only ones who matter. Monty couldn't care less what other people have to say about him, because they don't have any idea what's under development in the Labs."

"Monty's going to make me a Corporate Fellow?"

"I guarantee it."

"Come on, Carl. You're hallucinating. Those guys are the cream of the crop."

"They are *now*. But let me tell you something. None of them, not a *one*, was considered a genius before being named a Fellow. They all were solid workers whose careers had inexplicably gone into the toilet for *years* before Monty rescued them. They were elected Corporate Fellows, and suddenly they became golden, brilliant. Smarter than smart-"

"Maybe Monty has an eye for latent talent."

"—and their personalities changed too."

This was ridiculous. Everybody *knew* that the Corporate Fellows were geeks and kept their mouths shut about Monty Meekman. Everybody knew that they were fabulously wealthy even by Silicon Valley standards. But everybody also knew that Corporate Research Fellows of Digital MicroSystems, Incorporated, were the best computer engineers in the world. They designed the coolest products on earth. Virtual reality systems with photo-realistic graphics, symphonic sound, and whole-body proprioceptive feedback. Neural nets that could predict stock market activity better than anybody on Wall Street. Holographic imaging systems used by neuro-surgeons to perform the world's most sophisticated brain surgery. Chess programs that no Grandmaster could hope to compete with. Language translation systems as accomplished as any linguist. . .

"The Corporate Fellows *are* weird," Nick said. "I'll admit that much. But you're saying that being made Fellows transformed them from nobodies into supermen? Come on. They're geniuses. *God* made them that way, not Monty Meekman."

"When an engineer becomes a Fellow it's like when an ordinary Mafia goon becomes a 'made man.' Or when a squire becomes a knight. It's like ordination, when a novice becomes a priest. After a long apprenticeship proves your mettle, you get elevated. Whereas before you could only receive the sacraments, now you can perform them. It changes you."

It was hard to believe that these words were coming from the man whose chief goal during their trip to India had been to experience the whole of the Kama Sutra in five nights.

"Carl," Nick said. "Are you on drugs?"

"I'm telling you what I know."

"What, that Monty put me in Siberia to see how I'd bear up?"

"Basically, yes. He was sizing you up. And weakening your resistance."

"What? How so?"

"Tell me, Nick. How's your personal financial situation?"

Nick looked at him intently, but the look on Carl's face didn't change. There was more to Carl Swirsing than Nick had realized.

"I'm fucked," he said. "I don't know whether to file for bankruptcy or what. I can't see any way out of the mess I'm in. But I guess you already knew that."

"Yes," Carl said. "I did know that. How does a guy with no dependents who makes your kind of income manage to go bust?"

"It's a long story."

"You guaranteed all loans for that children's co-op, didn't you?"

"Yes."

It was increasingly apparent that this meeting was not as casual as Nick had thought it was going to be. Carl had done a lot of homework, and he and done it for a reason. He wanted to sell Nick an interpretation of the last five years of his life. Carl's theory did have a certain perverse logic. But Nick wasn't ready to buy it.

"Monty Meekman might be doing weird things with his Corporate Fellows, but don't tell me that Monty Meekman caused the implosion of our children's co-op in Newcastle, Massachusetts. The Reagan-Bush recession caused that co-op to fail."

"How many members did the co-op start with?"

"Thirty-six."

"And there are five die-hards left, including yourself. Three of the remaining five are over seventy years old. The fourth is your wife Bartlett, who moved out of your house at the beginning of last autumn. In other words, it's down to you alone.

Why did everybody else fall off? You thought your crew was there for the long haul, but they've all bailed out."

"Even among starry-eyed idealists, the spirit of goodwill and cooperation tends to evaporate when local unemployment hits twenty-two percent," Nick said.

"Look, Nick. I'm going to be blunt, because there's big things at stake and there isn't a lot of time for dancing around. Here's the facts. Five years ago you were a hot shit. You were a fast rising star in a fast rising company in a fast rising industry. Then your best friend got shot and everything turned sour. You got married but your wife split. You threw yourself into this children's charity, which is great, but you managed to put everything you own on the line and now the loans are being called in. Meanwhile you're doing scut work for a no-op who couldn't code his way out of a paper bag. You're full of anger and doubt. You can't find a better job. You have good interviews outside the company but you never get the offer. You take out your frustration in gyms and bars. You bench press three hundred pounds, and you drink way too much. You are ripe for the plucking, Nick. Ripe. This afternoon Monty is going to pluck you."

Chapter 5

Dieter Steffen stared intently at the molecule floating in the air above his upturned palms. Like a magic fairy hovering over the cupped hands of a wonder-filled child, the molecule rose when Dieter raised his hands, sank when he lowered them. To Dieter Steffen, this molecule *was* a magic fairy, as wondrous as any mythical being that ever held a child enthralled.

The orthogonal Diels-Alder adduct: five benzene rings, some associated nitrogens, fluorines, and a solitary silicon. It was an exotic, and, Dieter thought, a profound molecule—profound in the way that a chessboard is profound before the first piece has been moved, as a piano is profound before the first note has been played. It was profound as DNA itself was profound: it embodied an infinitude of possibilities. This molecule, a billionth of a meter across, was the one he had been seeking for six years. It was, he dared to hope, the last piece needed to complete his and Pavel's machine. If Dieter's calculations were correct, this simple molecule was the key that would unlock the tabernacle in which resided the Holy Grail itself.

Nitrogen, carbon, silicon, fluorine—red, black, white, green: a perfect T, two walls intersecting at a right angle. It looked like part of a building made of colorful plastic blocks. Dieter was only vaguely aware that he was not looking at the molecule itself, but at an image of it on a computer screen. And it was not floating in the air in front of him; that was an illusion created by the visor through which he looked, just as the image of his hands was generated by the data gauntlets that he wore. He grabbed the model, one hand on each wall, and twisted it. He felt the resistance to this torsion through the data gloves: the molecule wanted to keep its shape. Using a foot pedal, he increased the power in the gloves— just a fraction, a factor of 1.1. He twisted the molecule again and felt it snap: the two walls now lay in the same plane, one on top of the other, like two sheets of multi-colored paper held by an invisible spring. He couldn't pry them apart more than a tiny bit without again increasing the power with the foot pedal.

An illusion: but to Dieter Steffen this molecule was more real than the chair in which he sat. It was more real than the visor and the speakers in his headset, or the twenty-five inch Digital MicroSystems graphics workstation in front of him, more real than the data gauntlets on his hands or the cradle in which his right foot rested. This molecule was reality itself.

A billionth of a meter. Even after all these years of working on nanomachines, Dieter had trouble imagining something so small. Compared to the devices that he and Pavel designed, a virus would look like a jumbo jet beside a Wright Brothers' flyer. And like the airplane, like the wheel, like the first tool used to create the first fire, Dieter and Pavel's machine would forever change the relationship of humankind to the universe.

As soon as Pavel and Dieter perfected the design and refined the manufacturing process, their machine would be able to change any one DNA sequence into any other DNA sequence. With this capability the age of the new alchemy would truly begin. With this technology all things would become mutable: oil spill would become fish food, smog would become clear air, the cystic fibrosis gene would become sound. Imagine: the dying child lies on the hospital bed, a simple injection into his blood, and *lo, behold the child arise and walk.*

All they had to do was complete the design and take it from simulation into the world.

"All they had to do. . .". It was like saying all they had to do was flap their wings and fly to Pluto. In computer *simulation*, it was possible to design simple nanomachines. It was even possible to *build* simple machines that worked in the protected, eutactic environment of the laboratory. Eutactic environments—such as perfect crystals, the interiors of protein molecules, or "machine-phase" systems—were characterized by precise molecular order. But Pavel and Dieter's machine was designed to work on DNA, and DNA wasn't generally found in eutactic environments. DNA was generally found in the disordered solution environment of biological structures on a cellular scale. To build a machine that could survive in that real, meat world—

that was the challenge. The real world, where hungry hydrogens came swooping from everywhere like demonic flying raptors; where ultraviolet light shone down like deathrays from the heavens; where the rise in temperature from *comfortable room* to *warm room* would have the same effect as a visit to the surface of Venus. To make a programmable nanomachine for DNA repair that could survive in the real world was to cure cancer, prevent genetic diseases, and possibly, to bring about an end to aging and bestow on mankind the gift or curse of immortality.

It was a dream that only the most ambitious and most gifted even dared to dream—even to experience it required mastery of twentieth century physics, molecular genetics, and human physiology. Dieter Steffen and his partner Pavel Isaacs were two of the gifted.

And now, today, Pavel had told Dieter that he had made not one, but *two* breakthroughs that would allow them, together, finally to complete the solution to the problem. This was Nobel Prize work, but much more than that. This was work that would make them gods.

The one small hitch was that Dieter did not really understand Pavel's break-throughs: a fractal compression algorithm for storing vast amounts of information, and a graphite laser evaporation technique for constructing a C_{60} buckminster-fullerene shell *around* a working computational element. Dieter had been in this sit-uation before, when Pavel had explained something beyond his grasp. And invari-ably, after he had thought about it, *zoned on it*, he had come to understand. This had been true when they first met at MIT during the fall of 1987, and it remained true today, nearly ten years later. All Dieter had to do was think. So this would be his task for the day: to concentrate and wait for insight. He was sure it would come.

But something wasn't right. What? It took him a minute to realize that it was the music coming through his headset that was out of place. It wasn't right because he could hear it—a single violin doing the work of a quartet, making a choir from a single voice: the Bach *partita in A minor*. When the music was right Dieter could-n't hear it at all: he could only hear the molecule speaking to him, like a lover. It was time to switch to a more invisible music. He touched his fingertips together and felt the pressure on his fingers release.

He glanced at his hands on the keyboard. The metallic-grey data gauntlets looked like electronic hockey gloves, and his pink fingers protruded beneath them-making his hands look like hermit crabs carrying their comically oversized shells above them. With a few quick keystrokes he changed the music coming through his headset from Bach to Eno. The A-minor partita was good for the transition to total concentration, from meat reality to virtual reality. But once his mind was in the zone even Bach seemed too bound to the leaden world, to tangible things. Eno was zone music. With a once-practiced, now habitual movement he raised his hands from the keyboard and slapped them outward, as if giving the back of his hand to two insolent cads at once. As the inertial digi-lock sensors swung around his fingers and the gloves engaged, he was vaguely aware of the music fading to invisibility.

He gave the molecule a flick with the index finger of his right hand and watched it spin in its virtual space. In the upper right hand corner of the screen a virtual clock showed 18:48 Basel Local Time. It was still early in the day; there was plenty of time. The hands he saw on the screen were *his* hands. The molecule was an extension of his thought. He was ready to go back to work.

Suddenly he was startled by the light flashing on the telephone in the right corner of his desk. With the exception of his colleague Pavel, virtually nobody ever called Dieter. And Pavel always sent e-mail first, to warn him that a call was coming. Since he received calls so seldom, usually wrong numbers, and since his calls invariably came when he was deepest in concentration, he had long since disconnected the ringer; yet even the faint orange light was a jarring invasion of his mental space. It took three flashes of the light until he had recovered sufficiently to remove his headset, and another flash or two before he could answer.

"Steffen," he said. He pronounced Steffen with a long sibilant "sh," his tongue back deep in his mouth: Schhhh-teffen."

"Hello, Doctor Steffen," said an American-accented woman's voice. "My name is Judith Knight. I am chief scientist at Human Potential, Incorporated, in Boulder, Colorado."

"Dr. Knight," Dieter said. "I am honored to receive your call. How can I help you?"

"Dr. Steffen, I wish to speak with you on a matter of some urgency. Could you make yourself available for an hour or so, in a few hours' time—that is, this evening?"

"Certainly, Dr. Knight. I am at your disposal. We can speak now, if you wish."

"No; I mean that we should meet in person. In fact, I have flown to Basel expressly to speak with you. I have only now arrived; I need only a little time to refresh. Can you suggest a place for us to meet?"

This was an extraordinary request. It took Dieter a moment to think what to say. And he was distracted by the noises coming over the line—conversations, music, the clinking of glass. Could it be that Dr. Knight was calling him from a public phone in a restaurant? A bar?

"There is a café near the art museum, in the old section of Basel that we call St. Albans," Dieter said, trying to ignore the distracting sounds. "It is called the Kunsthalle Café; it is on an inside terrace, so it is pleasant to sit in the air, even so late in the year. Any cab driver can take you there."

Dieter assumed that this was true; he had read about the place in a newspaper. He himself confined his meals to his apartment and the Hoff-Zeigy employee cafeteria.

"That sounds wonderful. Shall we say eight PM, or what do Europeans say, twenty o'clock?"

"Very well," he said.

"Good. I am tall, I will be wearing a dress with a floral print, and a hat with a flower in the brim."

"Can you tell me what we will be discussing, Dr. Knight?"

"We must talk; that is all I can tell you at this time. It is very important that you tell no one about this call, or that we plan to meet. Please, tell no one. And please forgive my rudeness. We should not stay long on the telephone, so I will say goodbye, until twenty hours."

"Goodbye," he said, as he heard the click at the other end.

He placed the receiver in its cradle, slowly. Then he placed the headset back on, trying to put this astonishing conversation out of his mind. What could it possibly be about? Well, he would find out soon enough; in the meantime he would concentrate on his machine and Pavel's algorithm.

But it did not take him long to realize that the necessary concentration would not be forthcoming. It wasn't like him to daydream, but that's exactly what he was doing. In his mind's eye he was already on his way to a chic café in Basel's Old Town to keep an appointment with a woman he had never met. *Scheiese.* He might just as well log off. He took off the headset, removed his foot from the torsion cradle, and switched off the computer.

His thoughts turned back again to the curious phone call. She had said that she wanted to talk to him in person, that it was very important, that she would appreciate it if he would not mention her call to anybody. Under other circumstances he would have dismissed her as a crank.

But it wasn't just any woman. It was Judith Knight, Chief Scientist at Human Potential, Incorporated, of Boulder, Colorado, the director of her company's participation in the Human Genome Project. He had known her, by reputation, for years. Her first paper had been presented at the 1973 Gordon Conference on Nucleic Acids, where her comments prompted other scientists to voice their concern about the potentialities of recombinant DNA. At the time of the Gordon Conference she had been fifteen years old, a sophomore in high school. The Gordon Conference participants wrote an open letter to the President of the National Academy of Sciences expressing their reservations, and this letter led to the 1975 Asilomar Conference on Recombinant DNA Molecules, where the ethical and practical problems of working with DNA were first explicitly addressed by the scientific community. There had been one hundred and thirty-five participants in the Asilomar conference, including fifty-two scientists from outside the United States. Of these one hundred and thirty-five participants, one hundred and thirty were Ph.D.-credentialed scientists. Of the remaining five, four were lawyers. The fifth was Judith Knight. She was seventeen. Her essay "Thoughts about the Human Genome" had appeared in *Science* in 1980, when she was twenty-two, and it was one of the one of the touchstone documents of the entire Human Genome Project. This worldwide effort to unravel the structure and function of every single gene in the human genetic blueprint was certainly the most ambitious undertaking in the history of science, and Judith Knight was one of its chief architects.

Her essay had not only outlined the science that would be required and the organization that would be needed to coordinate research activities, it had also anticipated the moral issues that the project would raise— from the ethics of research conducted on aborted human fetal tissue, to questions of resource allocation in a world where some people can live forever but some people must die. Since then Dieter had seen her name often; she had become one of the world's preeminent scientists. Although they had never met, she had been a professor at MIT when he was a graduate student. Judith Knight was no crank. Dieter could only wonder what she could have to say to him that was so urgent that she had flown from Boulder to Basel to divulge it, so private that it could not be discussed by telephone, even a telephone in an unnoticed corner of a busy nightspot, where nobody would be able to overhear her.

Chapter 6

Carl had said he was going to be blunt, and he had been. And evidently he was as good at collecting personal information as he was at collecting marketing research. Nick felt violated, but he had to respect any man with balls enough to tell it to him straight.

"Monty Meekman caused all this turmoil in my life and now he's going to 'pluck' me?" Nick said. "How? Why?"

"I don't know why and I don't know how. I only know the pattern. It's called Digital MicroSystems Corporate Research Fellow. Monty recruits these guys—guys like you: smart, decent— and somehow he transforms them into geniuses willing to die for him. There's a connection between Monty and the Fellows that goes deeper than money. It's more like the loyalty to Jim Jones that led six hundred people to drink cyanide at Jonestown, or the loyalty to that guy in Waco that made people fight to the death for his promised salvation."

"Koresh."

"Monty's like him, or that guy that led his 'flock' out in the desert to meet a space ship."

This was getting extreme. Nick had spoken with Monty on about ten occasions over five years. Sometimes Nick would go to a restaurant to keep a date, only to have the maitre d' bring a telephone so that Nick and Monty could "converse" over dinner. The 'conversations' were odd, lopsided: Monty did most of the talking, and most of it was about himself—his role in the computer industry, his role in the history of computer science, his thoughts on society, politics, art, music, history, the philosophy of science. . . He was a chirpy, squeaky-voiced, arrogant, self-satisfied pipsqueak of a man who had more IQ in his little finger than Nick had in his brain. Nick never *enjoyed* Monty's conversations per se, but he continued to accept Monty's invitations for the same reasons he always had: simple animal curiosity, and a vague hope that maybe something good for his career would come of it.

He tried to reconcile his experience of Monty with the theory Carl had just sketched. Monty was fascinating, there was no doubt about that. But there was nothing charismatic about him, nothing that would inspire the kind of devotion that led to mass suicide in Guyana and conflagration in Texas. Although. . .

"There *was* one rather odd evening I spent with the Fellows at Pajaro Dunes," Nick said.

The staff of Digital MicroSystems Laboratories was having a three day teambuilding retreat, and Monty invited Nick to join them for one evening. So Nick had driven his rental car down from Menlo Park to Pajaro Dunes, where the Fellows had rented a group of secluded oceanside condominiums. The fact that the team had gone "off-site" for a few days of rest, physical exercise, relaxation, and brainstorming was, in itself, not odd at all. It was standard practice for every engineering team he'd ever been part of. Nor was it especially odd that the engineers were all men, and all wearing identical sweatshirts. Commemorative team sweatshirts were as much a part of this kind of event as the after-lunch frisbee toss. What was odd was that the sweatshirts were plain purple tunics, almost like Star Trek uniforms. What was also odd was that the evening's activity was to watch the movie *Twelve O'clock High*, the story of a demoralized bomber squadron in the Second World War that is whipped into fighting shape by a no-nonsense Gregory Peck. Any ordinary group of computer engineers would have talked over the entire movie in nonstop satirical commentary. This group had watched in rapt attention until the final credit. Then they thanked Nick for coming and showed him the door, without so much as offering him a beer or pretzel. Monty, of course, had never shown up.

"Did you ever ask yourself *why* Monty had taken such an interest in you? Did you ever stop to think *why* a junior engineer from the Mill might have been casually invited to spend a few hours with the brainiest nerds on the planet?"

"Sure, I wondered. Of course."

"And what answer did you come up with?"

Carl had him there.

"OK," Nick said. "You win. Let's say it happens. Monty summons me from Siberia and anoints me with holy oil. He gives me millions of dollars, and in return

I take the Omerta, the Mafia vow of silence. Where do you fit in?"

Carl waited before answering, almost as if he had changed his mind about the whole thing.

"I'm the one to whom you betray him," he said at last.

"I betray him," Nick said, stunned by the oddness of the concept. "You're the one to whom I betray him."

"Yes. You're Judas, and I'm the chief Pharisee. You spend a few months insinuating yourself into Monty's good graces, then you start serious espionage. You let me know what's under development at the Labs. You tell me how he transforms ordinary engineers into Corporate Fellows. You sell him out. To me. That's where I fit in."

Nick's beer was empty; he signaled for another.

"So you do want me to do market research for you."

"No. I want to write a book about him. The real story. Not the press-release stuff, 'he led this team, he led that team.' There's something else going on, and I can't find out what it is without being a Corporate Fellow, which is not in store for me. You're as close as I'm going to get."

"Will you match the bucks I'll forfeit when he finds out I'm a rat?"

"Not even close. But I will split the book deal with you. We might make some money, but it's more likely that you'll get sued for breech of contract and perhaps thrown in jail for corporate espionage. The risk to you is infinitely greater than the risk to me, of course."

"Then why am I going to do it?"

"Because when you find out what he's up to you'll want to shake his tree."

As Carl was talking, Nick noticed two men in leather jackets with Harley-Davidson insignia gazing at him from a the side of pool table. One said something to the other; they walked over to Carl, each with a pool cue in hand, and before Nick could do anything one of them had put his hand on Carl's shoulder and spun him on the stool.

"Hey, man," said a boyish-looking man with brilliant teeth. "It's Carl, right?" He put his hand out. "Jim Boerr. Cybersuds!"

"Of course," Carl smiled, shaking Boerr's hand in the glad-hand way that showed Nick once again how perfectly Carl was suited to his profession. "Cybersuds, I remember. Jim Boerr. Kliner Cawkins. And your sidekick Kim Cardinal."

Carl nodded toward Nick.

"Say 'hi' to my friend Nick, an old college buddy of mine. Catching up, reliving the old times, blah blah blah."

"Hey, Nick." There were fake smiles and handshakes all around.

Boerr's gaze seemed to narrow at Carl, even as the smile on his face beamed.

"Did you hear what the Dark Angel's got planned?"

"I've heard talk."

"It's gonna be hot. Hot."

"It sure seems that way."

In the short silence that followed this remark, Nick thought he detected a contest, some kind of stand-off. After a further moment of silence, Jim and Kim simultaneously put up right hands to wave 'bye,' and stepped back.

"We'll let you get back to 'glory days,'" Jim said. "We were just on our way out when we caught sight of you."

"Great, man, take it easy," Carl said with a broad smile, as if delighted to have run into two of his dearest friends. They placed their cues in a rack and left, with their game unfinished.

"Friends of yours?" he said.

"V.C. vultures."

"*Viet Cong Vultures?* That's some bad-ass name for a motorcycle gang."

"Venture capital. Kliner Cawkins Partners. Those two guys are 'angels,' men with money to fund start-ups. That boyish little man that looks like Michael J. Fox is worth about three billion."

"Pocket change," Nick said. It was the only proper response for a man with negative net worth.

"Fucking vampires," Carl said. "Always looking for information."

"Unlike yourself. What's Cybersuds?"

"Sort of a high-tech movable feast in New York; a salon, if you will. Palo Alto in Manhattan. All the movers and shakers of Silicon Alley get together for beer, contacts, connections, virtual blow jobs, trendy talk about 'new media'; one-and-all looking for a ground-floor entry to the next Microsoft, the next Netscape. It's the world I live in. Engineers enter it at their peril."

"Thanks for the warning. Who's the Dark Angel?"

"He'll be picking you up in his ratty little Mercedes in about two hours."

Of course, Nick thought. The Dark Angel. Monty Meekman.

"They seemed to know you've got an eye on him," Nick said.

"Everybody's got an eye on Monty Meekman. Or at least everybody who follows money and technology has an eye on him. But nobody knows what he's up to. And with the Forum coming up they're getting skittish, like little woodland creatures before the storm."

"Forum? What forum?"

"The Biodigital Forum. It's an offshoot of the Digital Forum. You know, Rachel's Thing."

"Oh, yeah," Nick said, making the connection.

Rachel Tryson, the futurist and technology pundit, was, at thirty-seven, the most powerful woman in information technology. She had been to the infotocracy born: her father was a Nobel Prize-winning physicist who had been pals with Johnny

Von Neuman himself, and her mother was the architect of the Lovelace Programming Environment.

Once a year the most powerful people in the industry—CEOs, venture capitalists, and random visionaries— ritually set aside their weapons and gathered for the Digital Forum, otherwise known as Rachel's Thing. It might take place in Arizona one year or at Jackson Hole the next. Attendance was by invitation only, the invitees drawn from the subscribers to Tryson's newsletter, *Patch Process*. Whatever the setting, the modus operandi was the same: the billionaires relaxed in the sun with drinks in their hands, and, under Rachel's virtual-maternal gaze, they decided the future of mankind.

"OK," Nick said. "So I know what the Digital Forum is. What's the Biodigital Forum?"

"The same thing, only more hip: the number infocrats is cut in half to make room for the corresponding elite from biotechnology. People who want to know what's really going on in the Valley watch Rachel's Biodigital invitee list more closely than they watch the NASDAQ ticker."

"Where's it going down this year?"

"Saratoga Club: everything a harried billionaire could want in a Wine Country retreat, without the Wine Country or the hassle of the drive up to Napa. Two three-star restaurants, a ten-thousand bottle wine cellar, a PGA golf course, ten tennis courts, a world-class croquet field, and twenty masseurs—for two hundred guests."

"Doesn't sound like my kind of gig," Nick said.

"That's where you're wrong. Monty and Rachel have something cooked up for the Biodigital Forum. If Monty makes you a fellow, you'll be there. The timing isn't accidental."

"*What* do they have cooked up?"

"I don't know. Nobody does."

"Your friends the vultures seem to be in the know."

"They're bluffing."

Nick picked up the hundred dollar bill and held it to the light from a neon Budweiser clock.

"Down payment on my blood money?"

"Not at all. Remember, if you take the job I want it back. If you *do* go to work for Monty I won't call you. But if the time comes when you want to talk, call me." Carl reached into his pocket and produced a business card. "Here. Don't forget the zip code."

"You're serious about all this aren't you?" Nick said.

"Nick, I'm as serious as Tantric sex with a Hindu goddess."

"Cheesus," Nick said. "I'm going to be really disappointed if Monty just wants to say hello."

"I'll see you at Saratoga," Carl said, as he raised himself off the barstool.

"You're on Rachel's list, of course," Nick said. "I should have known."

"One more thing," Carl said. "Beware of icicles."

"Icicles? In Sunnyvale?"

"No fingerprints. Watch your back, Nick."

With that Carl was out the door.

Nick ordered another beer. Carl hadn't seemed deranged, but the words that had come out of his mouth were crazy. Perhaps it had been a joke, but who would have put Carl up to it? It didn't matter: within a few hours Monty either would or would not propose to Nick that he become a Corporate Fellow. Until then Nick would watch Buster and Mike.

Ironic, wasn't it, to think Monty might be the one to rescue him from oblivion? Bartlett had prophesied that Nick would never work for Monty. She also had pledged that she herself would remain faithful to Nick for life. She had left him. Monty had never promised Nick a thing, but had remained faithful, in a manner of speaking, for five years.

"God, Bartlett," Nick whispered to the empty stool beside him. "Has it really been five months? Five God damned months and I can't shake you for a minute; not even for a second."

Nick picked up the C-note, put it into his wallet and walked out of Mad Antonio's Nut House. The sunlight nearly blinded him.

Chapter 7

Twenty minutes before he was scheduled to meet Judith Knight, Dieter Steffen opened the lower left-hand drawer of his seldom-used desk and removed the lid from a sealed box of business cards. He withdrew a card and examined it: Dieter Steffen, Ph.D., Senior Scientist, Hoff-Zeigy, AG. *So that's who I am,* he thought. He put several cards in his shirt, closed the drawer, and left.

Ten minutes later he boarded the tram. The ride from Dreirosenbrücke to Barfüsserplatz took twelve minutes. He spent the time looking out the window at night-time Basel, occasionally catching glimpses of the river before crossing it on the Mittlere Brücke over into the Old City.

When the train went under an overpass he saw his reflection in the glass of the window. How jowly he had become! At one time, in his early teens, he had been a competition skier, an athlete. Now he was the very embodiment of unphysicality. He was embarrassed to find himself thinking this way: he never thought about his looks. It was only his going to meet a woman, an assignation in a café right out of a spy movie, that had gotten his mind going along this unfamiliar path. For two hours he had found himself wondering what she would look like— endless variations on the themes tall, floral-pattern dress and hat with a flower in the brim.

He got off the tram and headed towards Freie Strasse. The air was cooler than had anticipated, and he was chilly. He walked close to the buildings on the right side of the street in a largely unsuccessful attempt to find warmth. At Freie Strasse he turned left. Five minutes later he was on the terrace, looking nervously about.

Then he saw her.

It had to be her. She was tall, she was the right age, she was wearing a floral print dress and a hat with a flower; a jacket was folded over her arm. But why, if she had wanted to make sure that she would be recognized, had she said only that she was tall, was dressed in such a fashion, would be wearing such and such a hat? Why had she not said, "I am a Nubian princess, the color of Swiss milk chocolate, possessor of such grace and beauty that men walk into walls when they first see me?" He knew for a fact that she was thirty-seven years old. It was hard to believe. Had she, in her work, perhaps solved the mystery of teleomeres, the chromosomal timekeepers attached to each human cell's DNA chain, and thereby drunk from the fountain of youth? He took a deep breath and approached her.

"Miss Knight? I am Dieter Steffen."

"Hello," she said. "Thank you for coming."

"Of course. Shall we sit?"

They took seats at an open table; a waiter approached.

"Miss Knight?" Dieter asked.

"Campari, please," she said.

"Wartek, bitte." Dieter said. Yes, by all means, a beer. Quickly. "I am hoping you you have found your way here without too much trouble?"

"No trouble at all, thank you. It is indeed a lovely city."

The drinks arrived; Dieter resisted the urge to consume his in one gulp, to help him to regain his composure. The circumstances, her fame, his shyness had made him nervous enough already. Her being an exotic African beauty in the bargain was nearly more than he could handle. Her forehead was high and sloped back like a pharaoh's. Her eyes were dark, her nose aquiline, her teeth a brilliant white. She had a dimple in her right cheek.

"Well now," he said, "how is it that I can be helping you?"

"Perhaps you know me as a scientist with Human Potential," she said. "But it is not in that capacity that I wish to speak with you today. Are you familiar with ARB, the Association for Responsible Biotechnology?"

"I believe that I have heard the name, but I must confess that I do not now recall anything about this organization."

Do you know a Paul Aubrey, from your company?"

"We may have met. In what capacity he may work I am not remembering."

Dieter! What is it with this accent? You speak English every day!

"Paul Aubrey is a matchmaker," she said. "Like all the pharmaceutical companies, Hoff- Zeigy wants to know as much as it can about the Human Genome Project. Paul Aubrey is your company's ambassador to the small biotechnology companies of the world, where much of this work is going on. Small companies like Human Potential—"

She paused, to make sure he was following her. Certainly he was following her. He would have followed her anywhere.

"—He met with the board of directors of our company last week. I sit on the board of directors."

Dieter nodded.

"He came to us to propose a collaboration between Hoff-Zeigy and Human Potential. To be precise, Doktor Steffen, he proposed a collaboration between your nanotechnology laboratory, and my genetic research laboratory."

Oh *merde,* he thought. *Doktor* Steffen. And I have been calling her *Miss* Knight. *So ne duubel!* What an oaf!

"I must admit to being at somewhat of a loss, Dr. Knight. This is the first I have heard of this proposed collaboration."

"So I thought; that is no matter. My board has declined the offer. The reason that I have called upon you is that Paul Aubrey is still casting about for a corporate partner to provide research results on the human genome. His proposal to my company was rejected, but there are other companies. As a member of the board of directors of Human Potential, Incorporated, I can do nothing with this knowledge. It was divulged to me in strictest confidence; I cannot ethically share this information with anyone who wasn't part of that discussion. Many people, including your corporation's lawyers, I am sure, would consider that I have already broken my agreement by speaking with you. But you are not an uninterested party, Doktor Steffen. The whole reason for Paul Aubrey's quest is your work."

"Please go on, Dr. Knight," he said. "Only, I would ask a favor. If it would not make you uncomfortable, I would prefer that you call me Dieter. I am Swiss, but I have spent much time in the States. I am more comfortable with the American form of address."

"Very well. And you should call me Judith."

"Thank you. Please continue—Judith."

"As I was saying, as a member of the board of Human Potential I have nothing to say about Hoff-Zeigy's corporate research strategy. But as a human being, as a founding member of the Association for Responsible Biotechnology, I am very concerned about the kind of partnership that Aubrey is seeking to bring about. I don't think such a partnership should take place now, perhaps not ever. Humankind has not yet developed the wisdom necessary to manage the offspring that might come about from such a union.

"I don't know very much about your nanotechnology work, Dieter," she continued. "I only know what Paul Aubrey told me. I am certain that he intended to divulge only enough information to see whether we would be interested in proceeding further. So I only know the general outlines of your approach."

"Tell me then, please, what you understand of it," Dieter said.

"You and your team are working on a nanomachine for DNA repair. This machine would be smaller than a virus, yet capable of storing the information equivalent of the human genome, all forty-six human chromosomes, fractally condensed. This machine would be programmable, so that any portion of the stored genome could be used as a template for repair of a damaged chromosome in a target cell. Finally, this machine would be strong; strong enough to live outside of laboratory conditions, strong enough even to live in the air."

"It seems that you know a lot about my work."

"Dieter, this is very, very dangerous work. I am sure that you can see that."

"If you mean that there exists the possibility for misuse of this technology, certainly you are right. But that is true of any science, of any technology. Steel can be used to make surgeon's scalpels or, what do you call them, dum-dum bullets. Fertilizer can be used to grow crops or to make terrorist bombs. Computers can be used to explore the ocean bottom or to manipulate the stock market. It is up to society to determine how technology is put to use, not up to the scientist."

"That is certainly a common argument, and a convenient one. But sometimes it begs important questions. It took the scientists of the Manhattan Project two years to invent an atom bomb, and yet fifty years later Iraq cannot do it; they must seek to buy their bombs elsewhere. What would the world be like if atom bombs were not so difficult to make, if you could get one as easily as you can buy a toothbrush? What moral burdens would rest on the shoulders of those first bomb-makers? Your work is perhaps as much in advance of the world. If you stopped working now, it might be fifty years until some other team reached the stage that you are now at. Fifty years is a long time. I would rather take fifty years to get ready, to think through what we are about, than to go ahead and make something dangerous now, just because we know how to make it."

"So my work is like a Manhattan Project, an atom bomb? I was under the impression I was working on a universal medicine, a cure for Cystic Fibrosis and cancer," he said.

"Of course it could be used for that, and I am sure that is your intent. But you cannot escape the fact that this technology could also be used for biological warfare of the most sophisticated, the most evil kind. Assume you succeed in making your device, your nanomachine. You could release these—" she hesitated, looking for a word— "these *things* in the air, and they could be programmed to seek out people who had a certain gene, say, a gene for blond hair. When they find that gene they change it to the 'right' gene. Or they launch another program to kill the 'defective' person who has that gene. These machines would be so small that they could pass through any gas mask. They would be virtually undetectable. And if they were enclosed in a sixty- carbon, flexible-diamond shell they would be virtually indestructible. There would be no way to stop them."

"In theory what you say is correct. But how likely is it?"

"How likely does it have to be? How likely was it that the HIV virus would jump from monkey to man?"

She was leaning over at him now, speaking very rapidly in a loud whisper, as if restraining herself from yelling. Dieter noticed her hands gripping the sides of the table; she almost looked ready to release it and slap him.

"How likely that HIV would be able to penetrate the immune system?" she said. "When you are talking about the most powerful weapon in history, the perfect terrorist weapon, the answer to Hitler's prayers for a final solution—the likelihood doesn't have to be very great before it becomes frightening. How would you feel if Saddam Hussein were loading warheads with these devices?"

Dieter was taken aback by her intensity, but in a moment he found a way to answer.

"Well, you can rest easy for a little while, Judith," he said. "We have not figured out how to make these things, as you call them. In computer simulation, it is possible to design simple nanomachines. But to build a machine that could survive in the real world? The real world, where a two degree rise in temperature has the same effect as a nuclear explosion? No, you can rest easy, Dr. Knight. We are not there yet," he said.

In truth, he had had inklings of some of these same concerns from time to time, but he had always put them out of his mind. Thoughts like Judith's could drive you crazy. Start down this path and you might never get back on the right track, never regain your momentum. And once a scientist loses momentum, it's all over, *kaput*.

"That is reassuring, certainly," Judith was saying. "But based on what Aubrey told us I would have to conclude that you are getting close. Otherwise why would Hoff-Zeigy go shopping for a partner? I would add that when Aubrey met with our board he mentioned money available to the right partner. Very large amounts of money. Enough to make every person in the room a millionaire many times over, instantly. And that would only be the down payment if the collaboration succeeded. Not many boards of directors will be able to resist that lure. Especially a board of directors like mine, I might add, which holds title to remarkable technology, but hovers on the brink of bankruptcy."

"I don't suppose that many such boards of directors will be able to resist the lure. But it occurs to me, Judith, that perhaps you are talking to the wrong person. Why not talk to Aubrey himself?"

Judith Knight looked up from the table; her eyes fixed Dieter's for a long time before she spoke.

"Paul Aubrey is only an agent of Hoff-Zeigy," she said. "He is an ambassador, a salesman. Hoff-Zeigy must find a genome-research partner, the financial incentives are just too great to do otherwise. If Paul Aubrey did not want to pursue this work, the corporation would easily find somebody else to take his place. . . But without you, without the science, Hoff-Zeigy is dead in the water. You are irreplaceable."

She stared at him so earnestly that he had to look down for a moment before he answered.

"You flatter me. But perhaps I am not as indispensable as you might think. I have a colleague, perhaps Mr. Aubrey mentioned his name. He must be the source of Aubrey's knowledge, since I have not spoken with Aubrey myself, and my reports go only to this other person, the research director of the NanoSection. His name is Pavel Isaacs."

She sighed, then appeared to bite her lower lip, however briefly.

"I think I would like to try a sip of some authentic Kirsch," she said. "I have been told that the varieties available in the States pale in comparison to the real thing."

"May I suggest, then, a local product, made here in Basel."

Dieter turned to the waiter. *"Zweite Basler-Dybli, bitte."*

"Thank you," she said. "I'll just need a few seconds to collect my thoughts."
In the space of those few seconds the waiter reappeared, bearing a tray on which were two large shot glasses filled to the brim with clear liquid.

"Brost," Dieter said, raising his glass to his lips. They each took sips, and Dieter felt the sensation of the strong bitter drink, vaguely reminiscent of the taste of cherries, on his tongue.

"Well," she resumed. "What I am about to say is going to place an imposition on your goodwill. I cannot talk with Pavel Isaacs, as you call him. This 'Isaacs' and I have, how shall I say this, a complex and intimate history. I cannot go into details. But I can tell you this. I fear this man. I fear him greatly. It was when I became certain of his identity that I knew I must come here to speak with you."

Dieter was stunned. He took another sip of his brandy. How could this be? He had known the man for nearly ten years. It was true that in that time they had met outside of work perhaps four times. They were both extremely quiet and private people, each knew very little of the affairs of the other. But if he were indeed such a dangerous man, wouldn't Dieter have noticed *something*?

"You astonish me, Dr. Knight." His formality reasserted itself.

"Dieter," she said. "Listen to me carefully. You must not let Pavel Isaacs know that we have met. I apologize for putting you in such an awkward position, but I assure you that I am in earnest. Carry on with your work, if that is what you must do. I hope that I can convince you otherwise, but that is something that you will have to decide for yourself. But please, do not let him know that we have spoken. You may choose not to look at the potential for evil embodied in these machines you are trying to build, but Pavel is aware of this potential. That is his motivation."

"Judith, I am speechless." he said. "Are you telling me that my colleague, my collaborator at MIT and here in Basel, the most brilliant scientist I have ever known, is a *terrorist?*"

"Dieter, please. The more I tell you, the more I endanger you. Let us not talk about Pavel Isaacs. Why don't you imagine that he was an old boyfriend of mine and that the wounds are too deep for me to bear to see him again. We can leave it at that. Please. But let us talk, as scientists, about your work, and about the collaboration that Aubrey is trying to bring about."

"Very well," he said, hoping his voice sounded confident.

"I am guessing that Isaacs designs the computer. These will be as powerful as a supercomputer but one hundred thousand times smaller. They will be very fragile. They could not survive outside of a vacuum chamber, much less in a human body.

"You are a very astute observer, Judith."

"But a *fullerene* shell, a hollow graphite sphere would be impregnable, wouldn't it? A buckminsterfullerene sphere could protect the computer."

"That is something we do not know," he said.

"The problem is, a graphite sphere is impregnable from the inside as well as from the outside. You would need to modify the sphere, to create an injector, a tunnel back and forth."

"It seems there is little you have not guessed."

"So we would have a sphere with a long tunnel coming out at one point. It would look a little like a water tower, or a blade of onion grass gone to seed, perhaps, shall we say, like a bacteriophage? The T4 strain would be a good model— "

"Judith," he interrupted, "would you care to join me for another taste of kirsch?"

"Yes, I think I could use it. And I think I'll take the opportunity to excuse myself for a moment."

She left, leaving Dieter in a mild state of shock. The nature of his collaboration with Pavel Isaacs was something intuitive; he had never discussed it with anybody. Nobody but Pavel had seen the fullerene-with-tube design, which was, indeed, based on the model of the bacteria-infecting virus known as T4. And yet Judith Knight had just sat there and told him all these things, as if she were reading from a cue card. This woman was more than smart, she was clairvoyant.

She returned as the second shots of Kirsch arrived.

"Well now," Dieter said. "If I am not to discuss our conversation with Pavel, and if Aubrey is, as you say, only a salesman, then what is it that you would have me do? Should I become suddenly stupid, and sabotage my own work? Should I run away from this research, and take up residence on a desert island? What are you asking of me?"

"There are several things that you can do," she said. "As you say, you can abandon your research. Honestly, I think it might be better for everybody if you did that. But we both know that that is not going to happen. Another thing you can do is make sure that there is a way to disable the device you are building, and publicize it widely. Make the device vulnerable to salt water, or laundry soap, or weak radiation. Your machine could still be used for medicine, but would be less attractive as a weapon. I know that this makes the job more difficult, but you must consider what is at stake."

"Why did you turn down the offer to work with Hoff-Zeigy? You could have built these safeguards in yourself."

"Because we of the Association for Responsible Biotechnology do not believe that there are *any* safeguards strong enough for such devices. The only way to get rid of the threat is to never build them in the first place."

Dieter paused a second to take this in.

"You say I cannot talk to Isaacs, that he is some kind of dangerous person. Can I raise these concerns with Paul Aubrey? Can I tell him that one day after he divulged Hoff-Zeigy secrets to Human Potential I received an urgent phone call from Human Potential's chief scientist?"

"That is something that you will have to decide for yourself. I believe that Isaacs has collaborators, but I don't think Aubrey is one of them. I think it is more likely that he is being used. Just as you are being used."

"I hardly know what to say. I came here to meet a famous scientist, perhaps to talk over some recent scientific developments of mutual interest. Instead I find myself invited to intrigue."

"I can imagine how crazy this must all sound. Take time to think over what I have said. I won't intrude upon you again unless you e-mail me first. If you use two precautions, an anonymous e-mail account and simple encryption, our correspondence should be safe from prying eyes. Anybody poking around in your files is going to assume you've got a secret correspondent for some excitement in your life and probably not get suspicious of anything else. Have you got a card? I don't want you to have anything with my name on it."

He fumbled in several pockets before locating one. By the time he handed it to her the cap was off her gold-nibbed Mont Blanc pen.

"Here is an address, an anonymous address at a server in Sweden."

She wrote:

anon7432@anon.tippi.swed

"The server will assign you a new account number, so I'll know how to get in touch. Now, we'll need a password."

"Basler-Dybli," he said, smiling for the first time today. "It's the brand name of the Kirsch we've been drinking." He reached in his pocket for another card and wrote the words on the back.

"Thank you, Dieter. Please don't call me; my phones may not be secure," she said. "Well, that's what I came here to say. Perhaps it would be better if I left now. It has been a pleasure speaking with you, Herr Doktor Steffen."

She arose quickly and put on her jacket and hat. He stood as quickly as he could, nearly upsetting his chair. She offered her hand and he shook it. She smiled pleasantly, as if they had just agreed to a future date at the opera. Then she turned, and in an instant disappeared into the crowd.

Chapter 8

Pay no attention to that nerd behind the curtain, Nick thought. *This* was Monty Meekman, the great and terrible? *This* nonentity? Talk about anticlimax.

Carl was right: Monty's Mercedes *was* a ratty little rattletrap. Before Nick could even get into it he had to wrestle with the stubborn passenger door, then toss books and papers from the front seat into the back. It was bad enough that the car was so gross; what was worse was that it was unsafe. It had started to shimmy as soon as they hit twenty, and now that they were approaching highway speed a mass of empty coffee cups jostled about Nick's feet like a sea of writhing snakes. It was hard to believe that this was it—the first face-to-face encounter of the mysterious billionaire genius and his reluctant protege: Monty had simply driven this pig-sty on wheels to the hot-dog stand where Nick was waiting for him and tooted his horn. He hadn't even said hello yet.

Monty Meekman might be one of the richest people in the world, but clearly it wasn't a passion for fine automobiles that had driven him to amass his wealth. For that matter, Nick couldn't think of any material goods that attracted Monty's interest, much less passion. Monty was not a person who wanted wealth for the usual reasons that people wanted wealth. Which raised the question: what *did* Monty want?

That's what Carl Swirsing wanted to know, and it was a question that had intrigued Nick, too, for half a decade. Today would present Nick with his best chance to find out, but he had somehow lost all interest in the question. Screw Meekman, Nick thought. Who *cared* what that weirdo wanted out of life? Today Nick was interested in discovering what *Nicholas Aubrey* wanted out of life. And the sad fact was that he hadn't a clue.

Once upon a time Nick thought he knew what mattered to him. He would have said that the meaning in his life came from taking part in the redefinition of human nature. The technology that Nick and a few dozen engineers at Digital MicroSystems designed would have thousandfold bigger impact on the human prospect than Aristotle, Shakespeare, Gutenberg and Henry Ford put together. The Information Revolution was bigger than the invention of agriculture, the Renaissance and the Industrial Revolution added and cubed– who wouldn't leap at the chance to be at its forefront? Moreover, it was fun. The bozos leading this insurrection were a crazy fruit salad; oddballs, free-thinkers, and geniuses. And although Digital MicroSystems was only one banana in the bunch, it was undoubtably the Top Banana. The hottest box was always the Dijjy-Mike box; the coolest code was Dijjy-Mike code. Check out the Internet—developed on Dijjy-Mike machines— a distributed egalitarian thinking engine. Check out chips that helped the crippled to walk, the deaf to hear: if Jesus were alive today he'd be a VLSI designer at Digital MicroSystems. Power to the people, baby: technopotheosis. Nick's business card said Director of Software Engineering, but it should have said Spiritual Alchemist.

He lived on the ramparts. With one office in Newcastle, Massachusetts and another Mountain View, California, Nick Aubrey had spent so much time on the Boston to San Francisco run that he knew the TWA flight crews better than he knew the people who lived next door to him, knew the regular business-class upgraders better than he knew the volunteers at The Magic Box. For years he had spent twenty hours and more each month lashed to an uncomfortable seat inside a smelly contrivance ping-ponging between Logan and SFO, assaulted by white noise as his feet swelled. He had spent endless hours swapping UNIX-wars gossip with the marketing dweeb from the Open Software Foundation whose cologne stuck to Nick's clothes through three washings, or chatting with the stalking-horse delegates to the IEEE Floating Point Standards Committee about how underflow exception handling differed from straight divide-by-zero. This was the thing: even the boring parts were interesting.

There was a down side to his cyberlife: as it flourished, his meat life evanesced. His involvement with the Magic Box children's co-op switched from volunteer work to financial backing; his involvement in his own house switched from volunteer work to financial backing. He worried that Bartlett grew colder. . . He worried that his life was slipping away from him. But he never dreamed of stopping. He rather too much dug the buzz from the Juice.

The Juice, man. Residual perfume, fat feet and yuppie marriage angst were the price you paid to be plugged into it. The Juice was the adolescent Net, the nascent Web; it was intelligent agents, distributed objects, the Human Interface to cyber-whatever. You could pick it up by induction just walking down any street in Mountain View; it was so strong every where in the Silicon Valley that it messed up radio signals from unhip stations. They even used it to heat burritos at the *Dos Hermanos* trailer in the Longs Drugs parking lot on Rengsdorff Avenue and to recharge the leaf-blowers of the landscapers who ate there. It was intoxicating. The gizmos that would turn the world on its head in 1999 were dreamed up by Dijjy-Mike microkids in the eighties and prototyped by them in '90, '91, '92. To be a bi-coastal manager of software engineering for Digital MicroSystems during those years was truly to have your finger in the socket.

So yes: present at the creation, check. Consequently today Nick's finger was charred black all the way to his shoulder. He had sacrificed his life to his addiction to the Juice. Sometime in the next hour or so Monty Meekman would either fulfill or belie Carl's prediction, and either way Nick would know that he had wasted the last five years in pursuit of that buzz. For if Monty did do the utterly fantastic, if he did offer Nick ten million dollars to become a Corporate Fellow, that could only mean that Nick had been played like a marionette. But if, on the other hand, Monty did not offer Nick a fortune; if, indeed, he wanted nothing more from Nick today than he had wanted on other occasions— somebody to talk to, somebody to listen in awed silence to Monty's self-absorbed explanations of Life, the Universe, and Everything—then what was the point of that? Was that all Nick had accomplished in his career? To have become an unpaid word-sink for a wealthy old crank?

Nick's high-tech life was a high-tech grind. Juice? Nonsense. Let *Wired* keep all that technohip bullshit. Information technology was an economic centrifuge, a wealth-and-power concentrator. This was the reality of the Information Revolution: efficiency, productivity, and downsizing; NAFTA, and the Walmartification of once-beautiful downtowns like Newcastle's; the strengthening of multinational conglomerates relative to poor people, human rights workers and small countries; the end of privacy, the eclipse of democracy, and realistic mayhem in video games.

From the front seat of Monty's Mercedes rattling down the frontage road Nick gazed out to the east over a sea of tall marsh grass that extended from the macadam all the way to the edge of San Francisco Bay. Amid square miles of vegetation he could see tiny figures jogging—distant people taking toy-scale exercise in the bright winter sun. It almost looked as if they were floating atop the cattails, but Nick knew they were walking on earthen levees that snaked through the estuary. He himself had just returned from a long walk on those dikes in a desultory effort to sober up. The sound of an unmuffled down-shifting tractor-trailer brought his attention around to the left side of the Mercedes, where, beyond a chain-link fence, four lanes of traffic on Highway 101 North paralleled the path of Monty's car at twice its speed. Nick turned his gaze forward, and, out of the left corner of his eye, regarded Monty Meekman.

Monty was a perfectly ordinary-looking white person, Nick thought—with the qualifying words 'whatever that means' forming themselves as a detached commentary on his own half-inebriated observation. Monty was perhaps fifty-five years old, with dark wavy hair and a three-o'clock shadow that was somewhere between Lieutenant Colombo's and Fred Flintstone's. He was a slightly-built, unathletic man who had developed the small paunch typical of slightly-built unathletic men at middle age. He was wearing a nondescript dark suit that had probably fit him better at one time than it did today. Leaning forward as he drove, grasping the steering wheel with both hands, smiling the smile of the self-satisfied—he rather resembled the engineer in Dr. Seuss's *Green Eggs and Ham*, Nick thought, nonchalantly sailing his locomotive through the air. At the traffic light where Frontage Road met Oregon Way, Monty pulled to a stop.

"Do you know what those buildings are over there, Nick?" he chirped.

Duh, Nick thought. Everybody knew that those perfectly anonymous two-storey brick-and- glass office buildings in the little office park across the street had once housed the Mountain View Research Center, MVRC. During the late 1960's, Duplicon—the giant photocopying company—had operated an R&D lab there. The free-thinkers of Duplicon MVRC, "Emverk", most of whom had some prior association with Thomas Engleton and the Santa Clara Research Institute, developed the Duplicon DataStar, the precursor by two decades of the modern personal computer. Meanwhile, back in Syracuse, Duplicon's incredibly dim corporate management somehow didn't notice that Emverk had just laid a golden egg, and they shut the place down. Emverk's engineers scattered—to Apple, Hewlett-Packard, Intel, and of course, Digital MicroSystems. Nick had heard this legend a hundred times before, ninety times from the lips of Monty Meekman, who, at the age of 25, had been Emverk's Director of Research.

"Was that the garage where Steve and Curt started Apple?" Nick deadpanned.

"No, actually, heh heh . . ." And so began the hundred-and-first telling of the Emverk legend.

It was inescapable: like a captive altar boy to an ancient priest saying a Latin mass, Nick's role would be to mutter responses at lulls in the sacred text as the liturgist and acolyte transversed Palo Alto. Nick knew that it didn't matter if he said inappropriate things in the wrong language at the wrong time: Monty was ordained, Monty was conducting the rite, and nothing Nick did could fuck it up. Nick was superfluous. *"Introibo ad altari Dei,"* he said.

The Old Testament readings came first: Monty began today with the chronicle of Alan Turing, who wrestled angels of improbability up and down a ladder-like virtual machine in his mind. Then came the story of John Von Neumann, who had led the chosen people from the captivity of analog to the heights above a land flowing with digital bits. This part of the oratory took them down Oregon Expressway to Alma Street, where they turned right, north, along the Cal Trans tracks.

Monty's virtual tape droned on. Now it was at the 'sh'-boys: Shannon of information theory, Shockly of the transistor. These two proto-hackers went together in Nick's mind like prophets from the late-middle Bible: Ezekial and Ezekiah, or Zephaniah and Zechariah.

A quick left jog on University Avenue took them under the railroad tracks and across El Camino Real, as Nick mouthed random responses to Monty's monologue. "Oh yes, entropy," Nick said, or "the transmission of any message is necessarily accompanied by a certain diminution of the information it contains," or "surprise equals the negative logarithm of probability." If he had had a hand bell he would have rung it.

They cut through the Stanford campus, skirting the Packard Children's Hospital, until they came to Sand Hill Road, where they turned west, left, towards the rolling dry hills. Quarks and leptons drag-raced alongside them underground in the Stanford Linear Accelerator, "SLAC," as Monty picked up the pace of his recitation, getting to the early part of the New Testament— which was conventionally said to begin on the day that Thomas Engleton appeared at the Santa Clara Research Institute, SCRI, wearing sackcloth, eating locusts and wild honey, preaching Usability. From his earliest days at the Rengsdorff creek he foretold the kingdom of Emverk, making smooth the way for Monty. Nick gazed at the familiar sights and did his best to tune out.

The rolling hills became the steep wooded hills of the Santa Cruz ridge, and still Monty chirped on, coming, inevitably, to the story of Engleton's famous 1966 broadcast from SCRI to the Association for Computing Machinery assembled in San Francisco. Monty had been Engleton's chief assistant at that epochal event; it had been his baptism. But Nick didn't need to hear this part again, not now.

"Where are you taking us?" Nick asked, as a dread of Pajarro Dunes came over him. The Dunes were over the mountains, an hour south of Santa Cruz. Nick's flight didn't leave until ten o'clock tonight, but there still wasn't time to get down there and back to the airport before the red-eye left. "I'm flying back east tonight," Nick added, to make sure Monty understood the constraints on his liberty.

"Flights can be changed."

Nick didn't suppose he would ever get used to this billionaire's presumption.

"I change my flights when I have a good reason to," Nick said. " I don't have any reason."

Monty didn't seem concerned about Nick's travel plans.

"What do you like about selling toys?" he said.

"I don't do too much of that any more."

"That wasn't the question."

"I like children."

"That wasn't the question either."

Until today Nick had never really thought about why he put up with Monty's breaches of common etiquette, but since his conversation in Mad Antonio's, Nick knew the truth: he sucked up to Monty because Monty had money and power. Well, screw that. It was time to change the terms of their relationship by the simple expedient of acting like a man instead of a doormat.

"I don't like selling toys," Nick said, resuming the conversation. "I like watching children play with toys, and I like the toys themselves."

"You don't have any children of your own."

"Do you?"

"Your wife left you. Why was that?"

"Keep your nose out of my personal business, Monty."

"Her company works with recombinant DNA to research the human genome. Is that her way of sublimating your refusal to have children with her?"

"How many children do you have, Monty? I've never heard you mention any."

"Oh, I have many. Many. You'll see."

"How many?"

"Bartlett's company needs another infusion of cash," Monty changed the subject.

"I wouldn't know."

"She wants to retain control, but control is the one thing capital never relinquishes. She doesn't understand capitalists."

"You don't have any children," Nick said. "You're full of baloney."

Monty slid a cassette into the player, and presently piano, bass, drums and trumpet sounded, barely audible over the squeaks, rattles, and road noise.

"The best way to understand Miles Davis's music is as a pentatonic stochastic process, with each instrument a simple Markov chain. . ."

"You still haven't said where we're going."

"People are generally stupid, Nick. That's the important thing to remember if you want to have fun."

"Baloney," Nick said. The snakes at his feet were writhing again.

In Portola Valley Monty picked up Skyline Drive and headed south on the San Francisco peninsula along ridge of the mountains that separate the Silicon Valley from the Pacific coast. Although Nick had been down Skyline Drive several times before he had never gotten used to its drama. Up and up the road rose until eventually they were at almost three thousand feet, amid sequoias ten yards thick and a thousand years old, a forest primeval. There were places where he could see the San Andreas Fault, like a hiccough in the terrain; had he gotten out of the car he could

have touched it. The Mercedes rounded a turn, the forest gave way, and a spectacular view opened up to them. There was a little parking area with a sign stating the
obvious. Monty left the road and pulled to a stop at the edge of the scenic overlook.
As they were getting out of the car Monty said, "Sometime in the next half hour."

"What?"

They walked to a guardrail at the edge of a cliff. The Silicon Valley lay beneath
them, flush against the shallow waters of the South Bay: Sunnyvale. Cupertino. Palo
Alto. Mountain View. Menlo Park. Santa Clara. Los Gatos. Los Altos. And at the
south tip of the bay, to the right, San Jose.

There wasn't much smog that day. Looking north Nick could see the
Dumbarton Bridge over the bay, and seven miles north of that he could faintly make
out the San Mateo bridge. Across the water lay the towns of the East Bay and the hills
behind them—Mission Peak, and way off in the distance, high on a mountaintop in
the southeast, those two white domes of the Lick Observatory, with their two giant
telescopes pointed up to the heavens: the Moon, Mars, Jupiter, the Milky Way,
Castor, Pollux, the Horsehead Nebula; pulsars, quasars, galaxies upon galaxies, dark
matter hiding the uncomputed mass of the unseen infinitude, neutron stars, black
holes, the end of time. Somewhere to the east of the observatory lay Massachusetts.

"Knowledge is power, Nick," Monty said.

"A commonplace," Nick answered. "You're boring me. Power bores me."

"Of course it doesn't. You love power. That's why you're no longer living in
Fanaye, a mud-hut village on the edge of the desert, with Ousmane Diop and
Amadou N'Diaye and Sediou Tall and Ama'sy N'Dongo. They may be nice people;
I don't know and I don't care to know. You seem to believe that they are nice people. But you are a sentimentalist— a great failing. The point is that you left the pow-
erless peasants behind. You found your way to Digital MicroSystems, the forge of
human destiny. Would you like to know why?"

Nick's breath was taken away. How would Monty have learned the name of a
small African village Nick and Todd had visited nearly twenty years ago, much less
the names of its inhabitants?

"Why?" The word came out involuntarily.

"You love knowledge, power. That's why I've taken you here—to give you
more of it."

"I never told you about Fanaye," Nick said. "I never told you their names."

"I notice that you recently filed a bug report on the mail program," Monty said.
The conversation was back to normal—random comments apropos of nothing at all.

"I file bugs when I discover them," Nick answered.

"You fixed the bug yourself and then you filed the report about the fix."

"Nothing unusual in engineers fixing bugs, is there?"

"It wasn't your code."

"The guy who owned the code couldn't see the problem. I fixed if for him."

"The bugtrack protocol is that he who owns the code files the fix."

Monty Meekman, primordial codeslinger, knew damn good and well that the bugtrack protocol was honored in the breach. The bugtrack protocol was about as sacrosanct as the admonition on a box of Q-Tips to use them to clean the outside of your ears only.

"I'm surprised that the Vice Chairman of the corporation is reading bug reports," Nick said.

"Do you think it's possible that someone might have sown bugs throughout the system, like bread crumbs in the forest, to see who would come to eat them?"

"You tell me," Nick said.

Monty *wouldn't* tell him, of course. Monty rarely answered a direct question. But there must have been a reason that he brought the subject up.

Chapter 9

Bartlett Aubrey skated down Lansdowne street with Fenway's left field wall, the Green Monster, on one side, and a row of silent nightclubs on the other. The streets were clear of ice, but the air was cold. It was the dead of winter, and Fenway Park was quiet in the fading sun of the late afternoon. She had gotten off to a late start today; she needed to hustle. Boston drivers lived up to their reputation, and rollerblading in the dark was a suicidal gambit.

It was just as well that there was no baseball to distract her. Her work and her workouts were all she needed. She had no time or energy for anything else. Work and workout. Period, full stop. No entanglements, no distractions. Not even baseball. She had no desire to become a well-rounded Cosmo Girl. She was a scientist, and science was all she needed in her life. In particular, she needed to find a cure for Fitzgibbon's Disease. If she didn't need marriage she certainly didn't need *hobbies*.

It had been fifty-five minutes since Dr. Bartlett McGovern Aubrey, Ph.D. had taken off her lab coat, blouse and blue jeans, and slipped into her skating outfit—baggy green shorts with a faded Kirkland College logo worn over orange and black Bruins sweatpants and topped with faded but still eye-catchingly purple "Purple Aces" sweatshirt from the University of Evansville. As usual, she had followed no pre-set route. Starting out from the exit on Kneeland street she had skated through Chinatown to Downtown Crossing. Pedestrians had been thick on the mall in front of Jordan Marsh and Filene's, and that had slowed her down.

From Downtown Crossing she improvised her own version of the Freedom Trail: she made her way along Tremont, cut down the hill at Government center, skirted the crowds at Fanneul Hall and went by the back of Haymarket, under the tunnel beneath the Central Artery to the North End, through narrow streets thick with the smells of bread, garlic and tomato sauce, back to Mass General, up Beacon Hill (for this she took off her skates, slipped on some black canvas Chinese shoes stored in her waistbelt pack and walked), down Beacon Hill past the State House and into the Common. From the Common she had taken a long detour out to Fenway, trying to force herself not to go by the Public Garden.

It hadn't worked. Like the drunk making a U-turn to go to the roadhouse, she doubled back from Fenway to Kenmore Square and from there went down Commonwealth to the place she couldn't avoid. Now she stood on the little suspension bridge in the Public Garden looking down to the little pond where, come spring, the Swan Boats would swim. She knew better than to come here, but she still did it once a week or so. Inevitably, she remembered that day in the spring of '91. Every person in the Public Garden that day had carried a radio tuned to the Celtics. The team was playing poorly that year, at least by the standards of the mid-eighties teams, but every true Bostonian was drinking up those last games of the Big Three—Parish, McHale, Bird. She had been seated on a Swan Boat bench with Jackson on her lap; Nick stood on the bridge with his camera, his silly camera. He never remembered to take any pictures, unable to imagine a day when photographs might be all they had left.

Jackson had just been discharged from Children's, and the doctors thought they might have had the infection finally beaten. He looked healthy, laughing with the college girl who paddled the boat. If his arms hadn't been so black and blue from the IV needles, if the back of his hands hadn't been so covered with little scabs, he would have looked like any other child in the park that April morning. Just another child come to visit Mr. and Mrs. Mallard. To make way for their ducklings. Make way! Make way!

That's what Jackson had been after all: just another child. Just some kid, a ward of the state, with an orphan disease that nobody much cared about—no movie stars had died of Fitzgibbon's Disease, no fashion designers. He was just some kid, a subject in a clinical investigation, an orphan kid with an orphan disease, somebody Bartlett never even would have met if she had followed proper scientific protocol. He was just some damn kid, who died.

She could feel her throat tensing, the sensation at the tip of her nostrils as if she were about to sneeze, the tears beginning to well up in her eyes. *Oh hell* she thought, *stop coming by these imaginary boats!* She resumed skating, heading back to the molecular genetics lab at medical center and the tiny shower in the ladies' room.

Night had come. It was fully dark as she skated down Kneeland.

She knew she would be here again next week.

She was going to have to get some new basketball shorts. Despite the safety pins, despite the bulky sweatshirt tucked into the waistband, these shorts were just too big. Three and a half months had done the trick. Three and a half months of walking two miles to work, an hour of rollerblading every lunchtime followed by a lunch of raw vegetables blended up each morning in her Waring blender. Three and a half months of orange juice, dry toast, and boring cereal with skim milk for breakfast. Three and a half months of nine-mile walks along the Charles every Sunday, rain or shine. Three and a half months of boiled brown rice and steamed fish for dinner. Three and a half months of sit-ups. She had lost thirty-three pounds, and only had four to go.

Robert DeNiro had put on fifty pounds for *Raging Bull*, then promptly taken them off and had made it look as easy as taking off an overcoat. *Be like Robert DeNiro,* she had told herself that Thursday in November, and stopped unpacking in mid-box to walk down Commonwealth Avenue in search of a sporting goods store. *Get back, Girl,* she had admonished herself. *Get back to where you once belonged.*

That had been her mantra whenever she had felt like giving up and driving to work instead of walking, or when she was on the verge of succumbing to a pint of Ben and Jerry's, or taking a cab back to the lab from the North End—exhausted, out of breath, too tired to skate another step. Get back. In the early days, when she had been obese, uncoordinated, catching stares and the occasional jeer as she made her ungainly way down Washington Street: Get back. Two months into the program, when she was starting to get compliments from co-workers in the lab, when she could have told herself that she had done enough for a woman of her age, a woman who would never again see her girlish figure. But she had kept on, and now she had her figure back.

Passing Jakob Wirth's pub she remembered, as she had not done for nearly half a decade, her so-called job interview. Some interview. All she had had to do was show up and verify that she was the same Bartlett so glowingly recommended by her doctoral advisor Eddie Fessman. She had been almost disappointed that she had not been asked to explain her research on overlapping gene products of the T4 bacteriophage, or her breakthrough work on the Trojan gene. That she had been recommended by Eddie was all that Irwin Goldberg needed to know. Eddie (orthodox) and Irwin (reform) had grown up in adjacent Brooklyn neighborhoods, and had been classmates at Bronx Science. But it wasn't allegiance to neighborhood, school or tribe that mattered to Irwin as he staffed his laboratory. If the person was from Pluto, he should care? No. But if Eddie Fessman said she was a scientist? Eddie Fessman, who as everybody knows, the Nobel committee, *they* ask his opinion? She got the job. Neat trick for a white-bread *shiksa* from Carbondale, Illinois.

On her way to the interview, with her hair in a bun and wearing her most conservative suit, twenty-five years old, two weeks a Ph.D. and one week married, she had literally stopped traffic. The lout in the Boston Gas truck had leaned on his horn and yelped, and the Boston Edison bozo had answered. It had caught on, and she had run across the intersection clutching a copy of her dissertation to her chest to a chorus of wolf yells and whistles. Welcome to stately, dignified Boston, the Hub of the universe.

Out of the shower now, she ran a comb vaguely through her hair and thought about her work—as usual, she would be working late tonight. Her team at the Medical Center was attacking the problem of Fitzgibbon's Disease from three sides—Bartlett was studying the molecular biology of the organism that caused the disease; anatomists were studying physiological evidence of disease in the brain; and neurobiologists were experimenting with approaches to brain-cell regeneration. Tomorrow Bartlett would be meeting with a pathologist to go over some results from stained slides to see how they correlated to PET results from before the patient died. Tonight she would study the patient's history. What a delightful prospect.

She walked down the hall past open door of Irwin's office; he saw her and motioned to her to come in. He was sitting at his cluttered desk, just finishing his nightly tunafish salad. Papers, journals, notebooks were everywhere. There were even bench apparatus: flasks, beakers. Bartlett had to disguise her shudder. How could such a serious scientist be such a slob?

"Come on in, Bartlett," he said, after swallowing. "Take the seat of honor."

"Gee, thanks," she said, sitting on the broken-back swivel chair.

"An article in the New York *Times* today that I thought you would find interesting."

"Yes?"

"There's a couple of researchers over at MIT who're doing work on that Gulf War stuff. Very bizarre. They say their funding was cut off and they were harassed and that their tenure was even threatened because they were investigating an unorthodox line of research that evidently somebody didn't want them to investigate."

"People with unorthodox ideas sometimes say things like that when they lose their funding," she said.

"Sure. But here's why I thought you might be interested. Number one, they're investigating bacteriophage as the cause of the disease. And two, they used to work in Eddie's lab. I thought you might know them."

"How could they think bacteriophage caused Gulf War illness? Trying to make a biological weapon from phage would be like trying to make a broadsword from a stick of butter. Who would think of such a thing? Some crackpot maybe. Not a real virologist."

"I only know what I read. Did you know Chris and Janine Garbougian, husband and wife?"

She grabbed the paper out of his hand with more violence than she had meant to.

"I know them quite well. I haven't seen them in years, but I know them."

"Crackpots?"

"No. They're real scientists, not crackpots."

Sure enough, there were Chris and Janine on page one of the science section, posing in a laboratory, looking very serious and much older than Bartlett remembered them.

"What does the article say?" she asked. "Why do they think it's phage?"

"They say they found markers from some industrial phage sold by a Swiss pharmaceutical company. But nobody's been able to replicate their work, and all their remaining blood samples were ruined when a freezer failed. They say it's sabotage."

"How very odd," Bartlett said. "Very odd."

"Give them a call."

"I think I will."

"Keep the newspaper. Are you ready to get back to work?"

"Sure," she said, forgetting that she had not yet eaten her meager vegetable delight dinner.

The next hours were typical, as far as research on incurable diseases went: the patient records reconfirmed things she already knew; she read an article with a promising title that turned out to be far off the subject, and she helped a post-doctoral fellow tune her gel. Another quarter inch of progress on a million-mile journey.

At nine in the evening she decided to call her friends.

Chapter 10

Above the Silicon Valley, a Dark Angel hinted at untold powers and Nick Aubrey was beginning to regret that he had come along for this ride.

"You are familiar, of course, with the work of Abraham Maslow," Meekman said.

Nick wanted to think more about the villagers of Fanaye Dieri, or about the bread crumbs—Monty's hint about bugs deliberately strewn in the system—but evidently those lines of the conversation had evaporated. OK then; Nick would talk about Maslow. The name evoked memories of a college girlfriend, a tall psychology major with strawberry-blonde hair. Nick's first love: she had had freckled breasts and sharp wit and passionate sense of justice. Why had they ever broken up?

"Maslow's the one with the theory about the hierarchy, right?" Nick said. "How did it go? Need food, need shelter, need achievement. . ."

Monty seemed pleased with Nick's answer.

"At the most basic level, people need food, shelter, sex. Once their biological needs have been met, more subtle social needs present themselves—for companionship, stability, love, a feeling of belonging. And once these needs have been met, people need achievement, a sense that they have accomplished something. Their sense of self is *actualized* by the regard of others."

"Fascinating," Nick said. He knew there was a reason he had broken up with that girlfriend.

"At the highest level of human development are self-actualized people," Meekman said. "Those who have attained a perfect indifference to the scorn or acclaim of the rest of the world. There are fewer and fewer people at each successive level of development, so the whole of humanity makes a pyramid, with self-actualized people at the peak."

"Gotcha," Nick said. "Like the TransAmerica Building."

"How far up Maslow's pyramid would you say you are, Nick?"

Nick thought. He didn't care about cars, clothing, social standing, achievement—basically he didn't care about anything. Outside of a vague and very faint hope that he would someday reunite with Bartlett, the only things that interested him were lifting weights and drinking beer.

"I guess I'm at the top," Nick said. "Self-actualized."

Monty looked at Nick with lowered, pitying eyes.

"Oh no no no no no," he said, like a songbird instructing its young. "No no no no no. No, Nick you have a long way to go until you're self-actualized. No no no."

"Well then maybe I misunderstood the concept," Nick said. "Can we talk about getting me down from this mountain in time to get to the airport?"

"Let me give you an example of some self-actualized people. Albert Einstein. Abraham Lincoln. Bill Gates. Saddam Hussein. Alexander the Great. Adolf Hitler. Henry David Thoreau. George Soros. Mahatma Gandhi. Rupert Murdoch. Michael Eisner. Napoleon. The directors of the Cali cocaine cartels and the Russian Mafias. Alan Greenspan. And myself."

"What about the Pillsbury Dough Boy?" Nick said. "He seems pretty self-satisfied."

It was pointless, of course, to use sarcasm on Monty. Once he got going there was no stopping him.

Monty said, "Understanding Maslow's pyramid is the first step in understanding how the world works. Understand the pyramid and you'll understand why oil, weapons, and cocaine are the three greatest commodities in international trade."

"Do the guys at the top have a dating service and get together to play Scrabble like they do in Mensa?"

"We play, yes. But to we who are self-actualized there's only one game worth playing: Rule the Roost. The object is to make the other players cry, 'yield'. And, of course, to do so stylishly."

"So that's your idea of fun," Nick said. "Who's winning?"

"Gates is winning on paper. Hussein has the most style points. Eisner is my biggest threat, especially if he hooks up with the cocaine cartels. But I'm winning."

"Eisner? The chairman of Walt Disney is your biggest threat to world domination? By selling drugs?"

"The Television Reform act of 1984, by which Ronald Reagan gave America's children over to the care of the Telescreen, was the most significant political act of the twentieth century, and I include Hiroshima and the decoding of DNA as political acts. Reagan blew the locks on the door that separated the nursery from the whorehouse, and Eisner rushed in first. Under Eisner, television has perfected the way it brainwashes children into the modern cult of sex, violence, fear and individual entitlement— which will make religion, family, and government moot within a generation. Disney's children have grown up addicted to Little Mermaids, Michael Jordan, suburbia, MTV, and ABC news. All Disney needs now is a narcotic supply to complete its portfolio of dopamine enhancers and he'll have an army of two hundred million of the best fed, best educated people in the world eating out of his hand. That's why he'll cut a deal for a narcotics supply. The Cali cartels also provide a more risk-free route to atomic weapons than the Russian Mafias do. Eisner and Disney have a very compelling game plan."

Nick had to admit that as far as sociological theories went, this one explained a lot.

"What about you?" Nick said. "Where's your bomb? Where's your army? How can you expect to rule the world without an army?"

"Not rule the world. The game is rule the roost. To deny your opponent what he wants."

"Ah," Nick said. "That explains Saddam's style points. Because Bush didn't get two terms, the only thing he wanted."

"Some day Saddam may be acknowledged as the greatest military strategist of all time," Monty said.

Nick thought that was a reach.

"I'll grant him political style points," he said. "But military strategist? No way. Saddam's boxed into a corner. His army is decimated."

"Subedai," Monty said, significantly. "His maneuvers are still studied at West Point."

Monty was baiting him, another favorite conversational ploy.

"OK, I'll bite," Nick said.

"Ghengis Khan's most able general. Subedai perfected the feint, the false attack to lure the enemy's forces where he wanted them. Then he did as he pleased with his prisoners—which usually meant conscripting them into his own army."

Why was Nick even having this conversation? What were they even talking about?

"The Gulf War was a *feint*?" he said. "Give me a break."

As Nick spoke, Monty clambered atop a guardrail post. There he stood, like an Olympic diver on the high platform, with his feet pointing ahead touching each other and his arms at his sides. Beyond the guardrail the ground tapered steeply down one or two yards to a chiseled edge. Roll off that and it was fifty stories straight down.

"What would *you* do," Monty said, while looking northeast from his perch to Devil's Mountain thirty miles away, "if you had a programmable biological weapon that could put millions of the world's best soldiers under your command, but no way to deliver that weapon?"

Nick himself had no especial fear of heights. On the other hand he was no daredevil. Harold Lloyd movies with breathtaking stunts filmed atop unfinished skyscrapers literally made him shiver—as if someone had taken fingernails to a dusty chalkboard.

"Hmmmmm. . . . ." Nick said, refusing to acknowledge that Monty was one good gust of wind from certain death. "What would I do if had a programmable biological weapon that could put millions of the world's best soldiers under my command, but no way to deliver that weapon? Let's see, what would *Subedai* do? Would I attack Kuwait?"

Intellectually Nick knew the importance of maintaining sang-froid. But exactly how was he supposed to disregard this demonstration of ice-water in Monty's veins? However Nick did it, he had to act cool. To do otherwise would be tacky, like pointing out to Titanic's gallant orchestra that the barky, she was a-goin' down. It would be tantamount to ceding the game on the opening play.

"Stylish, isn't it? " Monty chirped from his aerie. "Even Gates was impressed."

Maybe Nick hadn't given Monty enough credit. Perhaps he was a syphilitic madman. Not only was he walking on a trapeze without a net, he apparently also believed that he was playing a real-life board game with Saddam Hussein, Ghengis Khan, and Bill Gates. Nevertheless this was turning out to be an amusing conversation—if you ignored the fact that it might end in free-fall at any moment.

"How about you?" Nick asked. "How are you going to rule the roost?"

"That will be revealed to you if it becomes appropriate," Monty said.

With those words the spell broke. The sun was starting to slip behind the mountain ridge that rose behind them, and the air was getting chilly. Nick was about to force the issue when he noticed, out of the corner of his eye, something moving. About fifteen or twenty yards to Nick's right, at the far end of the parking lot, two bicyclists had stopped and dismounted. A man an a woman, both in spandex and clearly in great physical shape, took off their helmets and riding gloves. As if choreographed, both of them shook their heads, then ran hands through long shiny blond hair, his as long as hers. Venus and Adonis: for a moment Nick couldn't take his eyes of them, and he had to force himself to remember his train of thought.

"You didn't drive me all the way up here to give me this little Kissinger's eye view of global power relations," Nick said to Monty, taking his eyes off the New Gods. "You want something from me. I don't know what it is, but you're not going to get it without a little honesty. Tell me your strategy for winning Rule the Roost."

"Stand beside me," Monty said, and indicated the next post, six feet to the right of his own.

Backing out was impossible now: Nick had come here for information, and it was obvious that he wasn't going to get it without passing this first test. Monty had issued a challenge, and dread or no dread, Nick was going to have to pick it up. He stepped forward and placed his hand on the thigh-high post.

"How nice of you to invite me up," he said.

He focused his eyes on the spot where he was going to put his feet, and before he knew it he was crouching there. Quickly he stood erect, keeping his gaze straight ahead across miles of air to Mission Peak, from whence Europeans had first seen the mirror view and proclaimed God's salvation to the indifferent bay.

"Chuckie Johnson was fired today," Monty said. "Your project will be discontinued after the next stable build of the source tree."

There it was. All this talk about a global conspiracy of self-actualizers had been a goof. Nick had been taken up to the mountains simply to be whacked. But why was Monty doing the hit? Nick turned his head to the left and saw Monty slowly, silently, raise his arms from his sides until they were straight across, like Christ's on Sugarloaf above Rio de Janeiro.

Nick turned his gaze one more to the front, but was distracted by something out of the right corner of his eye. He couldn't believe it. The two perfect Aryans, as if playing "Simon Says" with Nick and Monty, had clambered atop guardrail posts at the far end of the lot and were raising their arms as well. Despite the spandex and the distance, Nick could see the size and symmetry of the man's muscles, right down to his abs—and the woman's form was, in its own way, even more remarkable.

"I am offering you the position of Corporate Fellow of Digital MicroSystems," Monty said. "You will be special assistant to me, to work on projects at Digital MicroSystems Laboratories, Incorporated. The salary is two hundred and twenty-five thousand dollars per annum."

"Jesus," Nick said. His thighs began to tremble. He imagined Harold Lloyd stepping off a girder into thin air fifty stories above Times Square, catching himself on a shoestring.

"Let's jump, Nick." Monty said. "Have faith. We can fly if you touch your finger to mine."

The blood pounded in Nick's temples as he found himself involuntarily lowering his head to look to where the earth met the sky at the cliff edge. Infinitely below was a pile of boulders. Nick imagined his own and Monty's bodies lying atop the rubble, like tiny little Sistine dolls with arms outstretched, index finger to index finger, separated by a breath.

"You first," Nick said.

"I have with me a bonafide offer, signed by Scott Beckwith. If you accept, ten million dollars, net of taxes, will be deposited today in account that has already been set up in your name. And you will receive bonuses at regular intervals."

Nick's legs weakened worse than before and for a moment his field of vision went completely black. Everything had happened just the way Carl had said it would: Johnson fired, Docudisc canceled, and Nick offered preposterous sums of money to accept a position for which he was probably not qualified—all wrapped in Monty's thesis that the chairman of the Walt Disney Corporation was personally responsible for modern narcissism and the general shape of late twentieth century capitalism.

"That's my job title," Nick asked, weakly. "'Special Assistant to Monty Meekman?' At ten million down and two hundred and twenty-five thousand dollars a year?"

"Yes."

"Why? Why me?"

"Genius is innate; it cannot be taught, only shaped. You are not a genius, but you have a genius for certain kinds of fluid algorithms."

"Bullshit," Nick said.

"Don't seek flattery Nick; it's beneath you. If I went to the trouble to learn the names of the Fanaye-nabay don't you think I've read your code? We both know what you're good at, and we both know how good you are. Now, do you want the chance to really use your talent, or do you want to spend the rest of your life writing Novell emulators? That's the choice before you: spend the rest of your life coding Novell emulators, or come with me to design the most complex and beautiful objects in the history of human creation."

"With no interference from the Software Architecture Review Committee, I assume?"

"You'll have total freedom of design—and a lot of money."

"And what will I be doing to merit such generous remuneration?"

"You must accept the offer before I can tell you that."

Nick should never even have along for the ride. From Mad Antonio's he should have gone directly to the airport and caught the next flight out. He'd be nearly home by now, instead of getting a visceral lesson in the true meaning of the word "afraid."

"And here's your first opportunity for a bonus," Monty said, nodding towards the spandex-clad mountain-bikers. "Push those vain imbeciles off their perches. They'll never see you coming. I'll give you two million dollars for each one."

Nick said nothing. He could not remember how to speak.

"Well, son?"

Nick jumped backward, nearly losing his balance as he hit terra firma. Upon his perch, Monty turned to face Nick, his arms again at his side. Nick looked up at Monty like Dorothy looking up to Oz, the Great and Terrible—only not even Dorothy could have felt the terror that Nick now felt. But at least he had remembered how to speak.

"I knew you couldn't do it, Nick," Monty laughed. "You're not self actualized; not yet. But the offer still stands. How about it? How would you like to reside at the very frontier, the very apogee of human knowledge?"

"You just told me that you're locked in mortal combat with cocaine cartels and Saddam Hussein," Nick said. "You offer me ten million dollars for no good reason at all to do a job you won't describe. Then you make a joke about killing people for hire. Do I have 'idiot' stamped on my forehead?"

"The offer is genuine. It is no joke and the Fellows are no joke. You're now one of them. Corporate Fellows have interesting jobs and very much money. None of the Fellows are working on Novell emulation, and none of them are bouncing checks. You've noticed, surely. "

Yes, Nick had noticed. He had also noticed that the Corporate Fellows wore matching Star Trek tunics and watched movies without drinking beer. So far Carl had been absolutely right about Nick's rehabilitation. He had been right about everything. Which meant, Nick was now quite sure, that Carl had been right about Monty's role in the destruction of his career, his marriage—heck, his entire life. In compensation for which Nick was now being offered, what? the chance to run off with the Pied Piper of the nerdoids? The chance to invent the future while committing random homicide?

"Monty," Nick said. "Shove it up your ass."

"You're making a mistake."

"Well, that's the way it is. Get down. Let's go."

"The instant you accept this offer I can begin to help you achieve the thing most dear to you. Decline this offer, and you'll see what the world brings you."

There was no mistaking the meaning of that remark. Nick had begun to recover from the tussle of wills on the guardrail posts. Monty wanted to play power games? Fine. Nick was ready to play.

"Are you threatening me?" Nick said. "I'll smash your face, you pipsqueak. I'll throw you off this cliff."

"Bartlett is finding venture capital very hard to come by," Monty said. "With ten million dollars you could provide a substantial lift to her and her colleagues."

The bastard.

"I repeat: take me off this hill before I throw you off—and your shitbox car on top of you."

"It's a very short contract," Monty said, as he reached into his jacket and withdrew an envelope. "It basically says that Digital MicroSystems will give you enormous sums of money, and that you will work only for the Labs—no consulting on the side, no projects of your own at home. You are free to leave the employ of the laboratory after five years; if you resign before then you will have to pay the corporation back for all monies you may have received by that time. It obliges you to total confidentiality, for as long as you live, about the projects under development at the Labs."

"Lifetime confidentiality? Even official government secrets have expiration dates."

"Their contracts don't pay tens of millions of dollars. And I'm afraid that this offer expires in two minutes. You have only to say, 'I accept,' and I will place the contract in your hands. Sign it and the money, the Fellowship, are yours. So think about it, Nick. But don't think too long."

"You want me to take your money so that I can offer venture capital to Bartlett Aubrey, my own wife."

"You can use the money however you like."

"No strings?"

"There are none."

"Capital never relinquishes control," Nick said.

An tiny smile appeared on Monty's face, and for an instant Nick thought he was going to be congratulated for spotting the contradiction. Not a chance. With a grand gesture Monty swept his right hand out, indicating the panorama behind him.

"I made this," he said.

Nick didn't think he had heard him right.

"What?" he asked, still trying to comprehend the horror of his situation.

"I made this," Monty said again. "I created the Silicon Valley."

There was a look of rapture on his face as he began to recite the names of Silicon Valley companies: "Intel. Hewlett Packard. IBM. Advanced Micro Devices. Oracle. National Semiconductor. Silicon Graphics. Apple. Adobe. Next. All the others. All of them! Without me there would be nothing below us but a bunch of Mexicans picking fruit. All those companies, all that wealth, it all sprang from *me*, from *my* thought, from *my* inventions. Silicon is nothing but sand, and the Silicon Valley is nothing but my sandbox. Without Monty Meekman there would be no Silicon Valley. And you, Nick, are the one I have chosen to help me design what it will look like a hundred years from now."

Monty was smiling from ear to ear, like the Grinch, like Pat Robertson. Nick had no doubt now: Monty was a danger to Nick, to Bartlett, to the world. Nick wished he had listened to his wife. He wished he had never met this crazy billionaire. He should have never abandoned agriculture for the intellectual seduction of systems and algorithms. But past was past, and 'should have' was shit. This was now, and Nick knew what he had to do. Anger was a useless emotion, a self-indulgent emotion. Carl Swirsing had been right: if anyone was going to get the better of Monty Meekman, it was going to have to be an inside job. No one but a Corporate Fellow would ever get the upper hand on this madman.

"I accept your offer," Nick said, even as he battled the impulse to vomit. Monty glanced at his watch.

"Right," he said. Then he stepped off the post and placed the envelope in Nick's hands.

Suddenly the ground beneath Nick's feet melted away, and he had the sensation that he was falling out of the sky. At first he thought the insanity of everything Monty said had caused him to faint, but in a moment he realized that it was an earthquake.

Nick had been in earthquakes before, but he had never felt anything like this. It lasted about fifteen seconds, and the whole time he was quite certain that he was going to die. But he didn't die, and eventually the terrible shaking ceased.

Nick looked up. Monty was standing above him, smiling.

"The world is a very predictable place, Nick," Monty said. "Events are predictable. People are predictable. Arise."

Once again Nick asked himself if he had lost his mind.

"How?" Nick asked. He was not expecting an answer, but Monty gave one.

"With a little knowledge of stochastic processes and strange attractors you can pretty much tell when Saratoga earthquakes are going to happen just by looking at what the Calistoga geyser is doing, modulo the seismic data from the Heyward fault."

Nick stood, uncertainly, like a toddler who has fallen after taking his first step.

"'You can tell when an earthquake is going to happen to the precise minute?' he said.

"I can tell to the exact minute with a thirty percent degree of confidence. The degree of confidence goes to ninety-nine percent if I only specify the hour. That was four point six, by the way. It felt worse because you're standing at the epicenter." Monty looked increasingly serene, like a Dr. Seussian Dalai Lama.

The Lama said, "You're not astonished by somebody who can predict a hurricane a week in advance or a lunar eclipse a hundred years in advance. Why should you be surprised that somebody can predict an earthquake a day in advance? Here's a pen. Sign."

Somehow the contract was still clutched in Nick's left fist. The fist was trembling.

"Thirty percent degree of confidence?" Nick said, as the implication sank in.

"Thirty percent? That earthquake could easily have come when I was standing up there. If you want to commit suicide, that's your business. And when you play around with murdering me, well, I don't like that."

"The world is what it is, Nick," Monty said. "People who are nothing, who allow themselves to become nothing, have no place in it."

Only then did Nick remember the bicyclists. He looked to where they had been, but they were not there. Only their mountain bikes remained, one thrown atop the other.

"Sign the contract, Nick. You'll be a multi-millionaire by the time we reach sea level."

Behind him Nick heard a car approaching. He tore the envelope in half and dropped it, then turned and ran, with his arms waving in the air to flag down the rather battered Buick station-wagon that was rounding the curve.

Chapter 11

Two and a half hours after hitching a ride into Los Gatos, Nick Aubrey had made it back to Mountain View, retrieved his car from the Dijjy-Mike lot, and driven to Palo Alto. Dusk faded into night as he parked the rented white Taurus on Hamilton Street, near Alma, and walked through the warm Palo Alto evening towards Emerson. In a few minutes he was in the back section of the Gordon Biersh mircrobrewery, chomping on a salty breadstick and watching the opening tip of the Knicks -Warriors game on the chest-high television. He had downed a pint of amber before the first time-out was called.

The interior of the beerhall was rectangular, more deep than wide, and decorated in 'earth tones' that Nick found abhorrently tasteful. Along the right wall and across the back there was an L-shaped bar behind which stood bartenders at regular intervals — improbably handsome men and women in crisp white shirts, like lifeguards at a very formal beach. Behind the back bar, framed by a two-story window, there was an enormous copper tank with pipes, tubes and gauges all about it. Nick was tall: from where he stood, even slouching with his back resting on the back bar, he could look over a standing pride of standard-issue Silicon Valley yuppies. They were mostly young, white, casually-dressed and smiling able-bodied people, all scrubbed and prosperous. The occasional Negro face (smiling like all the others), the clump of Japanese men in suits, the few people here and there who looked over fifty and vaguely chaperonish all added just the right California touch. Like the bartenders, they looked happy and confident, at ease in the material world.

Anybody who didn't speak English would never have guessed that they had all just been through a respectably-sized earthquake. Nick, however, understood English, so he knew that the people around him were talking about the bridge collapse over 101 North, with attendant death, and what was worse, bad traffic. These people were as foreign to Nick as air was to a lobster. Beyond this gaggle Nick could see a dining area on a raised terrace, and beyond the terrace there were tables on the sidewalk near the front entrance. It was seven PM on Friday night; Nick's flight left in three hours, which meant he had about an hour to kill.

He had come here out of habit: Gordon Biersch was a Dijjy-Mike hangout. Nick often came here with some of his Left Coast posse before heading for the airport. And why not? He had to go someplace, after all. The beer was good, and the alienation he always felt here was in its own way comforting. Right now Nick could stand some comforting. He was half hoping to run into Eduardo or Suzy or Maceo, half hoping he wouldn't encounter anyone he knew. But the Valley was so incestuous that trying to avoid people you knew at Gordon Biersch was like trying to avoid people named "Lee" in Beijing.

Nick had been there another ten minutes, long enough to feel the kick from the beer diffusing into his arms and legs, when Maceo arrived. In his hopelessly tacky vest, with his razor-thin lips, androgynous features, pallid skin, and thinning hair pulled into an unstylish ponytail, he stood out in this crowd like Dracula at the beach. Nick approached Maceo from his blind side and poked him in the ribs with a bread stick.

"Is this a banana in my pocket, or am I just glad to see you?"

"So Nick, what gives? I thought your ass was out of California."

"I'm on the red-eye tonight," Nick said. He took a long pull on his third pint. "I stayed around for an extra day at Monty's request. Big mistake."

"A pox on that asshole," Maceo said. "What's he up to?"

"Nothing worth talking about."

Or rather, Nick thought, nothing that I have the least idea how to talk about. But there were some subjects that he was able to talk about, subjects that he would *force* himself to talk about in order to keep from thinking of what had transpired in the Santa Cruz hills just three hours ago.

"Did you ever meet Carl Swirsing?" Nick asked. "He used to work over in Marketing Communications."

"I don't talk to Marketing," Maceo said. "It's against my religion."

"He started his own company a while ago. Public relations, market research."

"Yuppie. Why are you asking about him?"

"I'm thinking of going to work for him."

Maceo sucked on this factoid as if it were a sour candy. Nick, waiting for Maceo's response, continued to watch the crowd. Actually he was only pretending to watch the crowd; in reality he was having a hard time keeping he eyes off one beautiful blond bartender—in particular, her neck, where it met her jaw: the spot where her earring touched her skin as she turned and smiled.

"What's the gig?" Maceo finally spit out.

"Writing flack. 'The Glorious History of Company X, from an idea in a Stanford Business School hallway to twenty billion annual sales.' That kind of shit."

He needed some reason to be asking about Carl. Maceo would forgive him a white lie.

"Since when are you a writer? You sling code."

"English is code."

"What are you telling me? You're on the outs with Dijjy-mike?"

"Johnson got whacked today."

Maceo turned his head to look where Nick was looking. On the tube above the earring'd goddess, Patrick Ewing drove to the hoop and was fouled.

"I guess we better watch our ass."

"The Operating Systems group has a few open reqs. Grab a job while you can, brother. Our ship's going down."

"How about you?"

Yeah, Nick. How about you? He took another long drink.

"I'm alright," Nick said.

Over Maceo's shoulder Nick could see the ridiculously attractive blond bartender with the long earrings, each a silver spider web with miniature feathers dangling from it. What a great notion, he thought, the dream catcher:—sort of a still for the astral plane, modeled on the way a spider web catches dew, for catching dream essence from the lively air, distilling it into pure dream, and guiding it to the receptive sleeping mind.

"What I mean is," Nick clarified, "I'm a fucking wreck."

He looked away from Maceo and the angel over his shoulder to survey the bistro, now completely full. At the far end of the bar there was a man who appeared to be staring at him and Maceo, but when Nick returned his gaze the man quickly turned and left, as if afraid of the least hint of intimacy.

"White people," Nick said. "They give me hives."

"You're white, Kimosabe."

"You know what I mean. Yuppies."

"You're a yuppie too," Maceo said. "We're all yuppies now."

Then Maceo, bored, drank.

"So you're going to be a hack on retainer," he said, not bothering to look at Nick.

"I'm thinking about it."

"Why don't you ask Monty for that job he keeps hinting at?"

Good idea, Nick. Why don't you go work for Monty?

"No, thank you," he said. "I just put myself on his shit list."

It took all of Nick's self-control not to scream out, 'Monty's a freaking madman, Maceo. Steer clear! Steer clear!' But the encounter on the mountaintop would remain Nick and Monty's little secret, for now. Not even Maceo got to hear the story. The question was, did Carl?

"Once you're on Monty's shit list," Maceo said, "you're on it for life."

"I esteem it an honor. You got no more dope on Swirsing?"

It was funny, Nick thought, that of all the friends he had made in ten years with Digital MicroSystems, Maceo was the only person he cared to see now that he didn't work there anymore. Nick had been Maceo's boss for five of those years, and managing him had been like managing a mule. Maceo showed up for work whenever he felt like it, contradicted Nick in public meetings, interrupted him, put his feet on Nick's desk, and sometimes answered Nick's managerial directives with a fart. It was no secret that Maceo's unconventional political activities sometimes followed him to work—when looking through the office window at Maceo staring intently at his computer screen, Nick had never been able to tell whether he was programming or writing another short extracurricular piece for *The Nation* or *Cybertopia*. Maceo had covered every subject from virtual sex to the politics of Laotian cocaine, and had lately finished *Blood for Oil*, a book about what he called the "the marketing extravaganza known as Desert Storm." Nick was well aware of the real identity of the prankster known as Exxon Tanker. During the Gulf War "E.T." had disrupted San Francisco rush-hours with life-sized puppet shows set up at busy intersections, using cohorts in the crowd to dismantle the stage and disperse within thirty seconds whenever police got close. ET/Maceo could sometimes be found patching a compiler while still dressed as an oil-soaked cormorant.

Maceo was basically unmanageable. But he also wrote mass quantities of the most solid code of anybody in the Silicon Valley. Maceo's programs were on-time, bug-free, well-structured, commented, compact, and fast. So what if he was a pain in the neck? Nick was glad to have him on his team. With Maceo there was no bullshit, and that was an attribute that Nick had come to prize.

"I don't know nothing about Swirsing," Maceo said. "Want me to see what I can find out?"

"Yeah, do that."

As Nick finished speaking, Maceo fixed his gaze on the front entrance.

"Oh no, here comes trouble."

"What?"

"Peter Barlow. He just walked in the door."

"Who's that?"

"Crazy Peter. I know him from my Gulf War stuff. He used to be a technician for CNN, he says, but got fired for putting himself on the air to explain his theory about computer chips and multinational corporations and biological warfare and

Saddam Hussein and you name it. Kind of a poor man's Ross Perot."

"A friend of yours?"

"He's just some guy, a nut-case. He heard me talk at a symposium at the Santa Clara Research Institute, and ever since then he's tried to adopt me."

"What did you do to earn that high honor?" Nick said.

"I don't know, Nick," Maceo said, loudly. "I said he was crazy, didn't I? For four years he's been tracking down this imaginary professor that he says was behind the whole Gulf War. It's like the fugitive tracking down the one-armed man, only this time the bad guy really is all in his head. He's got some kind of proof he wants to give me for safe-keeping, and somehow I didn't say 'no' loud enough. Says he's got it hidden someplace and won't give it to me until he's sure nobody's following him. He'll lurk in a corner for ten minutes to make sure nobody's on his tail—he usually thinks there is, but maybe he'll manage to give it to me tonight. I hope so; he's been on me like a god-damned leech for four months. So whatever you do, don't say anything nice to him. This is not a friendship we want to encourage."

There was no need for Maceo to worry about that. One Gulf War conspiracy crackpot at a time was quite enough, thank you.

Nick slowly looked around the room staring at first one face, then another, wondering if he could spot Maceo's crazy friend among all these eminently sane yuppies.

It wasn't hard. A short, stocky, perspiring man with thinning hair was hurriedly making his way toward Maceo, all the while pretending to look in a different direction. He was wearing a light tan suit, rumpled. His garish red polyester tie was askew, and he was carrying what appeared to be a manila envelope, soiled, about an inch thick. He seemed to take no notice of anybody other than Maceo, although certainly others had noticed him barging his way through the crush.

"Here," the man said, placing the envelope in Maceo's hands. "The professor's going to be on the flight tonight. I'll have to figure out which passenger he is while we're in the air. But I'm sure he's on to me, and will probably try to take me en route."

He continued holding both of Maceo's hands with his, staring into his eyes.

"Everything's in here. The diskette's in here too. Unix. Do not try to copy it; it will blow up your system. And remember: nine three two three three. A million soldiers are counting on you. Farewell."

He turned and quickly made his way through the crowd.

Maceo placed the package on the bar, and Nick picked it up. It was covered with illegible writing in different inks smeared by what appeared to be coffee and water stains, and the frayed edges were taped. One note he could read, however: the block letters were large and thick, gone over with a ballpoint a hundred times:

Thou art Peter, and upon this rock I will build my church; and the gates of hell shall not prevail against it. Matthew 16:18.

Nick tossed the envelope back on the bar. Maceo picked it up then patted it on both sides, feeling its thickness, then pursed his lips, opened the clasp and looked in.

"Balls," Maceo said.

"What is it?"

"No diskette. Now he'll tag around after me for another month until he finds a good time to complete the rest of the drop."

Chapter 12

Thirty minutes out of San Francisco Nick Aubrey had had enough. He liked to think of himself as a peaceable man, but if he didn't change seats soon he was liable to kill somebody. The plane had reached cruising altitude and the cabin lights were out. The flight attendants had been up and down the aisles dispensing pillows and blankets like kindergarten teachers at nap time, and white noise from the enormous jet engines provided a familiar lullaby to the very important big boys and big girls resting before their next busy day. Conditions for sleep were nearly as good as they were going to get on a transcontinental flight, and if only the two loud business boys up in First Class would shut up, maybe Nick could get some rest.

It was true that running into Monty just before the boarding call had set Nick's nerves on edge. Set his nerves on edge? Scared the living piss out of him was more like it. Freddy Kruger, right where you least expect him. And Monty's smirk had made Nick angry too: it was obvious that he had planned to be on this flight all along. On the other hand Nick's adrenal system was so cooked that the effects of this chance encounter with his own personal Antichrist had already worn off by the time Nick took his seat in the first row of the business section, just behind the bulkhead, and stretched his feet before him.   After all, he reminded himself, soldiers who cannot train themselves to sleep during lulls in the battle eventually die of exhaustion anyway.

Monty was only three yards away—out of sight, in First Class—but Nick was simply too spent to give the man another moment's thought.   Rather, Nick *might* have been able to put Monty out of his mind if it weren't for the for the blow-hards in seats 4A and 4B blabbing on with Monty— beyond the curtain that separated first from business class like a paper-thin bordello door— about Internet stocks and founders' shares. Monty's conversation with these power-dorks was so inane, so Gee-whiz-*Business-Week*, that Nick could only assume Monty was taunting him. Screw this, Nick thought, and headed west.

Towards the back of the plane he found an unoccupied spot—a vacant aisle seat, with another empty seat next to it. Against the window, separated from him by the two empty seats, there was a balding man wearing a light business suit, perspiring. Nick had the feeling that he knew the man from somewhere, but couldn't place him. In a minute it came to him: it was the funny little man from Palo Alto, the one who had given Maceo a package and left after a short, odd conversation.

"Anybody sitting here?" Nick said.

"I'm not going to stop you," the man answered. It wasn't a red carpet, but so much the better. Nick was interested in rest, not chat.

He quickly stowed his things, then slouched down into the aisle seat and tried to make himself ready for sleep. It was pointless, of course. For the first few hours after the quake he had been in shock, but now he was slipping into after-shock and guilt was already starting to gnaw at him. He had not told the police about the two people who fell. He had not even gone over to the edge to make sure that they had not miraculously landed on a ledge or clung to a branch. As soon as Nick landed in Boston, he decided, he was going to have to report the incident to the police. Nick's eyes had been closed for about half a minute when he heard the voice from his right.

"How are you going to do it? LSD in my Coca-Cola? Sodium Pentothal in an oxygen mask? Or were you planning to put some of your nanomachines into me and watch me turn into a robot?"

Nick opened his eyes and looked to his right. The man was huddled against the window, with his legs curled up. He looked pale but defiant, as if Nick had him cornered but could not make him surrender.

"Say what?" Nick said.

"Save it," the man said. "You're here to drug and kidnap me. So do it."

It took Nick a few seconds to comprehend that the man was not joking and that he, Nick, was sitting next to a bonafide crazy person who was afraid for his life.

"My name is Nick Aubrey," he began, cautiously. "I'm no kidnaper. I'm just a washed-up computer geek. . ."

"A computer geek who just happens to be an expert in nanotechnology," the man sneered.

Clearly this conversation wasn't going to be easy. Nick drew in his breath, paused a second to collect his thoughts, and tried again.

"OK," Nick said. "Suppose you help me out. I've forgotten your name?"

"Sure you have. I'm Peter Barlow, remember? The guy you're supposed to slip a mickey finn? But you can call me whatever you want, Mister Aubrey. Or should I say *Herr* Aubrey."

Yes, Peter Barlow. *Crazy Peter* Barlow, Maceo had called him.

"Hey, Peter, no need to be alarmed," Nick bluffed. "I forgot your name but I remember you. You're Maceo's friend; I'm Maceo's friend. We're friends. Nobody's going to hurt you."

"Maceo's friend? Bullshit. I know why you were with Maceo tonight."

"Why?"

"To see what I look like. How are you going to kidnap me if you don't know what I look like?"

Oh, brother.

"Why do you think that I want to kidnap you?" Nick said.

"You want to kidnap me," Barlow said, "because I know about your cabal. I know about the computer chips and Gulf War Syndrome. The CIA hand in hand with the Butcher of Baghdad. You need to find out how much I know. Do you really think I don't know what 'brain dump' means? You want to wire me up!"

Play along, be careful, Nick told himself. Crazy people sometimes did crazy things.

"How do you know all this?"

"As if you didn't know. I was stationed in Iraq, remember, with a CNN technician job as cover. Until you busted the play. You do fine work, too—it's not easy to fool the people who invented disinformation, but you pulled it off. Now everybody thinks I'm crazy. Ollie North and Aldrich Ames and now you. Another sterling product of the Langley Home School for Traitors."

Ollie North? Aldrich Ames?

"Do you think I'm in the CIA?" Nick said. This was too weird.

"I know a Company joke when I hear one, *Herr Aubrey*. Aubrey, Burgess, Carr, Delcourt. You think I never saw that film? I was *with* the Company! So I know about the Company and I know about the Corporate Fellows. I know about the Emverk Alumni Association."

Jesus Christ, Nick thought. Who put the LSD in my Coca-Cola? Was this coincidence or was it fate? Was Barlow an angel sent to enlighten him, or just a random nut?

"What do you know about Corporate Fellows?" Nick asked, unsure whether he wanted to hear the answer. "What do they have to do with Emverk? What film are you talking about?"

Barlow ignored him, and his face took on a look of even greater venom and disdain as he spat out the next words:

"I know about Orson!"

"Orson? Who's Orson?"

"Shut up, asshole, and listen. I told everything I know to Iraqi intelligence. You probably never thought a loyal soldier would do that, did you? You can kill me, but they're gonna get you."

This was classic paranoia. Nothing that a shot of thorazine couldn't handle, but Nick didn't happen to have any thorazine on him. The best he could do would be to see if he could get the guy calmed down long enough to make a break for the flight attendants. He would tell them that they had a delusional person on board and let *them* handle it.

"Honest to God," Nick said. "I don't know what you're talking about. But maybe I can help you. Maybe I can get the captain to land and let you off. You can escape whoever is hunting you."

"Very funny," Barlow said. "Escape. I know about your biometrics lab. You've got me scanned into your system. You've got my fingerprints, voiceprint, DNA, PETscan, brainwave patterns. You've got my credit card records, cable TV records, grocery store records. You know what I watch, what I eat, where I go, how much money I have. Cameras in ATM machines recognize the lines in my iris. My image is in the public domain. Escape, ha! As if you wouldn't scan for my voice on the telephone. As if every video camera in the country isn't programmed to recognized my face. As if you couldn't find me in ten seconds! You've got a simulation of me in your lab, predicting what I'll buy next, say next, think next!"

"Calm down Peter," Nick said. "I'm concerned about privacy too. You're concerned about the government turning into Big Brother? I am too."

"Privacy! *Privacy?* Privacy is a bogus concept. It's more archaic than the Roman gods. Government is a bogus concept. Who has more power, the President or Bill Gates? Microsoft controls the CIA, everybody knows that. Gates bought it from Reagan."

OK, Forget the angel hypothesis. This here is a classic random nut.

"But I don't work for Gates or Reagan. Here," he said, withdrawing his wallet from his pocket and offering his laminated identity for Barlow's inspection. "This is who I am. A fellow traveler, just like yourself. Only I bet I'm deeper into MasterCard than you are."

"*MasterCard!* MasterCard owns the National Security Agency! You think I don't understand the 3D face scanner in every store? That I don't know about mass suicide and the spaceship behind the comet? Government is not big brother; *MasterCard* is Big Brother! *Disney* Is Big Brother. *Microsoft* is Big Brother. *Orson* is Big Brother. *You* are Big Brother."

"Peter, I am not Big Brother."

"Go ahead, tell me I'm lying. You have gesture analyzers that can tell whether I'm lying by the look on my face. Come on, tell me I'm lying. Tell me, you bastard. Then fucking kill me. I don't want to live in a world without freedom. Escape? Fuck you. Escape to where? Your satellites encircle the globe. There are no degrees of freedom left."

Nick looked up and saw a stewardess walking down the aisle towards him. If he could find a way to signal her. . .

"Another one of yours, coming for back-up?" he heard Barlow say.

"Listen," Nick said, turning to face him. "I'm a *good* guy. I don't know her, I am not going to hurt you, and the only Orson I know is Orson Welles. '*We will sell no wine before its time.*' You're frightening me. Please let me help you. Do you take any medication? Maybe you've forgotten a dose or two?"

"Save your breath," the man said. "You're no good guy, and I'm a dead man. Do you hear me? I'm a dead man. You can't touch me. You can't plug my brain into your system. I'm dead already."

Then, before Nick realized what was happening, the man flashed his palm towards Nick, showing him something small.

"Here's my *medication*," he sneered. He put his hand to his mouth, bit hard, and swallowed. Then, with a sick but somehow serene smile Barlow turned and kneeled in his seat, looking beyond Nick towards the aisle of the jumbo jet. He took a deep and labored breath, then called out above the dull roar of the engines, "If I may have your attention please."

As Nick looked at the man, amazed, he could see others turning to look at him as well.

"Give me your attention. Please, I do not have much time. Let me have your attention."

Here and there a few lights went on. Nick noticed that the man's hands were trembling.

"My name is Peter Barlow. I am going to die in one minute. This man sitting next to me has murdered me. He works for Hussein Kamel, of the Iraqi Defense Ministry. The Iraqi secret weapons is not nerve gas. It's tiny robots to control our minds. Gulf War Syndrome is only the beginning. I have left proof and a plan for the cure on a diskette with a friend in California. Cincinnati Tuskegee Bikini. LSD. MK-ULTRA. The radical uprising. Radicals. Free radicals at forum. Stop them. This man is a murderer."

With a sudden jerk of his arms, as if impersonating Boris Karloff in *The Mummy,* Barlow reached across the empty seat that separated him from Nick. Nick flinched and tried to put his hands up to protect his neck—he was sure the man was going to throttle him. But instead Barlow's hands now rose to his own throat, and he began to convulse, sending something small and flat flying from his shirt pocket onto the intervening seat. The convulsions momentarily ceased, and, with his hands still clutching at his own throat, Barlow toppled towards Nick, like a mast snapped in a gale. As passengers all around began to scream, Barlow lay across Nick's lap, his head dangling in the aisle, with a ghastly grimace stretched across his blue-tinted face.

Chapter 13

Having read Nick his rights, the two gentlemen from the Airport Police said that they would be back soon to hear his story, then left. As the door opened Nick heard the sounds of the airport: the rumble of jets, the announcements on the PA system, the cry of a disappointed child, the footfalls of someone running. Then the door pulled shut and the small dingy room became amazingly quiet.

Alone with his thoughts, Nick now found himself reliving the ordeal of Barlow's theatrical exit. Nick had never experienced anything like the power-assisted descent that the jet had made into Salt Lake City International. The seat belt lights had just come on and the first officer had been calmly telling the flight attendants and passengers to strap themselves into the nearest available seats when the plane pulled away from underneath him, like a roller coaster accelerating downwards, but harder. The aircraft was in no danger, the first officer had serenely continued; there was a passenger on board with a medical problem and they were making an unscheduled stop in Salt Lake City to let him off. *Some 'medical problem,'* Nick remembered thinking. *He's dead.*

Oblivious to the screams all around him, Peter Barlow lay stretched out in the aisle with his mouth frozen in a grin and his eyes rolled back. It was a hideous discolored deathface, a Halloween mask. Yet somehow his tired suit and cheap tie made him look more pathetic than frightening. A drink cart had slipped its moorings and its brakes were not engaged; it rolled down the aisle and hit the dead man's feet, tipped in the air, and deposited soft drinks, cups, coffee and ice on his plainly lifeless body before somehow righting itself as the plane leveled to land.

And now Nick sat alone in this sparsely appointed interrogation room— four drab yellow walls, a black-and-white linoleum floor, a table, four old futuristic plastic chairs, a telephone and a wall clock that showed half past twelve—waiting to see whether he would be arrested for murder.

At first Nick hadn't been nervous. The police had wanted to ask him some questions; that was only normal. They had advised him of his rights. Well, that was unnerving, but a dying man *had* accused Nick of murder, so *of course* the police had had to read him his rights. That in itself it was nothing to worry about. But why this long delay?

How long had they been gone? Ten minutes? *An hour* and ten minutes? Half past twelve: was that Pacific Time? Rocky Mountain? He couldn't think.

Finally the door opened again and the two detectives came back in. The taller of the two—a heavy-set, grey-haired man with a silver moustache—had introduced himself as Lieutenant Ivan Marki. The other man was younger and slimmer, with bright red cheeks; he was carrying a small tape recorder. He had said his name was Detective Sergeant Carelli. Both men were wearing sports coats and ties. They confirmed again that Nick didn't wish to have a lawyer present, and began the interrogation.

"OK," the younger man, Carelli, said. "What happened?"

Nick told them everything he could remember, minus the fact that he had met Barlow in Palo Alto, and that Barlow had remembered their encounter. He also neglected to tell the detectives that Barlow's insane ranting bore a uncanny resemblance to a theory advanced earlier that evening by Monty Meekman. Nick had a feeling that mentioning these coincidences would vastly complicate things, so he left them out.

"OK," Marki said, when Nick had finished. "Let's back up."

There was a hint of an accent. Hungarian?

"Sure," Nick said.

"That was the first time you ever met this guy, on the airplane, when you sat next to him?"

Nick tensed.

"Yes," he said, trying to sound positive.

"Then why did he think you were an expert in these 'nanomachine' things?"

"I don't know where he got that idea." Nick said. "I know what the word means, that's about it."

"What does it mean?"

"Atomic scale machinery. I work in the computer industry, and 'nanotechnology' is the latest buzzword, like 'Internet' or 'cyberspace' a couple of years ago."

"How does it happen, then, that witnesses say you're an expert? They heard you talking about it."

Was this a curve ball? Were the cops toying with him?

"Who said I was an expert? Where?"

"In the terminal. You were introduced as an expert."

Nick was perplexed. Who, besides Crazy Peter Barlow, would mistake Nick for an expert on atomic machinery? Then he remembered.

"Somebody must have overheard Monty when he said that. He was joking."

"Who is Monty?" Marki said, deliberately, biting his words like a Hapsburg Poirot.

"Monty Meekman. He's my ex-boss. I ran into him in the terminal."

"Ex-boss?"

"He hired and fired me on the same day."

Should Nick tell them that this hire-fire incident had happened less than twelve hours ago, that it involved ten million dollars and a contract abrogated by an earthquake? He didn't think so.

"Fired you from where?" Marki said. "What does he do?"

"From Digital MicroSystems, where he is Genius without Portfolio, and Power Behind the Throne. Monty Meekman, as he will be glad to tell you, is a legendary figure in the history of the computer, a founding member and three-time chairman of SIG-CHI."

"Siggy *what*?"

"SIG-CHI, rhymes with pig sty. Special Interest Group for Computer-Human Interaction. It's a world-wide professional organization," he said, then added in his best Ed Grimly voice, "highly regarded, I must say."

"Why did he fire you?"

"Because he's a lying scheming asshole," Nick said. "Is this relevant? I really want to be able to get out of here in time to catch that plane. Am I going to be able to leave?"

"Why did he tell people that you were an expert in these things?"

"It was a joke," Nick said, with exasperation. "He said it to humiliate me. Years ago he promised me a job on a nanomachine project, but he didn't keep his promise. Anyway he put me on something else and then he fired me. He's totally fucked up my life. So of course he tells random strangers that I'm a genius. That's the kind of person he is; he thinks it's funny. What does this have to do with the guy who killed himself?"

"That's what we're trying to find out."

"There's no connection between Barlow and Meekman. Monty Meekman screwed me. That's life, I'll get over it. Is it a felony in the state of Utah to dislike your ex-boss?"

"It's a felony to kill people."

The reality was starting to sink in.

"You think I murdered Barlow," Nick said.

"You have been accused of that."

Marki did not appear to be joking. This was turning out to be worse than Nick had anticipated. Should he stop now and ask for a lawyer? Not yet, he decided. For the time being he would count on logic and common sense to clear up this little misunderstanding.

"I didn't even know Barlow," he said. "Why would I kill *him* to get revenge on Monty?"

"People who feel resentful about losing their jobs often exact revenge in odd ways. And I have to say that you seem very, very resentful."

Nick thought, You'd be resentful too if you'd been boxed into a corner by an ingenious madman who killed people with earthquakes.

But what Nick said was, "Sure I'm resentful. But I don't work for the Post Office. Nor do I work for the CIA or the Mafia. I do *not* kill people."

"Why are you so antsy, Nick?" Carelli chimed in.

"See if you can guess," Nick sighed.

The detectives glanced at each other, and there was a bit of a pause before Carelli spoke again.

"We'll be done with our questions in just another few minutes," the younger detective said, "then you can go."

"Thank God."

"But we're going to have to ask you not to leave the vicinity until the autopsy has been completed," he added.

"*What?*" Nick said. "How long will that take?"

"It shouldn't be longer than twenty-four hours."

Oh, Christ.

"Officers," Nick said. "Surely you don't believe I murdered him? You must have a dozen witnesses who can tell you what he said. It's clear that he was crazy, isn't it? And anyway, you've got my name and address. I'll be happy to leave my fingerprints. I'm a very findable person."

"Sorry," Carelli said.

"God damn it," Nick said. "You can't keep me here."

Carelli got out of his chair and leaned close to Nick. He was visibly angry.

"We can't keep you?" he said in a loud voice. "We can't keep you? Let *me* tell *you* what we can do, Mr. Aubrey. We're the Airport Police, and this is our turf. But we can always cede jurisdiction to Salt Lake City Homicide. Then you'll see what police can and cannot do to a person fingered for murder."

At that moment the door opened and a uniformed officer handed a piece of paper, obviously a fax, to Detective Marki, who looked at it, then passed it to his partner. Finally Carelli nodded at the door.

"I'll be back in a few," Marki said, as he rose out of his seat.

Carelli reached under his jacket and removed a small gun, which he handed to the other detective. "Better hold this for me," he said.

Oh no, Nick thought. *Here comes 'good cop-bad cop.'*

Marki left, and Nick heard the sound of the door being locked from the outside as Carelli turned his chair back-to-front and straddled it.

"What do you know about Iraqi biological weapons, Nick?" he asked.

"Just what you hear on the news," Nick said. "I haven't followed it very much."

"Your friend Hussein Kamel knows a lot about it. Only I thought he was dead."

"Who's he?"

"Your employer, Nick. The guy who hired you to hit Barlow. Saddam Hussein's son-in-law. He ran the Iraqi weapons program for Saddam, then defected to Jordan. Ring any bells?"

"I remember," Nick said. "He went back to Iraq and got murdered by Saddam's family."

"Says who? Iraqi state television? Mr. Barlow seemed to think that Kamel was still alive, and that you were working for him. So now I'm thinking that maybe that whole defection-murder story was a scam."

"Oh for Pete's sake," Nick said. "Barlow also said that I was in the CIA. So now I'm a double-agent, working for the CIA *and* the Iraqis? I must be damn good. Or here's another possibility. Maybe the guy was just nuts, and maybe I was just unlucky enough to sit next to him."

"You're a smart-ass, aren't you, Nick?" It almost seemed like Carelli wanted the answer to be Yes, I am. Stay calm Nick, he told himself, He's trying to provoke you.

Nick took a moment to summon his most even-tempered voice and said, "I'm not trying to be a smart-ass, Sergeant. But put yourself in my place. I'm sitting there in my airplane seat, minding my own business, when the guy next to me decides to kill himself—"

"But it *wasn't* your seat. Your seat was up front."

Maybe relying on common sense and logic had been a mistake. This guy needed yelling at.

"Jesus Christ, I changed my seat," Nick said, raising his voice. "People do it all the time. That makes me a murderer and a terrorist? You might get a little testy if you were in my shoes."

"I see your point," the detective said, again rising out of his chair and leaning over the table. "Now you put yourself in my shoes. See these ruddy cheeks?. . ."

Carelli pointed to his face with both hands. 'Ruddy' was a fine word to describe his cheeks, Nick thought. 'Scarlet' or 'crimson' or 'screaming neon' also would have been good.

". . . I never had them for the first twenty-seven years of my life. Then my reserve unit got called up for Desert Storm, and now I got a constant aching back, a ruby-red face and a two-year old son with only two fingers on his left hand. I'm a walking, talking poster boy for Gulf War Syndrome. And before me sits a man accused of murdering a CIA agent on orders from the man in charge of Iraq's biological weapons program. So what do you think about my shoes? Well, Nick? How about my fucking shoes?"

"Jesus," Nick said. His indignation, which had been rising just a few seconds ago, had disappeared. "I didn't kill the guy," he said, quietly. "He killed himself."

"We'll see about that," Carelli said.

The door opened and Marki came back in. He nodded at Carelli, then spoke to Nick.

"OK, Mr. Aubrey, we're going to let you go," Marki said. "Your story checks out. And it appears that Mr. Barlow has a long history of dramatic exits. Apparently this was just his last shot to get himself on the news."

Then he thanked Nick for his cooperation and opened the door. Nick was taken aback, unsure whether Marki was joking.

"Can I ask you something?" Nick said. He remained seated in the Jetsons chair. "Shoot."

"Who *was* Barlow? Did he really work in Iraq?"

"CNN confirms that a man by his name and matching his description worked in Baghdad right until the eve of the war. Then he was let go."

This wasn't the answer Nick had wanted to hear.

"Mental health?" he asked.

"They wouldn't put it in writing, but they hinted."

Well, that was a plus, anyway.

"What about the CIA? Did you ask them if he had worked for them?"

"I asked," Marki said. "They ain't saying nothing."

Nick stood, still unsure whether the interview was over.

"Am I really free to go?"

"I'm making a judgement call," Marki said. "But if something comes up and I need you back here for questioning, you're going to come back under your own power. Agreed?"

"Sure." What else was he going to say?

"And if you don't come back when I call you, you become prime suspect in murder one."

"It wasn't murder, Lieutenant," Nick said. "It was suicide."

It was obvious that Carelli didn't want to let Nick leave.

"I'm taking a very personal interest in this case," Carelli said, jabbing Nick in the chest with his finger. "And if I ever find out you lied to me, *about anything*, I'll track you down myself."

"I'm sorry about your son's hand, Sergeant," Nick said. "I'm sorry about your back. But Barlow's death wasn't murder. It was suicide."

"You better pray I never catch you in a lie, Aubrey," Carelli answered. "I'm taking a very personal interest in this case."

Drenched in perspiration, Nick walked to the gate where the passengers of the interrupted Flight 44 to New York and Boston had been waiting. He arrived in time for the final boarding call. As he walked down the aisle of the now-less-crowded plane he was aware of hostile stares. Nick wondered what his greater offense was: murdering a man, or causing the red-eye to be almost three hours late. He took his originally-assigned seat just behind the bulkhead separating first class from the main cabin, and fastened his seat belt. A few minutes later he was looking down at the receding city lights as the plane headed up over the Wasatch mountains.

The police had asked him if he had ever met Barlow, and he said no. They had asked him if there was a connection between Barlow and Meekman, and he had said no. That made two false statements right there, and Nick was pretty sure he had told a few more. The red-faced cop had sworn to chase Nick down if he found out that he had lied. But what were the chances of that? *The hell with it*, Nick thought, *no harm no foul.* It had been a patch of rough ice, but he was through it. He put his seat back and closed his eyes. He tried to think of other things, but his brain wouldn't let go of the incident in Gordon Biersch. Over and over he saw Maceo, the yuppies, the fine deep amber pints, Peter Barlow in his ratty suit, the man at the end of the bar turning his gaze away. . .

Oh God!

He sat bolt upright, his chest pounding. He knew who that man was, oddly familiar, turning away the instant Nick looked up. It had been seven years since Nick had seen him, and Nick had never seen him with a beard. That was what had thrown him: in Nick's memory he was still a beardless youth. Besides, he was supposed to be in Switzerland, not in California. But Nick had no doubt now whom he had seen. It was a man Nick had betrayed and deeply wounded. It was his best child-hood friend and only living relative. The man from whom he had stolen Bartlett: Paul Aubrey. Nick's own baby brother.

He reclined back in the seat and closed his eyes, but sleep remained elusive.

Chapter 14

Nick Aubrey sat slumped in his seat, looking out the L10-11 window onto the JFK tarmac. He was unshaven, his hair was greasy, he felt scaly, his clothes stank and he had a headache that throbbed just behind and above his left eye, about one inch back under his skull. Not only did his head throb, his heart felt like it would eject itself right out of his chest in time to the tune lodged so deeply in his head.

Because I'm made of flesh you can't wear my armor down.

As usual, the worst part of the flight was this one-hour layover in New York at five AM. He could have gotten out of the plane to stretch his legs, but what would have been the point of that? His neck was sure to remain stiff whether he stayed on or got off, and even if he had gotten off the plane, walked through a wall of stale cigarette smoke and up the ramp to the concessions and there found the best coffee in the world, it still would have tasted like crude oil. The experience of eighty red-eyes had taught him that nothing could make him comfortable until he got to Boston.

Because I'm made of flesh you can't wear me, wear me down.

His armor damn sure *felt* worn down. The heart-race of the New York Wait: cof-fee, booze, and sleep deprivation wreaking their terror. He hated it with a passion.

You just pound.

If he so hated the New York Wait, some Millers asked, why not switch to American? There was no New York Wait on the American red-eye.

Pound.

It was like asking the heroin addict why he didn't just switch to crack. Because my miles are with TWA, you moron.

Because I'm made of flesh.

Because the American red-eye has its wait in Los Angeles, and I would rather take a wagon train through Death Valley than fly cross-country with Angelinos.

You just pound.

Trapped in seat 9B with hot itching ass and swelling feet, he ineluctably replayed a mental conversation with some precious Los Angeles yuppie:

Precious Yuppie: "I never check luggage. I put everything I need in carry-on."

Nick: "You don't say! I never use hot water when I shower!" *sotto voce:* "Asshole."

It was a point of pride with Nick that he *always* checked his luggage. He brought his own boom box—in its original Styrofoam and cardboard, now held together with duct tape— to make sure he would have a decent radio. Nick couldn't stand a hotel room without KFJC—the station from Foothills Junior College that played grunge-punk, movie sound tracks, acid-surf and conspiracy talk shows. He always brought a stack of CDs, too: Human Sexual Response's albums had just come out on Rykodisc, and the one song, *Pound*, was worth a wait at the baggage claim. He brought his gym bag, Franco Colombo memorial weightlifter belt, and a nearly complete set of Balzac because he never knew which volume he would feel like rereading.

Pound. Pound.

Half an hour into The Wait, twenty or so early-risers boarded for the continuation to Boston. Nick couldn't help overhearing them talking about the throng of reporters who had been waiting for the 'Agatha Christie Flight.' Was it suicide or was it murder? Stay tuned for details at eleven.

Pound. Pound. Pound. Pound. Pound. Pound. Pound. Pound. Pound. Pound.

There had been a media ambush in New York, but the hit-man fingered by Barlow had remained on the plane. That meant there was bound to be an even greater media mob in Boston. Nick envisioned a phalanx of floodlights and microphones, a piranha school of junior reporters looking for a chance at the big story. He could just imagine himself on the front page of the afternoon *Herald*, the lead story on the evening news with Chet and Natalie.

Eighty minutes later, as he pulled his dented Volvo out of the long-term parking lot onto the airport access road, Nick felt silly at all the worry he had put himself through. Sure, there had been a TV crew and some reporters waiting just outside the security checkpoint. But no frenzy. It seemed that the arrival of Flight 44 wasn't the equivalent of an attempt on the President's life or Princess Diana frolicking *au naturel.* It was more like a house fire in Revere, with some bored reporters at the end of their shift going through the motions. Nick had simply ignored them, and none of his fellow passengers had pointed him out. As simple as that.

By some miracle there was hardly any traffic. The drive from Logan Airport to the Sumner Tunnel took only four minutes, and the trip under Boston Harbor only five. Before he had had time to really think about where he was going Nick cruising down Route 16 in Medford, and then he was on Route 2 West, barreling towards

Newcastle. He got off at the Sudbury exit and turned towards Newcastle. He needed a UNIX machine, but his regular home computer ran DOS. Having no choice, he headed straight for the Mill.

It was a beautiful morning: stark and overcast. Leaveless lilacs and dogwoods lined the roads and surrounded the white farmhouses that each had a little understated sign, white on black, somewhere near the front door: 1742. 1777. 1695. 1854. It was good to be back home in Massachusetts, where things were allowed to get old.

Little more than an hour after collecting his luggage from the Terminal C carousel, Nick Aubrey stood on the bridge that led to the Mill's west entrance, hypnotized by the sound of rushing water and the sight of light snow swirling into the torrent. He alternated between nibbling on a corn muffin and sipping hot coffee while gathering the courage to go inside.

Bartlett had said that the Mill was like Dracula's castle, but she was only partly right: from this approach the Mill resembled a *Saxon* castle, not a Gothic Carpathian. It was massive, not airy—with its drawbridge extended over a turbulent moat. Architecturally, of course, the red-brick home of Digital MicroSystems' East Coast Division had little in common with the squat grey fortresses of pre-Norman Britain. But like the great houses of Arthurian legend, the Mill was massive, defiant, and permanent.

These falls were meant for mills. Flour mills and sawmills had come first, sipping the smallest taste of the available force. The first cloth mill had appeared on this site in 1804, and it had grown like Topsy. By 1925 Newcastle Textiles had become the largest manufacturer of cloth in the world, and prosperity had reigned right through the Depression and the decades that followed. But then the modern mills of South Carolina and South Korea had appeared, whittling away at Newcastle Textiles, shuttering one wing after another until, in 1960, the last lonely light had gone out. The Commonwealth of Massachusetts took title to the building in lieu of back taxes. For years the mill stood vacant. Then Ben Golson bought it, for one dollar, and created a legend. In 1952 Golson had founded Digital Data, Incorporated, and by 1958 his manufacturing plant in Kendall Square, Cambridge, was shipping so many computers that the surrounding streets could not handle the traffic.

In 1963 Golson bought the Mill and began the never-ending process of turning the dark relic of a bypassed industry into the home of the most advanced computer makers on earth. There were jobs aplenty, for carpenters, painters, electricians, furniture movers—and for the world's brightest computer engineers, who were drawn to Newcastle like moths to a candle. All went well, until 1989.

Stanford MicroSystems, a California start-up with incredible new technology and a charismatic twenty-five year old chairman named Scott Beckwith, was eating Digital Data's lunch. Two rough quarters cut Digital Data's stock price by 63%; Drexel, Burnham put a junk bond deal together, and in the blink of an eye Stanford MicroSystems—all six hundred and twelve smart-asses of it—became parent to Ben

Golson's twenty-thousand employee baby. Digital MicroSystems was legally born, and Golson's resignation was "reluctantly" accepted. Champagne was poured on Wall Street, and the flood of pink slips began.

At first Nick's luck had run contrary to the pattern. Instead of being laid off, he was given a second group to manage, this one in California. It was as if a promising Indian of the Colonial Police had been given responsibility for a London precinct in addition to his beat in Bangalore. He hired the hottest software engineers, and they made millions for the company. But Nick's reward had been the slow dismantling of his career. Bartlett predicted it, but she didn't stick around to see it to its conclusion. How had Nick missed the writing on the wall that she had seen so clearly? That was a question for Nick to ponder at another time. He finished his muffin and entered the house of his liege lord.

A complex as large as The Mill could be confusing to anybody, and even after nearly ten years, Nick was grateful for the street signs on the corridors. He followed "Shay's Highway" the length of Building One. At Two he went up four flights of stairs, then down Publick Alley 4754 to Three. Once in Three he turned at Turners Falls and walked ten yards until he came to an unmarked firewall door on his right. The next door on the left was his office.

As the door shut behind him he tossed his briefcase in the corner, displaced the stack of memos, post-its, phone slips and code listings from his chair to his desk, and logged on. About nine million e-mails had arrived since yesterday—when he had logged on from the guest terminal in the Menlo Park office. He would read them tomorrow, maybe. But what was this new icon up in the corner? System administrators were forever cluttering up his screen with egregious clutter. Didn't the word 'trespass' mean anything in this electronic age?

He clicked on it, and almost immediately a pornographic film of a man and two young children began playing in the upper left corner of his monitor.

"What a sick bastard." Nick instinctively started another window, found the links and nuked the vile program. The headache, which the coffee and corn muffin had partially subdued, was back, stronger than ever. Why was some freak harassing him? All Nick had wanted to do was read Barlow's diskette and clear out. Was that too much to ask?

He was assuming that this diskette was the one Barlow had forgotten to put in Maceo's envelope, and he was hoping that it might shed some light on what had happened last night. Normally Nick would have made several backup copies before trying to read the original. But Barlow had said that any attempt to copy it would hose his system. How? Maybe there was some kind of magnetically-activated explosive on a track that wasn't used for storing files, but would be accessed in a copying operation? Reading or executing files would be OK; copying would literally blow it up? Good morning, Mr. Phelps. Something like that?

He clicked over to a Bourne shell window, stuck the diskette in the drive and typed

```
ls -a /dev/rst0 | file
```

He heard the whirring of the disk drive, and in a few second the screen showed

```
>      orson  program
       data1  ascii text (encrypted)
       data2  ascii text (encrypted)
```

Bingo. An executable file. With a very familiar name.

But should he run it? Common sense dictated that one should no more run an executable of unknown origin than one should have unprotected sex with an unknown partner. On the other hand. . . Did he really care, at this stage in his so-called career, whether he might blow up a little bit of Digital MicroSystems's physical plant?

He was reveling in the imagery when there was a knock on his office door. Not now, go away he thought, as he swivelled to see who was there. It was Lynette Evans, from Human Resources, and some dweeby-looking guy Nick had never seen before.

Well that answered that question, anyway: he was toast.

He motioned for them to come in. As they opened the door and entered, Nick quickly ejected the diskette and slipped it into his shirt pocket. The nervous-looking woman perched on the edge of a chair; the unknown man remained standing. Nick extended his hand; she shook it but the man studiously avoided it, with a Clint Eastwood stare.

"Lynette," Nick said. "My favorite angel of death. Who's your friend, a mortician in training?"

"Nick, I'm afraid I have some bad news for you. . ."

"Christ, Lynette, I know that. How much severance pay do I get? It used to be two weeks, plus an additional week for every year I've been here. That would make eleven weeks' pay."

"That's not a option," the Eastwood wannabe said. "You have fifteen minutes to clear out your effects and leave the premises. And you are not to re-enter the premises for any reason, whether alone or accompanied by an employee."

"Who is this guy?" Nick asked Lynette. "He's got the personality of a quahog."

"Corporate security," the wannabe said.

"I'm not talking to you, security. I'm talking to Lynette."

"*I'm* talking to *you.* Start packing."

"Lynette, would you tell him to go fly a kite for a minute or two, please?"

"Nick, as you know, Digital MicroSystems competes in a very aggressive marketplace. But competition is not a bad thing; it's the source of our product innovation. . ."

"Oh spare me, Lynette. We've known each other for seven years."

"Fourteen and a half minutes," Quahog said.

"In a global economy, companies, especially high-technology companies like

Digital MicroSystems, must maintain flexibility. . ."

"Enough already. Please just tell me, how many weeks's pay do I get, and when do I get it?"

"You get nothing," Quahog said. "Consider yourself lucky that you're not walking out of here in handcuffs."

"Shut up, clam-boy. Lynette, will you tell him to shut up, please?"

But Lynette had temporarily ceased to be a person. She was already in Human Resources mode.

"Experts predict that in our working lives, each of us will not only experience several jobs, but several careers. The old model of the employee who stayed in one job at one company for their entire career isn't realistic in today's economic environment—"

"What about my severance?"

"Fourteen minutes," Quahog said.

Lynette was trying to finish singing her paean to downsizing, but seemed distracted by the cross-currents.

"—although losing a job can be traumatic, many people find the experience to be very beneficial in the long run. It provides an opportunity to take an inventory of your strengths and weakness, to update your resume, perhaps take some courses to augment your skill-set—"

Nick decided it would be better to ignore her for a moment and concentrate on Quahog.

"What did you mean about handcuffs?"

"Trafficking in child pornography is a serious offense. The authorities have been notified."

"What, that porn clip on my machine? I didn't put that there."

"On every machine in Digital MicroSystems intranet."

"Every machine in the company? Give me a break."

"Thirteen and a half," the clam said.

Nick needed some information from Lynette. He clapped his hands in front of her.

"Hello? You mean I'm getting fired, not Reduced in Force? No severance pay? No notice?"

"I would advise you to stop asking questions and start packing," the serious man said.

This clam-boy meant business.

"Lynette, why is this guy making noises about child pornography?"

"It came from your machine," Quahog said.

Evidently Lynette had entered the second Human Resources mode, the thousand mile stare.

"That clip was posted from an anonymous server," Nick said. "I checked before

I nuked it."

"Corporate security knows how to penetrate anonymous servers."

"Then you also know that anybody could have made it look like it came from my machine."

"It bore your digital signature, which can be generated only by the fingerprint reader on your keypad."

"Lynette," Nick tried, but she continued to stare blankly, as if waiting for somebody to hit her reset button.

"I'm not adding any time to your fifteen minutes. Once they're up, they're up."

"Lynette, hello? Lynette? Are you going to let him slander me like this?"

That seemed to reset her.

"Nick, maybe you should consider relocating. Dataquest predicts that demand for computer professionals in the Sun Belt can only continue to go up between now and the end of the decade—"

"Lynette! Lynette!" Nick shouted. "For Pete's sake! Would you please stop talking to me as if we've never met? We've known each other for seven years!"

The room fell silent for about ten seconds. Ten very long seconds. Through the glass next to his door Nick could see the curious slowing down their walk as they passed, glancing discretely at the scene playing out in Nick's office, like motorists checking out the overturned car at the side of the road.

"I'm sorry Nick," Lynette said. "We've prepared a press release saying that 'Flash' has been canceled, and that you've been dismissed. It was the best compromise I could work out."

"Thank you," Nick said. "Now we're starting to get somewhere. But as you know, Lynette, I didn't work on the Flash project. Not once, not ever. Why am I the fall guy in a press release?"

"It was the best I could do, Nick. I'm sorry."

"Eleven minutes. It's not too late to tell the police where those film clips originated."

"There was a bug in the digital-signature software," Nick said. "I'm sure you know that."

"Any security consultant will testify that our signature software is robust."

"It required a very intimate familiarity with the reverse-address-resolution protocol, but anybody who knew RARP inside-out could have forged a signature."

"Save it for the District Attorney."

"Any *espresso* applett compiled with the common-object request broker flag set to "false" could use the reverse address-resolution protocol to fake out the polynomial checksum by sending a lightweight thread through the kernel to reset the floating-point microcode. I fixed that bug, but somebody could have stockpiled signatures before I did."

"Tell that to the DA too. Unless you'd rather take the option of a quiet dismissal."

"The economy really isn't as bad as it seems, Nick," Lynette helpfully added. "There are jobs to be had out there. Chuckie Johnson. . ."

"The only job Chuckie Johnson is qualified for is professional hodad in the James and Carly fan club. Now you, mister," Nick added to Quahog, "you know damn well how that bug worked. And you also know that I could never explain it to a jury. So I'm well framed, well and truly. But why am I being allowed an out? Couldn't you find another fall-guy for Flash?"

"What's a hodad?" Lynette said.

"A hodad, Lynette, is a puffed-up jackass who drives a Cadillac and walks along the beaches of Martha's Vineyard sucking farts out of dead seagulls. Lynette, why did they go to the trouble of framing me? Did they really go to all that trouble just to have a scapegoat for Flash?"

"I did the best I could, Nick."

"Monty Meekman, by the way, designed the RARP architecture," Nick said. "But I guess everybody knows that too."

"I would be very careful before I started making public conjectures about Mr. Meekman's knowledge of security bugs and pornography," Quahog said. "The corporation will not allow malicious slander of its chief technologists."

"Maybe I'll file suit for wrongful dismissal. Then you'll hear all about Monty Meekman."

"I would be very careful if I were you. You now have two minutes."

"Where'd the other ten minutes go? Oh fuck it all. Nevermind." He opened his desk drawer. Amid broken pencils, piles of post-its and some parking tickets he found a small photo of Bartlett, from their wedding day. He went to get his briefcase.

Quahog yanked it out of Nick's hands.

"I'm going to have to search that," he said.

Before Nick could say no, the man had grabbed it from his hands. There was nothing Nick could do about it now unless he felt like fighting him for it, which seemed a bit much. Folders, notebooks, and Nick's work diary came out. What else was in there? Nick couldn't remember.

"What's this? Oh. Indeed," the Clam from Corporate Security said, as he removed the High Society magazine from the back fold of the case, and thumbed through it, studying illustrated reviews of ten recent triple-X features. It seemed to Nick that the man was taking a lot longer than necessary to make sure there was no Digital MicroSystems intellectual property hidden in the back pages among the phone sex advertisements. Everybody in the hallway, not to mention Lynette, now knew something about Nick's taste in non-Balzac leisure reading.

"Here's your magazine and your Human Sexual Response record," the man said, with a snicker. "You can take your photo of your girlfriend—"

"My *wife*," Nick corrected.

"Whatever. Let's go."

"Wait a second."

Nick reached into the drawer and rustled until he found what he was looking for.

"Now let's go," Nick said.

He walked down the hallway with Lynette at one elbow and the Corporate Security quahog at the other, like a prisoner being escorted to the electric chair between a sadistic executioner and a bewildered chaplain. People parted to let them pass, like a human Red Sea.

As they walked though this twentieth-century gauntlet, Nick understood that Monty had been right about one thing, anyway: Nick wasn't self-actualized. He didn't want to care what these people, mostly strangers, might think of him, but he did care. His face burned with shame. He couldn't even muster anger—the shame extinguished it like salt on a grease fire.

Check him out, K-mart shoppers; Nick Aubrey: hungover, smelly, fired, broke—being escorted to the door carrying a rock-n-roll CD, a porno magazine and a photo of his estranged wife. Check him out. Lynette and Security left Nick at the front door, by the bridge. He walked to the middle of the bridge, then remembered something, and stopped.

Watchful eyes looked out from every window as he fumbled with the item he had grabbed from his desk drawer. In his awkwardness and self-consciousness, he dropped it while trying to place it on his finger. It fell, bounced off the bridge surface and through a hole in the fence. He watched in disbelief as his wedding ring glittered, then disappeared into the dark icy waters of the Mill stream.

Chapter 15

Nick drove home thinking about his briefcase. Why was it, actually, that he had left it behind? It was his own damn briefcase, after all. Bartlett had given it to him for Christmas years ago—a fake-leather K-Mart deal which she, by the simple expedient of a bogus tag, had tricked him into thinking was a genuine Coach and thus five hundred dollars over their budget. He had laughed when he figured it out, but he had also been ticked-off that she had so easily gotten his blood going. She knew she had ticked him off, and was happy about it. They laughed, then screwed three times before the fireplace. Screwed three times very forcefully, to be quite exact; each trying to figure out who really was the boss in this new marriage of theirs.

And while Nick was on the subject of things left behind, why hadn't he taken his pictures off the wall, or the little bronze man from Dahomey, or the files of doodles and sketches from boring meetings? Why hadn't he slugged that corporate bastard in the mouth? Why, why. Who cared. It was over. Did he really want to work at a place where Monty Meekman was the guiding light? Fuckit. They could keep his doodles. They could keep his little bronze man from Dahomey. The could keep all of it: his career, his dreams, his money, his technoid life. They could keep it all so long as they left him the hell alone. He was going to go home, take a shower, put some clean sheets on his bed, and go to sleep for about a week. When he woke up from that nap, then—and only then—was he going to begin figuring out the next phase of his life, the post Dijjy-Mike phase.

He pulled into the forlorn driveway over a quarter-inch dusting of snow and parked near the big spruce. He grabbed his suitcase, gym bag, boom box and ten-pound laptop from the front seat and headed for the front door. It was open a crack. The name "Goldilocks" came to mind. Being goofy-footed, he kicked the door all the way open with his right.

Welcome home, Papa Bear. Tag, you have been touched. Burglarized, home-broken, violated, ransacked, visited, imposed upon, trespassed against, raped. It was a flipping fiasco, with furniture overturned, bookshelves emptied, cupboards spilled, dead plants smashed. The perfect homecoming for his recent little excursion through hell. Mary, mother of God, the Catholics said. He dropped his bags amid chaos in the front room and stepped over the scattered remnants of his material life.

He consulted his watch; it was ten-thirty-two in the morning. That meant it was seven-thirty-two in California, and he had been awake for twenty-five and a half hours. In that time he had been told a fantastical tale by Carl Swirsing about a quasi-religious cult centered on Monty Meekman—a cult, moreover that required absolute debasement by Meekman as a precondition for membership; he had been spied upon by leather-wearing venture-capitalists in a Mountain View low-rent dive; he had taken a ride up Skyline Drive with a seriously deranged Monty Meekman and there been inducted into said cult—whilst being subjected to mind-manipulation and earthquake; he had encountered another crazy man in a yuppie beer place and then again on an airplane, where said crazy man had flamboyantly committed suicide; he had been held for questioning on suspicion of murder; he had been framed for dis-tributing child pornography and summarily fired by a marine bivalve; he had dropped his wedding ring into an abyss and come home to a ransacked house. He had no wife, no job, and hardly any money. And now, evidently, no home.

Nick felt certain that there was a thread to these events, some kind of connec-tion between all this random craziness. But he would never find that thread until he got cleaned up, sobered up and rested up. All he had wanted was a chance to sleep and regroup. But now this: vandals in his living room. The craziness had stopped merely following Nick; now it was anticipating him, beating him to his destination.

"Bite me," Nick Aubrey said.

He went to the kitchen and opened the refrigerator: Three Genesse Cream Ales and six Sierra Nevada. Thank God for small miracles. As he cracked open a Genny he saw his UNIX box, the old junker, sitting on the dining room table.

He was sure that he had left it in a closet, but there it was, plugged in and humming amid debris left by thoughtful housebreakers. Neatly perched on his keyboard there was a handsomely embossed business card that bore only two words: "True Patriots." On the reverse, in pen, were the words, "give it back."

"Fat chance," he said, and put the card in his wallet, next to Carl's. One thing was abundantly clear: It really *was* time to crack Barlow's diskette.

He typed a few commands but nothing happened. Locked keyboard? Hard reset, why not.

He turned the computer off, waited ten seconds, and turned it on again. There came up, in the place of the usual boot sequence, a color screen showing two flags crossed and rippling in a simulated breeze. One was the flag of the United States. The other was, in Marine Corps red and yellow, the large letters PV above an inscription, evidently in Latin, which he couldn't parse. Whoever had done this was pretty hardcore, since Nick had done a full security check before packing this machine into the closet. Nobody should have been able to get on without the root password, and it was unlikely that anybody had guessed E#j9uUi@b randomly. He tried typing this command and that, to no avail: he was locked out of his own computer.

Something snapped. "ARRGH!" he screamed, throwing his head back like Chewbacka the Wookie as he stood, grabbed the chair he had been sitting on, and smashed it into his china cabinet. Then he destroyed, in a similar manner, every chair in his dining room.

"Fuck you, *and* the horse you rode in on," he explained to the universe, then went off in search of a Philips-head screwdriver and another beer. In the end he had to take off the skin and, kneeling on the seat of a busted chair, toggle in a new boot path to regain control of his own system. By the third beer he had a bastard UNIX limping along in single-user mode.

Now he stood with the diskette in his teeth, unsure whether to put it in and try to read it. Rest now, hack later, his prudent self counseled him. This prudent self was making a lot of sense. But on the other hand, his beer-fed, true self whispered, what was the worst that could happen? The program on the disk might hose his system—this old war-horse prototype that his late friend Todd had cobbled together from spare parts years ago. Big Fucking Deal. Even setting the house on fire would solve a certain class of problem.

The prudent self never had a chance.

He took the diskette out of his mouth and stared at it, as a gambler might look at his dice before rolling them, then stuck it in.

He typed

```
cd /dev/rst1; orson
```

and pressed the return key.

After about two seconds a message appeared:

```
ONE MINUTE TO TYPE PASSWORD (160 CHARS)
OR SELF-DESTRUCT
COUNTING SPINS
TIME REMAINING 60
TIME REMAINING 59
TIME REMAINING 58
```

It took him a few seconds to read and interpret the message: the orson program was counting spins of the disk drive and was going to erase itself if he didn't type in the password within one minute. *Hell's bells.* He needed to stop the thing from spinning. What command should he type? He couldn't think. *When finesse doesn't work, there is always brute force.* He reached over and pressed the button to eject the diskette. It peeped a slender edge out of the drive, like Hunca Munca the mouse cautiously checking Lucinda Doll's house to see if the coast was clear.

That answered one question, anyway: there was no way he was going to read it until he had figured out the password. Now he was in a *really* bad mood. He felt like Daffy Duck taunted by Bugs Bunny. The right thing to do would be to walk away, but his sense of dignity compelled him to do otherwise. He closed his eyes and tried to reconstruct exactly what had happened in the back section of the Gordon Biersch microbrewery on Palo Alto's Emerson street yesterday evening. If he could just remember exactly what Barlow had said last night, perhaps he could figure out how to convert the number into a sequence that was exactly one hundred and sixty characters long.

Maceo might have some idea what Barlow had meant, but it was pretty obvious that Nick was going to have to figure the password out for himself. Maceo hadn't wanted to have anything to do with Barlow and had only agreed to take his manuscript to get rid of the guy. If Nick asked Maceo for help with this thing, Maceo would tell him to go fuck himself. There was nobody else Nick trusted. For now, however, Nick was beat. He picked the damn thing out of the diskette drive and put it back in his pocket.

He wouldn't bother reporting the break-in to the police, since it was clear that whoever had done it was looking for the diskette, and Nick didn't want any more police scrutiny on that score than he already had. He spent half a day tidying up the mess, killing the Sierra Nevada, and proving to himself that nothing was missing. As far as he could tell, nothing was. So the house was OK. But what the hell was he supposed to do about his life?

At around two PM the phone rang; it was almost a mercy.

"Hello, Mr. Aubrey? My name is Susan Carr; I'm with the New York Times. I was wondering if you would have a few moments to talk with me about what happened on Flight 44 last night? I have a copy of the flight manifest. . ."

"No thank you, Ms. Carr. Not today. Goodbye. . ."

"Have you seen the discussion on the alt dot conspiracy newsgroup, sir?"

"What are you talking about? I don't read that paranoid crap," he said, and hung up.

In a moment he wished he hadn't been so curt. He didn't want to talk with any news people, but a brush-off like that would only whet a reporter's appetite. He reminded himself to be civil when she called back, as he was sure she would. And what had she meant about alt.conspiracy?

But before he could figure out how to get his UNIX box on the net the phone rang again.

"Mr. Aubrey, my name is Gene Burton; I'm with the Associated Press. We're looking into the story of Flight 44, on which a man, Peter Barlow, either committed suicide or was murdered. Were you on that flight, Mr. Aubrey?"

Here we go again.

"Yes," Nick said.

"Did you see the incident?"

"Not really. No."

"Did you get a look at the man who was sitting next to Mr. Barlow?"

"No. I was at the front of the plane. It was all very disturbing. I would rather not talk about it. Thank you."

He hung up. There, he told himself. That was a somewhat more polished performance.

Another ring. Already?

Yes?"

"Mr. Aubrey, this is Susan Carr of the New York Times. Earlier you and I were speaking of Flight 44."

"We most certainly were not."

Click. Ring.

"Mr. Aubrey, this is Kathleen Gerbens of the New York Times. We're covering the story of Flight 44, and our research seems to indicate that you are the so-called 'Mystery Passenger,' the one who was sitting next to Mr. Barlow and later questioned by the Salt Lake City police. Would you care to comment on this?"

"What research? Did the police give you my name?"

"Can I take that as a confirmation, Mr. Aubrey?"

"No. No you cannot. Ms. Gerbens, you are the third reporter to call me in the last two minutes. I am trying to get some work done. I don't want to talk about that flight, but I'm sure that you can find fifty people who do. Please find one of them."

"But none of them are the man who was sitting next to Mr. Barlow, are they?"

"I've got to get back to work."

"What do you know about Hussein Kamel, Mr. Aubrey? What about Iraq's biological weapons program?"

"Nothing. Not a god-damned thing. See you later."

He hung up. The phone rang again. He lifted the receiver, quickly put it down again. Then he grabbed his coat, hat, suitcase, gym-bag, boom-box and laptop and headed for the door.

The faded elegance that was the Newcastle Hotel was located across the street from the Mill's main entrance, next door to the anachronism that was the Newcastle Diner. Seventy years ago, during the roaring twenties, the Hotel had been a grand place. All the bigwig visitors to Newcastle Textile stayed there, and the swells from Boston took their dates there too, driving out in their Packards or Cords for a night of dancing. In the nineteen-seventies and eighties there had been rumors that somebody was going to buy the hotel and restore it to its Gatsby glory, but nobody mentioned those rumors any more. The Newcastle had accepted its fate as a last stop for old-timers and way-station for transients, and the last of its neon letters had gone out.

Harris, the clerk at the Newcastle Hotel, was nice enough, although clearly he had been drinking at least at much today as Nick had. A hundred and seventy-five dollars the week for a room, Harris said, and you could just sign over your SSI check and he would refund the balance.

"SSI? What's that?"

"Supplemental Security Income. Disability. You know, for being a drunk."

"I'm no drunk. I'm not disabled."

"That's what you think. Sign here. After one week of good behavior you can get a key to the front door. Until then, you better be here by ten PM cause I don't like to get up."

Nick took the tiny slow elevator to the third door and checked into his new digs: a corner room with one window onto First and another window that looked out across Main Street and the falls to the Mill. It wasn't a bad room, as end-of-the-line dives go. He dropped his bags and lay face-up on the bed.

"West and wexwaxation at wast," he said. One problem: Mr. Sleep hadn't checked in yet. Mr. Sleep was three time zones and one lifetime to the west of New England.

∞III∞

SMALL
MIRACLES

Chapter 16

Christian and Janine Garbougian lived on Conwell Avenue, Somerville, near the Tufts campus in Medford. The afternoon shuttle-bus from the Medical Center to the Tufts campus left twice daily, at 4:00 and again at 6:00. Bartlett decided to take the later one.

It was 6:15 when the bus passed by the Boston Gardens—the old Garden looking weary unto death in the pale light of all the construction kliegs, and the new Garden going up right alongside, its skeleton within inches of the bridge. When the bus was halfway across Charles River the rain against its window turned to sleet; it was snowing by the time they reached Bunker Hill. *They probably have five inches in Newcastle by now,* Bartlett thought. Then she turned from the window and stared blankly ahead, thinking about bacteriophage.

Phage were tiny viruses that infected bacteria. Because they were such simple organisms, and harmless to humans, they had been studied in biology labs for decades—Watson and Crick had been studying bacteriophage DNA when they came to their epochal insight. These viruses came in countless species, with names like T3, T4, and ΦX174. You could order the variety that exactly fit your research needs from a commercial supplier and it would arrive UPS the next day. Phage were as common as dirt, as exotic as skim milk. How could Christian and Janine Garbougian possibly have thought bacteriophage were the key to the Gulf War mystery?

The newspaper article had prompted her phone call, but this was to be a social visit with some old friends, not a truth-commission inquiry. How wonderful it was going to be to see them again. She had lost touch with many of her old lab-mates after she got married and came East with Nick. If only she had known that two of them were working just across the river, only a few miles away! If she had stayed at MIT instead of going to the Medical Center, they might even have been her coworkers these last several years.

Bartlett had never been to the Medford campus before, but it was easy enough to follow the directions she had been given, and after a five minute walk she came to Jay's Deli. Chris and Janine had staked out a little booth and called to her as soon as she walked in the door. Bartlett felt a surge of joy and fairly flew to hug them, shaking snow off her hooded sweatshirt as she went. In some ways it was as if she had seen them only yesterday. But oh, how they had aged. Christian's blond hair, which he had once worn in a gorgeous ponytail, was nearly gone. Janine's black hair had been cut short, and her face looked tired around the eyes. They were still an exceptionally good looking couple—but they were definitely grown-ups, not the hot-shot kids that Bartlett had led to a stunning scientific breakthrough. Even Janine's earrings looked like grownup earrings. Was Bartlett herself that much older?

They appeared glad to see her, but more clearly anxious to share their story. That was fine with Bartlett—she wasn't in the mood for talking about herself, her failed marriage, her lonely apartment on Commonwealth Avenue. She ordered a cup of herbal tea from a very Greek looking waiter in a white apron, and Janine launched into her narrative before the tea arrived.

They had gotten into Gulf War research for an obvious reason, she said: it's where the money was. Like all university scientists they spent half their lives filling out applications, and the NIH seemed primed for Gulf War grants. Besides, Janine's sister had been in Tel Aviv when a SCUD fell almost on top of her, and now she was beset by skin rashes and backache that her doctor told her were caused by post-traumatic stress. If there were more to than that, Chris and Janine wanted to know what it was.

"But what made you think of looking for phage?" Bartlett said.

"We weren't looking for phage," husband and wife said in unison. "We were looking for a retrovirus."

That made more sense. A doctored retrovirus—doctored to make it less dangerous for its handlers, not less noxious to its intended targets—would be a whole lot more likely than a phage.

"We found evidence of phage by accident," Christian said, leaning intently. "And like the article in the Times said, almost immediately the ceiling came crashing down all around us."

"I didn't read the whole article," Bartlett confessed. "What happened?"

"We thought we found phage in the blood of five different soldiers," Janine said. "It seemed odd, and we were confused. So we posted a little note to the Internet asking if anybody else had found the same thing—"

Chris picked up her thought. They had completed each other's sentence for as long as Bartlett had known them.

"The next day when we came into work the freezer was off, all our samples were melted—"

"The files on our computer were corrupted, and the box of backups had a magnet sitting next to it—"

"The head of the department asked for a review of our project, and the next day he announced that our methodology invalidated any results we might have had."

"I can't believe you would use poor methodology," Bartlett said.

These had been two of the most methodical people on a very methodical team.

"It was our experimental design that they jumped on, not our lab technique. Our first approximation was seat-of-the-pants," Christian said. "We figured that if we found anything interesting, we would bring a biostatistician on board to design a more rigorous approach. After all, if it looked like we had gotten a fix on Gulf War Syndrome, finding additional funding wouldn't be a problem—"

"We knew, of course, that we had to work with numbered samples only, to prevent us from projecting what we expected to see. But we didn't think that meant that we couldn't meet any of the soldiers. There was no quicker or easier way to get the histories than to take them ourselves—"

"That sounds reasonable to me," Bartlett said. Or did it? If she herself had followed a pure double-blind protocol, maybe she never would have met Jackson. Maybe that would have been better.

"It didn't make sense to them." Janine said. "They raked us over the coals. Not only for the experimental design, but for the loss of our samples, not having back-up copies of our files—"

"—and then, when they checked out one of the references we had cited—"

"What reference was that?" Bartlett asked.

"We've brought it; I'll show you in a minute. But first let me tell you the oddest thing. Right in the middle of all this, when the chairman of the department was calling for our heads, he took us aside and told us that Hoff-Zeigy had endowed a chair a the school, and that we could share it."

"If you stopped your inquiry?"

"Exactly! So on the one hand, 'We're ready to fire you for incompetence,' and on the other hand, 'We nominate you for this high honor as long as you stop what you're doing.'"

For the moment Bartlett was more interested in the science than the politics.

"Are you sure that you didn't somehow contaminate the samples?" she asked.

She was having a hard time getting over the idea of phage protein in soldier blood.

"That was our first thought. But it was a strain we've never used in our lab. It was a version from Hoff-Zeigy Laboratory Products Division. Each variant is well marked; you know that. This particular little guy has an extra carboxyl group right at the end of the alpha helix. It's like a billboard, you can't miss it. So we were sure it was phage, we knew where it came from, and we were certain that we hadn't put it there."

"So, however unlikely as it sounded, we had to explore the possibility that maybe phage had caused Gulf War Syndrome. After all, why couldn't you build a biological agent based on a phage?"

"Good question," Bartlett said. "And there are a couple of good answers. One: phage attack bacteria, they don't attack human cells. Two: phage cannot survive in the human system. Three: There is no epidemiology that has ever associated outbreak of illness with exposure to phage. Four: every molecular biology laboratory in the world uses phage. Countless scientists have exposed themselves to phage infection. But we do not see an outbreak of Gulf War Syndrome in biology departments. Five: phage used in research have been engineered to die outside of the most extremely limiting test tube conditions—"

Janine interrupted.

"—that's all true. But nobody was having any luck with any other explanation for Gulf War Syndrome, unless you count that fertilizer-insecticide work, and that seemed dubious. People talk about nerve gas, mustard gas, Anthrax—but there's no physical evidence. And even if there was evidence, the symptoms that the veterans report are not explained by any of those things."

"But why phage?" Bartlett said. "To you and to me, phage are like our native tongue. We're fluent. Maybe too fluent. They say that when the only tool you have is a hammer, everything you see starts to look like a nail. Our particular hammer happens to be bacteriophage, and Gulf War Syndrome, to me, looks suspiciously like a nail."

Christian seemed annoyed by Bartlett's tone.

"If you were captured by a mad dictator and ordered to engineer a variant of bacteriophage that could work as a biological weapon, could you do it?"

That was one way of looking at it. Bartlett considered the question.

"I suppose you could engineer phage to attack people," she admitted. "You could also breed alligators thirty feet long in the sewers of Manhattan. But phage are so weak. It would be like attack by wet noodle."

"Precisely," Chris said, with unusual intensity. "But that got us to thinking about it. If we wanted to devise a biological warfare agent that nobody could find, how would we do it? We would start with a very small agent, and a very weak one. It would be like invisible ink. It wouldn't last very long in the body, just long enough to cause some symptoms in *some* of the affected population. The symptoms would be so weak that many people would deny they existed at all. This would be a great morale attacker. Soldiers would fear it, the military brass would not be convinced that it even existed. You see? It's as much a psychological weapon as a battlefield killing weapon. How would we build such a thing? With a tiny thing not associated with harm to people: bacteriophage."

"That's ingenious," Bartlett said. "But I still suspect hammer-nail syndrome. Tell me about the references."

It was like being back in the old days. In a coffee shop—surrounded by under-graduates earnestly talking about sex, music and sports—Chris, Janine and Bartlett were earnestly talking about phage.

Janine reached into a bag on the bench next to her and removed a few thin small booklets; they looked very flimsy even by the standards of obscure academic journals.

"*Journal of Applied Virology?*" Bartlett said. "Not exactly *Nature*."

"Published by Eastern Appalachian Christian College," Janine said, smiling. "It's sort of the National Enquirer of scientific journals."

"More like the *Weekly World News*, actually," Christian clarified. "Less celebrity gossip and more UFOs. There's an article in here by one Dr. Pascale Pacheco, enti-tled, 'Short-Lived 'Monster Cells' as Transport Vectors.' That's one of the references we cited."

"OK," Bartlett laughed. "Let me have it. What does Dr. Pacheco have to say?"

"She claims that she has devised a way to create artificial cells large enough to be seen without a microscope. They're only as stable as a soap bubble, but after she creates them, she fills them with small DNA sections—plasmids, or even phage. Inside this artificial membrane is a perfect environment for the precise, electrical engineering of DNA."

"Electrical engineering of DNA," Bartlett echoed.

"Electrical currents precisely controlled by a computer chip allow her to create hundreds of thousands of minutely different versions of a given section of DNA."

"That's ridiculous. How can you electrically engineer DNA in a big bubble?"

"You know about DNA diagnostic chips, glass wafers that can passively match genes up to eight base-pairs long? Five years ago, who would have said that was pos-sible? Pacheco seems to describe an active version of the same thing."

Obviously Chris and Janine knew how silly it sounded too, but they must have thought there was something to it, or they wouldn't have bothered to mention it.

"OK, How does it work?" Bartlett said.

"The monster cell is attached to a chip, the DNA inside is customized accord-ing to the program built into the chip."

"It sounds like alchemy."

"It is like alchemy. She doesn't tell how to create these cells or even what they're made out of. She doesn't explain how to electrically arrange DNA. There are no pro-tocols, so you can't replicate her experiments."

"In other words, it's crackpot stuff."

"It certainly has the look and feel of crackpot stuff. But even the Weekly World News breaks a big story from time to time. And she's serious enough about one thing, her own citations. She cites a lot of your work. And our work."

How lovely, Bartlett thought.

"That's nice, but it doesn't mean anything," she said. "Besides, I'm not sure that having crackpots cite our work as inspiration is career-enhancing."

"It gets better. Pacheco seems to recommend clinical trials on hundreds of thou-sands of human guinea pigs. She doesn't come right and call for germ warfare, but she says that possible research partners for future work were the governments of Iran, Iraq, China, and North Korea."

"And you cited this article in your grant application?" Bartlett asked, incredu-lously.

"We cited thirty-one articles," Christian said. "Two by her. In retrospect it was-n't such a smart move. But scientists are not supposed to prejudge. It seemed like it might be clue. Farfetched, but a clue."

"So where do things stand now?"

"We're on administrative leave at half-pay pending a peer review of our work."

"Oh, guys!" Bartlett said, and put her hands out to touch theirs. It was time to stop judging them and start showing some sympathy.

"The worst thing is not that we're under a cloud," Janine said.

"The worst thing is that we don't know whether we're crazy. The instant we discover a Hoff-Zeigy strain of phage in Gulf Vets, Hoff-Zeigy endows a chair for us—and at the same time our work runs into several coincidental accidents and we become subjects of an inquisition. So we start to wonder, Is somebody trying to shut us up? Who, Hoff-Zeigy? But Hoff-Zeigy is the one Swiss pharmaceutical company that everybody agrees is squeaky clean—no deals with Iraq, no Nazi skeletons in the closet—"

"— But their vice-chairman was involved in the BCCI bank scandal, and so were the CIA, Noriega, and Saddam Hussein. So on the one hand we feel like we may have stumbled on something very sinister, a pharmaceutical giant developing a brand new kind of weapon, selling it to Iraq and then blackmailing a university to shut up the scientists who discover it; and on the other hand we can almost understand why the department would want to shut us down. Between our discovery of phage—"

"—that nobody can reproduce—"

"—and the Pascale Pacheco articles—"

"— that nobody can believe—"

"— they may think they have a 'cold fusion' on their hands, or an alien abductionist. They might really believe we've gone around the bend. Plus, ever since that article appeared in the New York Times, every Gulf War fruitcake wants us for his poster children. We're swamped with E-mail. Half of it says, 'You're right! You're right! It is phage, and it was developed by aliens that landed at Roswell.' And the other half says 'Do me a favor. Go buy a biology textbook, you dumb stupid cunt.' What do you think Bartlett? Are we crazy?"

"No," Bartlett said. "You're not crazy. You're doing science, and science is political. Just try to relax. I'm sure it will work out."

"Bartlett, we're so glad you came," they said simultaneously.

"But we're being rude," Janine said. "How are you? How have you been? You look great. How's your husband?"

It had been bound to come up sooner or later.

"Actually, we're separated."

There was and awkward pause. Then Janine smiled and said,

"Tell me what it's like being single!"

But Bartlett wasn't single, was she?

"We only just got separated five months ago. I'm still rather in shock."

"No children?"

She paused. Should she say, that's rather a sore point? That that was a prime reason I couldn't take it any more? Nick's refusal to deal with our future? No, she shouldn't say that.

"No children," she said. There was no need to say anything else. But she found herself going on. "Nick is a dreamer, which is why I married him. A beautiful dreamer. But. . ."

But what? What was she trying to say?

"But at our age the line between dreamer and loser gets hard to see. Oh, I sound so bitter. I hate to hear myself calling him a loser, but I don't know how else to describe it. He's so smart, so gifted. But he fritters his life away, waiting for something to happen for him. He flies off to California in search of I don't know what, and comes back empty-handed time and time again. He would have been happier, we would have been happier if he worked on a garbage truck. Why could we never even talk of having children? He *loves* children. But whenever I brought up the subject of our having children, all he would say was, 'enna boubi,' which means 'it's cold' in some African language he knows. It got old."

What an eruption. Did she feel the better of the worse for it?

"Life happens to all of us," Chris said.

And Janine asked, "Do you ever hear from Paul?"

"Paul is at Hoff Zeigy, in Basel, Switzerland. But I haven't seen him since I got married."

"Hoff-Zeigy," Janine said. "Small world."

"It's hardly surprising," Chris said. "That company is so big. They must have a hundred thousand employees. They're everywhere."

There was another pause, and to fill it Bartlett told them about her work—the investigation of Fitzgibbon's Disease, and also about her new company, The Neuro Group. The founders of the company were the neurologists, neurophysiologists, molecular biologists, psychologists and computer engineers that Bartlett worked with. Their product was a neural-network that was proving very useful for testing hypotheses about diseases of the brain. Many medical schools and drug companies had expressed interest in buying it. Bartlett didn't know anything about computer simulations of brains, per se, but she did know a lot about the etiology of Fitzgibbon's disease, which had been used to validate the model. And she also had made some promising discoveries about the genetic regulation of nerve cell regeneration. The Neuro Group was incorporated, but unless they found a source of money to develop the company, their tool would remain a prototype, suitable for in-house use, but not ready for prime time.

"This is fascinating," Janine said. "Shall we stay here for dinner, or do you want to go somewhere else?"

But Bartlett wasn't in the mood for dinner. She was ready to go.

Chapter 17

X number of hours after checking into the hotel, Nick was drinking his n^{th} cup of coffee in a booth at the chrome castle called the Newcastle Diner, thinking: Well now what, Nick? Back at his house the phone would ring and ring. Flight 44 was not going to be something that would just blow over, after all. The key question, though, was whether these reporters actually had any evidence that Nick was the man who had been detained by the police, or if they were just taking an alphabetical walk down the passenger list. He could imagine Kathleen Gerbens using that same "our research seems to indicate. . ." line on every passenger with a male-sounding name, hoping to scare up the actual mystery passenger. On the other hand, maybe the police had leaked Nick's name. Maybe he was due for six months of reporters calling every two minutes, camping out on his doorstep waiting for that big scoop. What should he do? He would figure that out tomorrow. For now the Newcastle Hotel, even if it was a dump reminiscent of some places he had stayed in Benin and Burkina Fasso, would be his refuge. Let the reporters call his home number all they wanted —he had arranged for voice mail and would take great delight in nuking their messages. For right now, only Nick Aubrey and Harris Drake had any idea where Nick would be sleeping tonight.

But something was bothering him: Susan Carr. Gene Burton. Kathleen Gerbens. *Times*, AP, *Times*. No, that couldn't be right. The *Times* wouldn't assign two reporters to such a trivial story. One of them must have said the *Globe*, or *USA Today*. He consulted the clock above the counter. It was nearly one in the morning, time for all good reporters to be putting their papers to bed.

Taking his coffee with him, he walked to the pull-shut phone booth. In a minute he had retrieved the 800 number for *Times* news desk, and faintly penciled it on the wall.

"Kathleen Gerbens, please. She's a reporter."

"Kathleen Gerbens? Just a moment; I'll put you through to her voice mail."

He waited until hearing her greeting before hanging up.

He dialed the same number again.

"Susan Carr, please. She's a reporter."

"Just a moment. How are you spelling that?"

No luck. Nobody named Carr or Karr or Karp at the New York Times. Three more phone calls confirmed that there was no Susan Carr at the *Globe* or *USA Today* or the Associated Press. Something about that name, Carr, bugged him. What had Barlow said? *'Aubrey, Burgess, Carr, Delcourt. You think I never saw that film? I was with the Company, remember?'* Could the CIA really be looking for Nick? Not bloody likely. But even if they were, he was safe for now.

Or was he?

There was somebody sitting in Nick's booth, on the bench opposite where he had been sitting. As Nick watched through the glass of the phone door, the waitress brought a cup for Nick's guest, and the guest filled it with coffee from Nick's pot.

She was a slender woman, about thirty, with a narrow face, wearing gold-rimmed glasses. Her brown hair was long, and pulled into a simple braided ponytail that rested on a plaid shirt worn open over a white turtleneck. She seemed bemused as she reached for the little silver pitcher. As she finished putting milk in her coffee she looked up, and her eyes met his. She wore no make up. The bemused look on her face didn't change at all as he stared at her; it was a little turned-down smile that seemed to say, you wouldn't remember me. I'm nobody. She was Tom-boyish, if one said that of a thirty-year old woman, but she was pretty.

He left the phone and walked to where she sat, neither of them averting their eyes.

He sat down opposite her.

"Hey stranger," she said.

Chapter 18

Dieter Steffen lay on his bed in the dark, staring at the glowing red numbers. It was 3:17 Basel local time. A new day had begun, a day with no prospect of rest. *Scheiese*, he thought. *Ich stand hüt nacht im bett.* Tonight I am standing in my bed. There will be no sleep for me.

Thirty hours ago Judith Knight had spoken to Dieter over cherry brandy on the terrace of the Kunsthalle café, and he had been in torment ever since, as the projector in his mind replayed, endlessly, the series of facts and conjectures that kept him in his current distressed state:

In Basel, Switzerland, at the laboratories of pharmaceutical giant Hoff-Zeigy, Dieter is hard at work on a "nanomachine" —a programmable mechanical device smaller than a virus—that will be able to repair and rearrange DNA. This is how the device works: a DNA pattern is first programmed into a computer chip. During the manufacturing process, the DNA pattern is transferred from the chip into a "nanocomputer" within the device. The nanomachine is then injected into living organisms, where it re-arranges DNA according to the instructions that have been programmed into it. This work, potentially worth billions of dollars, is a closely guarded corporate secret. Only a handful of people know about it, and only one other scientist—another young loner, an American named Pavel Isaacs—works on it with Dieter.

Elsewhere, the Human Genome project is making rapid progress. This is a worldwide collaborative effort of universities, private companies and government laboratories, greatly assisted by the Internet, to identify the function of the approximately 80,000 genes in the human genome— to decode the human genetic blueprint, which is written in the universal language of DNA.

Dieter's machine is being built in anticipation of the results from the Human Genome Project. If his machine ever moves from the drawing board to the real world it will revolutionize medicine, providing an instant cure for cancer and hundreds of genetic conditions such as Cystic Fibrosis, Down Syndrome and Sickle-cell Anemia. Indeed, this machine will change the human condition, theoretically opening the door to personal immortality and the creation of whole new forms of life— 'designer' plants, 'designer' animals, 'designer' people.

Dieter is deep in concentration, enmeshed in the computer-created virtual environment that he uses for molecular modeling, when he is interrupted by a call from Judith Knight, one of the leading lights of the Human Genome project. She requests a secret meeting.

The stunningly beautiful Judith tells Dieter that for the good of mankind he should stop the work to which he has devoted his life. She also tells him only the other person on earth who is capable of understanding this work is a dangerous sociopath. Dieter must not let Pavel know that he has spoken with Knight. Paul Aubrey, who probably does not understand the danger of this device, is trying to create the team that can build it.

Pavel cannot create the machine by himself; he needs Dieter's help. Thus the fate of mankind rests with Dieter Steffen: a shy, slightly overweight, Swiss scientist and proper citizen. Dieter must decide what he is going to do. Over and over, this endless series, always ending up in the same place: *Jetyt muss er sich eutschrade was er machen will.* He must decide what he is going to do.

He needs to decide soon: over the last ten weeks he and Pavel have made remarkable progress on the two remaining design problems for their nanomachine: the compression algorithm, the fullerene sphere. And yesterday, only yesterday, Dieter completed the redesign of the tube. But he has not yet told his partner Pavel. That is the question that keeps him awake: will he tell Pavel? For the chance of saving humanity from the ravages of disease and starvation will he risk unleashing the demons of hell?

He knows that once he shares this design with Pavel there will be no turning back. It will be time—after patient years of research, of regular failures and small incremental successes, years of computer simulation—time at last build the real device.

But first Dieter must decide about Pavel.

Is he what he seems to be: a brilliant scientist obsessed with discovery and invention? Or is he what Judith Knight has darkly hinted: an evil person working with evil people to devise a doomsday weapon? Was Judith Knight a guardian angel sent to warn him, or was she a delusional woman with an obscure score to settle?

Judith implied that Pavel had misled Dieter for as long as they had worked together. Now Dieter finds himself wondering whether Pavel's decision to collaborate with him had been based on an ulterior motive. Dieter admits that there had been some odd aspects to Pavel's decision to leave MIT for Basel. But on the whole the move made sense. Dieter had secured a position at Hoff-Zeigy, and had encouraged Pavel to apply for a job to work with him. Pavel and Dieter had worked well together in graduate school. Their two doctoral dissertations provided a roadmap to a brave new future; it was only natural that they would continue to travel that road together.

Pavel had seemed curiously anxious that April, nearly six years ago, the last time they had been in America together. He had had two jobs: in addition to his work as a graduate fellow in the department of Molecular Computation at MIT, he had also been an intern at a computer company. Dieter had expected that Pavel would move to Basel in the summer of 1995, but one day in early spring Pavel had announced that there was no further need for him to stick around: his dissertation was complete and his computer project had been canceled. He was moving to Europe immediately, he announced; he would be moving the very next day.

He was sick of the racism, he said; he wanted out of America *right now*, to give Europe a try. He didn't care about graduation—they could mail him his diploma.

The comment about racism had seemed odd. Pavel had dark complexion and wiry hair, it was true. But to Dieter Steffen he looked Mediterranean, not Negroid. Dieter had assumed, given the last name, that Pavel Isaacs was Jewish. It would have been less surprising if he had complained of anti-Semitism. But to Dieter it was astounding that Isaacs could complain of ill treatment at all. As far as he could tell, the MIT community had recognized in him another Feynman, a future Nobel Prize winner. They sucked up to him like groupies to a rock star.

That had been in 1990; now it was years later and yet Dieter knew next to nothing of Pavel's private life. What Pavel did on his own time, where he went on those long absences, sometimes months at a time, were his own affair. Dieter turned away from the clock and shut his eyes in a last attempt to sleep. Five minutes later he admitted defeat. He was at his lab before 4:30.

But this brought no solace either.

Out of his laboratory, down one flight of stairs. As always, he took the route that cut across the molecular genetics laboratory on the third floor. Once upon a time Dieter had worked in labs like this, with colleagues like the white-smocked scientists who worked here, amid these pungent smells. These days Dieter worked mostly alone; the molecules he worked with were odorless, 'virtual' molecules made of 'virtual atoms,' simulations on a computer screen. Maybe that was why he walked through this laboratory twice daily—to remind himself that a real world truly did exist, a world in which human beings used *all* the senses, sometimes even to communicate with each other.

The lab was slowly coming to life. Technicians in white lab coats were tidying their already orderly lab benches, preparing ice baths or Luria broths amid the smells of ethers, mercaptans, and alcohols. Doodles —chemical equations, structures, formulae written in marker pen— filled the glass doors of the enclosed hoods used for work with dangerous evaporators. Ceiling ducts pulled away the fumes, and the enclosed hoods hummed. Dieter liked it here; his worries became lost in the noises of the laboratory: the whirr of a centrifuge down the hall, the rattle of a shake table, a faucet turned on, a fan humming. In a few minutes he was at the lab's far side, running his feet past the Geiger counter at the door to check his feet for trace P34 before leaving.

But where would he go? All he knew was home, such as it was, and the laboratory.

He decided, almost in desperation, to go to Kaiseraugst. As a young man he used to go to this site of Roman ruins from the time of Caesar (Kaiser) Augustus. It was a tram ride of less than twenty minutes. But the trams were not running yet. He would walk. It would clear his head.

But his anguish went with him on his walk along the Rhine. And it remained with him three hours later when he took the return ride. The open air of the scenic arches on the banks of the Rhine no longer comforted his soul. He had become an indoorsman, if there could be such a thing. The molecular biology lab comforted him more than rivers, birds, trees and clouds. He would go there and strike up a conversation with some junior scientist, find out what she or he was working on. By engaging his mind with somebody else's puzzle perhaps he could free himself, if only briefly, from his own.

To his astonishment, however, that possibility had disappeared during the few hours he had been at Kaiseraugst. He returned to the third floor laboratory to find the usual cadre of scientists gone, and a small army of technicians in white lab coats, rubber gloves, goggles and gas masks hurriedly packing the contents of the lab into boxes marked with warnings of chemical and biological hazards. In dismay he walked through the commotion, unnoticed, as a scuba diver might pass through a school of hammerheads.

Hours later, still staring blankly at his screen, he could hear an incessant hammering and whining of motors coming up through the floor. Immediately below him the molecular biology laboratory was being demolished. Presumably, to make room for something.

What?

Chapter 19

"Casey," Nick said. "Casey Montgomery. Won't you join me? How've you been?"

No wonder it had taken him a few seconds to place her. He supposed that he hadn't seen Casey since the week Todd had been shot. That was what, almost six years ago? He remembered running into her at Spaulding Rehabilitative Hospital after they moved Todd there. Nick had only gone to see him once. What was the point of visiting a vegetable?

"So you're not sailing on the Mother Ship anymore?" she said.

Casey never had been one for beating around the bush.

"Good news travels fast," he said.

"Did you jump or did you get pushed? I heard you got riffed, but maybe I caught the wrong rumor. It wouldn't be the first time."

It was her air of sympathy and concern that Nick found so touching.

"Partly wrong. I didn't get riffed, I got fired."

"Mazel Tov. I've been trying to pull that off for years."

Then silence. Apparently it was his turn to speak.

"So how about you Casey," Nick said. "What have you been up to?"

"Hardware, you know," she said. "Just hardware. I'm working on a hyperscalar CPU. Sixty-four bits. Gallium Arsenide, remember that? G.A. The wave of the past. Me and Seymour Cray."

Again that self-deprecation, that turned-down smile. Her upper right lateral incisor was turned about fifteen degrees, creating a very slight gap that gave her a pleasingly asymmetric smile.

"Have they figured out how to make that economically yet?" he asked.

That had been the problem with gallium arsenide, right? The cost? Or was it the heat dissipation? Or susceptibility to EMF? He couldn't remember. He basically knew nothing about chip substrates. GeeAy, EnMoss, CeeMoss, Nickel Oxide. When Todd had been alive he had explained to Nick the feel of each chip technology. To Todd they were as different from one another as a Formula One racer was from a Volvo station wagon. But to Nick they were all just hardware. He was a software boy.

"Ask me in a month," she said. "Got any plans?"

"Think I'll go work for this friend of mine who does market research."

"Spill your guts on every Dijjy-Mike project you know about?"

"Precisely. The guy who fired me would shit."

"Who was that?" she asked.

"Monty Meekman."

The look on her face was awe.

"Monty? He slimed you too? I'm impressed."

He didn't think she was joking.

"It wasn't a distinction I had actively sought out," he said.

"At least you're in good company. If you work with him and don't get slimed, you're pretty suspect, as far as I'm concerned."

"You sound like you speak from experience."

"I got slimed a little on the Kali project."

"You worked on that?"

Nick thought he had done great to remember her name. You couldn't expect him to remember her entire work history.

"I worked on Kali until Monty took me off and put funny boy, what's-his-face, Pavel, on it. But fundamentally I didn't have enough talent for Monty to even notice me. Also, I'm not a guy. Monty was always finding these guys with real talent and taking them under his wing, grooming them to be the next Dalai Lama or something. Then at some point he would either make them Corporate Fellows, or decide that they had let him down and set about to cut their balls off."

"Sounds familiar," Nick said. Had he been the only one not to notice this pattern?

Casey continued, "The way he scapegoated Todd really caught my eye. Here's Todd lying in intensive care with half his head shot off, and Meekman's making a speech to the team about how Kali is being canceled because Todd fucked up. Which was absolute bullshit, of course. Then the next day Monty's at the hospital, the picture of piety, hovering over poor comatose Todd."

"What did happen to the chip?" Nick asked.

"Want to buy me a beer?"

"Beer," Nick said, raising his hand to this forehead. "Please not to mention that word."

"Oh," she said. "I see. Well you can be forgiven. I'd get drunk too if they ever cut my umbilical cord to the Mill."

"I don't care about my umbilical cord to Digital MicroSystems. But the fact that I totally, irremediably fucked up my marriage while simultaneously going bankrupt has kind of gotten me down."

Not to mention the incident in the Saratoga hills, the interrogation in Salt Lake City, the reporters, the burglary. . . Nick's memory was finally engaged now, the cobwebs having been dusted from a long-unused corner. He was remembering Casey, and her connection to Todd.

Like Casey, Todd said what was on his mind or he said nothing. You asked him a question; if he didn't feel like answering it he ignored it, and sometimes he just walked away. It was as if his brain simply filtered out anything that his higher self would consider inane. Women who preferred conventional relationships with men didn't last long with Todd. They might spend an hour with him, or an evening. Then they would pronounce him "cold" or "weird" and that would be that. There were others, though, like Casey: Suzy Creamcheeses to Todd's Frank Zappa. "No one could understand our bizarre relationship," Suzy says on the Uncle Meat album. "I was his intellectual frigid housekeeper. . ." Nick couldn't remember the rest of the way Suzy put it, but he could recall perfectly her blasé tone of voice, talking about her intimate life as if she were reading a shopping list. He imagined that she had a turned-down smile to go with it.

Todd and Casey were hardware hackers. Sometimes they designed chips together. Sometimes they slept together. Sometimes they went their own ways for months at a time. The parameters of their relationship were determined by them alone. It wasn't the kind of thing that Todd and Nick would have talked about under any conceivable circumstance. It was no surprise, then, that it had taken Nick a moment to remember Casey's name. Todd had similar relationships with two or three other unconventional women. Nick couldn't remember their names either.

"Hey Casey," Nick said, after getting another memory refresh from somewhere deep beyond the locus of his headache. "Whatever happened to the Shrine?"

Was that a smile? On a micron scale. Maybe.

"It still exists, although I had to move it. Now it's kind of in the museum annex."

"The Shrine's in the museum annex? What museum?" he said.

"The Bonehead Computer Museum, of course. Don't tell me you you've never been to the Bonehead Computer Museum?"

"Perhaps you could enlighten me sometime."

"Let's go see it right now. It's in the Mill."

"I appreciate the offer, but not today. I have to figure out a way to get Bartlett back."

"No, now. Come on, you're wallowing." She spoke with sudden authority, as if she were a cop rousting him from a nap on a park bench.

"Well, let me try another line of defense," Nick said. He really was in no mood to go back in the Mill only hours after his disgrace. Not to mention the fact that he didn't want to get arrested for posting child pornography on the intranet. "Corporate

Security has enjoined me from re-entering the Mill. I'm *persona non grata.*"

"Corporate Security?" she said, incredulous. "All the more reason to go back right now. You've got to get back in the saddle, son. Jesus Christ on a Pogo stick, Corporate Security? Spit in their lemonade, Nick. Come on. Let's go."

She had a point.

"You're right," he said. "Let's go."

They left a few dollars on the table and walked out onto the Main Street sidewalk. How long had he been in there? The sidewalk was already covered with snow about five inches deep. Nick headed left, towards the main entrance, but she pulled his sleeve.

"No, this way," she said, and led him in the opposite direction, towards the upper mill pond. "The main entrance is probably the only place you have chance of getting nabbed."

They crossed at an angle to the opposite sidewalk, which ran parallel to the series of falls that began at the upper pond and continued along the whole west face of the Mill to the lower pond. A low black iron fence separated the sidewalk from the cataract. By this route it would take them at least fifteen minutes, Nick figured, to get around the upper pond and the south parking lot. They had gone about twenty yards when she said, "O.K. Hercules, up and over," and with surprising agility, did a one-handed vault over the fence.

Nick vaulted after her, awkwardly, and followed her as best he could down the steep, dark, slippery rocks along the falls. Eventually she stopped under the main bridge. Nick was breathing hard, as much from his fright at almost falling as from the exertion. Here, directly under the bridge, there was a relatively quiet pool that he had never noticed. Was this perhaps where his ring had come to rest?

"Take my hand," she said. "This is a little tricky."

"I'll say."

But he took her hand, and she led him over a path of rocks, some of them barely visible, to the other side. In the dark he never would have seen the door, but she obviously knew it quite well; in fact, she had a key for it. They entered into a dank sub-sub-basement illuminated by naked bulbs, but within a minute they had climbed three flights of stairs through increasingly less sinister surroundings, and soon they were in the hallway that began just behind the main reception desk.

They followed "Shay's Highway" the length of Building One. At Two they went up four flights of stairs, then down Publick Alley 4754 to Three. Once in Three they turned at Turners Falls and walked ten yards until they came to the unmarked firewall door on the opposite wall just before Nick's office. Nick turned his head so as not to be recognized by the new tenant already moving in.

"And they cast lots for his garments," Casey said, as she pushed the firewall door open.

Nick couldn't remember the last time he had seen anyone use this door. He followed her through it into an area of old-style cubicles, long vacant. In Nick's glory days as a manager this area had been part of his demesne. Then came the merger, the layoffs; before long this was just another void, one of numberless unoccupied sections that sprouted all over the Mill like spots of January mildew on a summer-house wall. Some cubes contained obsolete equipment—keyboards, mice, monitors, printed circuit boards—like rubble-strewn rooms beneath a pyramid before the archeologists have gone to work. Nobody cleaned them up. Who would have bothered? It would have been like sweeping out a dustbowl farmhouse before decamping to Salinas to pick lettuce.

"My Void and welcome to it," she said, and her voice reverberated.

He followed her to a distant corner, where there was a door there that he didn't remember. Instead of a push-bar there was a two-foot long spatula-like device, and above it a printed sign had been pressed onto the door:

> ## EMERGENCY EXIT ONLY
> ## ALARM WILL SOUND

She pressed the door and it swung open, noiselessly.

"What did you do, disconnect the alarms?" he asked.

"Nothing so renegade," she said as she led him up a flight of dusty stairs. "Somebody probably forgot to turn something back on when they shut down the Alpha Annex two years ago."

"Does anybody else know about this?"

"I've never seen anybody," she said. She stopped at the next landing, the top. In front of them was a door, padlocked. To their left was a window that ran nearly floor to ceiling. "Here, this way," she said, as she opened the window and stepped out into the freezing night air.

He stuck his head out and found her standing on a slightly sloping roof. Nervously, unsure of his footing, he stepped out to join her. What little light there was came from the upper stories of Nine, the tallest of all the Mill buildings about thirty yards away, but the falling snow blocked most of it. As his eyes grew accustomed to the dark he began to make out rooftops of the various mill buildings all around him. Casey led him to a three-foot parapet at the edge of the roof. "Listen," she said. He could hear the muffled sound of the half-frozen falls coming from below.

"I'm trying to make out where we are," he said.

"We're on the roof of Seven, right above the Klingon fab lab. Come here, I'll show you something. They extended the clean room under the skylight; you can look down to see all the Klingons in their space suits."

She set off at a trot and Nick loped after her. In a minute she had wiped a swath and he was looking down through a raised skylight at three or four people dressed in white smocks, hair nets, white gloves and elastic slippers milling about in a blindingly lit room.

"I thought we shut this down operation when the equipment became obsolete. Don't we outsource all our chips to Texas and California? I swear, I remember the layoffs."

"We outsource all our new stuff. This is an old line. Makes chips according to 1990 specs, and older. You're looking at the computer equivalent of Henry Ford's original assembly line."

"Who could possibly want that?"

"It's mil spec. Military specifications. Chips for tanks and jets. They change slower than the glaciers. And they generate scads of cash. Dijjy-Mike just pulled its old machines out of mothballs and got into the business."

"Do you suppose they can hear our footsteps?" he said.

"I doubt it," she said. "There's all kind of white noise in that lab. Come on, I'll show you something else." She walked down about fifteen yards, put two hands on the parapet and vaulted over. For the third time that night she scared the breath out of him.

She stood a foot below, where the roof of an adjoining building met the wall. If she had vaulted a few feet earlier she would have fallen five stories onto the rocks by the lower pond. She led him for another five minutes and he lost track of the turns before they came to a stop at another low wall. Beneath them was a street, and across the street was the Newcastle Hotel. He could see the windows of his darkened room; the hotel was close enough that he had no trouble seeing what people were doing in the rooms above and below his.

"I thought you would find this amusing," she said, as she reached up and let her long hair out of its braid. "I look from time to time thinking maybe I'll find something I can post to alt dot sex dot voyeurism," she said.

She was looking right at Nick's room.

Her lips parted just a little, revealing the twisted incisor. Didn't she ever smile without a tinge of irony? The wind blew her hair back, and a little light glinted off her snow-flecked glasses. *She looks like a boy*, Nick thought, *but she's really very pretty.*

"I was surprised to see that door at the top of the stairs padlocked," he said, deliberately changing the subject. "What if there were a fire? People might run to the roof and get trapped."

"Well, I padlocked it. It opens on to nothing. Maybe there used to be a ledge there or something, but now it's a doorway to nowhere. Walk through it and it's five stories straight down."

"Jesus," he said. "What is this, Winchester Mystery House East? Doesn't the Mill have a director of safety?"

"I don't know," she said. "Ask Corporate Security. I guess that's why those Californians ate our lunch. We're just too damn disorganized."

He was trying to keep his teeth from chattering, but she seemed perfectly comfortable. Was she, perhaps, a ghost?

"What about the Museum?" he said. "Or are we doing an experiment in hypothermia?"

"Follow me."

A few moments later, by a path that he could never have retraced, he found himself back inside, walking next to her down a corridor that he eventually recognized as Charles Street, building Nine. She excused herself to the ladies' room. When she came out her hair was again braided.

"So you see where we are—Building Nine—here's Todd's old office. Some geek has it now." Nick glanced into an anonymous office: family photos, a college pennant.

"Here's my office," she said, tapping on an office door as they walked past. After six years of working in the same room, Nick wondered, had she suffused it with her personality, as Todd had done with his? Or had she left it sparse, undecorated, enigmatic?

"Recognize this?" she said, pressing a swinging door that opened to her right, off the well-lit corridor onto a darkened hallway.

"It's the delicatessen, isn't it?" he said.

"Used to be. Here, this way."

She flicked a switch and a light came on at the far end of the thirty-foot passage. Nick remembered that there was a little lunchroom there. There would be a little counter on the right wall, where two brothers from Coolidge Corner had once served kosher fare. Nick wondered how long the delicatessen had been shut down. How isolated he had become, taking his meals in the main cafeteria, or more frequently at the Diner, alone. Going back to this little lunchroom was almost like going back to his kindergarten classroom. What memories would it bring back?

He wasn't going to find out. Casey stopped half-way down the hall.

"Here we are. Ta-da," she said.

On her right was a door that, as he now recalled, led to the kitchen behind the counter. He looked at the door, and saw, affixed to its center, a small neat etched plastic sign:

The Bonehead Computer Museum

Open Midnight to Midnight - Monday Thru Sunday

And By Appointment
Donations Welcome

"Please, I would be honored," she said, and indicated for him to push the door open. He did, and entered, and immediately tripped over something on the floor and fell.

"Shit," he said. "Watch out."

She turned on a light.

At his feet he saw a hunk of electrical equipment: metal cage, wires, circuit boards, and what appeared to be a stack of tan dishes connected by a spindle.

"Oh look," she said, evincing no recognition of his fall, "another foundling left on the cathedral steps. This is a prize specimen. The curator has coveted one for years."

"What is it?" he said, rubbing the sore spot on his right shin. "Looks like an old disk drive."

"Correct," she said. "Second generation, a DSU19. It's probably nearly twenty-five years old. Are you OK?" she said, and extended her right hand to give him a help up.

"Now this, this is a truly bonehead piece of work," she continued. "This is an exquisitely poorly-engineered kludge. These things never worked, you know. They were Digital Data's first flop, their first Edsel. They broke, they caught on fire. But they were at the time the only option customers had for disk storage. I think they held, like, ten K or something. Just nothing. And they sold for like ten thousand dollars. Do you know what Ben Golson said about them? 'The good news is, you sold one, you sold two.'"

"Where did it come from?" Nick said.

"Who knows? Most of my donors are anonymous. When I get things like this I suspect Golson himself is sneaking in here at night. How's your leg?"

"I'm alright," he said, and looked around him. Affixed to the wall were mounted printed circuit boards, dog-eared manuals, reel-to-reel tape drives; on small tables he saw odd-looking personal computers. There was an industrial range and oven in burnished steel against one wall, and in the center of the room there was a large table with a butcher-block top. The room ell'd to the right; he could not tell its size from where he stood but guessed it was not very large.

He began to wander through the room. The first article he came to was a printed circuit board about sixteen inches square, which projected out perpendicularly from the wall. The board itself was hard laminated green plastic an eighth of an inch thick. Mounted on it were tens of brown chips and tan chips, each looking like a rectangular ant with eight or sixteen or however many little silver feet frozen to the board. Connecting the ants were little sharply-angled rivers of solder. Capacitors, resistors and heat dissipaters sat on the board like miniature railroad tank cars, tiny robots, and Christmas trees on the world's smallest train set. And on front and back of the board there were scads of wires held in place with dollops of hardened green glue. The back of the device, in particular, looked like an electronic bird's nest that had been sneezed upon.

The description mounted on the wall adjacent said:

Mosaic Technologies, Inc. CPU (1983-1984) - NS16016 CPU board for the Mosaic Graphics Workstation. One of the great marvels of boneheaded design, this module, despite its uncanny resemblance to a prototype, was actually the third pass board being produced by manufacturing. It is obvious from inspection why Mosaic failed after only two years of operation. "Never before have so many taken so long to produce so little."

Gift of K. Thompson

Even a software boy like Nick could see the boneheadedness of this design. It must have cost a fortune, and the number of wires would make it almost impossible to correctly manufacture.

"So you don't just have Dijjy-Mike designs here?" he said.

"I started out with just one or two egregiously kludgey Digital Data designs. One of them was my own first board, a total crock. But people kept giving me all the great kludges of their own careers. Why should the Museum be provincial? Bonehead design is a universal human right." Next to the Mosaic board was a smaller printed circuit card, crammed with chips, about five by fifteen inches. Its card read:

S-100 Cassette Interface Card (?) - A beautiful period piece. Note the design such that chips were more expensive than sockets. This is a fine example of excessive engineering to the point that not even Digital Data could sell it.

Gift of C. Montgomery

Arched over the two small cards was a heavy grey cable that appeared to be singed at one end, and at the other a card read:

ECD Bomber (1989) - Cable. This cable single-handedly flamed several peripherals in its short but hideous life.

Gift of Barry J. Folsom

Casey was standing back, fastidiously avoiding comment. In her turtleneck pullover, red flannel shirt, faded blue jeans and Topsider shoes she was the very vision of the rugged, outdoorsy New England woman, straight from the pages of LL Bean. And indeed, he noticed again, she was handsome. But her femaleness was entirely unlike Bartlett's: she was taller, had fewer curves, stood with a more athletic posture. But the curves definitely were there. She should be hiking in the Adirondacks, he thought, or canoeing Moosehead Lake. Why did she spend so much time within this monastery-like expanse of the Mill?

The next object he came to was a square of thick wire mesh, about five inches on each side, and on this there was a donut shape of heavy gray dust, grown up like coral. The caption read;

Filters (1986-1989)   These were the non user-replaceable filters on the 386ie. It is not clear where dust this big comes from.
Gift of T. Griffith.

"Have you ever been back to visit Todd at Spaulding?" she asked.

"Not in years," he said. Suspecting that she still went, he didn't add, What's the point?

"Prepare yourself, then, for the experience of his simulacrum."

"OK. Where is it?" he said.

"Look behind you," she said.

"Yah!"

Floating in the air behind him was cross-legged, four-armed Kali, Hindu goddess of death.

"Got you again," she said.

Just a damn poster, he thought. It was mounted on a massive stainless steel door, which obviously led to the walk-in cooler dating from when this place had been a working restaurant.

"I thought Kali was supposed to be beautiful," he said, after his heart had resumed beating.

"That's what Todd thought too. He was thinking of Shiva. Kali's a hag. Just look at those saggy tits. Shiva's tits are like Teri Hatcher's: big and firm."

"Casey, you frighten me."

"Moi?"

"Maybe I'm just jumpy," he said.

She looked at him quizzically, as if he were a bonehead kludge that she was considering adding to her collection, then opened the door.

Chapter 20

At 7:30 that morning Dieter still sat in front of the Dijjy-Mike graphics workstation. He hadn't moved in the last four hours; his hands were still on his lap. Little more than a day of bone-crushing worry had brought him to this: complete inertia. It was no use putting it off: he had to talk to Paul Aubrey.

He had no idea where Aubrey might be in the eighteen-building complex that was the central office of Hoff-Zeigy Pharmaceuticals AG. *Quel drole de type que je suis,* he thought. What a funny little man I am. I have worked here all these years and I know nothing about the place. How does one go about finding Herr Paul Aubrey among all these buildings, all these employees?

He walked across the parking lot to the guard station and asked for directions. Ten minutes later he was on the fourth floor of the Executive Building, standing before Fraulein Claire Mason, secretary to Herr Aubrey. She would see if he was available for an unscheduled visitor, she said, if Herr Doktor Steffen would care to be seated.

Two minutes later Paul Aubrey emerged from his office.

"Hello Dr. Steffen, Paul Aubrey. I was wondering when I might meet you," he said.

That American presumption of friendship, the clasp that squeezed his knuckles as if a handshake were a test of strength: so far Aubrey was true to form. He was wearing a double-breasted suit; his styled hair was grey with some vestigial black, as was his closely-cropped beard.

"I may as well get to the point, Mr. Aubrey," Dieter said. "It comes to my attention that you are seeking a partner with whom Hoff-Zeigy can collaborate on nanomechanical systems; a partner that can provide a research capability on the human genome. Am I correct?"

"Doctor Steffen," Paul said, "please come in. Sit down."

Dieter perched himself uncomfortably on the edge of a chair, as Aubrey continued:

"You are correct: on behalf of Hoff-Zeigy, I am looking for an appropriate partner with whom to share the work of the NanoSection. Your machine is a brilliant invention, but without the genome structure to program it, it has no therapeutic value. It's a toy."

"A toy?" Dieter said. "A programmable computer only a few atoms wide is a toy?"

"A scientific marvel, no doubt. A fundamental advance in the understanding of physical-chemical systems. But to make something practical, we need a partner who is as far ahead in human genome work as you are in nanotechnology. Together, we can create a universal drug, something that will revolutionize medicine more than antibiotics, vaccines and anesthesia combined. It will be worth billions. And it will win for you the Nobel Prize in Medicine."

"That is a long way off," Dieter said.

"We'll never know unless we try," Aubrey said. "The corporation has decided that the time has come to reach out."

"And what of me, whose work you propose to sell. Were you planning to keep me in the dark indefinitely?"

"In the preliminary stages Doktor Isaacs thought it best to keep the discussion small. These projects can go through a lot of false starts; sometimes it's best if there are fewer people involved."

"So. I am the young prince for whom the King and his court will find a proper marriage; no need to worry the child until we have found the right match. Is that it?"

"Doktor Isaacs is the one who decided not to distract you with talk of joint research. If you are upset at having been excluded, you should speak with him. But since you now know what we are trying to accomplish, I would be glad to hear your opinion about how to proceed."

"That's the problem," Dieter said. "I'm not sure we should proceed at all."

"But at some point Hoff-Zeigy must get something for all its expense, don't you agree?"

No, I do not agree, Dieter thought. He was a scientist advancing human knowledge, not a financial instrument whose maturity date was approaching.

And now, on the threshold of a new world—a world of his own creation—he was experiencing what the Americans called 'cold feet.' But was Paul Aubrey, corporate venture capitalist, the person with whom to share his worries? All Aubrey seemed to care about was the return on investment, the billions to be made. Dieter thought about ending his visit right there. Conversation was hard for him, and confrontation was harder still. But he had come this far, he had to speak his mind.

"There are grave dangers here, Herr Aubrey. It is one thing to create 'toys' in simulation, and quite another to build them and release them into the world." There, he had said it. Sort of.

"Any new technology brings dangers with it," Aubrey said. "When it was proposed to electrify New York City a hundred years ago, the anti-electricity people used to electrocute a dog every day in Central Park just to show how dangerous electricity was. And they were right. Electricity is very dangerous. Would you have been with the dog killers a hundred years ago?"

"Perhaps," Dieter said, as he rose from his seat. "Thank you for your time, Herr Aubrey. I will ask that you keep confidential the fact that we have spoken."

Paul Aubrey looked at him quizzically for a second.

"Ah," he said. "So it wasn't Doktor Isaacs who spoke to you."

Dieter said nothing.

"Judith Knight," Paul said, with a bemused smile. "She is a brilliant scientist, and she provides a moral ballast that the world sorely needs. . . "

Dieter hoped that the look on his face remained neutral.

". . . she, however, would have been in Central Park."

"Good day, Mr. Aubrey," Dieter said.

"Let us continue this conversation at another time."

"Certainly," Dieter said. But he was far from certain. He was unsure of everything.

Chapter 21

A musty odor greeted them, mingled with a smell of jasmine incense and rose-petal potpourri. The shelves had been removed; the empty cooler was the size of Nick's bathroom at the Newcastle Hotel: slightly longer than an old-style bathtub and three quarters as wide.

In front of him, covering the wall from floor to ceiling, was a picture of a chip: thousands of impossibly thin blue, black and red lines that looked chaotic but somehow gave rise to a marvelous order. On the floor in front of it: some candlesticks with melted candles in them, wands of incense in small buckets of sand, the Mothers of Invention's Uncle Meat album on vinyl and CD, a paper-flower lei, two "matchbox" Formula I race cars, a pair of drumsticks, a pair of earplugs, a Cheech Wizard comic book, an unopened can of Jolt Cola, a whiteboard covered with saw-tooth and square-tooth timing diagrams scribbled on top of each other in blue, black and red marker, stacks of unread memos from management about uniform coding practices. On the left hand wall was the needlepoint sampler:

```
Running Round and Round
     In Tiny Circles
   At Very High Speed
```

and resting on the floor beneath that was Todd's framed two-photo sequence of a Formula One racing car exploding into a wall, with tires flying like heat-seeking missiles.

Mounted on the right hand wall there was another small pea-green printed circuit board, about five inches by ten. In the middle of the front face, dwarfing everything else, was a squat postmodern skyscraper: an inch-tall square stack of dull brown clay and shiny silver metal, about two inches on each side, that rose from the surface of the board like a colossal hotel in the desert. Thick wires of black, red, and copper were crudely soldered into the stack at various places, and capacitors and resistors joined them, all held in place by solder, black tape, transparent tape and that snot-green glue. Atop this crude ceramic tower there was a little square well, and situated in that, connected by gold wires impossibly fine, there was a single silver iridescent chip.

A gold half-inch-square sliver was attached to the tower by a piece of tape. It bore the Digital MicroSystems logo and the notations

8808V

VM374

VC2964-0001

KALI 1.0

Proto   USA

Nick turned his attention from the chip to the caption:

Kali - (1990- Canceled) Cache controller for the Roadrunner Workstation. A good idea one day too late. "From hush-hush to irrelevant in one incandescent whoosh."

Donated by M. Meekman

Nick looked over his shoulder; the wall behind him was covered by a large photo mural of a beach at sunset. It was a remarkable illusion; even with the outline of the door clearly bounding the declining sun the mural conveyed a sense of calm, a journey's end, a destination. He returned his gaze to the enormous reproduction of the chip that filled the wall in front of him. This shrine indeed performed spiritual work. Over the years Todd had become a memory to Nick; not even that—an abstraction, a notion. This place made him real again.

He closed his eyes against his will and tried to smile—which had the opposite effect.

"God damn," Nick said. His eyes stung from the effort not to cry.

From his left he heard a single short sob. So: her irony could crack, after all.

"He's been gone a long time, Casey," Nick said. "You're going to have to let him go."

Her answer was one long exhalation.

"I know I know I know I know I know."

"That's funny, 'donated by M. Meekman.' Does he know about this place?"

"I'm sure he doesn't, the asshole. Right after he canceled that project, while Todd was still in intensive care, Monty was here collecting prototypes. He wanted all chips accounted for. I had to hide this one from him, like an innocent from Herod."

"Why did he want the chips?"

"He had some story about how we were going buy the cache-controller from Intel, and part of the deal was that we had to give them all our specs and chips. He even wanted the plots," she said and nodded at the wall. "That slimeball."

"What's a plot?"

"Like this here. It's just a picture of a chip, blown up a hundred times."

"You don't think that's plausible?"

"It's bullshit. What does Intel care about our plots? They've got their own design. It's not like they're going to reverse-engineer ours from a *drawing*."

"What do you think his real reason was, then?"

"He was covering up for funny-boy, you know, Michael Jackson."

"Michael Jackson?"

"What's his name. Pavel Isaacs. Whatever he calls himself now."

"Why do you call him Michael Jackson?"

"You don't remember?"

"I never met the guy. I was pretty busy back then. I only saw Todd a few times a year."

"Well," she said. "It was just like Michael Jackson: He was here two years. The first year he was black. The second year he was white."

"Get real."

"You really never heard about it? Boy, you must have been out of the loop. He didn't start out like Robert Parish or Malcolm X; he was more like one of those not-so-black Black guys. And he came out white, but not blond-hair-blue-eyes Aryan Youth. It was more like Mediterranean."

"This really happened?"

"For a while it was all people could talk about. Then the novelty wore off, like when Jamie had the sex change: people just got used to the idea."

"And you think Monty was covering for Pavel?"

"You figure it out. The first year Pavel was here, he was doing I-don't-know-what. Todd and I started on Kali. When Todd and I were working on it, it was going pretty smooth. Todd used to get chips right on the *first spin*. They say a UNIX wizard is a guy who writes a compiler using the 'cat' command. That was Todd and silicon. He was the Bobby Fischer of chip design."

"You must have been pretty good too." He noticed that the air was getting close, and kicked the door open behind him.

"I'm a good chip designer, but not like Todd," she said. "He did the architecture on this thing, he did the geometry, he did the layout; divvied up the big chunks, figured out all the tricky timing and race conditions. It was going to be one cool chip. Then Pavel came on and they went to four spins. Four spins. And they still didn't get it right. It looked like it was Todd's logic that was fucked. He couldn't figure it out. But the more I think about it, the more I think it must have been the other guy's logic that was fucking up Todd's. Todd never took four spins for *anything.*"

They turned, left the cooler and began slowly walking out of the old kitchen.

"By the way," Nick said. "It's really musty in there. Doesn't the cooler's circulation fan work?"

"No, I just ran a wire for the light. The fan doesn't work because they closed off the vent. Don't close the door behind you, you might suffocate."

"Please tell me you're joking."

"Yes, Nick, I'm joking," she said. "You could kill somebody in there, but not by accident. You would have to lock it from the outside.

"Well anyway," she continued, "I did all the garbage logic. I-O, data alignment, that kind of stuff. It's like I was the sous-chef, and he was the chef. I snarfed the bits off the bus, got them ready for him. Just like the sous-chef gets the ingredients ready for the chef. Then I fed them back out to the bus when he was done cooking them, like that. Like telling the waiters when to pick up their orders. Also I did the BIST."

"What's a bist?"

"Built-In-System-Test. On-chip diagnostics. It was pretty new and cool back in 1987. Standard practice in 1990. Old hat now. That's where I think Pavel fucked up."

"And you think Monty was trying to hide it?"

"Look. The project is on schedule, doing fine. Monty takes me *off* the project, he puts Pavel *on* the project, and the chip slips six months and still isn't right. We never saw Michael Jackson after Todd got shot. He never even came in to clean out his desk. Just whoosh, gonzo. And the next day here's Monty canceling the project, looking for specs, prototypes, plots. We couldn't even figure out how Monty got here so soon. You remember, there was a storm? Logan was *closed*. They must have had planes delayed for hours. By looking at the time that Meekman showed up at the Mill, we figured he would have had to have been on the first plane that landed and raced like hell from the airport. It was obscene. One would hope for a little more class from a Messiah."

Messiah?

"OK, Casey. I'll bite. Why do you call him a Messiah?"

"You never heard of the New Gospel?"

"No. What is it?"

"Allegedly there was this famous computer scientist who was given a guest editorship of an issue of the *Communications of the Association for Computing Machinery.* He wrote a long article that had some kind of obscure title, but people quickly started calling it the New Gospel."

"Yes dear, but why?"

"You know who Vannevar Bush was, right?"

"The guy who wrote that *Atlantic Monthly* article in 1945? I've heard about it, never read it."

"It's called 'As We May Think.' It's astounding. Vannevar Bush was like Jules Verne and Leonardo. Twenty-five years before the first microprocessor was invented, Bush predicted the Internet and the World Wide Web—he called them by different names, of course. But his descriptions were pretty right-on, fifty years ahead of his time. He looked beyond that too, to a future when people would communicate brain-to-brain, electronically."

"Like a built-in Internet."

"Precisely. And thoughts would be trackable through their evolution from one person to another. As you shared ideas they would become part of an electronic archive that he called "the record of the race," which would keep track not only of ideas, but who started them, who improved them. The best thinkers would be 'Masters' and the less gifted thinkers would be 'Disciples.'"

They were walking through a corridor in hardware land now; the gizmos and gadgets were a dead give away. Corridors in software land, or God Forbid, Marketing, didn't have little robots making observations about your gait as you walked past, or coffee machines that tried to guess how you liked your coffee by analyzing your face. The engineers on this hall looked about fourteen years old and very chirpy.

"*That's* the New Gospel?" Nick said. "The Vannevar Bush article?"

"Be patient. You also know who Thomas Engleton is, right?"

"Lord God Emverk, patron saint of SIGCHI, inventor of the Engleton glove?"

"And the brainwave parser, and the larynx sensor that knows what you're going to say a millisecond before you say it, and about fifteen other inventions that marry people to computers."

"*Engleton* wrote the New Gospel?"

"'anonymous' wrote the New Gospel. The ACM article allegedly took the ideas of Bush and Engleton to the next step: linking all the computers and people on earth into one giant organism."

"I'd like to read it."

"You can't. The ACM board of directors pulled the plug. Officially speaking, the New Gospel never existed. They went out of their way to destroy all traces."

"Why?"

"This article talked about social policy as well as computer stuff."

"Lots of *Communications of the ACM* articles do that."

"Not like the New Gospel. Apparently 'anonymous' embraced a very Nazi-like philosophy, a hierarchy in which some people were more valuable than others."

"That doesn't necessarily mean he was a Nazi. It might just have been a capitalist."

"No, Nazi. He proposed things like rounding up 'unnecessary' people to provide a supply of brains for neurophysiological research, and factories for growing fetuses to use in DNA research, and using genes from birds to grow magnets in people's heads so that they could navigate and develop primitive radios. There were lots of other cool ideas straight from Auschwitz and De Sade, only updated to reflect the latest technological developments."

"And the ACM wouldn't publish that? The cowards."

"They cobbled together a replacement issue, and it was bad, but it was better than letting the New Gospel see the light of day in an official ACM publication. Legend says that copies of the original 'anonymous' article still exist, passed hand-to-hand like holy relics, pieces of the true cross."

"You would think somebody would have posted it to the Internet by now."

"According to the myth, only the initiated get to read it. Nobody else can be trusted. It will never be posted to he Net."

Nick really disliked this legend. He had had enough of hierarchies of human worth, and of Masters and Disciples and things only the initiated get to know. He wished he had never met Carl Swirsing. But there was no unknowing what he knew, so he asked the obvious question.

"Why do you think that this 'anonymous' is Monty Meekman?"

"It fits," she said. "Few people are brilliant and weird enough to have written such a thing. Monty was Engleton's understudy for five years, and his godfather was, you guessed it, Vannevar Bush. So some people refer to Monty as 'The Messiah' and they call those drones of his—"

"The Corporate Fellows?"

"Yeah, them. They call them 'The Apostles.' They're the keepers of the flame. Of course, it's probably all bullshit, a story Monty made up and circulated about himself in order to add to his mystique. But the Bush article is real enough. I've got a copy of it at my house. Why don't you come on over and read it. I'll make you a cup of coffee," she said, putting her arm through his.

He thought again of their prowling over the darkened rooftops and realized that it had been the single most enjoyable thing he had done for over a year. How striking she had looked with her hair blowing free in the dim light; how quickly she had braided it as soon as she was inside. It was as if she must go out of her way to deny the least hint of prettiness. A goddamn Joan of Arc, that's what she is, he thought. He imagined her: sword in hand, *fleur de lis* unfurled on a standard beside her as she gazed into the distance. And as he held the image in his imagination she suddenly became naked, still holding her sword; her small breasts upturned, nipples erect in the bracing wind, her legs impossibly long, like a Barbie doll's.

"Come on," she said, giving his elbow a tug. "Live dangerously."

Nick felt, suddenly, a tingling from the small of his back through his thighs to his knees. If he didn't do something quick it was going to be the mother of all erections. He shook his head, as if to undo a stuck solenoid.

"Here, this way," Casey said, and pushed open a door he hadn't noticed. They emerged from the Mill out into the cold night air near the edge of the lower pool. She led him up a rocky path onto a lighted pavement, and after a few looks around he recognized First Street. Five minutes later Casey stopped walking, bringing them up just outside the light-cone of a streetlamp. He turned towards her and tried to get a look at her face, but the shadows were too dark.

"Nick," she said, staring straight at him. "Let me tell you something about Monty and the Kali project. Meekman shot Todd."

Nick finally realized what had been going on for the last few days, ever since Carl had called him. He had been going insane. And now the process was complete.

"Meekman shot Todd?" he echoed.

"Oh I can't prove it, of course. But dig it, OK? The police established that Todd's last phone call was to Monty, at nine PM. Todd must have told him something that made Monty think he had to kill him. *That's* the reason he arrived at the Mill so early on the day that Todd was found dead. *He was already here.*"

Todd's last call had been to Meekman at nine PM, and he had sent Nick the cryptic e-mail, "I fear these things," at nine-eleven. What had Todd been trying to tell him? What things had he feared? At the time Nick hadn't been able to think of anything, but now he was beginning to wonder if Todd had been referring to Meekman. Nick was in no mental condition to accept this line of thinking. Not now, maybe not ever. It had to be wrong, because if it were right the implications were unthinkable.

"It isn't possible," Nick said. "Todd was shot in the middle of the night. The first flight came in late, delayed because of the snowstorm. You already told me that."

"The corporate jet, Nick. With a good tail wind that Gulfstream can cross the country in four and a half hours. Commercial flights were delayed, sure, but if Monty came on the Dijjy-Mike jet he could have gotten here before the airports shut down. He wouldn't even have had to land at Logan. The jet could have landed at Hanscom, which is closer to Newcastle. That would have generated another hour."

"Meekman fired up the jet, raced out here and murdered Todd? Why?"

"What if Todd discovered something in the chip, a hidden function—you know, a Trojan horse, like that RARP trap door that you found in the in the mail daemon?"

"How do *you* know about that?"

"Bugtrack, Nick. Any engineer can read bug reports."

"I just closed the bug. I never sent out a press release saying that it was a damn trap door."

"What, only Nick Aubrey knows how to read between lines?"

"I guess not."

Indeed. It was clear that Casey Montgomery was a pretty good interlinear reader, herself.

"What if Monty instructed Pavel to insert a trap door in Kali, but Todd figured it out?"

"Have you ever told the police this hypothesis?"

He was cold and not cold, and his stomach was a mess.

"Sure. Logan had no record of the Dijjy-Mike jet landing. They checked all the airports that can handle that size jet. No record of it. Case closed."

"You think Monty covered his tracks."

"Two things Monty Meekman is not: he is not stupid. And he is not careless."

"They why would he have killed Todd himself? That would have been pretty reckless."

"He might have done it himself because he is evil. Or maybe he didn't do it himself; maybe he had an accomplice. In either event, now that you've been slimed too maybe you'll be willing to help me find out."

"How?"

"Let's spook him and see how he reacts."

"What do you want me to do, waltz into his office and accuse him of murder?"

"All I want you to do is see if you can flush some bunnies out of the woods."

"I don't know," Nick said. What else could he say? He was cold, he was confused, he wasn't even quite sure where he was. He loathed Meekman as much as he had loved Todd, and the notion that the one was responsible for the other's death had an oddly attractive symmetry to it. But he couldn't figure anything out at this stage. He was tired beyond exhaustion, he was still half drunk and on top of that he was feeling an electrical, sexual charge across every square inch of his skin.

"You'll do it for me, right?" she said, squeezing his arm. "I'll do anything in return." That smile. God help him.

They walked another ten steps, her arm still through his. She stopped, grabbed him with both hands on his right arm to stop him. Snow went down his collar.

"I want to tell you something else," she said. "One of the many things De Sade was *right* about: Everybody has an animal nature. Everybody knows lust, and the need to dominate from time to time." She leaned towards him, standing on her tip-toes, and put her lips to touch his right ear. She put her left hand on the back of his head, fingers splayed. She put her opened right hand on his face, gently cradling his head as if it were a cantaloupe that she was sensing for ripeness, careful not to bruise it. He was totally unprepared for the sensuousness of her touch; he felt the hair stand on his arms as her tongue, ever so lightly, quickly, darted in his ear. Then, without warning, with her left hand she grabbed a handful of his hair and pulled down sharply, while with her right hand she pinched his lips shut. Her teeth bit into his earlobe. He was taken totally by surprise. The pain was sharp, from everywhere at once, and he felt simultaneous urges to pull his head forward and backwards, even as something extremely pleasant but equally embarrassing very nearly happened elsewhere in his system. Then, still holding his head immobile, with her lips touching his right ear she whispered "am I right?" and let go with both hands.

Before he could say anything she smiled and said,

"Well, here we are at my house. Won't you come in for tea?"

"Is it safe?"

She shrugged. "Depends on what you mean by 'safe,' I guess."

"OK, but don't forget. I'm a married man." Technically, anyway, he thought.

"How could I? You wear it like a purple heart."

Three steps led up to the porch of a small wood-frame house. At the top of the stairs she motioned to him to stop and be quiet. He did, and within a few seconds he heard laughter from inside. Was it two voices? Three? Definitely female. How old? Teenagers, perhaps. He listened.

"No listen, I am so serious," a voice said. "I am like *totally* serious."

Across a darkened room came light from a doorway through which Nick could see three teenaged girls seated at a kitchen table. A blond girl with an angelic face was talking.

"So we go into the house, right? and the old lady just stands there, looking at us. And we're like, 'um, it's *Halloween*, you know, like dress ups? Like trick or treat? Like, candy?'"

Casey opened the front door quietly and stepped inside, motioning to Nick to follow. They stood in the dark, unnoticed by the girls in the kitchen.

"She was, ohmygod, she was about one hundred years old," the girl went on. "I am *not exaggerating*. And we're like 'Nevermind, we came to the wrong house,' cause we just wanted to get out of there, right? and that's when like, *doink*, this light goes on over the old lady's head and she says 'Oh, *Halloween*!'" And we're like '*Finally!*' And that's when her teeth fell out, and they scooted across the floor and she couldn't see them because they *slorped* under Kirsten's sheet—like she's a ghost, right? And we're all going 'give them to her' and Kirsten's like, 'no way, they're gross,' and we're like, 'give the old lady her teeth, she's already deaf she might totally fall apart.'"

"No way! Then what happened?" said another voice.

"Kirsten wouldn't pick them up. And the old lady was getting more and more pathetic, looking at the floor like a puppydog that couldn't find its squeakytoy, so finally I lifted Kirsten's sheet and picked the teeth up, and they're all slimy and dirty from the floor and I'm like, 'um, excuse me, did you drop these?' and she's like, 'mank moo,' and that's when the *other* old lady walks in the room! Ohmygod, she was like *two* hundred years old. And she goes 'Oh, *Halloween*. Let me go look. I know we have some candy from Easter."

Nick burst out laughing, and three girls' voices shrieked in unison "Ohmygod! Ohmygod!"

Casey turned on the living room light and called out "No panic! It's me, Casey!"

Nick followed Casey into the modest kitchen where three breathless girls of about fourteen or so were seated around the kitchen table. "Nick, meet Kirsten, Danielle, and Kate."

"Hi Kristen. . ." Nick started to say.

"It's Kir-sten, not Kris-ten," she said brusquely. Then she turned to Casey and said, "You've got to let us crash here. OK? Please?"

"You know the rules," Casey answered. "Do your parents know you're here?"

There was some discussion of the protocol that Casey required before opening up her home as a youth hostel. It was clear that this was not the first time that these girls had been there.

"Wait here," she said to Nick. "I'll go get your stuff."

Nick stood awkwardly in the enforced silence. It was clear that the girls were not going to say anything while he was in the room, and of one mind, they got up from the table and removed themselves to the parlor. He busied himself looking around. On top of a bookcase he saw a stapled booklet that appeared to be about twenty pages thick. He picked it up for a closer look. On its cover, above a poorly-reproduced depiction of two crossed flags were the words

The Gulf War Coverup
By
The True Patriots of the Natural Law

"Enough, already," he said. It was time to find out what was *really* going on.

He grabbed the largest knife he could find from a wood block on the counter, and waited for her to come downstairs.

Chapter 22

Bartlett Aubrey awoke in the middle of the night when a truck sounded its horn—the kind of noise that city-born folks slept through. Bartlett wasn't a city person and probably never would be. Instead of drifting back to sleep, she found herself thinking about her trip to Tufts.

It had been good seeing her friends Christian and Janine, and she expected she would stay in touch with them. But Chris was right: life had happened to all of them; things had changed, and it was tiring to act as if nothing had.

Haven't we all changed, Bartlett thought. Nick has changed, Christian and Janine have changed too. What about me? How have I changed? How has Paul changed? Paul used to be so innocent; Nick so worldly. Now Nick seems so naive, and Paul is in Basel. Have their roles reversed?

She remembered now the last part of their conversation at Jay's Deli.

"We'll give you a ride to Davis Square," Christian had said. "You can catch the Red Line back to Boston."

As they stood to get ready to go, Janine looked deeply at her.

"Paul was so in love with you that it was nearly impossible to watch," Janine said. "It was like a force of nature that he was trying to restrain."

"I figured he had a crush on me."

"'A crush,' you say. Bartlett, if you only knew."

The three old friends had left the Deli at 7:30. Bartlett got on the Red Line train at 7:55 and headed home for steamed fish and brown rice. By 9:30 the dishes were dried and put away, and she sat down to write in her diary. Half an hour later she had gone to bed, and there she had read some analyses of the coming season. No matter who wrote it, baseball writing in late winter was pretty bland fare, and she had been lights-out by half-past ten.

But now she was awake. Usually if she woke up in the middle of the night, pre-occupation with her work in the laboratory was the culprit. But that wasn't the case this time; not exactly. She was thinking about a lab, yes. But she was thinking not of Irwin's lab, but Eddie's—of Chris and Janine and Paul Aubrey.

Lost in recollections, she absentmindedly again got herself ready for bed: used the toilet, scrubbed her face, brushed her teeth. She got back in bed but somehow forgot to get the ceiling light in her bedroom.

In remembering those times she could recall the intense camaraderie of the team in the lab—the around-the-clock work, the blending of day and night, the indescribable surges of adrenaline as they realized—as she realized, for the funda-mental insights had all been hers—how the Trojan gene worked. She remembered the exhilaration of realizing that they had made a publishable discovery; then that they had made a discovery that would be published by Science; and finally that her article would be the top story, the cover article.

In those heady days of constant work and occasional parties fueled by lab-pure 200-proof alcohol punch, of nineteen-hour days rushing to set up new experiments, ignoring safety in the name of speed, mouth-pipetting enough dangerous chemicals to obliterate a small city, followed by five-hour nights of dancing to Little Feat until the sun came up at one grad student's apartment or another; days and nights of sleeping wherever it was convenient to catch an hour or two—whether on a friend's bed or on the couch in the basement of the Catholic church near the Life Sciences building—in those circumstances, was it in any way surprising that she had made love with the handsome undergraduate who was a peripheral part of their circle?

She didn't think of herself as having being especially libertine in those days, but she wasn't the prude that her Baptist preacher uncles from the Illinois coal region would have wanted her to be either. She had had sex with a few men as an under-graduate, been played for a fool by a professor and experimented with the concept of "boyfriend" as a grad student. The experiment had failed. Sex to Bartlett was no big deal, certainly not when compared to serious science.

So she had gone to one movie over the course of a few months with Paul, and made love a few times, giggled with him about it in the laboratory. No big deal. Not to her anyway. But now she felt bad at how big a deal it had been, without her knowing it, to him. Evidently he had been in love with her. How was she to know?

The simple fact was that she herself had never been in love until she met Paul's brother Nick. And from the day she met him she had never known the touch of anyone else.

By the time she met Nick it had been two months since she had last seen his younger brother. Paul's semester-long undergraduate internship in the lab was over and her path no longer crossed his. Paul had called her several times at the lab (always missing her, which was statistically nearly impossible). She didn't return the calls. She hadn't meant to be cruel, but by that time she was working harder than ever, furiously putting together the final pieces of the puzzle. She seldom remembered to eat or bathe, so if she didn't remember to return his calls it didn't mean she was avoiding him. It just meant she forgot.

She lay on her back on her bed in the winter night. The landlord had yet to get the heating system under control, and tonight, even with the windows open onto Commonwealth Avenue it felt like August, and she was naked. The curtains were open and the light was on, but it wasn't like anybody was going to see her. Across the street there was an architect's office, always empty at night. And it was a wide street, anyway. Her plants swayed in the window.

Two more pounds to go, she thought; maybe they'll be gone by the time I weigh myself in the morning. She placed her hands on her stomach and flexed. All those situps had worked, and she felt proud. She hadn't been in such good shape since before Jackson died—and she fell apart.

If Nick were to see me now, what would he think? She knew just what he would think.

Her sex life had died along with her young friend. She had continued to go through the motions, but the passion had evaporated once it had become apparent that this time there would be no recovery for Jackson, that the disease had him and wouldn't let go, not this time. How could she make love when her every moment, her every waking moment, her every sleeping moment was filled with thoughts of her lovely boy, her sweet lovely boy, who sang her songs and made her pictures and hugged her and told her it would be alright? An abandoned child had comforted her while her husband went off chasing chimeras in California and then returned to chase the chimera of that stupid children's co-op. How could she make love with her little boy of a husband while her other little boy lay dying in that goddamn cheerful anteroom of death, Children's Hospital on Longwood?

It had been years, then, since she had felt an erotic thought. Her left hand cupped her left breast, and she ran her thumb over the nipple. She was dispassionate, the scientist examining her own responses, taking her own case history. Oh if Nick could see me now, she thought. Poor horny Nick. But when she closed her eyes she didn't see Nick.

With her eyes closed she was surprised to realize how vividly she could call his face to her mind, the face of the shy young undergraduate sitting in the corner at his first team party. Her right hand slipped along the inside of her thigh. With her left hand she found herself pinching her nipple, as she whispered his name.

Chapter 23

In the minute that Casey had been gone, Nick had come to his senses. Yes, it seemed that Casey had planned the whole evening to lead up to his discovering the True Patriots' literature. There were too many 'just happeneds.' Having not seen Nick in years, Casey *just happened* to bump into him—and *just happened* to know an awful lot about his recent experience, *just happened* to have a perfectly laid out plan to recruit him to a "get Monty" campaign. But that was no reason to go *stabbing* her. He threw the knife in the sink, disgusted with himself. As he did caught his reflection in the window over the sink, and he didn't like what he saw: bad posture and a hang-dog mien. A victim.

"It's time, Nick," he told himself, "to assert a wee bit of control over your life."

He stood erect and threw his shoulders back, closed his eyes and took a deep breath. If he was going to assert control, he needed to know what his ultimate goal was. That might take some thought. . . but his next step was pretty obvious: he needed to determine if Casey was on the level. Simple objective, simple approach. He opened his eyes.

"Once more, into the breach."

He turned to find Casey standing in the doorway, Spockishly raising an eyebrow. *Cute.* Too cute. With all the deliberation he could muster, he grabbed the True Patriot's pamphlet and held it to her face.

"What's this?" he said, trying to keep his tone neutral.

"What's what?"

"This 'True Patriots' stuff. What the hell is this?" His voice was raising. This 'neutral tone' stuff was going to take some practice.

She looked perplexed. Or, perhaps, he thought, like somebody who was trying to look perplexed.

"Just some stuff," she said. "You know, Gulf War Syndrome stuff."

"No, I don't know," Nick said. "Where did you get it?"

"I snarfed it off their web site. It's wacky."

"Come along then," he said, grabbing her sleeve.

Casey said a word or two to the girls as she and Nick headed out the door.

"Wacky stuff on the net interests me," she said, to his silence. "Like Unabomber manifestos and plans to hook up with space ships. Like that guy Barlow, who died on the airplane. Have you heard about him?"

What, she *just happens* to know about Peter Barlow? This was too much.

Nick stopped and turned to her. They were standing, once again, under the streetlamp in front of her house.

"Are you yanking my chain? Did you know I was sitting next to that guy Barlow when he killed himself? Did you know that the police suspected me of murdering him? Did you know that these True Patriots, whoever they are, are breaking into my machines, breaking into my house?"

"No, I didn't know all that," she said.

That was one very evasive answer.

"God damn it, Casey, what *did* you know?"

She made a caught-with-hand-in-cookie-jar face.

"I saw you get off Barlow's flight," she confessed. "But I didn't know you had been questioned."

"You saw me get off Barlow's flight? You were at the *airport?*"

"No. You were in the background on the TV story. I followed the Barlow story on the Internet and discovered the True Patriots' web site."

He decided to believe that she was telling the truth. It was easier than believing she was lying. He flipped through the pamphlet.

"What's in their stupid manifesto?"

"Evidence of a coverup of the real causes of Gulf War Syndrome."

"What kind of evidence?"

"Evidence like the Pentagon changing its story six times about exactly what happened at the Kasimiyah ammo dump in March, '91—everybody now admits the US Army blew up something, but nobody can quite agree what it was. And evidence like the CIA having no records of any reports of chemical weapons—even though the Czechs and the French sent a constant alert to allied headquarters. Evidence like eight days missing from the log that Schwarzkopf's air command used to record reports of chemical or biological weapons attacks—the same eight days that Kasimiyah was hit from the air by Navy bombers. Like medical researchers who claim that they had been fired or that their work had been sabotaged when their results started to veer away from the party line. Like paper-trails that lead from Swiss pharmaceutical companies to Iraqi chemical plants, and UN weapons inspectors sitting on their hands while Saddam plays hide the salami. That kind of evidence. One could make a pretty compelling argument that somebody's covering something up."

"If you're paranoid to start with, everything looks like a conspiracy," Nick said.

"Call me paranoid."

"Okay, who is covering up what?"

"The who is the American government, and the what is nerve gas at Kasimiyah. Americans blew it up during and after the war, thereby causing Gulf War Disease."

"Is that what you got from the stupid True Patriots pamphlet?"

"I got the evidence from them, but they draw a different conclusion."

"True Patriots. . . assholes. Who *are* those guys?"

"I don't know. But 'True Patriots of the Natural Law' has a Montana-militia ring to it."

"Alright already. You say the Pentagon is covering up nerve gas, which the Army and Navy accidentally unleashed when they blew up an Iraqi ammo dump. What do the True Patriots say?"

"The Patriots believe that the Gulf War was a test of prototypes of microscopic machines that will forever rearrange the fabric of our souls."

"How, exactly," Nick asked, wearily, "is this conspiracy of boogeymen going to rearrange the fabric our souls?"

"By rearranging our brains," she said.

There were one or two brains that Nick felt like rearranging himself.

"Why didn't you mention Barlow and the True Patriots earlier tonight when we were talking about The New Gospel?" he asked.

"I respect your privacy," she said. "Whatever happened to you on Barlow's flight is none of my business until you make it so."

Forgive me, that's bullshit.

"What the hell are you talking about?" he said. "You look in people's hotel windows."

"With my eyes, not with a television camera."

She was staring right at him, as innocent as a child in the swirling snow.

He started walking, and she matched his stride on her Barbie-doll legs.

"Well, speaking of invasions of privacy," Nick said. "How do you feel about cracking the True Patriots?"

She put her arm through his.

"I hope it's more challenging than Corporate Security's machine."

They walked on until they came to Richard and John's house. Snow enveloped the enormous Tudor edifice, softening its curves, smoothing its shadows, somehow dimming its grandeur, in the night, like a death shroud on a once-feared king. It blew off the slate eaves and gables in spectacular flares all the way to the intersection of Westford and Edgell streets, where it entered the street lamp's serenely illuminated cone and drifted gently to rest. A Himalayan drift stretched from half-way up the mansion's four-foot-wide oaken front door all the way to the white mountain that the snowplows had made at the corner of the yard.

It had been during such a storm that Todd had been murdered, at the fag end of March, 1990, while two miles from here, in the unheated vacant storefront that was to become The Magic Box, Bartlett had walked through the door in the middle of the night and straight into his soul, showing him places within himself that he had never known were there. At dawn she had finally let him go to sleep, and when insistent rapping woke him up at eleven, Nick took one look around the white room, with snow drifted above the sign paper, and imagined for a moment it was angels coming for him. But it wasn't angels, it was the Newcastle police. They told him that Todd Griffith had been shot in the back of the head at about five AM with a silenced nine-millimeter handgun from a distance of three inches, a botched execution, and they wanted to ask Nick, said to be one of Todd's closer friends, whether Todd had any enemies and if he did drugs. Two days later it had been seventy degrees out, and Nick had stood in a tee shirt outside the yellow crime-scene tape that surrounded Todd's house as the police watched footprints and tire tracks melt into nothingness.

It had been years since Nick had given any thought to the mystery of who had shot his best friend. Now, with Todd's lover's arm through his, Nick looked at the window through which the would-be murderer had climbed, and he tried to decide if it really could have been the little billionaire pipsqueak who did it.

"Gulfstream jet?" Nick said.

"Four and a half hours from San Jose to the Gardner navigation beacon," she said.

Nick remembered standing on the guardrail, the smile on Monty's face after the earthquake.

"Meekman might have ordered Todd's death," he said. "But pull the trigger? I doubt it."

"No you don't," she said.

Minutes later Nick and Casey were stealthily approaching a door by the South lot, hugging the wall just out of the video camera's sweep. Casey climbed onto Nick's shoulders and gently dusted a miniature drift in front of the lens, then clambered down and slid her card through he reader. When the door clicked open, they went immediately to the Void. Casey led them to a corner cube. There was an old DD-12 with an Ethernet drop there; clearly Casey had hacked from here before. She hooked up a second terminal so that they could work side by side. In a minute the True Patriot's home page appeared on Nick's screen, with the two flags waving.

"A little game of chess," she said. "Name your opening."

"You run 'Whois' against the Internic's master records to get a list of DNS servers on their domain and see if you can figure out their subnet structure. I'll write a script to try telnet socket connections—and do port scans if we get lucky. I've got an idea for an espresso script too."

Nick began to write the programs. It was so automatic that it seemed as if his fingers, rather than his brain, were doing the work. Ten minutes had passed without a word between them when Casey said, "OK, got it. Looks like most of their machines are in Utah."

"Here's the path," Nick said. "Bang on the sockets while I finish this up."

"Looks pretty secure," she said. "Hey, wait a second! I got 'Admin' on this gator box."

"See if you can find an IP address for the Justice Department's militia watch group."

"You want me to set up a man in the middle?"

"You bet. I think both parties will be amused when all the True Patriot's mail gets redirected through Washington. Wait, holy cow."

"What?"

"They're using the Apache webserver. PHF query client."

"That hexadecimal hole?"

"Precisely. This is a wide open door. Almost makes me think it's a trap."

"Create a shell before they spring it on you."

With just a few minutes of furious typing Nick had made copies of the user account files and zone dumps of the mail routing tables. Using this information, with enough time and patience, he could probably figure out who these people were.

"OK," Casey said. "Ready to re-route. Just tell me when."

"First I'm going to fuck up their boot logic."

"You *are* pissed, aren't you?" she said.

"Tit for tat. It's what they did to me."

This was almost fun, in a primal way; yet Nick didn't feel good about it. It was like popping valve stems on the car tires of the local bully. It could only lead to more trouble.

"OK, done." he said. "Re-route them while I type in my valentine. *Fuck you. I don't have what you want. Leave me alone. Nick Aubrey.*"

"Poetic."

"Let's blow this pop stand," Nick said. "I don't like being back in the Mill."

"First we have to go down to Corporate Security's 'new-hire' room. You need a badge."

That done, they left by the front door. At the bridge over the falls, Nick stood watching her go until she faded, wraithlike, into the whiteout. It was a short walk to the Newcastle Hotel's front door, and in a minute he was rapping with his room key on the glass. A light appeared in a room behind the registration desk, and eventually there emerged a disheveled, unshaven man sporting the bouquet of a fine New York State sauterne.

"Goddamn Aubrey, I told you I go to bed at ten o'clock."

"Give me my own key."

Harris wouldn't dignify this request with an answer.

"There was a call for you."

"There couldn't have been. Nobody knows I'm here."

"OK, I made it up," the man said, and turned toward his room behind the desk. "Asshole."

"Wait," Nick said. "Sorry. Who called? What was the message?"

"About three hours ago. She didn't leave her name. Said to check alt conspiracy."

"That's it? Did she say how she found out I was here?"

"Don't sweat it. I told her you wasn't registered. Said I never heard of you."

"Why did you do that?"

"Hotel policy. I always say that. Unless it's cops with a warrant."

"You have no idea who she was?"

"She had an accent, I think."

"What kind of accent?"

"Who the fuck am I, Professor Higgins?"

"Merry Christmas to you too," Nick said, as Harris trundled off.

Who could have called? Nick hadn't told anybody that he was coming here, had he? On the way out the front door he toggled the lock.

The snowdrift on the bridge over the falls was already so thick that he could barely make it through. Nick ran his new card through the reader and listened for the click. With snow whirling behind him he stepped into the silent narthex of the Mill.

Seven minutes later he was sitting in the half-darkness before the computer at Casey's desk in the Void. He called up the net browser and clicked to the newsgroup alt.conspiracy. One topic predominated:

```
watch@1step_beyond.org      RE: Flight 44 Assassination.
Skeptic@bozo.com            RE: Flight 44 Assassination.
TOMA@Hamilton.edu           RE: Flight 44 Assassination.
Nosy_parker@aol.com         RE: Flight 44 Assassination.
```

If there was one thing the Internet was even better at than anonymous pseudo-sex, it was rumor amplification. Nick didn't want to poison his mind with any of it, but he knew he had to. He clicked on a message at random:

```
FROM: skeptic@bozo.com
Summarizing what we know to date:
    1) The person originally sitting next to Barlow moved
from his seat as soon as the plane reached cruising altitude.
The hit man, a tall white male with dark hair, then moved next
to Barlow and completed the job within five minutes.
    2) As Barlow died, a diskette fell out of his pocket. The
hit man picked it up and placed in his own pocket. (See orig-
```

inal post from Frightened@TIAC.net)

    3) Police claim that the cause of death was acute cyanide poisoning from an orally ingested pill, but the observed symptoms (convulsions, etc,) are more consistent with injection of a curare-like agent.

    4) After his "interrogation" by the police, the killer reboarded the plane, remained on board during the stopover in New York, and got off the plane in Boston.

Obviously the 'interrogation' was a scam. This was a hit designed to send a message, and clearly was sanctioned at a high level: The killer got back on board the airplane in front of a hundred witnesses. It's silly to scour the passenger list looking for the killer. One thing we can be certain of: this guy left no tracks.

Nick remembered how he had actually picked up the diskette: timidly, like a little mouse, after glancing all around to make sure nobody was looking at him. Reflexively he felt his shirt pocket; the diskette was still there. A part of Nick wanted to stay and read the entire discussion, but he had no doubt that it would only make him agitated and depressed. He logged off and trotted down the Mill's empty corridors to a seldom-used exit.

The snow was so deep that sidewalks were impassible, so Nick ran in the street where the plows had cut a swath. He felt like an arctic explorer, and by the time he pulled open the main door to the Newcastle Hotel he barely had the strength to stand. He took the creaky, smelly elevator up to the third floor and walked to room 301.

The door was open, the light in the bathroom was on, and the entire room was turned upside down.

Chapter 24

Bartlett Aubrey stood before her closet with a decision to make. She had lost another six pounds; her goal now was *not* to lose any more despite her increased level of workout. For a week she had been adding an hour of karate every night to her undiminished skating regime. She was in better shape than she had been since high school. What should she wear to celebrate? It wasn't as if she were going to do a Lady Godiva: she would walk to the lab wearing a winter coat, and as soon as she got to work the white lab smock would go on over whatever she decided to wear. She was playing dress-up for an audience of one, herself.

So what would it be? Her wardrobe didn't give her many options: she was a modest girl, and she had spent virtually her entire adult life, whether fit or fat, trying to disguise her shape. She decided on the scallop-necked black bodysuit, with her tight-fitting black jeans. It wasn't really dressing up at all, she told herself. How dressy was it to wear black Danskin and black Levi's? It only counted as "dressing up" because it varied her routine.

That was a lie, of course. She knew very well that this ensemble accentuated her figure, especially her breasts. Actually, now that she looked in the mirror, it showed her derriere to good advantage too. Was this any way for a modest girl to act? She got down on her knees and looked in the back corner of her closet; there she found the little white train case that housed her jewelry. She took out two necklaces, a jade collar and an amethyst pendant, and walked to the dresser mirror. The jade, well, it was nice. But the amethyst pendant, that did the trick. A large stone on a narrow chain, it hung to the middle of her breastbone. Yes, she smiled. That would draw men's eyes where they were going to go anyway.

"Girl, you're a mess," she laughed out loud. "You will leave your jewelry in the closet, where it belongs. And tomorrow you will wear the same outfit you always wear: loose jeans and a looser flannel shirt. Leaving one button, one button only, unfastened." But when she put her necklaces away she saw her ring; that made her wince, and her mood changed.

She hadn't spoken with Nick, but they had exchanged a few mail messages— about the break in, about selling the house. She had wanted him to handle it, she said, to get it over with quickly. The burglary was distressing even through he had found nothing missing. But she had resisted the urge to go out to Newcastle and check it out. Her independence was fragile enough; she didn't want to, couldn't bear to see him yet. He had priced the house low and accepted an offer on it in three days. The proceeds would be enough to cover, barely, the store's debts. And to keep all their things in a warehouse for a year. He had hired movers to box it up; he didn't have the time or the courage, he said, to do it himself.

And now he was staying at The Newcastle Hotel.

Ten years ago he had captured her heart with his swagger, his *elan*. On the night they met, he had told her stories from agricultural experiment stations in Senegal and Brazil while dancing with abandon, then recited Martin Luther King's *Letter From Birmingham Jail*. Now that same Nick was living in a drunks' flophouse with a majestic view of dark Satanic Digital MicroSystems. She quickly closed the case and threw her coat over her shoulders.

Down Commonwealth to Kenmore Square, thence past alphabetic blocks of Backbay brownstones: Exeter, Dartmouth, Clarendon, Berkeley; right at Arlington and left on Boylston, skirting the Garden and the Common, right on Tremont, left on Kneeland towards Chinatown and the Medical Center. Once she got there it didn't take long to find out whether her black outfit was as revealing as she had presupposed.

"My goodness, Bartlett," her friend Bobbie from the next lab said as they made their ritual trek for morning coffee. "Cleavage. Is there something going on that I should know about?"

"No," she answered, blushing crimson. It wasn't exactly a lie: there was something going on, but Bartlett didn't know what it was.

A package had arrived for her that morning; Irwin had put in the freezer. He didn't approve what she was going to do with it, but he generally granted her whatever leeway she needed. So now they labored on through the morning at benches at opposite walls of the laboratory, he listening to Pinkus Zuckerman playing Mozart, she listening to a *Waiting for Columbus*; the sounds of each cassette player reaching midway across the chamber where they met and canceled. At noon she put on her new black-and-orange Bruins sweatpants, her new green Kirkland College shorts and her same old University of Evansville Purple Aces shirt and went to skate. Fifty minutes later she was at the suspension bridge in the Public Garden, thinking, as always, about her young friend Jackson—and about Fitzgibbon's Disease which had killed him.

The illness was caused by a clever little shape-shifter. Happy in a bird's gut, it swam around like a guppy in a tank. Then out the door in some bird feces, it retreated into a stronger, uglier form, which sometimes got ingested into humans— from some unwashed lettuce, say, or maybe from a licked finger that had touched a contaminated baseball. When that happened the little parasite would try to multiply and cause some damage, usually without much success. Unless that human happened to be pregnant.

If the Fitzgibbon's parasite made its way into a human fetus, then by God it really went to town. By the time the baby's immune system had kicked in, the little beasties had beat a leisurely retreat to the brain, like a microbial Sherman marching to the sea, damaging as much nervous- system tissue along the way as they have had time for. Like bullies throwing icicles from a snowfort, the little death-star spheres mounted their assault from the safety of the blood-brain barrier and dared the immune system, the body, the doctors, the mothers, fathers, friends, machines, medicines, radiations, spells, Presidents, Popes, prayers, and angels of God to do one damn thing about it. But none of them ever could.

It was a new disease, as new as AIDS. Dr. Joan Fitzgibbons, the first person to prove the cause of the disease, was still in her thirties. It was hard to imagine how this thing could have just suddenly appeared. But as AIDS had proved, these things happened. How Bartlett loathed birds! Filthy pigeons, vermin-infested robins, shitting seagulls. *Oh for a world without birds*, Bartlett thought. A world without birds, and their wretched screeches. What a blessed place it would be.

She resumed skating, heading back in the general direction of the Medical Center, and thought about another medical mystery. She was trying to understand how phage protein could appear in human blood. Maybe, it occurred to her, phage protein in the blood didn't mean infection by phage after all. Maybe the phage protein was an artefact of something else.

What if there were some new little life-form somewhere in these soldiers, she thought, not reproducing, not setting off the immune system, just living undetected and generating phage proteins? Little machines, microscopic little factories, producing phage proteins?

Yes. And what if there's a *teeeeeny-tiny* little man in there with a *leeetle-tiny* radio transmitter sending messages to the president about the price of grapefruit? *Do me a favor, go buy a biology textbook you dumb stupid cunt.*

After her shower she went back to her bench. She pulled up a stool and half-stood, half sat as she picked up the negative, a still-wet image on x-ray film stock the size of a sheet of typing paper. She held it up to the light from the window and looked at the image: little black bands a quarter of an inch across at irregular intervals in ten numbered columns across the sheet. She had made and studied a thousand such sheets as an undergraduate, grad student, post-doctoral fellow in Molecular Biology. She knew how to make a gel, and how to read one. She knew the patterns of the reference proteins better than she knew her own face. That's why column seven bothered her. The spacing of its black bands had not changed during the hour she had been roller skating. Nor had the identity of the protein that it identified changed during that hour, any more than her own fingerprints had. Column seven was an old friend. Column seven was T4. Bacteriophage.

Irwin had said, "if you find phage, you had better double-check your results before showing them to me, because I am a skeptic." So she had double-checked, then checked again. She was sure.

Breathing hard, with water dripping from the hasty ponytail gathered in the purple and white scrunchy, she stood at Irwin's door for just a moment, then walked in without knocking. He was reading the newspaper, and only glanced at her for a second before going back to his reading.

"Hello Bartlett," he said.

"I know you're skeptical, so I want you to do a gel on this sample yourself."

Irwin put the paper down on his desk. He looked like he was thinking hard, searching for the exactly right words.

"Bartlett, tell me something," he said, and thoughtfully took a bite out of a tuna sandwich.

"Yes?" she said. Was he going to point out that he didn't appreciate desperation ploys like having him do a gel for her when they weren't even working on this project?

Slowly, excruciatingly slowly, he finished chewing and wiped his lips with a paper napkin.

"What the hell should the Red Sox do about Jose Canseco?" he said.

"Ask me after spring training," she said quickly, as if answering a child's insistent question while navigating the Fresh Pond rotary at rush hour. "Irwin, will you run this gel for me, please?"

"Alright, Dr. Aubrey. I will run your gel. Kindly allow me a few minutes to finish reading the box scores."

"Here's the blood," she said, and stood the test tube of blood in an empty coffee cup, miraculously clean, that sat atop a pile of photocopied articles from *Cell* and *Journal of Virology*.

She felt relieved yet anxious: relieved that Irwin had agreed to do the gel and confirm her finding; anxious that he would not find what she had found— that by some inexplicable mixup she had contaminated her sample, and that Irwin would prove it. Because despite the evidence, she was having a hard time believing that she had actually found phage protein in Janine's sister's blood.

"Some interesting news, by the way," Irwin said, picking up the sample.

"Oh?"

"A letter from Hoff-Zeigy to the Neuro Group expressing interest in exploring equity participation. Which I understand means they give us money in return for our firstborn children."

This was good news. Or so she told herself. Why didn't it feel that way?

"There's a conference in California next week where the people with the money go to meet the scientists with the ideas. In my day we had the Catskills. That's a joke. So we were wondering, how would you like to go on behalf of the Neuro Group? You're on the board of directors, after all."

Bartlett was on the Neuro Group's board of directors, but so was everybody in Irwin's lab.

"Me? Why me?"

"We think you need to get out more. But in truth it was the coincidence of name of the person who sent the letter that put us in mind of it."

Uh-oh.

"You don't happen to have any relatives in Basel, do you?" Irwin asked.

She made no answer, which, she hoped, implied 'no.'

At 1:15 she sat before the Digital MicroSystems computer with her right hand on the mouse, poised and ready to click on *bionet.protein.synthesis*. What should she have said? Yes, that's my brother in law, with whom I made love? Or, Please send me, I've been thinking of him a lot lately?

She banished Paul Aubrey from her mind and spent the next several hours reading *bionet* newsgroups. At four o'clock she stood and stretched. If Irwin had forced the gel it might be ready by now. She went in search of him and found him coming down the hall with a film in his hands, dripping. Irwin and chemicals. Good thing he did so little teaching; he set a terrible example.

"I owe you a nickel," he said, holding up the gel film. "Tail fibers."

"That's what I got too," she said.

"So. T4 phage protein from human blood. Have you determined what strain?"

"It has a Hoff-Zeigy marker. You can precipitate it right out; it's like they're putting on a neon-colored shirt."

Neither spoke for a half a minute. The developing chemicals dripped slowly off the film onto the linoleum floor.

"Well, this is certainly curious," Irwin said. "But it hardly seems like it's time to call up the CDC or quarantine the army. I suppose I should make an inquiry on the Internet."

"No!" she said, then collected herself. "Those friends of mine at MIT made a simple post— and it may eventually wind up costing them their tenure. I have another idea."

He waited for her to elaborate.

"I do know somebody at Hoff-Zeigy," she said. "Maybe he can help me out."

"Do you expect him to just come out and tell you that Hoff-Zeigy was developing biological warfare agents from bacteriophage?"

"We were quite close at one time," she said, and looked away from Irwin, to signal that the conversation was over.

Thank god there was Karate class that night. It felt good to get back into clothes that hid her figure. It was good to stretch, to concentrate totally. It was especially good to punch and kick the air in pantomime of mortal combat, to feel the weight of her partner as she threw him fall after fall, to feel herself upended as she was thrown in turn. But as good as it was at releasing her frustrations, the need for physical contact seemed to increase by the moment, and the karate increased her need instead of satisfying it. When she felt a friendly arm around her shoulder after the final bow to the instructor, she had to resist the urge to around and kiss its owner full on the mouth, not knowing whose arm it was. What did they say, cold showers could quiet this feeling? Saltpeter in the breakfast porridge? She showered at the Y; the water was icy. The fire abated for ten minutes. But as soon as she had toweled herself dry, there it was again.

That night she lay in bed, wondering how to break the thought pattern she had worked herself into. You're normal, she told herself. Single women get horny. But this had never been the way her mind worked. Why did she have to think of sex now? Why couldn't she get Paul Aubrey out of her head? Why couldn't she just go to sleep as she had all those thousand other nights of her life, thinking of phone bills, lab experiments, and off-season trades to strengthen the bullpen?

Chapter 25

Relative to the Gordon Biersch, the Wursthaus in Harvard Square had three things going for it: it was darker, there were fewer yuppies, and you could get three different kinds of potato salad with your bratwurst. On the other hand, the bartenders weren't as beautiful, the house beer wasn't as good, and the place was lousy with Harvard types talking about deconstructionism. So in the aggregate the two places were pretty equivalent, Nick figured.

Maceo had come east to interview at Data General. "Yes, that Data General. Tom West, *Soul of a New Machine,*" he had wearily admitted. "Yes, they're still in business."

"When in Rome," Nick had said, and they had agreed to meet at the Wursthaus. Now that Maceo sat before him, Nick got right to the point.

"Listen, like I told you, I got to ask you some questions about your friend Barlow."

"And like I told *you,*" Maceo asserted back, "he wasn't my friend; he was my stalker. Too bad he killed himself, but at least now he won't be pestering me around the clock. My book's gone to print, and I'm through with Barlow and all that Gulf War stuff. I'm on my next project."

"Yeah, but you owe me one, Maceo."

"How do I owe you one?"

"I saved your ass at great risk to myself. Those Salt Lake City police really grilled me about Barlow, wanted to know if I had ever met him before. I lied to them, man, just to keep you out of it. They would have thrown me in jail if they had found out I was stonewalling them. I was nearly down for murder, and I may go down yet. So you gotta answer some questions for me."

"I'll give you one question," Maceo said. "And I'll buy you a two-pint amber. Then we drop the subject. Deal?"

"What if I say no?"

"Then fuck you."

"Fuck you too. I bailed you out a thousand times when I was your boss, I bailed you out when I had cops crawling all over my ass. How many times do I got to bail you out before you answer a few questions for me?"

Maceo's face turned sour, but resigned.

"Why is it so all-fired important that you know about Crazy Peter Barlow? Let him rest in peace, why don't you."

"I think he may have been telling the truth."

"You're tripping."

"At least about being in the CIA. I've been getting some funny phone calls. People calling me from the New York *Times*, only they don't work at the *Times*, and they have the same last name Barlow told me the CIA uses for hit men."

"What are you *talking* about, Nick? That guy was a looney tune. I don't know who's calling you, but I can guaran-fucking-tee you it isn't the CIA."

"Don't be so sure. These people know where I'm going before I know myself. I'm talking about people luring me out of my room at one in morning and then ransacking the place. Stuff like that. I don't know who these people are, but they seem to take Barlow very seriously. I want to know why."

"Ignore them. They'll go away when they find out you don't have what they want."

"OK. Next time they call I'll give them your number."

"All right, all right," Maceo said, "Ask your questions. Let me buy the beer first."

He signaled with two hands to an older gentleman who could have served ably as Bruce Wayne's manservant.

"What do you need to know?" Maceo said, placing a giant beer-filled glass before Nick.

"What happened to the manuscript Barlow gave you? Did you ever read it?"

"I didn't tell you?"

"No, man, you've kind of been discouraging conversation on the topic."

"Somebody pinched it."

"*What*? When?"

"That same night. I left it on the bar when I went to take a leak, and when I came back it was gone."

"Who would have pinched the book? Why?"

"How the hell would I know? Somebody probably picked it up by mistake. To tell you the truth I was kind of relieved."

Nick, however, was feeling anything but relieved. And he had the strong sensation that he had been premature last week, when he had congratulated himself for eluding the reporters waiting for him at Logan airport. He was beginning to think that he not seen the end of the Barlow story, not by a long shot.

"OK, let's talk about that number. When he gave you the package, he said, 'Remember, nine-three-two-three-three.' What did that mean?"

"Beats me. Something to do with the password for his diskette, I guess. The diskette which wasn't even there, remember?"

"I have his diskette. It wants a password of a hundred and sixty characters, and I'm trying to find some way to convert his number to something a hundred and sixty bytes long."

Maceo cocked his head to one side.

"You're full of surprises tonight. How do you have his diskette?"

"It fell out his pocket when he was dying all over me."

"Lucky you. And now you want me to help you crack it."

"Yes."

Maceo seemed to be evaluating how far to let himself get involved. He turned away from Nick briefly, then again faced him to answer.

"I have no idea what his password was. You're sure about that number?"

"Yeah. I remember thinking: 'Nine: three squared, three times three."

"It's probably a public key system."

"But you can crack, what do they call it, PGP, pretty good privacy, right?"

"In theory. If I enlisted all the idle time on every computer in whole company intranet and spent the next month working on it. But if he's really CIA, it won't be PGP, it will be something harder to crack, some kind of vector into a hash table, a one-timer; and if he wasn't CIA, who gives a shit what's on the diskette? My professional advice: find a dumpster and toss it out. Especially if you think the spooks want it. You might pass a strong magnet over it first."

"Can't do that. The cops want it too, and I don't want to go to jail for destroying evidence."

"Cops? What cops?"

"Salt Lake City cops. Somebody saw me pick it up; it's all over 'alt conspiracy'. I don't think the cops know yet, but they will. And they'll want the diskette."

"Nick, you are a looney tune. If the cops want it, give it to them. What's wrong with you?"

"I plan to."

"Good."

"After we crack it."

"Oh for the love of Christ."

"I'm going to crack it," Nick said. "You're going to help me."

"I'll try to see if I can come up with a password for you. But I don't want to physically come into contact with that thing. I don't want my fingerprints on it. It's probably all nonsense, but it's *your* nonsense now. Don't drag me in. Where is this mystery diskette?"

"Don't worry about it. Let's say you were Barlow."

"Scary thought."

"And let's say you wanted to rig a diskette like he said it was rigged. How would you do it?"

"How would I booby-trap it or how would I encrypt it?"

"Both."

"Alright, alright," Maceo said. He grabbed a coaster and turned it over. For the next three minutes he drew a picture of a the logical structure of a UNIX-formatted diskette: boot blocks, I-nodes, sectors, rings—and on a second coaster, in tiny hand, a meticulous flow chart.

"Now are you happy?" Maceo asked.

"Almost. Next question. Who's Orson?"

"Orson?" Maceo said. "*Orson?*"

"That's what Barlow told me: 'I know about Orson.' He thought I was going to kill him because he knew about Orson."

"Everybody knows about Orson."

"If everybody knew about Orson I wouldn't be asking you the question, would I?"

"OK, Nick," Maceo said, then sighed, and paused, as if trying to figure out how to explain that water was wet. "Orson is the theory that an evil force is taking over the brains of people all over the world, one by one, in order to eventually control the planet. It's an acronym: obedient remote servo-organic network. O-R-S-O-N. The conspiracy people believe that there was some evil genius who wrote a plan for taking over everything, and that now a bunch of his followers are putting the plan into play. There's a version of the Orson story that some of the Gulf War vets are into. They think it explains the Syndrome."

"What's that?"

"They believe that there are computer chips implanted in their buttocks by the government. George Bush and the oil companies are usually behind the plot. You know those guys they arrested for the Oklahoma City bombing? One of them claimed he had the scars on his ass to prove it, until his lawyers shut him up. Said the government was trying to operate him by remote control, and that's why they blew up the Federal Building."

"And this is what Barlow believed?"

"Nick, did I or did I not tell you he was crazy?"

"And that's why he latched onto you, isn't it? Because you said the oil companies were behind the war, but nobody calls you crazy. You were Barlow's claim to respectability."

"I said *oil* was the reason for the war, not oil companies. That's why I called my book *Blood for Oil.* George Bush *was* a Texas oil man, so, obviously, questions arise in one's mind about the relationship between the multinational oil companies and the American government. But it doesn't mean that I think the chairman of Exxon was in the Oval Office dictating strategy to Colin Powell, or that George Bush is controlled by beings from the planet Pongo-pongo hiding behind a comet. I think I've answered enough of your questions now. I'm going to watch the basketball game."

Maceo turned his attention from Nick to the game playing on the television over the bar.

"Think the Celtics will ever break five-hundred again?" he said.

"What did Barlow think about Orson? Who did he say the sinister force was?"

"Time's up."

"Come on Maceo," Nick said. "Give me a break."

Maceo pointedly studied the game.

"How come every time Patrick Ewing takes a foul shot he looks like he's solving differential equations in his head?"

"You're not going to answer any more questions for me, are you?"

"No, but I'll give you a bonus answer. It's about your buddy Swirsing. I did some checking."

"And?"

"You ever notice how he's always got a gorgeous babe or two hanging off him?"

"He seems to have a discriminating eye for the ladies. What's your point?"

"Where do you think he gets all his 'market research' from?"

"I give up."

"Those chicks are his research associates. Mata Hari, baby. First I give you a happy, then you let slip a corporate secret or two, which I bring back to Carl."

"No shit. Where did you get this from?"

"My own research associates."

"C'mon Maceo," Nick said, but he knew his friend would never divulge a source.

"I think *Pervis Ellison* is from Pongo-pongo," Maceo said. "Did you see that rebound?"

"He probably is from outer space," Nick said, resignedly. "No Boston Celtic has boxed out a New York Knick since Robert Parish got traded to Charlotte."

An hour later Nick was back in his Newcastle Hotel room. He was so tired that he fell asleep with his clothes on, and he didn't stir until his wake-up call the next morning. Harris growled at him through the rotary phone, "Rise and shine soldier. Wake up and die right." Nick showered, walked down to the Newcastle Diner, ordered a corn muffin and coffee, went back to the pull-shut phone booth and called to check for messages at his home phone number. There was only one:

"Nicholas Aubrey, this is Detective Ivan Marki from the Salt Lake City Airport Police. I think you know why I'm calling. I need to hear from you within the next twenty-four hours. If I don't, I will swear out an affidavit and obtain a governor's warrant for your arrest for obstruction of justice."

Nick sipped his coffee and took a bite of his muffin. He could see Kathleen Gerben's number where he had penciled it on the wall.

"Big deal," he said, as he pressed the numbers to erase Detective Marki's message. "Big deal. Big deal."

Chapter 26

Dieter Steffen lay on his bed in the dark, staring at the glowing red numbers. It was 4:02 Basel local time. Why did he even bother lying down? He had always found it hard to sleep, but even for an insomniac like himself this unyielding wakefulness was extreme. It had gone on for weeks now—over and over the same thoughts cycled: Judith Knight, Paul Aubrey, Pavel Isaacs. Night after night, just two hours of wretched writhing with his eyes closed in a Jacques Tati pantomime of sleep. His body had determined the absolute minimum of rest on which it could maintain homeostasis and a pulse, and that was all it was going to give him. *Sheiese.* He got up and got dressed.

Half an hour later Dieter was in his office. Why the hell had he ever gone to see Aubrey? It had only made things worse. Now Dieter only felt *more* exposed, and no closer to understanding what he needed to do. Maybe he should consult, one time, with Dr. Knight. Then he would make up his mind about continuing with the nanomachine project. He opened his center desk drawer and looked for the business card that Judith had written her address on.

What had she said, that he should use the CIPHER command? Or was it DISGUISE? Such a bother. He knew how to use the Digital MicroSystems workstation for molecular modeling: ensconced in data gloves, headphones, three-D visor, foot cradle, he became one with the machine. But it had been years since he had used the computer for anything else. So it was possible that he would find the right manuals, type the right incantations, and send a message to Judith Knight. But what would he say?

The torment continued all day.

At nine that evening, he could withstand it no more. He decided.

At 21:00 Basel local time, Herr Doctor Dieter Steffen, Ph.D. walked into the office of Herr Doctor Pavel Isaacs, Ph.D.; Director of the NanoSection. Dieter was going to see Pavel, his friend. Pavel, with whom he had shared pizza at 4 AM in the Molecular Computation lab at MIT. Pavel, who had understood his ideas. Pavel, who had shared Dieter's dream for more than six years. Pavel, the smartest person he had ever met. Pavel, his best friend. His only friend.

He told Pavel the answer. He explained how he had modified the Orthogonal Diels-Alder adduct so that it could work as a non-immunogenic gate for a phage-like tube through the buckminsterfullerene shell. He gave him the last piece to the puzzle.

Then he went home, got in bed, and slept for twenty-seven hours.

Chapter 27

Nick Aubrey left his Volvo in a lot under the Central Artery and started walking through the slush toward Spaulding Rehabilitation Hospital. Casey matched his stride.

"Welcome to the Union of Soviet Socialist Republics," she said as they stepped into the drab, anonymous hall. The security guard said nothing.

There was no need to check the directory. People didn't move around too much in this place, and Casey knew the route by heart. Nick followed her to the elevator. At floor seven they got off and followed a mural, more depressing than bare wall, until they came to yellowed index card that told them they had reached Todd Griffith's room. As Casey stood back, Nick crossed the threshold briskly, knowing that if he hesitated he might turn around and never come back.

"Hello Todd," Nick said to the body on the bed. "Remember me? It's your old pal Nick."

There was no response, of course. Not the slightest flicker in the two glazed eyes pointed at the ceiling. Nick thought of Japanese veal calves kept immobile from birth and fed rich milk.

Nearly five years had gone by since Nick had last seen his old friend. They had made their farewells in the intensive care unit of Newcastle General Hospital, where the doctors had explained to Nick the various definitions of 'coma.' However you defined it, the bullet in Todd's brain guaranteed that 'coma' would become 'vegetative state,' and that that would be Todd's brain's fate until Todd died. Todd's heart, lungs, kidneys, and corneas, however, were in fine shape. Clearly, if it had been up to the doctors Todd would have been in the chop shop already.

But it hadn't been up to them; it hadn't even been up to Todd's family. Within hours of the shooting an obscure right-to-life group called "Lazarus" had filed an *amicus curiae* brief on Todd's behalf, and the court had issued an injunction against letting him die. Todd's entire family consisted of one exhausted sister, and she decided not to fight the ruling.

"I don't suppose he gets many visitors," Nick said to Casey, who was gazing out a grimy window over a highway, a gravel pit, and the Registry of Motor Vehicles.

"Just *moi*," she said. "And I've stopped too."

Light rain fell against the window from clouds that looked like folds in a cerebral cortex.

Nick turned from the window and forced himself to gaze upon his friend's impassive form. Todd was wired-up like a Soyuz chimp. It was easy to understand what the feeding tube was doing there, and even why there was an IV stub in Todd's withered arm. But was it really necessary to have all those electrodes on his head?

Above the bed a monitor traced the unvarying rhythms of his brain cycles—amber waves of nothingness. A lugubriously-turning spool recorded the patterns on paper. Nick leaned closer and saw, with a shudder, that one of the wires disappeared into a flap behind Todd's left ear. How convenient to have a bullet just there, Nick thought. A conductive probe deep in the noodle. But all this instrumentation was pointless, since Todd's brainwaves varied less than cosmic static. It was worse than pointless; it was insulting: this frail form had once been able to drum three against four against five, and had taken its Zappa loud. He never should have been subjected to this indignity.

"Alas, poor Todd," Nick said. "I knew you, Horatio."

Then slowly, gently, taking care to avoid the wires, he slipped his right hand under Todd's head, lifted it a fraction of an inch off the white pillow, and kissed Todd's forehead.

He removed his hand and sat down on a 1950ish Heywood-Wakefield armchair with state-bureaucracy-green vinyl upholstery. It was well preserved, which accentuated Nick's feeling of being trapped in a ghastly time warp: here in the 1950's the chair was nothing special; outside in the 1990's it would fetch a thousand dollars. Casey considered the rain.

"Hey listen, Todd," Nick said, as if resuming a conversation only momentarily interrupted. "Do you remember that Thanksgiving in N'Darr, at Sid's place?"

"Africa?" Casey asked, still looking out the window.

"Nineteen seventy-four. But we were friends before that, in high school."

"I remember," she said.

"We went to different colleges. I didn't keep in touch. Years later I'm over there in Senegal during a great drought and I run into Todd. He was organizing gardens with the Peace Corps, and I was doing research at an agricultural station up the river. Way out in the Fouta, the outback."

"He loved Africa."

"It's like an oven out there in the Fouta. But there's a river running through it; right through the middle of the god-damn desert. The water flows north from the jungles of Guinea Bissau. We were going to save the world with it."

"Nothing to be ashamed of," she said.

"On Thanksgiving we went over to this other Peace Corps guy's house. A real Johnny Appleseed: his place was full of seeds and tools. This wasn't in the Fouta; it was in St. Louis—the Africans call it N'Darr— where the Senegal River meets the ocean. When you come out of the Fouta and hit N'Darr, it's like leaving the oven and walking into the ice box.

"A few other Americans happened to be in the neighborhood. A couple of tourists, a freelance writer, a horticulturist from Rutgers and an alcoholic who had just spent nine dry months in a Mauritanian prison. A sandstorm came up and trapped us inside that big old cement house for nearly a week. Six men, six women, nine cases of *La Gazelle* beer, seven fifths of Johnnie Walker Red, and nothing to do but tell lies and play songs on a guitar with two missing strings. Anybody can drink Stork Beer, by the way. You've got to be real in-country to drink La Gazelle. Half the bottles had cigarette butts floating in them like little mescal worms."

"Sounds like heaven," she said.

"With the shutters pulled tight and towels shoved underneath them."

"Or hell."

"It wasn't hell, but maybe it was purgatory. A little expatriate purgatory. Sand filtering in under the shutters; we couldn't stop that sand. It was damn cold at night, too, for someplace on the edge of the Sahara. I said to him, 'freezing to death in a sandstorm. That ain't right.' At night I covered up with Sid's horse blanket. That was some funky thing—it smelled like horse sweat and it was loaded with fleas.

"The house had a concrete ceiling, and the water pipes ran right through it. I used to wait all day for the sun to heat them, so I wouldn't freeze my ass taking a shower. One time I'm in the shower with shampoo in my hair and all of a sudden that water turns to ice and I grab for my towel and somebody's gone and stuck it under the door to the balcony. While I was in the shower they did this. I pick it up, shake it off—man, it was like rubbing down with emery cloth—not that a shower did me any good with all that dust in the air. It was like living inside a vacuum cleaner bag.

"I came down with something—malaria, worms, dysentery, whatever— I was feeling awful. Todd and Sid were playing chess with the medicine. The pawns were lomotil, knights were nivaquine, rooks were aspirin. My hands were shaking, I had those fever shivers on top of a belly full of whiskey sours, and all the medicine was on the chessboard. Todd goes, 'Hold your horses, Nick, I nearly got him checkmated.' So I chuggalugged from a little brown bottle I thought was paregoric liquid."

"I guess it wasn't."

"Sid's crotch shampoo. He was rather fond of the girls at the Corniche, you see, and was beset by crabs. It was pesticide. I had to go make myself puke it up. . . with Todd in the background calling, 'Checkmate.' In the next room you could hear the drunk yelling at one of the tourists that it was her fault he couldn't get it up."

"How come I never get invited to parties like that?"

"After about three days I couldn't take it any more. I decided to go down to the Corniche. It was half a mile away. It was taking your life in your hands to go out in that sand, but I was ready to die rather than stay in the soap opera at Sid's. Todd said, 'I'm coming with you.'"

"Attaboy."

"Sid was chasing a mouse with a shovel when we left. BLAM! BLAM! BLAM!

That was twenty years ago and I can still hear that shovel reverberating off cement walls and seventy-five galvanized watering cans. And that harmattan wind blowing, just blowing blowing blowing.

"The Corniche was a dingy little cantina. There was a drunk Senegalese philosopher-poet who had a love-hate relationship with America. He wanted to be a Senegalese nationalist, a New York beatnik and an Oakland Black Panther all at the same time."

"No wonder he got drunk."

"He wanted to hate us, but he was too sweet to pull it off. He had this great big Bowie knife about a foot long. Said he was going to kill me and Todd because we were white. He was smoking *Craven A* cigarettes, and 'Get up, Stand up' was on the juke box."

Nick stared absently at the steady brainwaves. Amber waves of nothingness, indeed. But it was easier than looking at the body.

"So Todd says to the guy, 'Where do you think you are? America? Sit down and have a drink, for Christ sake. There, another friend for life. *Benin xarit ba abadan.*' That cracked the guy up. So instead of killing us, he joined us for a parlor game."

"What did you play?"

"We had a poetry contest. And I wrote a great poem, which Todd, God love him, committed to memory. *I fear these things. . .* How did it go? *I fear these things. . .* something something something. *And at night, the drear starry spaces.* I remember that line quite distinctly. *And at night, the drear starry spaces.*"

Nick stood and walked over to the bed again and gently gathered in one hand the wires that led from Todd's head into the machine beside the bed.

"What did you say was in that thing?" he said, nodding at the device.

"Data acquisition and control processor: CPU, analog to digital card, digital to analog card, floating point card, array processor, typesetting chip."

"Why all that fancy hardware just to put his brainwaves on a monitor?"

"Bonehead design. Some jack-leg tinker was using all those chips for side-effects. God knows I've done it often enough. You can't find the right chip for the job, so you contort some other chip into doing something perverse, like hammering in a nail with a pair of pliers. The person who designed this box either didn't know what she was doing or was very constrained in her access to chips. But the device itself is not clever. It's really a stupidly little box. The only thing it's doing is catching Todd's brainwaves and throwing them on the monitor."

"Give me a little credit, Casey. There's a reason you told me about this in the shrine. That's way too much hardware to be simply catching waves. You could make an EEG with a twenty dollar kit from Radio Shack. You don't need a fifteen thousand dollar setup."

"It wouldn't cost a tenth of that. This stuff is obsolete."

"But what would it have cost six years ago? Six years ago it wasn't obsolete."

"It's an EEG that catches and displays brain waves. It's doing nothing else."

That wasn't the reason she had brought Nick here. She had wanted him to see this and form his own conclusion. He was a software boy, but he wasn't blind.

Nick said, "You want me to imagine that this box allows Todd to communicate electrically, somehow, just like Vannevar Bush imagined. Todd might be wide awake right now, aware of everything we're saying. He might be screaming for us to rescue him. He might be trying, right now, to tell me the words I've forgotten from that poem I wrote at the Corniche. This box might be reading his mind, keeping him immobile, sucking dry everything he knows about computer design."

"You're crazy."

"Think about it. This device is not only reading his mind, it's making him write a book. It's even making him typeset the fucking thing. That's why there's a LaTeX chip in there."

"The box is a bonehead kludge. It belongs in the museum. Todd's dead."

"You're sure of that," Nick said.

"He's dead, and don't you dare try to bring him back. Don't you fucking dare."

"Why did you bring me here, Casey? I don't believe it was to see a dead person."

She walked to the cabinet over the sink, opened it up and began tossing books on the bed. *Göedel, Escher, Bach. The Life of the Bee. Simple Gifts. Brainstorms. Society of Mind. The Soul of a New Machine.* Adam Film World's 1991 *Porn Star Annual.* She was throwing books and magazines with a vengeance now; some of them stayed on the bed and some of them bounced off Todd's body and crashed to the floor.

She yelled at Nick, "I read to him. I spoke to him. I tried to jerk him off. I rubbed his fingers. I danced. I described chips I was designing, and I included very stupid logic errors. I brought in that VCR and watched movie after movie. *Dr. Zhivago. Buckaroo Banzai. Naughty Girls Need Love Too.*"

She was crying as she reached for the top shelf of the cabinet, which was filled with videocassettes.

"Not one blip on that monitor," she said. "Not one hiccough. He's gone. There's nothing."

"What was that last movie?" Nick said. He was trying to lighten things up.

"*Naughty Girls?* A fuck movie from the golden age of porn. I figured that would have gotten his attention. Hell, watching Honey Wilder fuck gets *my* attention. Honey Wilder Penfield fucks like a devil. So don't you go trying to sell me on some crazy idea about Todd being alive and under the control of that box. I've been down that road. It's a long road and it only leads to Crazyville. I'm not going down it again."

"Your subconscious betrays you. You said Wilder Penfield."

"I said Honey Wilder," Casey said, but the look on her face showed she wasn't sure.

"I've taken freshman psychology, Casey. I know who Wilder Penfield was."

"I was talking about Honey Wilder, a porn star. She fucks men and gives them blow jobs."

"Wilder Penfield was a neurosurgeon," Nick said. "He examined the reactions of patients whose brains had been operated on by inserting electrodes into various parts of their exposed brains, and then using small electrical impulses to stimulate the neuron or neurons to which the electrodes had been attached. He found that stimulation of certain neurons could reliably create specific images or sensations in the patient. These artificially provoked impressions ranged from strange but identifiable fears to buzzes and colors, and most impressively of all, to entire successions of events recalled from some earlier time of life, such as a childhood birthday party. Wilder Penfield gave you hope that Todd might still be alive. You wanted to believe that if Penfield could do it to his patients, somebody could be doing it to Todd too. That's why you took me here. You still believe. You believe that the wire from this box into the wall connects Todd to Digital MicroSystems Laboratories."

"Todd's dead," she said. "He's dead. He's dead. He's dead."

It was clear she didn't believe a word of it.

"Casey," he said. "Have you ever tried to crack the Corporate Fellows?"

"Of course I've tried."

"Not possible?"

"I need at least two of the following from a Corporate Fellow: voiceprint, fingerprint, retina scan, finger splay. And a badge."

"What would you do if you did get on their system?"

"Can you recreate that RARP bug?"

"Yes I can. But they know about that bug. Monty invented it."

"You could hide it in a ghost, like Ken Thompson's UNIX password trap door. Hot designers always let their guard down, because they can't imagine anybody's as smart as they are. We could use the RARP attack to create a ghost. Then we could nose around at our leisure to see what they're up to."

"Like controlling our friend who lies here."

"Shut up, Nick."

"Do you really think Todd's dead? Do you really think he's a living corpse?"

"Yes."

"Then pull the plug." Nick tightened the wires into a bunch. "You don't even have to do it. I'll do it; all you have to do is give the word. He's a living corpse. You tell me, and I'll pull his plug."

She looked away from Todd, away from the Soyuz monkey wires, away from the monitor, away from the amber waves of nothingness, and turned her gaze out the window to the rainy medulla oblongata in the sky.

"Fingerprints and voiceprints," she said. "And a badge. How are we going to get them?"

Nick reached in his pocket for his wallet and found Carl Swirsing's card.

"Market research," he said. "I'm going back to California. There's a Forum I need to attend."

Chapter 28

The newness of the room was palpable—from the smell of the paint to the gleaming counter tops to the stainless steel legs of bench stools reflected in the shining linoleum floor. Dieter could only marvel at his colleague's ability to get things done. Despite the reputation of the Hoff-Zeigy bureaucracy for its glacial pace and miserly disbursements, Pavel had managed to have this lab constructed almost overnight. And it must have cost plenty.

It was 8:30 AM, half an hour before the meeting time. Now, as he walked slowly, incredulously, around the machinery-filled room, Dieter thought back on the preceding months. Three weeks ago he and Pavel had devised solutions to all remaining problems and had built the first working model of a DNA read-write nanomachine. In an uncharacteristic display of whimsy, Pavel had christened it the Feynman 1, after Richard Feynman, who had spelled out the principles of nanotechnology twenty five years ago.

The Feynman machines were too small to be seen by any but the world's most powerful electron microscopes. But Pavel and Dieter had never even bothered to directly observe one; they had only inferred its existence by its actions. They no more needed to see the device to know it was there than they needed to see oxygen molecules to know they were in the air. Strike a match; it burns. Ergo, oxygen: Q.E.D.

The first trial of the Feynman machines, on bacteria, demonstrated that the machines existed, and that they worked. Or at least that they worked after a fashion: the experiment used sixty nanomachines. If every machine had done its job, then each should have created at least one colony of bacteria, and there should have been at least sixty separate colonies. There were thirteen.

They repeated the experiment, this time using an isotope of P34 in making the machines, again repeating the process sixty times. This time they got twelve colonies instead of sixty, and by precipitating radioactive salts out of the growth broth it was easy to discern what had happened: once let out of the protective nothingness of the vacuum jar, the other forty-eight machines had disintegrated like paper lanterns in a hurricane. It was obvious to Dieter that their marvelous new machines were so fragile as to be nearly useless. The flaw had to be in the tube, and he had assumed that Pavel would ask him to go back to the Dijjy-mike workstation for however long it took — a day, a week, a year — to devise a stronger one.

But Pavel had pronounced the experiment a resounding success and called for a new round of experiments: he wanted to try the Feynman machines on mammals. When Dieter had pointed out that the machines could barely withstand the benign environment of a petri dish, much less a mammalian immune system, Pavel had merely laughed.

"Then we use more machines, that's all. Like increasing the dose of a medicine. Once a machine changes one cell its work is done, like a little kamikaze. The fixed gene can replicate itself."

Well, that was true. But it had never been their intent to create a medicine; they had set out to devise a machine, a re-usable, long-lasting machine. If throw-away DNA repair engines were their objective, why go to all the trouble of inventing the world's smallest computer, when a simple drug would do? Why bother with all the work on the T4 bacteriophage? It was as if the Americans had started using their space shuttles for only one trip each. If the device were not meant to last beyond one use, the repair of one cell's DNA, then there were certainly cheaper—and safer—ways to get the job done.

"Come, Dieter," Pavel had said, briefly resting his hand on Dieter's shoulder with unusual— and to Dieter, uncomfortable—familiarity, "think of it as a disposable syringe."

"But if the machine is to be disposable, our approach is all wrong," Dieter had said. "With thousands or millions of half-broken Feynman machines floating around in a person's bloodstream, there's no telling what kind of havoc they might create. No, using many machines before we know how they work, how to fix them. . . it's. . . It's sloppy. It's. . . dangerous. Let's do it the right way. Let's make one good machine, a machine that doesn't break down. I. . . I must redesign the tube. It's taken us six years to get this far, why not spend a little longer to get it right? We don't even have a good mammalian genome to work with anyway. I do not understand the hurry."

"One can learn a lot from prototypes, Dieter. Believe me when I say that I speak from experience."

Dieter was taken aback.

"You confound me, Pavel. What prototypes? We have not made prototypes before these. What prototypes do you refer to?"

But Pavel had only answered that it was time to move on to animal experiments, and as Director of the NanoSection that's what he was directing Dieter to do. He then announced that the Hoff-Zeigy Board of Directors had approved funding for the NanoSection Test Facility, and that it was already under construction on the third floor of Hoff-Zeigy Building Two.

Dieter's familiar walk through the third floor biosynthesis lab was a thing of the past. The lab had been packed up wholesale and moved— where, he didn't know— and the door walled up. When Dieter walked down the third floor corridor, from behind the walled door he could hear the sounds of construction, and at all hours, as he sat at the Dijjy-mike workstation in his fourth-floor lab he could feel the floor beneath him vibrate. By the end of the second week the vibrations had ceased, and the heavy construction sounds had ceased filtering up from the floor below. A new door had appeared last week.

On the same day that the door appeared, Pavel had shown up at Dieter's office with a nurse and asked Dieter to roll up his sleeve so the nurse could draw a small amount of blood. He explained that in light of the extreme sensitivity of the work that would be going on in the lab, a new kind of DNA-reading lock was going to be installed. A small blood sample was needed to program Dieter's DNA into the system. Only those whose DNA matched the patterns on record would ever be able to get beyond the door.

This morning Dieter saw for the first time what the workers had been building.

The room itself was smaller than the sitting room in his studio apartment. But he was astounded at the amount of electronics that had been packed into the place. Three of the walls were covered with switches, dials, patch wires, television monitors; and along the fourth wall was a counter top in front of a large window: the room beyond was dark and the glass showed only his own reflection. Stools were pulled up against the counter, waiting. It was like one of those American altars of technology — NASA's "mission control room," the "situation rooms" of thriller movies— reduced to a manageable Swiss scale.

Everything that had happened in recent weeks troubled Dieter, and nothing more so than this room. Pavel was changing, and this room proved it. The words of Judith Knight kept coming back to Dieter. *I fear this man. I fear him greatly. It was when I became certain of his identity that I knew I must come here to speak with you.* Her words now seemed to him prophetic: it was as if one identity of Pavel were giving way and another asserting itself. Maybe the new extroversion that Dieter saw in his friend was the glee of a villain on the verge of triumph. *You may choose not to look at the potential for evil embodied in these machines you are trying to build, but Pavel is aware of this potential. That is his motivation.*

There were, of course, other explanations for Pavel's new behavior. Perhaps it was simple joy, even giddiness, in their recent breakthroughs. Was Pavel already imagining himself in Stockholm, giving his Nobel acceptance speech? Was he fantasizing about the millions of dollars (billions?) that could be his when the design was complete? Any of these explanations made more sense than thinking of Pavel as a terrorist.

And even if he was one, there was little danger. These machines couldn't break out of a proverbial paper bag, much less attack the planet. *Make the device vulner-*

able to salt water, or laundry soap, or weak radiation she had said. So far, there had been no need to do that, no need to build in additional weaknesses when the machines were so fragile to begin with. But he was glad that he had done so anyway, and glad that he had written to Judith about it.

It seemed like forever since Dieter's ineffectual meeting with Paul Aubrey. Forever since he had given Pavel the design for the tube: an eternity of improving the design, atom by atom; an eternity of avoiding serious discussion with his partner about the things that most troubled him. The whole time he had waited, futilely, for Pavel to mention Paul Aubrey or the search for a partner on the Human Genome project. But it was time for this evasion to cease. The issue had to be addressed head on, and today he would talk with this 'new' Pavel. As soon as the mammalian experiment was over, Dieter would do it.

The door to the lab swung open and Pavel Isaacs walked in, looking vibrant. There was a smile on his olive face, and his curly black hair seemed to have more life than ever. Even his clothes were different; he looked like a hip artist from the Kunsthalle, not like the earnest nerd that Dieter had met so long ago in the Lab at MIT.

"Good morning Dieter, ready for our big day?" he said. *Ready for our big day?* Where is my old taciturn friend, Dieter thought, the one who would never talk to me as if I were a four year old about to go to the circus?

"Hello Pavel," Dieter said. "How are you?"

"I'm great, Dieter," he said. "This is going to be some show today. Wait until you see what I have programmed our little machine to do. You are not going to believe your eyes."

"Let's hope it works," Dieter said.

"Oh, it's going to work alright," Pavel said. "In fact, I've invited one of our corporate guardian angels to see the show. I expect him at any moment."

"And what, my friend, is a guardian angel?" Dieter asked, trying to keep his inflection as neutral as possible.

"Why, the provider of our money, of course. The man who sees to it that we never want for wherewithal. His name is Paul Aubrey. He's an American who lives here in Basel and works for Hoff-Zeigy. Perhaps you know him?"

Was there irony in that suddenly serious look on Pavel's face?

"No, I do not know a Paul Aubrey," Dieter said, hoping his mannerisms did not give away his lie.

He wished more than anything that he could disappear before Aubrey arrived. His entire life he had been comfortable with chemistry, mathematics—never with people. The only time he had felt genuinely comfortable on the streets of Basel was during the three days of Fasnacht, when, safe in the anonymity of an oversized and garishly painted mask he could walk among the thousands of other nightmarish apparitions and enjoy the city's sights. Interpersonal relations, even ones that other people considered as natural as breathing, filled him with apprehension. And yet here he was in the middle of intrigue, with secret messages to anonymous addresses, hidden flaws kept secret from his partner, meetings that must not be divulged, deceptions, lies, evasions. He had to leave before Aubrey arrived, he suddenly decided. He would say that he had taken ill.

There was a knock on the door. He tensed in anticipation of Aubrey's entry.

"Come!" Pavel said.

The door opened, and a blond man of about twenty-five walked in.

Dieter felt his heart palpitate, he strained to maintain an equivocal expression. This was not Aubrey! What hoax was this?

"Dieter," Pavel was saying. "Say hello to Herr Kurt Alder. He is the designer of this studio. He will show us how to operate the equipment; soon we will handle it ourselves."

"Gut morgen, Herr Alder" Dieter said.

"Gut morgen, Doktor Steffen," the other answered.

Get hold of yourself, Dieter, he said to himself. You're panicking. Calm down.

Before the he could listen to his own advice the door opened again and Paul Aubrey entered the room. He was wearing a grey double-breasted suit, deep red tie. His beard seemed more grey than Dieter remembered, and he looked older, or perhaps simply more worn down.

"Hello Paul," Pavel was saying. "This is my colleague Doktor Dieter Steffen."

"How do you do," they both said, shaking hands. There was a moment or two of silence as each regarded the other. Dieter felt himself relax a tiny bit as it became apparent that Aubrey was acting as though they had never met.

"Gentlemen," Pavel began. "Let me explain today's experiment. As you know the Feynman Machine — I think we're up to version nine, aren't we?— the Feynman Nine is a device for finding a DNA sequence and converting it into another sequence. What gene it looks for and what action it takes are determined by me when I program it. To program it first I obtain the structure of a genome and load it into the controller chip. Then I make the Feynman devices by laser evaporation, downloading the pattern from chip into the new devices."

He gestured to Kurt, who pressed a button on a control panel. The light came on in the adjoining room behind the glass, revealing a table on which there were three glass boxes, each containing a mouse. Three glass tubes fed the boxes, one to each.

The mouse in the box on the left was brown, and appeared abnormally large for a laboratory mouse, almost the size of a rat. The mouse in the center box was white, and appeared normal. The small, oddly-shaped mouse in the right-hand box was brown and white.

"You notice that these three mice differ in color and in stature. For this experiment we don't care about color, only about body size. The mouse in the middle, the white one, is a normal-sized mouse. The other two have been genetically engineered.

The one on the right, the brown and white one, is a dwarf. Its size and body shape have been proven to be caused by a defect of a single gene. The mouse on the left has giganticism. Its abnormally large size is caused by a different defect of the same gene."

"We are now going to change the giant into a dwarf and the dwarf into a giant. To do this I have created two different versions of the Feynman Nine. The first one finds the giganticism gene and converts it into a dwarfism gene; the second finds the dwarf gene and converts it into a giganticism gene."

Aubrey was looking ahead, politely. It was impossible to read him.

"There are billions of cells in an organism of this size," Pavel continued, "so here is what we will do. Into the left and right mouse chambers we will introduce about a hundred thousand of the appropriately programed Feynman machines. If each machine changes ten cells per minute, then a hundred thousand machines should change a million cells per minute, sixty million in an hour. So within a couple of hours we should start to be able to see some real changes in these mice.

"A hundred thousand machines?" Aubrey said. "I had no idea."

"We make about one per second with the new laser process. But we get about fifteen per cent duds," he said, and smiled. "So that means that we create about three thousand Feynman machines an hour, seventy thousand machines a day. They're not very stable, even under the best conditions. They just break." Again that new, irritating laugh. "When you amortize in the cost of the labs, it probably costs about fifty dollars per nanomachine to make them. But that will change."

Fifty dollars per machine times one hundred thousand Feynman nines? This one experiment was costing five million dollars, at least. Dieter's nervousness was getting worse by the minute.

"OK," Pavel was saying, "here's what we'll do to start the process. Kurt, are you ready?"

"Shall I begin recording now?" he said.

"Yes, please. I suppose I should mention," Pavel said to Dieter and Paul, "that much of the equipment you see around you is for recording experiments. There are video cameras mounted on the ceiling and wall of the next room. There is a Geiger counter attached to each tube so we can count how many Feynman machines are introduced to each chamber; that information and much more is all recorded in an electronic log that is mixed in with the video signals."

The younger man pressed a few buttons at the bank of equipment on the wall.

"Recording," Alder said.

"Would you open the tubes please," Pavel said.

Alder walked two steps to the left and typed a few characters on a keyboard that rested on the counter in front of the glass.

"Open," he said.

"Gentlemen," Pavel said, "It would be tedious to stay here waiting for the pot to boil. I thought we might go for a ride in the country. By noon we might expect to see something."

●

They crossed the border and took roads Dieter didn't know, until, an hour later, they stopped at a small café. Where were they, Dieter asked. A village in France, Pavel said. Dieter could not comprehend such rudeness from his old friend! Couldn't he at least have told Dieter the name of the village?

A waiter set their *café au laits* before them, with a basket of croissants.

"Dieter," Pavel began. "I want to introduce Paul as more than a guardian angel. I want you to consider him a partner with us, part of our research team." He went on to explain the rationale for seeking a research partner that was active in the human genome project, the need for forming a joint venture, the importance of a properly structured corporate agreement, and the importance of having somebody with Paul Aubrey's experience and skill on the team.

No mention was made of specific companies. No mention of Human Potential, or the Association for Responsible Biotechnology. Or Judith Knight. It was now or never.

"You know," Dieter began. His throat was dry, his voice cracked. He began again. "You know, I have been thinking a lot about this work, and how the Feynman machines might be used on human beings. I think that they are potentially very dangerous things. I don't think we should even begin work on the human genome yet. We cannot do this alone; we need to publish our work and bring others into the discussion. For all these years I have put off thinking about these things because it seemed hard to believe that we would ever actually succeed. But now we are almost there. There are larger things at stake here than making profits for Hoff-Zeigy. In the wrong hands Feynman machines could be very dangerous indeed. I am not sure that I can continue to work on this project if we begin to program human gene patterns into the devices."

He had not intended to make such a speech, but in any event he had done it. He had stated his concern and raised the possibility of quitting the project. He felt relief, which was immediately followed by a new sense of dread.

Pavel spoke. "I've been having these concerns myself. But we can't stop work while we sort out the larger issues. Who knows how far along others might be in making their own nanomachines? You have read about Bill Gates, the wealthiest man in the world, underwriting the University of Washington to develop just what we have built? You know about the programs in Germany, Wisconsin, France, Tokyo? They are trying to go exactly where we are going, only we will get there first. We cannot simply stick our heads in the sand; that would not solve any problems. But let us continue this discussion. Why don't you and Herr Aubrey join me tonight, at my apartment, for dinner? I have already invited two other people who might like to discuss a little philosophy with us, and it will go a lot better after a couple of glasses of wine."

"And who would these people be?" Dieter said. "I thought our work was secret."

"Yes, it is very secret. But one person is already part of the project. An old professor of mine, he currently is director of Digital MicroSystems Laboratories, and he has developed the method that we use to collapse genetic information into so small a space. He is the co-designer, along with myself, of the little Turing machine computer that sits in every nanomachine. Truly he is a co-designer, along with you and me, of the Feynman device. But!" Pavel said, with a flourish. "He has another qualification, germane to the issues you have raised. He is guest professor of Bioethics at Stanford University, and he is quite concerned with topics like the ones you just brought up."

Dieter tried to absorb this new information. Certainly he had known that Pavel had some kind of special arrangement with Digital MicroSystems. Pavel had made no secret about the source of the compression algorithm, and he knew that Pavel sometimes went to the Basel facility of Digital MicroSystems Laboratories. But to call this man, this 'old professor' whom Dieter had never met, the co-designer of the machine that he and Pavel had collaborated on since MIT? After six years, he was hearing of him for the first time! He didn't even know the man's name!

"And who is the second person? Another unknown co-designer of the machine?"

"You'll be very happy to meet her," Pavel said. "She's quite a feast for the eyes."

Aubrey nodded, smiling awkwardly. What was he looking at?

"Well then," Pavel said, rising from his chair, "Let us say tonight, my place in Basel Town, at twenty hours? Good. Let's get back to the laboratory now and see how things have shaped up."

As he stood, Dieter looked behind him in the direction that Aubrey had been staring for the last fifteen minutes. He saw the back of a blond woman wearing a long skirt and white blouse disappearing from the sidewalk into the interior of the café.

Dieter had never even considered what might happen to the mice once the Feynman machines began to change their cells. He must have been so worried about seeing Aubrey at the new laboratory that he had somehow disengaged that part of his brain. He had simply never even thought about what it might mean to change a dwarf into a giant, a giant into a dwarf. But nothing he could have imagined would have prepared him for the sights awaiting him back at the third floor of Hoff-Zeigy Building Two.

In the right box, the brown and white dwarf had clearly changed. But it wasn't simply larger; it was distorted, grotesque. One side of its cranium was larger than the other, and the skin looked to be stretched over it, leaving one eye tilted up at an angle. Its legs were misshaped and unsymmetrical: on the left front leg, the foreleg had grown more than the thigh; on the right front the thigh had grown faster. The animal was lying on its side, its mismatched eyes open in anguish. Its little heart could be seen to beat furiously within its chest. If a mouse can wish, Dieter thought, this mouse is hoping it will die very soon.

If the mouse in the left box had wished the same thing, its wish had already been granted. But its agony before dying must have been extreme. This one had been the giant. Dieter tried to remember what color it had been. Brown, he thought. He could still see patches of brown fur beneath the blood. Deformed like the other, this one had suffered more, as the skin had shrunk while the bones could not, and eventually the bones broke and punctured through the skin. Dieter had seen squirrels after they had been run over by a truck that looked healthier than this mouse did after exposure to the Feynman Nine. Kurt was visibly distraught.

"Herr Isaacs," he said, as soon as the three men had entered the observation room and seen the carnage in the on the other side of the window, "can we not kill this miserable creature now? I could not find a syringe or already I would have let it out of its agony."

"Have you gotten everything on tape?" Pavel said. His tone was perfectly neutral.

"Yes. The blue tape cartridges are the final mixes. There is no point in allowing this creature to suffer any more. With the tapes you can witness the entire process frame by frame."

"But the process is not complete, Herr Alder. The experiment must continue. I appreciate your concern for the animal, but we must see this through. Who knows, perhaps it will live."

"Herr Isaacs, this is cruelty," Kurt said.

"This is *science*," Pavel said, looking at Alder but glancing at Dieter as he spoke. "This animal is not suffering in vain, nor will it die in vain. You have only to imagine a child cured of leukemia in the time it takes to drive to the country for a cup of coffee. Think on that, Herr Alder, and you will not be so distressed by the deaths of these animals. The experiment must continue."

"Well then you will excuse me if I leave the room for the next thirty minutes. The tapes are set; everything will run by itself without me here."

"Very well," Pavel said, and the angry man, veins showing in his neck, quickly left the room.

Once the door had closed after him Pavel turned to the remaining two men with an entirely new expression on his face. It was joy, pure radiant joy.

"Gentlemen!" he exclaimed. "What great success we have achieved today. Let us adjourn until eight tonight. I will bring the champagne."

Chapter 29

Three thirty that afternoon Dieter Steffen, fortified by four tall glasses of strong Belgian beer, presented himself at the office of Paul Aubrey and demanded an appointment.

"I am sorry, Herr Aubrey is in conference at the moment," said Fraulein Mason, Paul Aubrey's secretary.

"Fuck his meeting!" Dieter said. "Call Herr Aubrey this minute, *bitte*, or I will go into his office myself, meeting or no meeting." Why was he intimidating this poor secretary, a Basler like himself, with vulgar American English? Because it worked. He felt righteous.

"Do you call out Herr Aubrey or do I go in?"

As he spoke the door opened, and Rolf Steffen, Vice Chairman of Hoff-Zeigy, stepped out. Because the two men shared the same last name, people sometimes assumed that they were related. Unfortunately not, Dieter thought. If they had been, maybe he would be in line to inherit a few millions. The older Steffen was tall, nearly two meters, and looked the former athlete he was. His grey hair was combed and lightly gelled, and perfectly offset the deeply tanned and handsome face.

"Hello, Dr. Steffen," he said.

"Hello," Dieter answered. Good lord, now I *really* feel drunk, he thought.

Dieter stood for a moment, disoriented. The unexpected appearance of the Chief Operating Officer had disrupted his train of thought. What the hell was Rolf Steffen doing at Aubrey's office? Was he checking on the results of this morning's experiment?

"Come in, Dieter, come in," Paul Aubrey said.

Dieter snapped out of his reverie, remembering why he had come. He stepped into the office and the door closed behind him. Aubrey sat behind a large, sleek mahogany desk, and indicated a guest chair. Dieter remained on his feet, pacing.

"Herr Aubrey," he said. "First let me thank you for not telling Pavel about our earlier talk. Now, we must talk about this Feynman machine business. This is turning insane. Please do not tell me you do not find this project turning . . . turning crazy. Why was that animal laboratory built? We are years from understanding the how the machines work, even in bacteria! It will be years before we need to experiment on animals. Did you see the look on Pavel's face? He was in ecstasy! Two mangled dead mice and he proposes to discuss our 'success.' Aubrey, we must talk with him. This whole thing has gone to his head. Tonight we must bring some reason back to him."

"I have to agree," Paul Aubrey said, "those mice were pretty gruesome. On the other hand clearly their genes had been modified, so there was some measure of success in the experiment. Perhaps you and Pavel are both overreacting—"

"You cannot be serious—" Dieter interrupted.

"—but I agree that Herr Isaacs is trying to move things along faster than your results seem to call for. Perhaps, as you say, the thing to do is for you and I to approach him. Unfortunately, it appears that I will not be able to attend the *soiree* this evening."

At these words Dieter felt suddenly deflated. While sitting at the bar earlier that afternoon, amid the tough-looking truck drivers and warehousemen, he had imagined the whole evening. He and Aubrey would have rehearsed their speaking roles. They would argue for an entirely new approach to developing the Feynman machines: Dieter and Pavel would stop work now. They would organize a colloquium and invite the leading practitioners in the field to participate. To make sure that the fundamental issues of safety and ethics were not swept under the rug, they would invite Judith Knight and the Association for Responsible Biotechnology to co-host the meeting.

But in this daydream, which had become more vivid with each sip of the Belgian beer, Aubrey, not Pavel Isaacs, was Dieter's new partner. Dieter had come here to recruit him. And now Aubrey was bowing out before Dieter had even had the chance to spell out his plan.

"How, not attend?" he said, weakly.

"I have had a message from an old friend, from the States. She will be calling me later this evening, and says that it is very important. So unfortunately I must be at my home to take this call. Perhaps if she calls early I can join you for a nightcap."

"But surely Herr Aubrey —Paul— we have important business to attend to this evening. You can call her tomorrow."

"Well," he sighed, "I might if I could. But I don't know where she lives, or even what name she is using. You see, she is separated from her husband."

"I see —"

"And I have not spoken with her in a very long time. A very long time. But if she says that it is urgent that we talk, then indeed it must be urgent. I do appreciate your wanting me to attend this evening. It is nice to think that you value my opinion," Aubrey said.

"It is your influence I value, Herr Aubrey. You obviously have a lot of that. I cannot imagine our esteemed vice-chairman every paying a courtesy call on me," he said, and immediately regretted the tone. *If I am this drunk in the middle of the afternoon, how will I make it until this evening? I need to act more sober.*

"Do not overestimate my influence, Dieter. That was the first time Herr Rolf Steffen has ever been to see me, and his visit quite stunned me as much as it did you."

"Interested in the results of his brilliant scientist and the gold-plated laboratory, was he?"

"As they say, Dieter, I am not at liberty to discuss. But you know, as they also say, things are not always what they seem. It's wise to avoid hasty conclusions."

Dieter was only half listening, as he walked around the office. There was a diploma on the wall, and some innocuous floral prints. He was hardly listening to Aubrey, hardly noticing the office decor. Perhaps he *would* get good and drunk before he went to see Pavel tonight.

A framed cover of a magazine, sitting unobtrusively in the corner of a bookshelf caught his attention. Science, October 1986. The words "The Trojan Horse Gene" appeared on the cover, over a stylized rendering of a horse on wheels made out of twisted DNA.

"If I may ask?" he said, lifting the frame.

"My one and only publication," he said. "My fifteen seconds as a scientist. I may be a marketing man in a suit, but I used to know my way around a laboratory."

"I remember this article, the one on the cover. It was about DNA that serves multiple functions depending on how it is read. Plasmids use it for one function in a phage, then another function once insinuated into a bacterium. That's why they called it a Trojan Horse, the way it appeared to be one thing beneficial but is really just a disguise for an invader. It's a lot like AIDS in that respect."

"I know," Aubrey said. "That was my article."

Dieter found himself dumbfounded again. He remembered reading the article, remembered seeing its author present the results at the Cold Spring Harbor Symposium. He remembered what she looked like; she sure as hell did not look like Herr Aubrey. What was her name? McCarthy? McCraw? He couldn't remember. It wasn't 'Paul Aubrey'.

"I remember this paper being presented at Cold Spring Harbor," he said, "on Long Island."

"Oh yes? You were there?" Aubrey said.

"But you did not present it."

"Oh no," Aubrey laughed. "No, I didn't present it. Bartlett presented it. It was her work, her article. But I am listed as seventh of the nine co-authors."

"Oh?"

"I was an undergraduate, she was a Ph.D. candidate. I helped out in her lab. It was a joke, really, or a courtesy, for her to put my name on the paper," he smiled a forlorn smile. "It was a long time ago."

"I remember that she was very beautiful."

"That she was."

"I have forgotten her name?" Dieter said.

"Bartlett McGovern."

"Yes!" he said, "That's it. She must be a full professor by now. I wonder what became of her."

Dieter remembered so much of that Cold Spring Harbor weekend. His first trip to America. That dark- haired beauty and the Trojan Genes. The adolescent jokes among the men in the audience.

"She is investigating the Gulf War Syndrome reported by some American veterans. She thinks bacteriophage may have something to do with it. Hoff-Zeigy bacteriophage, in fact."

Dieter suddenly felt ill; and his right hand began to tremble. In America he and Pavel had developed a crude prototype based on genetically engineered phage. But that had been in 1988. They had only made one cell—Dieter called it a 'super cell,' but Pavel preferred the term 'monster cell'— and it had been hard enough to do that. Upon their arrival in Switzerland, could Pavel possibly have made copies without informing him? Might those copies have been used in weapons? He tried to imagine what symptoms would occur if soldiers had been somehow infected. But no, phage were not human pathogens. The whole notion was impossible. Or was it?

"So you keep in touch with her still?" he said, weakly.

"No."

"Then how —?"

"She called today while we were out, leaving the message that she would call again tonight."

Dieter smiled. "For a call from her I would wait at home this evening too." After a moment he added, "forgive me a question I would never ask if I were sober. I wonder if she had time for a boyfriend when she was doing all this science?"

"I thought she did," he said. "But I was never a very good judge of such things."

"And I suppose she married him and had some children. Like it always goes," Dieter said.

"No, as a matter of fact she married his brother. They grew apart. I've often thought that maybe she married the wrong one."

"Oh my God, so sad," Dieter said. "And what became of the brother, the first boyfriend?"

Aubrey looked out the window, and smiled.

"His hair turned grey and he moved to Switzerland," he said.

"Well Herr Aubrey," Dieter said, "in light of what you have just told me I will not attempt to persuade you to attend dinner at Pavel's this evening. But I am going to tell him what I think about all this craziness of animal experiments and human genome work."

"As you like, Dieter. But Pavel is a complex man. Perhaps this can wait another day until, well, until—"

"Until I am sober?" Dieter said.

"That might not be a bad idea. But I was going to say, Until you and I can discuss this further."

"My mind is made up, Mr. Aubrey. My entire life I have been too timid. If I need a few drinks to get my courage, then maybe I should be drinking more. But tonight I speak with him."

"Please watch your step."

"I will do that. And you," he said. "You give my regards to the lovely Dr. McGovern. And ask her how in the hell phage can infect humans. They're not a human pathogen. Unless she knows something nobody else knows."

"I'll ask her," he said, as Dieter Steffen, perhaps the slightest bit more sober than when he had entered, left. On the way to his apartment he stopped at the bar for two more drafts of beer and a shot of Kirsch, walked and took the trolley home, arriving at 18:08. From his house he eventually succeeded in placing a call to the States after much cursing, first at his phone book for the poor instructions, and then at the international operator. Dr Knight was not in her office, but if he left a message at the tone she would get back to him as soon as she could. Well, too bad. He had hoped that he could discuss with her his idea for a symposium before he talked with Pavel but that clearly was not going to happen. He told the machine what he planned to do, hoping that the combination of his slightly slurred speech, accent, increasingly awkward choice of English phrases, and less-than-perfect telephone connection would not make his message unintelligible. He chose some clothes and laid them out on the bed. Then he stripped, leaving a pile of his clothes on the floor, and stepped into the shower. The warm water felt good.

Lathering his penis, he said out loud, "This is for you, Dr. Knight. And for you, Dr. McGovern."

After two minutes of frantic manipulation he came to the reluctant conclusion that no erection was likely any time soon. *So this is what they mean about drinking and driving,* he thought.

At 17:32 the taxi arrived in front of his apartment. During the ride he drank the pint of Guinness Stout that had been in his refrigerator for three years. At 17:48 he got out, one block away from Pavel's apartment.

The door opened and Dieter found himself staring blankly at a stunning blond beauty, about twenty-five years old, as the sounds of a jazz quintet, Miles Davis?, came from within.

"*Bonsoir,*" she said. "*Soyez le bienvenu. Pavel arrive a l'instant.*"

"Good evening." Dieter said. "How nice to meet you too." Where was his French?

Dieter stepped into the room. It was not as he remembered it, but it had been a while, he told himself. It seemed more, what, studied. He looked about for the musicians; it took him a moment to realize that the sound came from a stereo. There were bookcases, pictures arranged just so on the walls. There were oriental carpets on the floor, and leather couches. This was not the apartment of the single-minded, obsessive graduate–student–turned–laboratory–director. *How is it that he has had time to acquire a personality while I have not?*

"Dieter! There you are!" he heard Pavel's voice calling to him. "Good of you to come. You know, Aubrey begged off. Well, screw him. We have had enough of bureaucrats for one day. This can be an evening for the scientists."

"Scientists," Dieter said. "Aubrey is a. . .well, whatever he is," he said, somehow managing to stop his tongue before saying "Aubrey is a real scientist."

"Yes, let this be an evening for us, the three creators of the Feynman machines," Dieter said. "And give me a drink, I want to make a toast."

Dieter noticed a middle-aged man in a poorly-fitting suit approaching from a back room.

"Certainly!" Pavel said loudly, displaying a broad smile. "A toast. But first say hello to my mentor. Dieter Steffen, this is Dr. Vannevar Engleton, of Stanford Divinity School. He is the professor of bioethics that I mentioned earlier today."

"Your mentor?" Dieter slurred. "Where is the damned drink? *J'ai soif! J'ai besoin de quoi boire.*" French? Why am I speaking French now? Who cares. Give me something to drink, I'm thirsty.

Somehow a champagne flute appeared in his hand; somehow it became filled with champagne, somehow he stood in the center of the carpet with the other three around him: Pavel in front, the chorus girl on the right, the puffed-up ethicist on the left.

"Stanford Divinity. That's it in a nutshell, isn't it?" he said, and laughed. "But let us not be joking. Let us be serious. A toast!" he lifted his glass.

"A toast," the three answered.

He raised his glass.

"To three blind mice," he said. "Two of them are dead. One of them is still alive." He drank his glass. The others smiled as if embarrassed, and after a nod from the one introduced as Engleton they all drank.

"Another toast!" he said. Hell, they can see I'm drunk, no need to hide it. Who cares.

"Fill the glasses," he said. Somehow they got filled.

"Another toast. Now that we have toasted the inventors of the Feynman machine, let us toast its victims." He held his glass over his head. "To the million dollar rodents of the third floor lab, God save their putrid bones." He drank. He did not notice whether the others did or not.

Somehow he was at the dinner table. He was not very hungry, but he ate a bite or two of something not Swiss. The wine was good.

Somehow the table was now cleared. Seated opposite him was the Stanford professor, a pompous ass if ever there was one, so full of condescending answers about every known thing. And shut up about the jazz already. I have ears of my own to hear.

"Dieter," he was saying. "You're drunk; that's understandable. It's been a very disturbing day for you. Tomorrow I can guarantee you that you won't recall a thing about our conversation tonight. But you have been saying some very interesting things. *In vino veritas est,* they say, in wine lies truth. So, let me suggest something. Here is a pad of paper, and a pen." He passed them to Dieter. "Now put down the date, then write down the things you are concerned about, and sign it. This can be a letter to yourself. After your hangover has cleared up you can look at it, to help remember the passion you feel tonight."

"Who are you, Zeegmund Fooking Vroid?" he heard himself saying. But the professor simply passed him the paper and pen, with a knowing smile.

"OK here goes. 7 February. Basel," Dieter said, writing.

"I believe that my work as a scientist poses a grave threat to the human race. I believe that my partners are madmen. Our tiny machines will change man into woman, woman into man, health into disease. There is no control over us. There should be an international commission to supervise us, and it should be headed by. . ."

The professor reached over and put his hand on Dieter's.

"No need to get too specific," he said. "You only need to capture the emotion, the feeling."

"Tonight I am with an asshole," Dieter said, writing. "An asshole who thinks he knows everything. His name is Vannevar Engleton." That was clever. He smiled and looked up across the table. Somehow there were three faces there now, somehow they all looked the same.

"I need to start my life over again, away from these monsters."

He thought of the woman from the Cold Spring Harbor symposium.

"I am in love with that Trojan woman with the big tits. There," he said, and signed the paper with a flourish. He passed the pad and pen to the professor with a dismissive shove.

The professor picked it up and read.

"Very good," he said. "This will answer a lot of questions." He folded the paper and slid it down the table. Somehow it was not there when Dieter glanced that way.

"Let me ask you a few more questions," he said. "Here, good American Bourbon is the best after-dinner cordial." Dieter took the proffered glass, sipped. *Scheissvasser.* What the hell, drink up.

"Now, tell me. You have been sending electronic mail messages to Judith Knight, in America, haven't you?"

"Nosey aren't we? What business is that of yours? Some ethicist. I think I will go to sleep." He put his head down on the table. He immediately felt it pulled back by his hair.

Dieter looked over his shoulder. Somebody was still holding his hair. Good thing I'm drunk or it might hurt, he thought. Could that be Pavel doing that? He felt like sleeping or vomiting, he couldn't decide which. Why would Pavel pull his hair? Too many questions. He would figure it out later. He tried to rest his head, but felt it pulled back again.

"Leave me alone."

"That's not my model, right now, Dieter. I need to know more about your messages to Dr. Knight. We have been copying your messages, but the encryption algorithm is too good. After all, it was designed by me. We simply cannot unscramble the messages until you give us the password. So come, what is it?"

"I don't think so. Drinking and driving."

He felt a sharp blow to the back of his head.

"The password, Dieter," somebody was saying.

"Basler-Dybli," he said. The room was spinning.

"What?" he heard Pavel's voice.

"Basler-Dybli, you assholes. Kirsch. Fucking Kirsch."

Pavel spoke to Engleton. "Kirsch, you know, the cherry liqueur."

"You are very drunk already, Dieter. Forget about the Kirsch. What is the password?"

"Basler-Dybli, I am telling you. You assholes. You mice-killers."

Ce n'est pas la peine. Forget about it," he heard a woman's voice say. "We let him get too drunk. I'll get the password from the other side."

His hair was let go; he felt his head bang on the table.

"Well Pavel," he heard the asshole professor's voice saying. "It's up to you. Can you take it the rest of the way from here?"

"Yes," he heard Pavel say.

"You are sure you don't need him any more?"

"I no longer need him for my model," he heard Pavel say.

"And Paul Aubrey?" he heard the woman's voice say.

"I need him for the genome deal. Another month or two."

"We're agreed to take care of this tonight? You don't think Aubrey will connect the two?"

"A coincidence."

"Alright. Wait for me here. Come on Dieter. Come on Herr Doktor Animal Rights, Herr Conscience of the World."

Somehow he was walking down the stairs with the professor. He was in the taxi with the American, he was in his house, in his bedroom. Tell the stupid American to go home.

These Americans and their Hollywood fixations. Now the black gloves. What, a pistol? Don't you divinity students hate guns? What? A silencer? I saw one of those in the movies.

∞IV∞

A CERTAIN CENTURIAN

Chapter 30

This time there would be no denying her motive, at least to herself. If she wore the black outfit, it would be to catch his eye. And what if she caught it? She had no idea. All she knew was that she was ready to be a woman again, not just a scientist. If Paul were the first man to notice, so be it.

The body suit felt good as she slinked into it; the black jeans were snug but not skin tight. She pulled her hair back, arranged the black Thai comb to keep it there. What the hell, as Nick used to say. In for a dime, in for a dollar. She put in the earrings, the monkeys with the sapphires. Then she threw on her Mr. Anonymous down coat and Mr. Anonymous knit hat and headed for the door.

At the stop outside her apartment building she hopped on the Green Line. Before Kenmore Square the trolley left the Back Bay grey daylight and plunged to into netherurbania. At the Park station under the Common Bartlett transferred to the Blue Line for Logan.

Paul would be flying in from Basel, via London. After a seven-hour layover he would be continuing on to San Jose; his ultimate destination was Saratoga, between San Jose and Los Gatos, where the Biodigital Forum was to be held four days from now. He was going out early so that his body would be adjusted to the time change before the meeting started, he said. He never worked while jet-lagged. Paul never made decisions after a long flight, or, God forbid, a red-eye.

It was Bartlett's idea that they meet in Boston. Paul had wanted Bartlett to fly out to meet him at the conference in California. It was to be held at the Saratoga Club, an exclusive resort in the lee of the Santa Cruz mountains that catered to oenophiles and hyperrich croquet players. At the Saratoga Club the lawns were well-tended and the restaurant was three star. *Croquet?* She laughed. *Yes,* he said. *Like polo without horses, and more money.* Hoff-Zeigy would be happy to pick up the tab if Bartlett wanted to go out a few days early.

At the Biodigital Forum Bartlett would see first-hand the convergence of genetics and information science. The Forum would be a good place for her to check out the competition—not only the Neuro Group's competition, but Hoff-Zeigy's competition as well. It would be open-kimono time, during which she, as the Neuro Group's representative, could meet and greet other moneyed angels like Paul. The Biodigital Forum was where the mating ritual of cold cash and hot technology took place, and if, after the dance, Hoff-Zeigy and the Neuro Group felt like getting in bed together, they would—and if not they wouldn't. But at least it would be an informed choice.

Bartlett declined. Somehow the Biodigital Forum seemed too intimidating. Was it stepping out of the laboratory and into the world of commerce that she feared? Or flying off to a resort with Paul? Both of these were considerations, but in her heart she knew it was something deeper—it was the *convergence itself* that put her off.

From the moment she had learned the austere magnificent trick of DNA she had known she was going to be a biologist. She had always found Nick's fascination with software hard to fathom: he had left agriculture for the computer business, but how could anyone choose 'computer science' over life science? Increasingly, however, that distinction seemed arbitrary and unimportant. At the molecular level, silicon chips and DNA molecules were the same thing: devices that shunted electrons by this path or that to create new information structures. Computer science and biology had converged; more accurately, molecular biology was now a subdiscipline of information science. That was the premise of the Biodigital Forum, and indeed it was the premise of the Neuro Group. But Bartlett, in her innermost heart, was repelled by this notion. That school girl who had felt a thrill to her soul the instant she understood the double helix; the-twelve-year old who had seen unutterable beauty in the Krebs cycle, the face of God in messenger RNA—that girl still lived inside her. She was not yet ready to concede. One could not see the face of God in Windows 95.

The Swissair monitor showed that the flight from London was on time, arriving in twenty minutes. Bartlett had a Boston *Herald* but was too nervous to read it. So she stood contemplating the glassed-in kinetic sculpture in the main terminal. Little colored balls rode up a conveyor, then fell, bounced and rolled along paths dictated by gravity and chance, hitting wood blocks, wind chimes, bells and drum skins all the way down to the collector at the bottom, where the ride began again. A playful concerto of bings, bangs and boings percolated out to the cavernous airport, reminding Bartlett of a similar sculpture in the lobby of Children's Hospital, where Jackson had asked her questions about atoms and molecules.

She strode away to find someplace else to pass the time.

Ten minutes of browsing in the bookstore found her in the science section. She stopped and stared at a photographic image, fascinating and perverse, on the cover of a book turned sideways on the shelf. Under the title *Convergence*, by Pascale Pacheco, it showed a computer chip with a nerve cell grafted onto it. *Monster cell,* she thought. *Pascale's Monster cell.* Indeed, the thing in the photograph was monstrous to Bartlett's eyes. It was Frankenstein on a minuscule scale—carbon brain and silicon brain in bestial communion. Is this what I'm doing with my life, she wondered, creating monsters? She turned and left the bookstore.

The Swissair monitor informed her that Paul's plane had landed. Paul would be in customs now, and any second she would see him. With all her heart she regretted having come. Why had she done it? For two reasons, she reminded herself.

On behalf of the Neuro Group, she wanted to find out if Hoff-Zeigy would invest enough money to develop their prototype. Years ago she would have called this whoring, the selling out of virgin academe to a multinational John. Her idols were Johannes Keppler, Isaac Newton, Marie Curie, Rosalind Franklin. Not Jay Gatsby. Not Bill Gates. She cared about science, not money. Time had softened her views—there was no such thing as pure research anymore, if there had ever been. She was part of the Neuro Group, and the Neuro Group needed money if it was going to survive. But she still felt like a whore.

The second reason had to do with the inexplicable discovery of protein from Hoff-Zeigy bacteriophage in the blood of American soldiers (and of one American tourist) who had been in the general vicinity of SCUD warheads in 1991. Bartlett had entertained hopes that Paul would help her—or help Chris and Janine Garbougian—to figure out how that protein had gotten there. But why in the world would Hoff-Zeigy as a corporation, or any of its employees as individuals, tell her how their genetically-altered bacteriophage had been used for biological warfare? For that matter, how would they know? It was like asking US Steel to solve a homicide because the fatal bullet had been made from their metal.

It was her third, unadmitted, reason that made her want to flee. How on Earth had she decided to dress provocatively for a meeting with her brother-in-law, a former lover whose heart she had broken? A brother-in-law who, incidentally, seemed to think about financing scientific research purely in terms of sexual conquest?

It was too late to change her clothes now. But at least, at the very least, she could get rid of the pendant that was caught between her boobs like a very large and uncomfortable cookie crumb. She was reaching behind her neck to unfasten the clasp when Paul walked out of the customs area. He was impossibly handsome. Nick didn't even own a suit, and Paul wore his like Cary Grant. She was still standing with her hands behind her neck when he kissed her on the cheek. She felt trouble in every cell of her body.

"Hello Bartlett," he said. "This is the most pleasant welcome I've had in a long time."

He exuded an unadorned masculinity that she found—contrary to her wishes, if not her expectation—to be almost overpoweringly sexually attractive.

"Do you have to go get your luggage someplace?" she asked. She was determined to do whatever it took to keep their conversation strictly impersonal.

He patted his shoulder bag with a confident touch. "I can't stand that wait at the carousel."

Oh. Well. Now what would she say?

She didn't need to say anything. She simply followed his lead. He walked across the floor to the revolving door and hailed a taxi; Bartlett got in as he held the door. Now they were in the tunnel, now in downtown, by King's Chapel. The cab stopped before the Parker House.

The doorman seemed to recognize him. Had Paul been here before? In Boston?

"Hello Richie. Put my bag someplace handy, will you? We'll only be a little while."

"Sure thing, Mr. Aubrey. Nice to see you again so soon."

Evidently the answer was yes.

Chapter 31

Somewhere over the Midwest Nick realized that he wasn't going to sleep. He opened his eyes, reached in the pocket on the back of the seat in front of him for Casey's bon voyage gift: a battered copy of *Motivation and Personality* by Abraham Maslow. The book fell open to page 143:

"Self-actualizing people are not well adjusted (in the naive sense of approval of and iden-tification with the culture). They get along with the culture in various ways, but of all of them it may be said that in a certain profound and meaningful sense they resist enculturation and maintain a certain inner detachment from the culture in which they are immersed."

Don't we all, Nick thought. What drivel.

Casey had also given him a copy of De Sade's *Juliette*, which he had left behind. Kinky sex between bishops and under-age nuns in underground chapels was one thing, but paroxysms of ecstasy on cannibalism, excrement, and the torture and rape of children were something else. But as Casey had said, it all flowed from a few sim-ple premises: that people are animals and should feel no remorse for following their nature, that the nature of every creature was to seek its own survival and pleasure, and that cruelty to those weaker than oneself was an excellent source of happiness. "Remarkably similar to reading *Forbes*, actually," she had said, "but with more sodomy and without all the blow-ins falling out as you turn the pages."

Nick had spent much of the last few days with the ever enigmatic Casey. Yesterday, as they stood in the cooler before the enormous portrait of the Kali chip, Casey said, addressing it, "OK, what do you do? What's your secret?"

"Any guesses?" Nick asked.

She sat down cross-legged before it, her braid resting on her shoulder.

"There's two hundred and seventy five thousand transistors on this thing. So, by doing the combinatorics we see that it will take me only nine trillion years to nar-row down the possibilities."

Looking to the plot on the wall Nick noticed, for the first time, Todd's tell-tale graffiti. In an empty space on the lower right hand corner, the words laid out as if on a bumper sticker:

> **IF YOU CAN READ THIS**
> **YOU'RE TOO DAMN CLOSE!**

On an actual chip those words would be, what, a hundredth of an inch across? In the upper right, an outline of Bullwinkle Moose, and the caption "This time fer sher." How many other jokes had Todd left for the intrepid sleuth?

"I must be out of my mind," Casey said. "Todd couldn't figure it out, and he had the specs, the layout program, prototypes to test—and it was his own damn chip."

"And none of that stuff is available?"

"Nope. Well, I've got the one chip," she had said, nodding at the circuit board on the wall.

"What about Todd's notebooks? Did he keep a log?"

She turned to look up at him, and he felt a rush. It was something about that turtleneck-and-bluejean combination, maybe.

"Son," she said, reaching her hand up for a lift, "that is an intriguing question."

At thirty thousand feet Nick turned his attention from the memory of her turned-down smile, and tried again to read Maslow. Somewhere over the Rockies he fell asleep.

The descent into Salt Lake City International Airport was more gentle this time. With his seatbelt fastened, seatback upright, tray table locked, carry-on luggage stowed, Nick was physically ready to land. Emotionally he wasn't so sure. He took the diskette out of his pocket and looked at it again, pondering the ballpoint 'Matthew.' Why had Barlow chosen that word? And more importantly, was Marki going to let Nick off the hook once he had this diskette in his hands?

From a phone in the terminal Nick called Marki to tell him he was ready to turn over the evidence. The detective didn't like Nick's attitude. The People of the State of Utah were halfway to a Governor's warrant to have the Massachusetts cops pick him. Why hadn't Nick called sooner? Nick had rehearsed his answer.

"There's nothing wrong with my attitude. I sat next to a man who killed himself. That's all I did. I'm not going to put my life on hold because some assholes have decided I'm the Antichrist."

"So now I'm an asshole?"

"I didn't mean you. I meant the people on 'alt conspiracy'."

"Taking that diskette was a crime."

"Removing evidence from the scene of a suicide is hardly enough to put me on America's Most Wanted."

"Why'd you take it?"

"I was curious."

True enough, in a Bill Clinton I-didn't-inhale kind of way.

"What's on it?"

"I don't know. It's password-protected, with a booby-trap. I couldn't unlock it."

Two honest remarks. Almost honest, anyway. He really wished he had figured a way around Barlow's booby trap, but he hadn't come close.

"If you want this diskette," Nick continued. "I need your promise with that you'll let me leave here on my scheduled flight, which leaves in forty-two minutes."

"Why should I agree to that?"

"Because I have the diskette in my hand and a magnet in my briefcase."

Back to bullshit. Oh well.

"Don't threaten me, Mr. Aubrey. If you're not here in five minutes I'm putting an APB on you."

"I'll see you in five minutes."

"And that diskette damn well better have Barlow's fingerprints on it."

"I appreciate your working with me, Detective Marki," Nick said, and hung up.

Six minutes later Nick was back in the interrogation room with the two detectives. Deja-vu, only this time it wasn't going to be good cop-bad cop. It was going to be bad cop-bad cop.

"Hand it over, Nick," were the first words out of Marki's mouth.

"My rights?" Nick said.

"You're a suspect in a murder investigation. You have the right. . ."

"I know my rights. I waive."

"You watch too much television, Nick," Carelli said. "Being a smart-ass gets you nowhere." Nick noticed that Carelli's cheeks were very red. It wasn't just his rash.

"Would you please give me the diskette, as you promised?" Marki said.

"Here," Nick said, taking it out of his shirt pocket and handing it to him. The detective grabbed it by its corners and deposited it in an already-labeled plastic bag.

"You've been trying to read this?"

"Yes," Nick said. "I've written a little report. May I open my briefcase?"

He withdrew a two-page memo, which he summarized aloud as he handed it over:

"It's in UNIX format. There's a program on it, called 'Orson,' and two encrypted data files. If you run the program it asks for a password one hundred and sixty characters long, and starts timing you. It says that it will self-destruct if you don't type in the password within one minute, of which I have used up seven seconds. The threat to self-destruct may or may not be a bluff. It also says that attempts to copy the diskette will result in self-destruction; that too may be a bluff. I have not tried to duplicate it. I think the safest plan of attack is to get somebody at the university to write a device driver that can copy the thing without blowing it up. Once you've done that you can make a couple thousand copies. Then you can write a shell script to throw passwords at the password checker, and a program to try to unscramble the data. With enough resources applied to it you can probably crack it in under a month."

Two months, if I'm lucky.

"Thank you," Marki said. "I like this attitude a lot better."

"Good. I'll be leaving now."

"Not so fast. Let's go over the events of the night Barlow died, just for old time's sake."

"I have nothing to add to what I told you then. I gave you the diskette. I'm outta here."

He stood to go, and Carelli pushed him back in his seat.

"You think this a game Nick?"

"Not at all."

Now Marki spoke.

"You've read the Internet discussion, so you know that Barlow's story doesn't sound so crazy anymore. Somebody might have wanted him dead; I might be looking for a murderer."

"It was suicide."

"Humor me. Assume murder. Give me one good reason to think the doer wasn't you."

Nick had been waiting for this question.

"Because my brother is a more likely candidate," he answered.

"*What?*"

He had thought that would get them.

"My brother Paul lives in Switzerland, where men are addressed as "Herr," which is what Barlow called me: *Herr Aubrey*. My brother is a molecular biologist who works for a Swiss pharmaceutical company. You know, the kind of company that supplied Saddam with biological agents? He probably even works with nanomachines. Ergo, my brother is a more logical murder suspect than I am. Maybe Barlow thought I was my brother, then panicked and killed himself. Or maybe my brother set me up."

"Why didn't you tell us this before?" Marki said.

"It never occurred to me. Besides, would you rat out *your* brother?"

"Where in Switzerland does your brother live?" Marki said.

"I ain't saying."

"What company does he work for?" Carelli asked.

"I ain't saying. But I am going to see him soon, and if I think he's guilty of anything I'll bring it to the attention of the proper authorities."

"You're investigating an international germ-warfare conspiracy alone?" Carelli said.

"That's right."

"I've had enough of this shit," Carelli seethed at Marki. "Let's lock him up."

"On what charges?" Nick said.

"I'll think of something, asshole."

"Incorrect," Nick said, rising to his feet. "There may be something going on here, with Barlow, and there may not be. But if you want to get to the bottom of it, I'm your only option. . ."

Carelli's punch to Nick's solar plexus was not unexpected, but it still hurt. The wind went out of him, pain shot up his spine, and the periphery of his visual field momentarily went black.

"You don't tell *me* what my options are," Carelli said. "I tell *you* what *your* options are."

Marki, impassive, looked on as Nick collapsed in the chair.

"Look, guys," Nick panted. "If I was a murderer, I never would have come back here, and I certainly wouldn't have handed over the diskette. You can lock me up, but you can't hold me long. And furthermore you will totally, completely piss me off, and there goes your best witness. Your own autopsy said Barlow died from a pill. Are you going to tell a jury I shoved it down his throat?"

"You could have injected something in his leg without him noticing it. Even good pathologists could miss something like that," Marki said. "The pill could have masked it."

"Then exhume his body and take another look. But if you think I'm hanging around for that one, guess again. Now, I repeat, I am leaving here in two minutes. I have given you the diskette, and I have told you the truth about my brother. Let me go and we all remain on the same team. Hold me against my will and I shut up, and that old *Habeas Corpus* clock starts ticking."

Carelli looked like he was going to hit him again, but Marki appeared to be it thinking over.

"OK," Marki said. "Two minutes. But they have to be two good minutes."

Nick nodded.

"First thing, asshole," Carelli said. "Forget doing a James Bond on your broth-er. We'll work that through Interpol."

"Sergeant Carelli, do you read the newspaper?" Nick said.

"What's your point?"

"Have you noticed the big stink over Swiss banks aiding and abetting Nazis? Safe-deposit boxes full of wedding rings and gold from teeth fillings?"

"So?"

"Do you *know* what the state religion is in Switzerland?"

"What?"

"Secrecy! They are *not* going to help you find somebody who will implicate their drug companies in germ warfare. Their tourism industry depends on images of quaint watchmakers and honest herdsmen, and their financial industry is based on keeping their yaps shut. They're worried enough about the Nazi fallout without copping to nerve gas. I repeat: I'm your only option."

"And I repeat. . ." Carelli said, his fist forming.

"Back off, Jake," Marki said.

"Yeah, back off, Rudolph," Nick said. "I'm leaving."

"Not so fast," Marki said. "You still owe me one minute."

"OK," Nick said, glancing at his watch.

Marki said, "Do you really think it's possible you were set up?"

Nick didn't have any problem answering this question truthfully.

"Yes, I can imagine that I was steered into that empty seat in order to freak Barlow out. Do I think that's what really happened? No."

"Why would your brother have set you up?"

"Because," Nick said. He reminded himself to take a big dramatic pause for emphasis.

"I stole and subsequently married his girlfriend. That was six years ago and we haven't spoken since. I think he's still angry."

Marki took a few moments to digest what Nick had told him.

"You haven't seen your brother in six years. He's mad because you married his girlfriend. You think maybe he's giving biological weapons to Iraq. You think maybe he murdered Barlow."

"Or at least set me up," Nick clarified.

"But you just told us you're going to go see him."

"Yes."

"Why? Why now? If I were you I'd keep the hell away."

"He left a message on my answering machine two days ago. He said he would be in California for the Biodigital Forum, and maybe we could get together."

"What's the Forum?"

"It's a conference. I just happens that I was planning to go there for my job anyway."

"Last time we spoke you didn't have a job."

"I do now."

"Doing what?"

"Market research. A fellow named Carl Swirsing. Want to see my card?"

It was a good thing Marki said no, because Nick didn't have a business card. He didn't even officially have a job with Carl until he sent him back the hundred dollar bill.

Nick was still shaking from the encounter when he handed his boarding pass to the agent at the gate. He didn't begin to relax until the plane was in the air. Now, as he glanced down at the snow-covered Sierras, Nick wondered if he had overdone the wise-ass routine. Maybe. But overall he was happy with his performance. The key thing had been to convince the police that he was cooperating with them, however reluctantly. That way, he hoped, when they didn't find Barlow's fingerprints on the diskette they wouldn't be too suspicious.

The question was, how long would it take them to crack Nick's forgery?, Pretty Good Privacy was, in fact, pretty good. But only pretty good. Depending on how aggressively the computer science people pursued the task, Nick's substitute might never get broken. On the other hand the chances were also pretty good that there would be police waiting for him at the gate when he landed in San Francisco.

If the Salt Lake City Airport Police *did* decrypt the bogus disk that Nick had so solemnly handed over, he hoped that Marki, at least, would get a chuckle from Nick's choices off the discount-bin CD, 'Disco Greats of the 70's.'

'Data1' was the Three Degrees, singing 'When Will I See You Again?'

'Data2' was the Bee Gees: 'Staying Alive.'

Chapter 32

Nick Aubrey sat at the Tied House, in Sunnyvale, waiting for his brother to show up.

They had both, in their own ways, loved the same woman. They had both lost her. Today that didn't matter. All that mattered was Nick was going to get a chance to size his brother up. Was he still the good kid Nick remembered, or had he become the kind of man who could have inflicted Gulf War Disease on a hundred thousand soldiers?

There had never been acrimony between the brothers, only awkwardness. But in point of fact, in terms of the contact between Paul and Nick, the last ten years hadn't been substantially different from the ten years before them. Back in Oneonta, Paul had been a child with a Tonka tractor when Nick had been a muscled teen with forty real acres to plow after school. Nick had been finishing college when Paul was just starting high school. Nick worked in France for a year, then three years in French-speaking West Africa while Paul was showing his high-school teachers the experiments he had learned at the Johns Hopkins summer program.

Their paths diverged again when Nick spent a year at home to let his aging mother get reacquainted with him. (Their father had died while Nick was working on an OXFAM project a hundred miles out of Timbucktu.) Paul went off to Purdue, for molecular biology. When Mother took ill Paul transferred back to the local branch of the state university—that was where he had met Bartlett, at SUNY. He had still been there during the year Nick spent at the Agricultural station in Brazil, the year that Mother died. Selling the farm had taken care of the medical bills and two sets of college tuition—there had been nothing more to talk about. Nick's marriage to Bartlett was all it had taken to push them into entirely separate worlds.

When Nick thought of his brother he could remember little: the toy tractor, the smile, and his fiddle playing. Paul had picked up the violin when he was five, and it had been clear he had "the gift." That was what Nick remembered about Paul. That, and the business with Bartlett.

Paul had said the back terrace, 4 PM. Nick got there at 4:10 and found the terrace empty. He went inside to the beerhall and ordered a pint of dark. This time let's stay a little bit sober, Nick, he reminded himself. He went back to an empty bench near some bougainvillea bushes, and waited. Paul showed up at 4:30. He was wearing a summer suit, the tie off. He looked great.

"I'm glad you called," Nick said. "It's good to see you. How are you?"

"That's a complicated question, really," Paul said.

It sure is, Nick thought but didn't say. *What were you doing in Gordon Biersh on the night Barlow killed himself?* His flash of recognition over the Wasatch range had been correct. Paul had seen him in Gordon Biersh, but left without saying hello. Why?

Nick looked toward Mission Peak across the bay, waiting for Paul to say more. There wasn't much of a view from the back terrace of the Tied House: a parking lot, and beyond that the tracks of Cal-Trans, where a double-decker commuter train was zooming towards San Francisco, half an hour north. Another train passed; this one heading south, to San Jose. Finally Paul spoke.

"There's something I need to ask you."

"Shoot."

"Have you ever heard of the Association for Responsible Biotechnology?"

Nick thought a moment.

"Nope."

"Here, look at this," Paul said. He reached inside his pocket and withdrew an envelope. He opened it and took out a piece of paper, a quadrille style that Nick remembered from his years in France and Africa. The penmanship was flamboyant, drifting carelessly over the page, and clearly European.

14 february, basel
i believe that my work as a scientist poses a grave threat to the human race i believe that my partners are madmen our tiny machines will change man into woman woman into man health into disease there is no control over us there should be an international commission to supervise us and it should be headed by
tonight i am with an asshole an asshole who thinks he knows

everything his name is vannevar engleton
i need to start my life over again away from these monsters
i am in love with that trojan woman with the big tits

There was an unreadable signature.

Nick felt as if he had seen a ghost. It was only hours ago in his hotel room that he had read the Vannevar Bush article in the nearly fifty year-old Atlantic. He had never heard that name, Vannevar, anywhere else. The only person he knew of named Engleton was Thomas Engleton, the computer visionary. They were the names that Casey associated with the New Gospel—and that Nick associated with "Orson" and Peter Barlow. And the person Nick thought of, inevitably, whenever he thought of any of these names, was Monty Meekman.

"What is it?" Nick said, passing the note back to his brother.

"I wish I knew," Paul said.

"What do you mean? Who wrote it?"

"It was written by a fellow I knew. A Swiss guy named Dieter Steffen. He was found dead last week with a bullet in his head and a gun in his hand. This note was next to him."

"Jesus," Nick said. "Was he a friend of yours?"

"I didn't know him well. He was a scientist, and he was working on some scary technology. I'm kind of involved with it myself. It worried him a lot, and he came to me to talk about it."

"'Our tiny machines will change women into men'? Sound like this guy was wigged out."

"His imagination was kind of running away with him."

"So he killed himself. Christ. That's rough."

"*If* he killed himself," Paul said.

"What do you mean?"

"Well, some things don't sit right with me. I don't know. Some things just aren't right."

"Like what?" Nick said.

"First of all, from what I can find out he hardly ever drank. But his blood alcohol was three times drunk that night."

"Maybe that explains it." Nick said.

"Maybe. Maybe somebody was egging him on. But here's another thing. The gun had a silencer. Why use a silencer to kill yourself? He's not the kind of guy who would have known where to get a gun, much less a silencer. And he never pulled a waafenschein, gun permit."

"I thought the Swiss all had guns. Aren't all men on call for the militia or something?"

"Most Swiss men do keep their army rifles in the house—kind of a ready reserve. But Dieter never served; he had some kind of medical exemption. And this was no military gun anyway. It was a custom Glock automatic with no serial number. A hit-man's weapon."

"What else?"

"The note. Who is it for? Why is it in English?"

"It's competent English," Nick said. "Wacky, but competent."

"Oh sure, he was fluent. That's not the point. His first language was German, second French. Why was the note in English? Who was supposed to read it? But what mostly bothers me is it doesn't read like a suicide note. I saw this guy that very afternoon. He was not suicidal."

"Go on."

Paul took a deep breath.

"There were four of us in a secret laboratory that day. I want to tell you about this lab, man. They have this lock on it, right? It's programmed to read your DNA by sucking blood out of your hand and matching it to a data-bank. You are not going to fool this machine with a fake fingerprint or dummy retina. It wants your blood."

"No shit."

"*Sans blague.*"

"Sounds like they mean business about keeping people out."

"Two of the people with me that day—Dieter and a guy named Kurt Alder—thought the experiments were unethical and should be stopped. Both of them were dead within twelve hours."

"God, Paul, now you're giving me the shivers. What happened to the other guy who died?

"Cut in half by a trolley in downtown Basel. Rush hour. No witnesses."

Nick drank flagged a passing waitress, holding up his fingers for two more.

"Both deaths were ruled suicides within thirty-six hours and the bodies were cremated."

"That's not that bizarre.. ."

"Dieter had no family. The cremation order was allegedly signed by Rolf Steffen, who was listed as an uncle."

"Should I know that name?"

"Vice chairman of Hoff-Zeigy AG. The third-richest man in the world. According to Forbes Magazine he's worth *seven, billion, dollars.* That's seventy times a hundred million dollars."

"Whoa. And this murdered guy, Dieter, was in line for it?"

"That's what I'd like to know. The official story is: same last name, no relation."

"Not a nephew?"

"No. And Rolf Steffen claims that he did not sign the cremation order."

"Creepy," Nick said. "How did you wind up with Dieter's note?"

Paul laughed, nervously. As Nick had laughed when lying to the police. "Dig this, man. You know that jillionaire? Rolf Steffen?"

"Yeah."

"He came to my office last week. Guess why?"

"I give up."

"Bluegrass, man. Bluegrass, can you believe it? Guitar, mandolin, but especially banjo. Five-string clawhammer banjo. He's really good, too."

"What do you mean?"

"What do you do if you're the richest man in Europe and your hobby is playing American bluegrass? You can't go clubbing; you've got to have the damn bodyguards with you all the time. So you find players and invite them into your private band, play in your goddamn chateau. I'm still the best bluegrass fiddler in Basel, but I hardly ever play so very few people know. Last week I got the nod, invited to join the Rhine River Rounders. Two days ago I was at his chateau; we played for three hours. He even does gigs sometimes, incognito. Calls himself Bob Smith, wears a false beard. But you gotta swear in blood not to give up his secret if you want to play with him."

"His secret is safe with me."

"He gave me Dieter's note. The police had given it to him; you see, they thought he was related. He's the one who told me about the falsified cremation order."

"Does he plan to do anything about it?"

"I don't know. He's a pretty inscrutable guy. His name came up in the BCCI business."

"I'm sorry?"

"Bank of Credit and Commerce International? Clark Clifford and those Pakistani guys doing a thirty billion dollar operation for criminals, terrorists, and the CIA. Ollie North territory."

"But why did he give the note to you?"

"Dieter was really private, didn't have many friends. And his co-worker seemed very anxious to get the note, which bothered the old man. This other scientist, I got to tell you, he's a weirdo. I stay out of his way. Steffen figured I was as close to Dieter as anybody, so he gave the note to me, asked me to hold onto it for a little while to see if any theories presented themselves to me. I'm supposed to give it back to him at the next Rhine River Rounders rehearsal."

"What theory have you come up with?"

"I can't pull it together; I'm missing pieces of the puzzle. But I don't think he killed himself. Anyway, on the night Dieter died, I was supposed to go to dinner with him and the other guy from the secret lab. But I canceled because I got the message that Bartlett was going to call."

"And?"

"She did call. It was pretty late. She wanted to meet with me. Some questions about the Gulf War, and something else. Nick, I hadn't spoken with her since before you two got married. So at the time I didn't say yes or no. I wanted to think about it."

What else had Bartlett wanted to talk about?

"It was pretty late by the time Bartlett and I stopped talking. I was off the phone for about a second when Rolf Steffen called. He wanted me to come over to practice, and he sent a limo to pick me up. When we got done practicing I went downtown—I figured I'd see if the dinner was still going on. I got there just in time to see a man and a woman helping Dieter into a cab. Dieter was obviously really drunk. None of them saw me, so I kind of dipped back into the shadows."

"And?"

"The police report said that Dieter had dinner with this other scientist, alone. No other man, no other woman."

"So?"

"I saw the man get in the cab with him."

"Christ."

"Who the hell is Vannevar Engleton?" Paul said. "Whoever he is, I think he killed Dieter."

Nick drank from a new pint. He had an idea who Vannevar Engleton was, but he decided not to say anything. Not yet, anyway.

"Did you get a look at him, the guy who got in the cab?" he said.

"I think I would recognize him if I saw him again," Paul said. "Here comes some more freaky stuff. Three of us from the laboratory had gone over into France that afternoon, a little drive in the country. We stopped at a café. There was a woman there who kept staring at me. I saw her today in Stacey's bookstore, in Palo Alto. Don't ask me if I'm sure; I'm absolutely certain."

"What's she look like?"

"Young, blonde, and very pretty. I was getting freaked out, you know? Kurt's dead, Dieter's dead, this woman is following me from France to Palo Alto—"

"It would freak *me* out."

"—So I called up this Judith Knight. She founded that group I mentioned, the Association for Responsible Biotechnology. Do you know what she told me?"

"What?"

"She told me A, that Dieter Steffen had been in touch with her. Dieter had called her that very day, before he got killed; B, that my life was probably in danger and that she could tell me more if we could meet in person, preferably in Colorado, where she works, and C, she was willing to meet me anywhere but the Silicon Valley. She said that there were dangerous people here who would recognize her, and it wouldn't be safe for me to be seen with her."

"Are you scared?"

"Paranoid is more like it. I even went out and bought a gun in a fit of panic. The next day I felt like an idiot, of course, and stuck it in the back of my closet."

"Do you think Dieter could have been bumped off because he actually did stand in line to inherit the dough? Could the old man have had him rubbed out, and invited you to play your fiddle with him to keep you out of the way for a few hours?"

"I thought of that too. But then why did he let me go home in time to witness the guy getting in the car with Dieter?"

"Who else stands in line to inherit Steffen's billions?"

"There are rumors, that's all. An ex-wife, a sister, a sister's child. . . will-o-the-wisps. . ."

Nick would add that to his ever-growing list of unanswered questions. There was one more for that list. He looked again at the note.

"Who, dare I ask, is the Trojan woman with the big tits?"

"Nicholas, you are going to love this. Remember that article Bartlett presented at Cold Spring on the Trojan gene? Dieter saw her, and was evidently smitten. The Trojan woman with the big tits is your wife, your ever loving wife. Seems like the three of us had that much in common. Me, you, and poor dead Dieter Steffen. Three suckers for Dr. Bartlett McGovern, Ph.D."

Nick made up his mind. If Paul was a terrorist he was a better actor. No, Paul was as baffled as Nick was. But maybe by working together they could get to the bottom of things.

"Well then," Nick said. "It would seem a toast is in order." He picked up his half-filled beer glass, and stood. Paul did likewise.

"To our fallen comrade," Nick said.

"To our fallen comrade," Paul answered.

They each took a drink, then poured the rest of contents of their glasses in the bushes.

"Nick, you gotta promise," Paul said, as they resumed their seats. "If anything happens to me, you've got to go to that lab in Basel and find out what the hell is going on."

"Brother, you're on," Nick said.

He put out his right hand to shake, Paul did too, and instinctively Nick grabbed his brother's forearm instead of his hand—the Indian handshake that they had used so many years before on the farm in Oneonta: big brother, little brother, mingling the blood they had loosed from cuts in their wrists made with Nick's pocket knife at their campsite at the bend in the creek. Nick thought a second, then decided: blood brothers. Maceo didn't want to help with this anyway.

"Here," Nick said. "I've got one for you."

He reached in his shirt pocket for Barlow's diskette, placed it on the table 'Matthew' side up and slid it to Paul.

"You're a smart boy, see if you can figure this one out. UNIX readable. It wants a password a hundred and sixty characters long. Once you figure out what it is you have fifty-three seconds to type it in. Your clue is a five-digit number."

He turned over a cardboard coaster and wrote '93233'.

"Hey," Paul laughed. "What's this all about?"

"If you can crack it, you get to tell me," Nick said.

"Tell you what. I'll stick it in my fiddle case and see if it picks up any vibrations."

"You bring your fiddle with you on business trips? You really are a fanatic."

"I'm not sure I'm going back. I may get dead there. I've been thinking of going back to Oneonta. But Bartlett. . ." He seemed to change his mind about whatever he was going to say.

"Bartlett what?"

"She said she said she was going to go back to Oneonta for a visit, to clear her head. That town's only so big, so maybe I better stay away."

"It is a rather small town."

"Let's you and I talk some more," Paul said. "But first I gotta pee, I'll be back."

Paul looked briefly at the diskette, then put it in his pocket. Was there a hint of a smile? Enough of a smile to give Nick second thoughts. He grabbed Paul's jacket by the sleeve. "Why are you really here, in the Silicon Valley?"

Paul looked perplexed.

"I told you. The Biodigital Forum. It starts in a few days."

"Why did you come early?"

"I was hoping to catch you," Paul said.

Nick released the sleeve, and Paul walked towards the interior, where the men's room was located. Ten minutes later Maceo showed up. Paul had not come back from the Men's room. Nick went to the men's room himself; there was no sign of his brother. Then he scoured the main hall, and stepped outside onto Villa street. There was no sign of Paul Aubrey. They boy had simply vanished. Nick walked back to the terrace, where, with a trembling hand he picked up the glass of beer that Maceo placed before him.

"You better drink up," Maceo said. "I have got some scary shit to tell you."

Chapter 33

Nick knew that everything Maceo was about to say would be at least as scary as advertised, but his friend's almost comical appearance softened the impact. Maceo

Burr—polemicist, loud-talker, kernel hacker, author, anarchist, and tweaker-of-noses to the highly-placed—still looked like a hippie version of Vlad the Impaler: pale white skin and razor-thin lips set off by the tackiest of hippie fashion accouterments—the vest, the extra wide watchband.

"Where's your brother at?" Maceo said. "I thought you were going to introduce me."

"Maybe he got sick. He was real tired and he put down a bunch of beer."

"Just as well. Dangerous waters, *hombre*. Wacky shit goin' down with this Gulf War stuff."

"Like the fact that our boys blew up some Sarin at Kasimiyah? That's not so scary."

"I guess you've noticed the CIA and Pentagon trying to cover that up?"

"A Pentagon-CIA coverup isn't scary. It's what you'd expect."

"The scary thing is not the coverup. The scary thing is that the CIA and Pentagon are advertising it."

"They *want* us to think there's a coverup?"

"Remember when that Japanese cult put Sarin in the Tokyo subway? Not one subway symptom matches Gulf War Syndrome. For that matter, Gulf War symptoms don't match any known chemical *or* biological agent."

"Maybe there's no such thing as Gulf War Syndrome. Maybe it's psychosomatic."

"Then why are the Pentagon and CIA working so hard to make it look like it's real? They're practically putting up billboards saying our guys got exposed to nerve gas. Why don't they stick to the line that there's no such thing as Gulf War Syndrome?"

"You tell me."

"Somebody wants us to believe that Gulf War Syndrome was caused by Sarin nerve gas at the Kasimiyah ammo dump that our ordnance disposal guys blew up after the truce."

"Why?" Nick asked.

"So they can put together an Agent-Orange type settlement and get everybody to shut up."

"Throw a few million dollars at the veterans and get them to go away?"

"It worked once, it could work again."

"So what's really going on? What really caused the symptoms?"

"I don't know," Maceo said. "But during the Iran-Iraq war in the nineteen-eighties we gave all kinds of help to Baghdad. William Casey was tight with BCCI, and BCCI was tight with Hussein. When Ronnie Raygun was around, the CIA and Saddam were good buddies. What if the Company happened to have passed Saddam some biologicals? After all, Ollie North gave missiles to the Iranians. Maybe somebody else gave biologicals to Iraq. What if Saddam was checking them out for us? What if Saddam then decided to use them *against* us? I'm sure that the Company would rather pay off veterans with bogus symptoms than deal with that the possibility of that revelation. Remember who was CIA director when Saddam was consolidating his power?"

"Who?"

"George Bush."

A pitcher came and Nick rapidly filled and drank his glass.

"What are you saying? That the Iran-Iraq conflict was used as a proxy by the United States government to test out biological weapons?"

"That's one hypothesis."

"A paranoid hypothesis."

"It wouldn't be the first time we used people of color as test subjects. Atomic tests in Micronesia. The Tuskegee syphilis study. Radiation tests on people with retardation in the state schools. MK-Ultra and LSD secretly tested on soldiers. Some people think AIDS came from a government project that went wrong. Some people say it's part of a plot to wipe out black people."

"What do they say about Cystic Fibrosis? A plot to wipe out Swedes?"

"Hey, who knows, man. People believe all kinds of wacky shit. But some of it may be true. My advice to you is to duck and stay ducked. This will blow over and nobody will remember your chance encounter with the late Mr. Barlow."

"I have to find out what's on that diskette."

"Why?"

"Todd Griffith. What that bullet did to him, it would break your heart. I owe it to him."

"What, now Barlow is tied to Griffith?"

"Long story."

"With all proper respect brother, that boy Griffith is not coming back. I thought you were going to give that diskette to the police."

"I gave them a fake. I took your algorithm and cobbled up a dummy."

Maceo gave him the sidelong glance he used to express disbelief bordering on contempt.

"Nick, you are dicking around with some very serious people."

"What I can't figure out is, why did Barlow make his diskette so hard to read? If he had proof of something, you would think he would have broadcast it, not kept it so damn secret."

"He probably wanted to keep it tamper-proof until he was ready to make it public. He got burned once before by public disclosure of things he couldn't prove."

"I'm damn well going to make it public, once I figure out what's on it. I'm not giving it to no CIA. And I'm not giving it to the True Patriots of the Natural Law neither."

Maceo spit out a mouthful of beer.

"*True Patriots?* Why do you mention them?"

"The True Patriots and I are kind of engaged in a little vendetta. They ransacked my house and hosed my system, so I fucked up their web site. They want Barlow's diskette too."

"You're fucking with the True Patriots? Do you know who those people *are*?"

"On the Internet, nobody knows if you're a dog."

"Those people are number three, Nick, number *three* on the Klanwatch hit parade. Jesus God. Serious military training, serious weapons, serious paranoia. The kind of people who would blow up a building full of people, only *these* guys wouldn't get caught. They have serious hacker skills. If you piss these people off you'd better make friends with Salman Rushdie, because you're going to live your life hiding from fanatics. The CIA and the True Patriots are like two mob families going after each other. Get out of the crossfire."

"They'll leave me alone eventually. I'm small potatoes."

"You have something they want, Nick, and they will make you give it to them. They may trick you with sex. Or they may use blackmail. They'll probably just kill you. You cannot handle these people, Nick. Take it from one who has tried and barely lived to tell the tale. Do you know what you should do?"

"What?"

"Call a press conference and bring a computer. Run Barlow's diskette until it blows up. Then they'll know that you don't have it anymore and that you never were able to read it. And bring along some kind of fingerprint expert to confirm that Barlow's prints are on it, so nobody thinks you pulled another fast one. You are playing with fire, Nick. Put it out while you can."

"Good plan," Nick said. "Only one problem."

"What's that?"

"I don't know where the diskette is. I gave it to somebody I trusted, who has vanished."

Maceo exhaled, long and deep.

"God have mercy on you, Nick." he said. "You have to go underground. I can get you fake papers."

"It's not that bad."

"Let's hope not," Maceo said.

Yes, Nick thought, let's hope not. But where was Paul? It had been nearly twenty minutes. Nick tried to convince himself that nothing was wrong, but it wasn't working. In his heart of hearts he knew that something bad was happening someplace. Something very bad.

"Let me ask you something else," Maceo said. "You still hanging out with Swirsing?"

"I'm not going to answer you without my lawyer present."

"Oh, man," Maceo said. "Engineering can *never* trust marketing, baby. You know that. I'm telling you Nick, the word on this guy ain't good. He's *el mysterioso*. Has he hooked you up with a girlfriend yet?"

"I'm married."

"Keep it that way."

"I'm going to my hotel," Nick said. "If my brother comes back, tell him where I went."

"Later," Maceo said. "Remember, if you get your hands on that disk, give it up. And duck."

Nick stood up and headed into the main building. First, the head. Then he would cut through the large beerhall and come out onto Villa street. The rented Thunderbird was on Castro, but he didn't want to drive it. Despite his good intentions, he had gotten drunk. *Hell's bells, wouldn't you?* The thought was addressed to nobody in particular. Well, it was only two miles to the hotel. No problem, he would walk, come back for the car tomorrow. Maybe that would give him time to sort out the paranoid questions threatening to drive sanity and common sense from his head. Nick had to get back on an even keel or he would end up as crazy as the guy on Flight 44 who thought he was in the CIA.

Nick, come on, he said to himself. Get a grip. Come up with a plan.

OK, here's the plan, he answered himself: Walk back to the hotel. Throw cold water on your face. Take off your clothes. Lie down on the bed. Remember Bartlett, that night in the store. Jerk off. Put ESPN on the television, and go to sleep.

It was a good plan. He was happy with it. He strode into the main hall; in a minute he would be on the street. Then he saw them.

Too late; they had seen him, he was being summoned. He had to go over and say hello.

Nick had heard that Scott sometimes hit the Tied House with an entourage. Once outside the executive offices, where he was a shark, he played the multi-millionaire bachelor playboy to the hilt. Somehow it never occurred to Nick that one day their paths might cross outside of work. But even so, it should have been easy to walk on by.

Yes, he might have ignored Scott Beckworth, President and Chairman of Digital MicroSystems, and Jim Bates, Founder and VP of Technology, Corporate Fellow numero-uno, the man who lived on top of a mountain in Aspen, Colorado, leading the espresso architecture team. Nick certainly would have ignored Monty Meekman and Jim Boerr, the boyish VC Vulture—they were making a show of ignoring him. And Nick had no reason to say hello to the six or seven women that Nick did not recognize, variations on a simple theme: young, gorgeous. So under normal circumstances he would have cast his eyes away and done a Snagglepuss, *Exit, stage right.*

But how could he ignore Carl Swirsing, the man Nick had flown out expressly to see, the man who had finagled for Nick the hardest ticket in all California? How indeed, when Carl was standing up and calling Nick's name so loudly that half the beer hall turned to see who was there?

Carl did, however, keep it short. There were no handshakes, no small talk. Carl simply introduced Nick to the party as a new market researcher on his staff, and announced that the two of them, Nick and Carl, would be representing CyberFlow at the Biodigital Forum in Saratoga three days from then. The confident arm that Carl threw around Nick's shoulder carried a very unambiguous message to nod, keep his mouth shut, and scram. Thirty seconds later Nick was on the street.

The walk back to the hotel was five miles, not two, and when he got back to his suite the phone light was on. The message was from Casey, at 6:07 PM. "Sorry to bother you, dude, but I need you to come back to Massachusetts, as quick as you can. I've got a lead that I can't follow up without you. I'll answer questions when you get here. Let me know your flight, I'll pick you up."

Chapter 34

Nick stepped off the plane at Logan, bought a cup of sludge at the first concession he came to, and proceeded to the baggage area, where Casey had promised to meet him. She wasn't there.

Businessmen and -women jockeyed for pole position at the carousel, grabbed their bags, and hurried off. Husbands met wives, college kids met friends with joyous hugs. A purple-haired teenaged boy in a sleeveless blue-jean jacket leaned against a pillar under a "thank you for not smoking" sign smoking a Pall Mall. Toddlers approached the moving belt and were rescued by older siblings; foreign-looking men grabbed cardboard boxes baled in twine and labeled in exotic script. Every stock figure from every airport scene ever filmed was there. But no Casey.

"Damn it," Nick said. "I do not need this."

Gradually the crowd thinned. It was down to just Nick and Mr. purple-hair. Now the kid was walking towards him, deliberately, and with a decidedly unfriendly look about him. Nick hoped it wasn't some kind of hustle, or worse. He felt his muscles tensing. The kid got closer, and as he did he began to look less intimidating, more lost, and yet somehow familiar. . .

"Hello, stranger," the purple-haired kid said.

Neither of them said a word during the ride out of the airport proper, nor as she drove through the Sumner Tunnel, then out and past the Boston Gardens and across the bridge. Ten minutes out of Charlestown the traffic thinned and she reached in the back seat and threw a few magazines on his lap. *Mandate, Out, Queer Times.* "Here, study these," she said.

With her short purple hair and a snake tattoo on her right shoulder she looked as inscrutable as ever. Maintaining the scowl had evidently been hard work: she had reverted to her habitual look of ironic detachment. As they made their way through Route 16 in Medford, Nick decided to give up the waiting game. He wanted to know what was up, and it was clear that she wasn't going to volunteer anything.

"OK Casey, where are we going?" he said.

"*Will.* My name is *Will,*" she said. Her voice seemed deeper than ever, but she was laying on a thick affectation. With limp wrists, she lit another Pall Mall.

"OK, Will," Nick said, "where are we going?"

"We're going to my house. I'm going to cut your hair and do you over. You're coming out of the closet tonight Nick. Or should I say, *Billy?*"

"Casey, will you please tell me what is going on?" he said.

"Will," she said. "The name is Will."

"Fine. *Will.* Halloween was *last October,* Will, remember? And my mom says I'm too old to dress up anyway, so, like, would you *please* tell me what the fuck is going on, Will, before I like get really testy?"

"I'll tell you in a minute. OK? I just cut off my hair, which was the last thing even *remotely* attractive about me, so a little consideration would be in order, don't you think?"

"What in the hell does that have to do with me? I didn't ask you to cut off your hair. What did you go and cut off your hair for? I *liked* your hair."

"Oh Billy you are a bitch," she said. "You are a total bitch."

Nick thought noticed a tear forming in her eye as she entered Route 2 West from the Alewife interchange. They rode the rest of the way in silence. In Newcastle she parked the Sentra

in front of the bridge at the main entrance to the Mill. When she spoke this time it was as Casey, not Will, without any affectation of her voice.

"Tonight I need you to act as if you're a gay guy, flamboyantly gay. I'm going to try to pass for a gay guy too. I want to make you over for the role—cut your hair, dress you up—and I want you to stay in character until you get back to California. If you don't want to play you can get out here. The Newcastle Hotel awaits."

What was he going to say? That there was a limit? But there was no limit.

"Drive on, Will," he said.

From Casey's he checked his voice mail. There was one message, from Paul.

"They told me you checked out of your hotel. I wonder if you'll get this. I spoke again to Judith Knight. Brother, I am living in the twilight zone. I don't want to go back to Switzerland right now. I've got something for you but I don't know where you are. Give me a call, will you?"

Yes, brother, Nick thought. Yes, I will be glad to give you a call. *Where the hell are you?* How about a phone number? How about a state? OK, a *country?* He would have to ask Judith Knight, of Someplace, Colorado. He tried directory assistance for all the Colorado cities he could think of. Denver? Boulder? Colorado Springs? Pueblo, Grand Junction, Aspen? No listing for Judith Knight in any of them. Damn! Maybe he could figure out a way to find Paul while Casey did his makeover.

Ten minutes later he was sitting in Casey's kitchen with his shirt off and a towel over his shoulders. She had just finished washing his hair and now she was drying it with a second towel, firmly tousling from the back of his neck to his forehead. Would she bite his ear this time too?

"You know, Will," he said, "'Casey' can be just as fine a name for a man as for a woman. Why do you need to be 'Will?'"

"Well the thing of it is, Billy? I have such a precarious hold on the Casey persona that I would just *die* if I fucked her up. You know? I mean, she's all I have?"

As she was saying this she was organizing her supplies on the kitchen table to his right: stainless barber's scissors, combs, hair gel, and a makeup bag.

"You remember the last time when we were in the shrine, right?" she said. "I was looking at the etch plot for the Kali chip, and you said 'I wonder if Todd kept any work logs,' and you know, he did, I remembered. So I asked myself, 'Where would they be?'"

She folded a magazine back to a picture of a muscular man with a pencil moustache and slicked-back hair and placed it on the table. Save for the scarf around his neck, he was naked.

"Oh darling, now *that's* technology," Will said.

"Tell me about the notebooks."

"Oh, all right," she said. "Where would they be, those notebooks? Well, Susan would know, Todd's sister? And you know what, she did know. Guess what— you'll die. Do you give up?"

"Yes."

"Last year she got a call from John. Do you remember John?"

"John who?" he said. She was combing his hair now, massaging his scalp from time to time.

"John, you know. I forget his last name. And Richard. John and Richard? You remember?"

"No," he said.

"They lived in the big house, Todd's house. Actually they own it. Do you remember now?"

"Vaguely."

"Well, ever since Todd got shot there they were kind of creeped out, you know? I mean, who wouldn't be? I know I would be? And they came to realize that the house was haunted! Haunted, can you believe it! Well it had to be Todd who was haunting them, of course. And they loved him, but he was driving them crazy. So guess what, you'll die."

She began to cut his hair, one small snip at a time. Nick slipped into a kind of languor as a pleasing gooseflesh developed on his legs and forearms.

"They had some parapsychologists in for a seance, to find out what Todd wanted. He said he was looking something, and he needed his room back just the way it had been before. He was looking for a horse! So! They put his room back together just the way it was on the night he got killed! You see, they loved him too. Now he's got two shrines."

"Christ," Nick said.

"These guys, John and Richard, they're about as queer as an eighteen dollar bill. And so were the parapsychologists who did the seance for them. Do you know what they told them? No more women or straights in the house! None! The ghostbusters accidentally woke up another spirit there when they were looking for Todd, a real trouble-maker. He was lynched for being a fag a hundred and fifty years ago! And he told them that if he ever saw anybody in the house that wasn't one hundred percent gay he was going to *poltergeist* them!

"And Billy, I have a friend who knows somebody who knows John and Richard, and they arranged for you and me to go over there for dinner tonight, at 8 PM. We told them that you're this great paranormal guy from California who heard about their place and you want to go check it out. After dinner, Billy and Will—that's you and me— we're going to spend the night in Todd's room! I've just got wear something so they don't think I have tits. I swear, sometimes I think I almost think I look like a *girl*."

At 8:05 they pulled up to the house on Edgell Street, and it *did* look haunted— Nick wondered if any children were brave enough to ring the doorbell on Halloween. He touched his mascara pencil moustache, then the silk foulard around his neck.

"This is never going to work," he said to Casey as they walked up to the front door.

"Oh hush!" she said. Her voice was noticeably raspier and deeper than usual; the cigarettes and the screaming had worked, at the cost of ringing ears and smelly clothes.

The enormous oaken door opened, and Nick and Casey were met by two men dressed in identical silk robes. The only way that Nick could tell the men apart was that John was clean-shaven, and Richard had an impeccably manicured Van Dyke goatee. The guests were escorted into the living room, which was dark and draped with heavy brocade. Nick sat next to Casey on an ornate loveseat before the fireplace; it was so small that Casey was practically sitting in his lap. There were three crucifixes on one wall immediately above a large Bible on a stand flanked by two thigh-high ornate vases from which exuded birds-of-paradise and long ropes of lustrous pearls.

At dinner Casey did most of the talking. She explained that Billy was very, very sensitive, especially in the presence of "other dimensions." Nick didn't eat much.

After desert Richard and John told the story of the night that Todd had been killed. He seldom socialized, they said. That night Todd had come home early, around 10:00 PM, because of the snow, and went to play drums, very loudly, in the basement. Since there was no escaping the noise anyway, John and Richard, earplugs in, had gone downstairs too. They had stayed in the basement until around 1:30 A.M. It was snowing hard, so they didn't set the alarm—no point in getting up for work if the roads weren't passable. Todd played in the basement until 3:00 A.M., his usual pattern; they could hear him all the way upstairs at the other end of the house. In spite of the snowstorm that night, March 28th, he left his window open. Todd always slept with the windows open. He liked his room cold. This trait did not always endear him to the women who spent the night in his bed from time to time but on the night of his attempted murder he slept alone.

John and Richard found him at 10:00 the next morning.

Will and Billy declined the after-dinner cordial. Billy was anxious to get to Todd's room to spend the night, Will explained. He could feel *the presence*.

"My God," John said. "I can't believe you're going to go *fuck* in a room with a ghost in it."

"We've never done it any other way," she said.

When they got to the room it was decidedly eerie. Everything was strewn about in an inexact recreation of how Nick remembered it from a visit eons ago, millennia ago. It would have been hard for the untrained eye to detect whether anything was missing. Todd had been known for the orderliness of his chip designs and the disorder everywhere else around him. "Entropy," he used to say.

The bed was two mattresses stacked on the floor under an enormous jumble of paisley sheets and faded quilts. The bookshelves were made of unpainted two-by-tens, red bricks and grey cinder blocks. The boards sagged under a confusion of titles that spilled onto the floor in front of and behind the shelves: *VLSI Design. Computer Architecture: The Vax 11.* A stack of comic books: *Uneeda Comix #1, Cheech Wizard, Howard the Duck.* A photo book on New York City subway graffiti. *Meditations of St. John the Divine. Knuth's Computer Programming Volume 3: Sorting and Searching Algorithms.* An illustrated catalogue from the Persian miniatures exhibit at the Fogg Museum. Drexler's *Engines of Creation: The Coming Age of Nanotechnology.*

There was a stereo system on the floor near the foot of the bed. Tall speakers of rough plywood, with covers removed, stood on either side of the bookshelves. Surrounding the stereo were piles of vinyl records and CDs—The MC5, Gang Green. Dumptruck. The Zulus. The Mothers of Invention's *Uncle Meat,* and Miles Davis's *In Blue.* And on the turntable, disk number two, the A minor, from the unaccompanied violin partitas of Johann Sebastian Bach. Atop the dresser were Todd's keys, Digital MicroSystems employee badge, and some guitar picks. Next to the dresser sat a laundry basket of clean clothes, not folded: blue jeans, T-shirts, socks.

An African mud cloth adorned one wall—Nick had given it to him years ago— with one corner sagging down where the pushpin had come out. Thrown about the floor were several composition notebooks with mottled blue and white covers. They were found to be Kali work diaries, numbered 1 through 7, containing sketches of timing diagrams, chip geometries, programmable logic, gate arrays—jottings that might be intelligible only to another chip designer, and probably not even to him—or her.

Casey collected the notebooks, put them in order, and began to read. Nick sat on the mattresses and read *Cheech Wizard* comics. At around two in the morning she said, "Listen to this: Response from memory too fast. Too slow is fixable. Too fast means fraud.'"

She gave Nick a meaningful stare.

"And?" he said.

"Somebody was cooking Todd's data."

"He didn't say that." Nick said. But he found it hard to concentrate on the comic book he had been reading. A poem was trying to force itself into the foreground. How did it go? *I fear these things.* . . something, something, something. . .

At 4:30 AM, having discovered many more intriguing clues but nothing that shed any definitive light on the Kali mystery, Casey finished reading. She opened her overnight bag and took out seven notebooks that matched Todd's originals, and began to inscribe their covers, using Todd's as models. She soon had made a plausible set of replacements and began to place them where the originals had been.

She moved with a remarkable grace, he thought; she made the simple act of bending over and putting a notebook on the floor balletic. Despite her best efforts, he realized, to him she was still a whole lot more woman than she was boy, and he had been experiencing mild degrees of erection for most of the night. For one sleep-deprived, jetlagged instant, he even imagined he heard Todd's voice telling him "Go for it."

Her voice called him back to the waking world.

"We're on to something here, aren't we?" she said. "Tell the truth."

"Probably not," he lied.

"Bullshit. Todd found Pavel's Trojan Horse. He told Monty and Monty killed him."

Nick didn't even want to think about it anymore. If he had wanted to think about anything, it would have been about peeling off his and Casey's clothes and doing what nature intended. But he didn't even want to think about that. He wanted only to sleep and forget. He was again sitting on the edge of Todd's mattress; all he would have to do now was to lie back. Sleep would be instantaneous.

Then he felt her hand on his knee, and looked to find her sitting next to him. Oh Jesus, he thought. What would he do when he felt her tongue on his?

"Casey. . ." he said.

"Sh. . . ," she said. "Don't worry, I'm not going to rape you. Tell me what you think."

He switched his concentration from sex to death.

"Monty is perfectly capable of murder," he said. "But that doesn't mean that he shot Todd. We haven't got the first bit of evidence that he did. We have hints that maybe Todd suspected a Trojan Horse. Hardly enough to secure an arrest warrant."

"He did it, Nick," Casey said. "And I'm making a promise to the ghost that's in this room: I swear I'm going to bring down Meekman if I have to tear down this world to do it. And you are going to help me, Nick. We are *going* to get him."

"What if I don't want to help you?"

"Love, can't you see? What you want has nothing to do with it. It's fate."

"Casey," he said. His voice was soft. "Do you really think there's a ghost in this room?"

"Do you?"

"I don't know."

"I don't know either," she said. "But I'll tell you what I do know. There's a Trojan horse in the Kali chip. And if Todd didn't tell John and Richard about it, who did?"

It was a question that didn't want an answer, but he answered it anyway.

"Let's get out of here," he said. "This place gives me the screaming heebee-jeebies."

It was still completely dark outside as Casey and Nick stole out the four-foot-wide front door and quietly slipped into the Sentra. To be on the safe side Casey didn't turn over the ignition; instead she let the car roll down Edgell and left onto Elm, where, coasting at fifteen miles per hour, she turned on her headlights and popped the clutch.

"Sleep at my house," she said as the car rolled to a stop before her house.

"I'm not ready for bed," he said. Had a bigger lie ever been spoken? "I'm going back to the Mill for a little bit. There's something I have to check out. Talk to you soon."

Five minutes later he was walking through the front doors of the Mill, and shortly thereafter he was at the desk in the Void, about to check the newsgroups. But if he was too agitated to sleep he was certainly too agitated to sit still, and there was no point in even switching on the monitor. After less than a minute in the chair he was up again and walking. Somehow his feet led him to the dusty staircase. Before he knew it he was wandering over the roof of the Mill as the first faint hints of daybreak appeared.

He walked to the edge of a low wall, and there, across the way, was the Newcastle Hotel. It was still nearly pitch black outside, and it took him a few moments to locate his room. Third floor, corner of Main and First. "Be it ever so humble," he said, "there's no place like. . ."

What the hell was that?

He concentrated all his energy to his eyes, straining as deliberately as he could to make certain that he was looking at the right room. That was his room alright, and even though all the lights were off he was sure that somebody was in there. Something glimmered. A knife? A gun? A Mylar balloon? Whatever it was, it didn't belong there.

He was off and running towards the stairs, running with all his might.

"I don't know who you are, joker."

In through the window, leaving it open behind him

"I don't know who you are," he reiterated in his mind, as he flew down the stairs, hardly aware of what building he was in. "But whoever you are, I am going to kill you."

Chapter 35

Wind sprints had never been Nick's strong suit, and he could feel the sharp stitch jabbing into his side before he had even crossed Main Street. The pain was almost enough to make him pull up, but the hotel's entrance was only a hundred yards away, so instead of slowing he ran even harder. He had to get to his room before the son of a bitch who was in there left. The cold air attacked his lungs, distracting him from the pain under his lower right rib, and as he reached the door the cramp melted away. This allowed him to focus on another problem: he was about to enter a room in which a presumably nasty person was preparing a presumably nasty surprise for him. This was not the kind of person that one would want to meet bare-handed. But how was Nick supposed to arm himself?

His key fit the lock and the old heavy door opened, its magnificent hinges swinging smoothly. Above the gilded letters in the door's dark glass he caught a glimpse of his mascara'd face reflected in the dim light of a single overhead bulb.

There was a glimmer coming from around the edges of the door behind the front desk. Was Harris up, or had he again fallen asleep with the light on? Nick crossed the lobby with a few short steps, rubbing the makeup over his face as he did, and threw his shoulder into the door. It gave way without the slightest resistance and Nick found himself on the floor of a tiny room furnished with a cot, chair, and dresser. There were a few photos, but Nick hardly saw them; he was looking for something else.

Harris was waking up.

"What the . . .?"

"It's me, Aubrey." Nick slurred, unsteadily raising himself from the floor.

"Get out of my room. What time is . . ."

"Thirsty," Nick said, wobbling like a drunk in a skit. "Here's twenty bucks." He reached into his wallet and threw a bill on the floor. "Buy a case."

He grabbed the unopened bottle of Oneida Vineyard's White Zinfandel by the neck and walked quickly from the room.

Stairs or elevator? The stairs would be quieter. Up he went, two steps at a time. At the fire door on the third floor landing he stopped to catch his breath. Count to ten. One, two, three; ten.

He opened the door; the hallway was dark, illuminated only by the exit sign above his head. He tip-toed to the door to his room and was surprised to find it unlatched, open about a quarter of an inch. As he tightened his grip around the neck of the bottle in his right hand, with his left he pushed the door open another inch or so. Darkness resolved into shapes. Nick made out a man's figure leaning over the bed, with his back to the door. He pushed the door full open, ran toward the crouching figure and swung the full bottle as hard as he could.

He had expected the bottle to shatter when it hit the man's head, but it didn't.

The sensation in Nick's right hand was what he might expect from slamming a baseball bat one-handed into a brick wall. Irresistible force (bottle) meets immovable object (skull). OK, Thompson, pop quiz. What happens? As the man collapsed at Nick's feet he was pretty sure he had just killed somebody. Quickly he walked back to the door and locked it shut.

He returned to inspect his handiwork. The man was lying on his side, motionless. Nick rolled him over onto his back. Even in the dim light Nick could see that it was Detective Jake Carelli of the Salt Lake City Airport Police.

So: no international terrorist, no CIA operative; just a cop. But was he really just a cop? Or was he a dead cop? Nick kneeled and put his ear to the man's face; he could feel the breath. Good. For now, anyway, the man was alive. What had he been doing in Nick's room? To find the answer to that question Nick would need a little more light. But not too much. After all, it was well known that every thing he was about to do would be visible from the roof of the enormous old mill building opposite. He went to the bathroom and switched on the light.

The mirrored door to the medicine cabinet above the sink was open. There, amid his generic deodorant, his Tom's of Maine organic toothpaste and his industrial-sized bottle of Star Market aspirin there was a prescription bottle that hadn't been there this morning. Using a washcloth to keep his fingers off the bottle, he opened it and poured its contents in to his hand. Ten small white pills.

He put the pills back into the bottle and gingerly put the bottle in his shirt pocket.

He ran back into the bedroom; Carelli was still out cold. Nick looked down at the detective and for the first time noticed the shoulder holster. *I'll be taking that weapon, fuck you very much.* Quickly he undid the safety strap and removed the automatic. It had been decades since he had held a handgun and he did not like the feel of it at all. He walked across the room, opened the top drawer of his dresser and put it there.

He knew his Swiss Army knife was in that drawer someplace. OK, there. He pried it open while running to the bed, tore the bedspread and blanket off with one motion and began to frantically stab at the sheet that remained on the mattress. The blade kept closing on his fingers, cutting him and spilling blood. After making fifteen or twenty cuts he folded the knife, put it in his pocket and hurriedly tore the sheet, using the incisions as starting places. Within a minute he had ten or twelve strips of varying length, most of them drenched with some amount of his blood.

He rolled the detective over on his belly, pulled his hands behind his back, crossed the wrists and tied them as tightly as he could. Then he pulled him up— Carelli was muscular, and heavy— and sat him in the worn-out old chair next to the bed. Within minutes, using strips of bed sheet and Carelli's own belt, Nick had made the unconscious man fast to the chair.

Now Nick looked around the room to see what other tricks Carelli had played. If he were going to all the trouble of framing Nick, he wouldn't stop at a few pills in a medicine cabinet. There would be weapons, disguises, false passports. . . all that crap from hackneyed thrillers. He opened the leather bag on his bed; Carelli had been peering into it when Nick clobbered him. It was empty.

Nick went into the bathroom, filled a glass with water, brought it back into the bedroom and threw it in Carelli's face. There was no reaction. Oh no, another Todd? But two more glasses of water in Carelli's face and two down his pants did the trick.

"Oh, hell," Carelli said.

"Welcome to my lodgings," Nick said. "How'd you know I was staying here?"

"Fuck you."

Nick showed him the prescription bottle, holding its cap between his thumb and pinky.

"Forget your medicine?" Nick asked. "What is this, cyanide?"

"Eat a few and find out."

"Mister Carelli," Nick said. "You're not in Salt Lake City any more. Either you answer my questions or I pick up the phone and dial 911. The local constabulary can help us sort this all out."

"Fuck you."

Nick was in no mood for this John Wayne stuff.

"Give me a break, Carelli. Why don't we cut this macho shit and talk to each other?"

"Get it over with."

"Get what over with?"

"Just shoot me, asshole. I'm sick of your face."

Not this again.

"What is this, a re-run?" Nick asked. "I'm trapped on Gilligan's Island with people who keep telling me to shoot them. Get it through your head. I am *not* a killer. I am a *nerd*. I'm a former manager of software engineering with a degree in farm management. I choose one wrong seat on an airplane, and now I've got people dying on me, tailing me, calling me wherever I go. I've got cops planting murder weapons in my room! Now that I think about it, maybe I *oughta* kill you."

"Go ahead."

What a routine. Peter O'Toole and Richard Burton: King Henry and Thomas Aquinas.

Nick said, "Will no one rid me of this meddlesome cop?"

He had only two alternatives: he could either kill Carelli, or find some way to bring him around. The second approach seemed a better place to start. Despite Carelli's efforts to shake Nick off, it proved remarkably easy to gag him with a strip of torn sheet. Then Nick opened the screw-driver blade of his bloody Swiss-Army knife, went to the light switch near the hallway door and removed first the plate, then the switch. "Motherfucker," he said, as the blade hit the hot wire and sent a shock to his elbow. "I hate it when that happens."

Once again he carefully took the prescription bottle from his pocket.

"Let's have some fingerprints, shall we?" he said. He stooped down behind Carelli and managed, despite Carelli's best efforts, to get enough of the man's fingerprints for any reasonably competent forensics team to find. Nick then walked to the door and dropped the brown plastic bottle down the hole in the wall. He picked up the telephone; a few moments later he was talking to Casey Montgomery, roused from a deep sleep.

"Get a pencil," he said. "Ready?"

"Jake Carelli. C-A-R-E-L-L-I. Of the Salt Lake City Airport Police. If you don't hear from me within an hour, tell the police that I've been kidnaped by him from the Newcastle Hotel. You'll find a bottle of cyanide in the wall underneath the light switch."

He hung up and walked toward the chair that Carelli was tied to. Nick's knife was sticky with blood, so it took him a few seconds to get the blade open. Carelli's eyes widened and he began to writhe. He was trying to scream, but all that came out was a low hum.

The knife was in Nick's right hand.

"Shut up," he said, slapping the back of the man's head with his open left hand. "You are turning into a broken record."

He stooped behind the chair and began sawing away at the cloth ties that he had fashioned to hold Carelli's hands in place. In a minute the ties were cut through. As Carelli dropped his hands to his side, Nick walked to the dresser and removed the gun from the drawer.

"Where's the safety on this thing? OK. Safety off. You told me to shoot you? Well, how about *you* shoot *me* instead? Here's your chance, Sergeant. Do the world a favor!"

He grasped Carelli's right hand with his own left and slapped the gun into it. The detective seemed too stunned to move; he sat motionless in the chair, even as his fingers instinctively curled around the grip and trigger, with the gun pointed at Nick's belly. Nick sat on the bed opposite him.

"It's your gun, man," Nick said, his voice rising. "You know how to use it. Go ahead. After all, I killed Peter Barlow. I also caused the Gulf War. I'm Saddam Hussein's right hand man. I invented Gulf War Syndrome. I'm the reincarnation of Adolf Hitler. I'm, the *boogey man*! Kill me!"

The silence took long enough for Nick to wonder whether Carelli was going to take him up on his offer. Then, after an eternity, Carelli placed the gun in his lap.

"If you're not going to use that cannon," Nick said, "then put the safety back on. It makes me nervous."

Carelli did, with confusion and distrust showing in his gagged face.

Nick picked up the phone again and dialed the front desk.

"Harris? It's Aubrey again. Listen, I've got a situation up here. If you don't see me and my boyfriend walk out the front door in the next fifteen minutes, call the cops."

He hung up and looked at the detective.

"You've got three choices," Nick said. "You can shoot me, you can wait here until the cops come, or you can come with me. Do you understand?"

Carelli nodded.

"Don't shoot," Nick said. "I'm just going to take the rag out of your mouth."

In a minute the strip of sheet was out of Carelli's mouth. His hands were free, but he was still bound to the chair. Nick returned to the bed and sat in front of him.

As he sat waiting to see what Carelli would say now, Nick noticed the rosy fingers of dawn plying around the window. God, what a night. Finally, the detective spoke.

"You're not going to kill me?"

"Albert Einstein," Nick said. "Untie yourself, Jake. I'm not going to do it for you."

Carelli reached down and began to untie the bloody rags that bound his legs to the chair.

"Let me guess," Nick said. "You wanted to get a warrant sworn out against me, but your DA told you to forget it. So you decided to take matters into your own hands."

"Yeah."

"What were you going to do about not having a warrant? Start a fire?"

"Something like that."

"Jesus God. Is Marki in on this?"

"He doesn't know about it."

"And all because Crazy Peter Barlow said I worked for Hussein Kamel, and Hussein Kamel caused Gulf War Syndrome."

"Yeah."

"Well, you fucked up, Jake. I don't know what caused Gulf War Syndrome, or even if there is such a thing. A lot of scientists think there isn't."

"Fuck them," Carelli said. "I got it. And my boy too."

That was the crux of the biscuit, wasn't it? The unfairness of it all. The innocent son.

Even though Carelli had beat him up and tried to frame him for murder, Nick could forgive him. He had to, forgiveness was a matter of necessity. For if Nick was going to find a way out of this predicament with Carelli, it was going to turn on compassion, on shared experience.

"How's your boy doing?" Nick said.

"He's alright, I guess. But he's missing half that hand, and it makes me so angry. None of this was his fault, but he has to pay the price. He can't do the stuff the other kids his age can do. He's the reason I got so crazy. You don't know what it's like to see the look in his eyes. . ."

Sympathy was one thing, but Nick wasn't going to listen to this crap.

"You sorry sack of shit. Using your son's missing fingers as an excuse to turn this country into a police state like Iraq? To send an innocent man to the firing squad? You Gordon Liddy bozos. You cowards. You give me diarrhea."

Carelli rubbed the right side of his head, as if just discovering that he had been hit.

"How's your head?" Nick said.

"It hurts."

"Mine don't feel too good neither. Wait a second."

He went into the bathroom and got the large bottle of aspirin. Then he came back into the room, found the wine and began to peel the wrapper from around the cork.

"Where's my knife?"

He found it on the floor and pulled out the corkscrew attachment. The cork came out of the bottle with a loud pop. Then, using his teeth, Nick uncapped the aspirin bottle and poured six tablets into his left hand. He threw them into his mouth and washed them down with a large gulp, then passed the aspirin and wine to Carelli, who repeated what Nick had done. They passed the bottle back and forth several more times as Carelli cut himself free using the knife Nick gave him.

"You were supposed to be in California," the detective said.

"You're wrong about a lot of stuff this morning," Nick said. "You said I don't know what it's like to see the look in your son's eyes? I damn well do know what it's like. I've had children die in my arms."

Carelli said nothing.

"Africa. Brazil. I've seen lots of children get sick. I've seen lots of them die."

Carelli held his head down.

"Even in the States. Did you ever hear of Fitzgibbon's Disease? I watched a boy slowly die from it. I loved him like a son. He would have *been* my son by now if he had lived."

"I'm sorry," Jake said.

"Save it. You're supposed to be in Utah."

"You probably won't believe me. But I've never framed anybody before in my life."

"Good thing. You suck at it."

Nick was now putting the light switch back where it had been, and as before he managed to catch the hot wire with the blade, again sending a shock through him. Even the wires in the walls were out to get him.

Carelli still seemed punchy. "I never even hit a prisoner until that day when I hit you."

"We're even now," Nick said, and grabbed the bottle to take another swig. "But don't ever hit me again. Next time I *will* kill you."

Now what? Nick had had all the adventure he needed from this particular dump of a hotel. It was time to get out and not come back. He had to think for a second what to take. Fuck it: two notebooks, some pens, a shirt, three changes of socks and underwear fit neatly into his new fake-leather briefcase. And the laptop; it might come in handy. He finished the wine in one long drink, half of which dribbled down his chin onto his clothes, and tossed the bottle in the cheap plastic wastebasket.

"Grab your shit, Jake. If I were you I'd burn it."

Carelli stared at Nick, still not grasping what was happening.

"Where are we going?"

"I'm asking the questions, remember?" Nick said, picking up his briefcase, his laptop, and his putrefying gym bag. "Let's go."

Chapter 36

Nick pressed the 'down' button and the creaky mechanism began to whirr. Carelli still hadn't come out of the room, and Nick wondered whether he was going to take this chance to beat it. But as the tiny antique elevator door opened, Carelli joined him and the two men squeezed in for the ride down to the Lobby. Harris, behind the desk, wore a look that said *'Boyfriend troubles at six AM? Been there, done that.'* Nick walked slowly by, to make sure Carelli knew he had been made. They left the hotel through the stately front door into the cold morning air. Nick's battered Volvo was parked behind a faded billboard. He threw his bags in the back, and Carelli's followed.

"When do I get to find out where we're going?" Carelli said, as he got in the passenger seat.

"Are you nervous? You've got the gun, not me."

The route that Nick chose out of town ran around the Mill on three sides, then down Chestnut street past a row once-stately Queen Anne houses that were entering their second decrepitude. A wham-bam farewell tour: Nick wouldn't have given a nickel for the chance that he'd ever see Newcastle again.

"So long, it's been good to know ya," he sang, "but I gotta be traveling along."

Chestnut took him to the Newcastle rotary, which he entered at full speed, cars weaving before and behind him.

"No wonder Boston drivers have the reputations they do," Carelli said. "I thought federal highway laws made these intersections illegal."

"It's going to be a sad day," Nick said, downshifting, "when Massachusetts highway planners finally get rid of the last rotary in the sate. The roads will be much safer, but they'll all look just like roads in Michigan or Nebraska. Which is worse, road death or soul death?"

"You're an odd duck, Aubrey," Carelli said.

"On the contrary, I'm just a Puritan. I'm as ordinary as mud."

They rode the next seven miles to Route 128 without saying anything.

Then Carelli said, "If you're trying to kidnap me, you're doing it all wrong."

"I'm not kidnaping you. I'm taking reasonable steps to get you out of my life."

"If you want me out of your life, why are you taking me with you?"

"Because, like Abraham Maslow, I'm such a great psychologist. Allow me to explain. Now you see, you, Jake Carelli, know that I could have killed you this morning, but I didn't. I could have run away, but instead I put a loaded gun in your hand. If I were a stone assassin, I never would have done that. So you figure maybe I'm being straight with you about not being a killer. But in the back of your mind, a part of you still isn't sure. You're thinking, 'Maybe Aubrey's doing a con on me.' Two days from now you'll have convinced yourself that I pulled a fast one. So I'm taking you someplace that will prove to you that I'm on the level. In the meantime you can answer some questions for me."

"What do you want to know?"

What Nick mainly wanted to know was whether Carelli was a True Patriot of the Natural Law. One piece of circumstantial evidence suggested an answer: the True Patriots had ransacked Nick's house before the New York *Times* had even obtained a copy of the Flight 44 manifest. Was Jake Carelli their source of information?

Nick also wanted to know everything that might bear upon Carelli's case of Gulf War Syndrome. And there was a lot more that he wanted to know, besides. The list of what he wanted to know could fill a small library. But there was no way Nick would be able to beat information out of tough soldier like Jake. He was going to have to sweet-talk it out of him.

"What branch of service were you in?" Nick asked, to get the ball rolling.

"Army. Mechanized Infantry."

"How long were you in the Gulf?"

"Thirteen months."

"What did you do there?"

"EWS. Electronic Warfare Support. I had a group of repairmen. We fixed the spying equipment when it broke down."

"Spying equipment?"

"GSR. Ground surveillance radar."

"Never heard of it."

They turned onto Route 2 East, heading towards Boston. With Nick acting as unarmed kidnapper of a passenger who had a loaded gun, this excursion had to rank among the more curious rides in Nick's life.

"Tank finders, TRQ-32, Turkey thirty-two's, we call them," Carelli was explaining. "It's like a pickup truck with a thirty-foot extension antenna, with a couple of Kuwaiti translators sitting in the back. GSRs make sure the guys in our tanks know where the bad guys are hiding."

"How do you do that?"

"By listening to white noise across a spectrum of radio frequencies. When you find some signal in the noise you fix on it. Iraqi tanks aren't very quiet; they're just standard issue T-72's. So you hear a lot. You might catch strategic information, but you're more likely to overhear some squadron commander bellyaching to headquarters about bad shoes. You need three GRSs to triangulate. You take an azimuth and you get your ass out of there. The bad guys can lock onto your radar in about 15 seconds, so you don't really want to be setting up a housekeeping.""

On the opposite side of the highway were the greenhouses of Arena Farms, where, a lifetime ago, Nick used to have his airport limo drivers stop so he could pick up flowers for Bartlett on the way home from Logan. Imagine: on one such day in January '91, while he was buying flowers, some Iraqi conscript sat sweltering in the cramped forward compartment of a tank half-buried in a sand embankment, listening to his commanding officer whining about shoddy footwear, both of them totally unaware that the full fury of an American armored division was bearing down upon them.

The Volvo was at Corbin's Corner now, on the way from Concord to Lexington.

"Hey Carelli," Nick asked. "You ever seen where the battle happened?"

"What battle?"

"Concord Massachusetts. What battle do you think I'm talking about?"

They made a slight detour down 2A, so Nick could point out the bend in the road where the British had detained Paul Revere, and the hill the Minute Men had climbed for a better vantage.

"You must have been pretty close to the front," Nick said. "What, a couple miles behind?"

"Nah," Carelli said. "We went out in front of the tanks. We had to tell them where to go. I was with the Third Mechanized, the spearhead group. We *were* the front."

"In front of the tanks? I thought you said you were a repairman."

"Can't have your equipment breaking down in the middle of an assault."

"If you're in front of the tanks, what are *you* in?"

"You ever seen a HumVee?"

"You mean one of those *jeeps*?"

"Yeah, basically. We got us some of what you might call bazookas, antitank rocket launchers. Strapped them to the roof with some duct tape."

"The Third Mechanized is sitting back there in their sixty ton tanks and they send you guys out there in front of them in *jeeps* and *pickup trucks*?"

"That's right."

"No shit. I would have thought the equipment would be reliable enough for a six day war."

"Turkey thirty-two's are pretty good hardware, but it's a rough terrain. So they break. And when they break, I fix 'em. Can't have a tank battle if the tanks miss each other."

"I thought they had airplanes and satellites to find the enemy."

Carelli made a little raspberry sound, "thppt."

"We never saw anything from them," he said. "You probably saw more on CNN."

Nick laughed; Carelli did too. He seemed to have genuinely relaxed. This was good. Now Nick could get to the heart of the matter.

"Did you have any exposure to chemical or biological agents?"

"Sure. And I can tell you where Gulf War Syndrome comes from too."

"Tell me."

"The Iraqi ordnance caches. Whenever you find an ammo dump you have to assume the munitions are all booby trapped. So the EOD guys — explosive ordnance disposal — they would just blow that shit sky high. They said there was no chemical or biological canisters, but they're just covering their asses. We got there first, us HumVee guys. It was my job to go into bunkers looking for documents. I saw that Iraqi stuff. They had *beaucoup* chemical-biological weapons, big time. The Iraqis probably never shot any at us. But EOD just went in there and blew all that stuff up. The sky was black, and it wasn't just from the oil fires."

"That would be the Kasimiyah dump?"

"Among others."

So. Carelli's story, at least, supported the official Pentagon/CIA party line.

At the Alewife rotary Nick bore right. He followed Fresh Pond Parkway around the edge of Cambridge, then took Memorial Drive along the Charles, past Harvard, all the way down to MIT, where he took the bridge over into Boston. Nick looked at his watch. They had made good time; twenty minutes remained before Casey would call to report that Nick had been kidnaped. Nick parked the car under the green girders of the Central Artery.

"You won't be needing your weapon," he said to Carelli. "We're going to visit a friend."

Carelli looked at him skeptically, then placed the weapon under his seat. In silence he and Nick walked across the vast lot and into the hallway of the impossibly drab building. Nick led them to the seventh floor, the familiar room.

On the soundless television mounted near the ceiling; a happy-news couple was miming the report of a father-and-son drowning at Revere Beach, switching from bright smiles to somberness to relate the sad details. Cut to a commercial: *Leggo my Eggo*. Nick could not imagine that the most foul cell in the deepest corner of Hell was any worse than this place.

"Carelli, meet Todd," he said. "Todd, meet Carelli."

Carelli looked at Todd's wire-covered, tube-spouting body.

"Poor guy," he said. "What happened to him?"

"Gunshot to the back of the head. Six years ago. He was asleep at the time."

"What's the connection between you and this guy?"

"He was my best friend. We grew up together. Went overseas together."

Carelli looked at Nick with what Nick thought *might* be a glimmer of respect.

"Why did you take me here?" the detective asked, slowly.

"To show you why Barlow committed suicide. This is what Barlow feared," Nick said, grabbing a handful of wires. "What did he say? 'Tiny machines to control our thoughts. No degrees of freedom.' That's why Barlow killed himself. He didn't want anybody inserting wires into his brain to control his thoughts. Nobody killed Barlow. He killed himself so he wouldn't end up like Todd."

Carelli's jaw actually dropped.

"What are you saying, that this guy's thoughts are being controlled by these wires?"

"That's what Barlow would say. That the CIA rigged Todd up for a medical experiment in mind control. Pretty crazy, huh?" Nick released his grip on the filaments.

Carelli asked, "Is it true?"

"Before I can answer that I'm going to have learn a whole lot about how minds and brains work."

"What are you going to do, go to medical school? You need to be a brain surgeon."

"What I need," Nick said, "Is a whole team of neurologists and neurophysiologists, and a software model of human brain functioning."

Carelli eyes followed the leads in to the data acquisition and control processor panel.

"But Barlow said 'tiny machines," Carelli said. "This machine isn't very small."

"Underneath those wires, sir, is a brain. Maybe the tiny machines are inside it."

"Don't call me sir. I work for a living."

"Right. Sergeant."

"Call me Jake. What's your friend's connection to Barlow?"

"I'm trying to figure that out. We'd better call Casey now before she launches a dragnet."

From the nurse's station Nick called off the pending manhunt. 'Roger,' Casey said.

"You think the hit on your buddy was related to Gulf War Syndrome, don't you?"

"Somewhere in Boston a light has just switched on," Nick said.

Carelli ignored the sarcasm.

"Does your brother really work for a Swiss pharmaceutical company?"

"Yes," Nick said.

"Did he kill Barlow?"

"No. But he is in danger because of what he knows."

The hint of a smile appeared on Carelli's face.

"You're going after them, aren't you?"

"Jake, I could have ended your career tonight. I let you off the hook. All I want in return is for you to leave me alone. You and Marki both. Look out the window: it's a short cab ride from here to the airport. Go. Get the fuck out of here. Don't forget your evidence and your gun."

"You can't take on the CIA alone," Carelli said.

"It's not the CIA. Or at least it's not *only* the CIA."

"Who is it?"

"Transglobal capitalism, the High Druid of Informationtology, and a crackpot cybermilitia."

If Jake got the joke, he didn't show it.

"I'll partner with you."

"Go home," Nick said.

"Two cowboys is better than one."

"Do you know how to run a gel?"

"A what?"

"Two-dimensional isoelectric-focusing sodium dodecyl sulfate polyacrylamide slab gel electrophoresis. You use it to separate proteins according to molecular weight and how electrophillic they are. It's a way to look for unexpected proteins in the blood of Gulf War vets when you don't have enough clues, or enough time, to run Monoclonal antibody titres. Understand?"

"No."

"First you lyse your cells in the ultrasonicator and spin them down in the centrifuge. Separate out the light stuff; put the remaining sample in a solution of non-ionizing detergent, inject it into a heavy gel of polyacrylamide, and pull it through a PH gradient of fifty thousand volts to separate proteins according to how attracted or repulsed they are by the electron-hungry gradient and freeze them in the gel accordingly. Finally, you wash the gel in sodium dodecyl sulfate to separate proteins by molecular weight and you x-ray the motherfucker to see what you've got. You get a distinct spot on the grid for each protein in the sample, just like a fingerprint. Now do you understand?"

"No."

"Then you can't help me. Go home and take care of your boy."

"I thought you weren't a biologist."

"I used to hang out in my wife's lab."

"Sounds like you paid attention."

"Let me tell you something, Jake. There was this woman, see, about twenty five years old. She was a scientist and she wore a white lab coat, which kind of went nice with her brown skin in the summertime. And she had a sweet smile and a quick wit and a pleasant way about her, and she wore her hair in a bun. She was as smart as the day is long and she had large firm breasts under that lab coat and a heart-shaped ass. And when she explained how a gel worked, you're damn right I paid attention."

"Where is she now?"

"She's working with a team of neurologists and neurophysiologists to develop a software model of human brain functioning. But you, buddy, are going to Utah. If I ever figure out the Gulf War mystery, I promise I'll send you a postcard."

Carelli shook his head slowly. The skin around his right eye was turning a deep purple.

"You would have made a good soldier, Nick. You've got guts."

"I'm not the type."

"You are. You like going different places, the rush from danger. You're that type."

Nick thought about that for a second. Had he really missed his calling?

"Jake," he said. "When I was in Africa I used to have a mailbox in a dusty little town called Podor. Every two weeks I would go there to pick up my mail. And there was this woman there, her name was Karen. She was a Peace Corps volunteer; she taught in the high school. She was the only white person in town, and the only white woman for a hundred miles in any direction. She had no telephone, no electricity, and the nearest English-speaking doctor was three days away. In two years she managed to get hepatitis, dysentery and malaria, but she never left her post. Who had more guts—her, or the guys in the sixty-ton tanks that the Iraqis never came within a mile of hitting?"

"If you ever decide you need a partner, *hombre*," Carelli said, "you look me up."

He walked down the hall and pressed the elevator button, leaving Nick standing by the nurses' station. The elevator came and Carelli got in before Nick remembered that he hadn't asked the most important question.

"Jake."

Carelli pressed the button to keep the elevator door open.

"Yeah Nick?"

"How'd you know I was staying at that hotel and that I was supposed to be in California today?"

"We had a tip last week."

"Did he mention that he could help you get a warrant by faking incriminating mail on the Internet? Perhaps suggest that I was peddling child pornography, something like that?"

"Nick, who's on your ass? Tell me his name. I'll get him off."

"Don't worry about him. You keep *Marki* off my ass and we're cool."

"That's a promise."

Nick took the next elevator down. He was trembling from head to toe before the cold air hit him. Then he opened the lobby door and stepped outside and began to shiver in earnest. His car was an icebox. But half an hour later, long after the car had warmed up, he was still shaking. The car was positively hot and he was still trembling so hard that the steering wheel wobbled. He liked the adrenaline rush. Yeah, right. He had been driving for more than hour before he realized where he was going. He was already a quarter of the way to Oneonta.

Chapter 37

By the time Nick reached the hairpin turn at North Adams he had calmed down sufficiently to pay attention to his driving. Good thing: the descent from the Berkshires to the Hudson River was as severe as the one from the Santa Cruz Ridge to the San Francisco Bay. He had had time to do a little thinking, and he had come to a few conclusions. He was going to die soon, that was apparent. It was therefor proper that his farewell tour should start at the place where he had been born: Oneonta, New York, the hilly little town where he had grown up and met his bride.

I left my heart in Oneonta, Nick sang. *High on a hill, it calls to me.* An image of an Aztec priest atop a pyramid popped into his head. The priest was holding high a bloody heart. "*To be where little cable cars . . .*" the bloody heart sang. Nick blinked and the singing heart was replaced by an image of Abraham holding a flint knife above a terrified Isaac. What was it about hills and human sacrifices? What was his subconscious trying to tell him?

Nick and Bartlett had made love, long ago, atop each of the four hills of Oneonta. Once in a parked car, once in a friend's apartment, once in a church that they had noticed open one weekday evening. But Oyaron was the best.

They had spent the afternoon in the Hartwick College library, halfway up the hill that palefaces called Table Rock. Lust drove them out the doors, across the springtime frisbee lawns, and scrambling to the flat top. Like Moses, they had looked down on the Susquehanna's city and farms beyond. Oyaron, usually about as private as the Public Garden, had been left entirely to them.

Memory, Nick thought, downshifting. *What a pain in the ass.*

Without taking his eyes from the road he reached into the back seat and picked a cassette from a shoe box and stuck it in the player. Soon a clarinet was bubbling a merry tune, and a pleasantly bland man's voice was singing—

Up and down the hall
Writing on the wall
Mommy come and look!
Uh-oh

Oh, God, Rosenshontz, detritus from the Magic Box. Not a good idea. Once you got a Rosenshontz tune in your head it might lodge there for days or even weeks. A sharp left bend in the highway momentarily required both hands. He couldn't switch the player off in time:

Rubby-dubby-dub
Filling up the tub
I can't turn it off!
Uh-oh

He needed something loud and jarring, quick. First he pressed the 'eject' button, then he reached into the back seat again for another tape; this time he looked at the label. Perfect. He stuck it in and cranked it up. Using Mission of Burma to eradicate Rosenshontz was like brushing your teeth with Ajax to get rid of the taste of pizza, but radical threat called for radical response. With the strains of "That's When I Reach for My Revolver" shaking his very rivets, he shifted into fifth and headed towards Williamstown.

It was at that exact moment, as he shifted the gear and let out the clutch, that he knew that Casey had been right: free will was an illusion. Not just in Todd's case, but universally. It no longer mattered, if it ever had, whether Nick wanted to solve the riddle of Barlow's diskette, or whether he wanted to find out why Monty had ruined his life—or why Todd had been shot, or whether Paul was an agent of some crazy conspiracy. It was Nick's fate, period. He knew now why his car seemed to drive itself. He was made of molecules; molecules were made of atoms, and atoms consisted of nothing but subatomic particles that followed a relentless logic. The *laws of physics* determined what Nick Aubrey would do next, not his volition. Not his "free will." He was no different than the SLAC leptons of Sand Hill Road. Free will? *Right.* What a crock.

By noon he was crossing Oneonta's City Line. He knew where Bartlett would be: at the house of Eddie Fessman, her retired mentor. But he couldn't bring himself to call her—something about the word "stalker" kept popping into his mind. Clearly Bartlett wanted Nick out of her life—and he loved her enough to give her that freedom. Either he loved her that much or he was just chickenshit. But the plain fact was that he was in great danger and needed her help. There was no one else he could turn to. Don't be a coward, Nicky, he told himself. Call your wife.

Ok, he would. But there was somebody else to see first.

The cemetery at the Second Swedish Baptist Church was a frozen green park, and even though it only covered a few acres it took Nick half an hour to find his mother's grave, for the markers were all modest, and the oldest ones were pretty-much indistinguishable from the newest. Her stone, however, would have at least this distinction: it would be the last addition to this collection. The fieldstone church atop the small adjacent rise was nailed shut, and plywood covered the windows. The Second Swedish Baptist congregation of Oneonta, New York, its collective soul and memory, was as dead as the deadest parishioner in this funny garden.

"Mom, I'm in a pickle," he said to the stone. "I wish you were here."

As expected, she made no answer.

Bartlett sat on the green corduroy couch in Eddie Fessman's modest living room waiting for him to bring the tea. As he shuffled in and placed the tray on the table in front of her she reflected again on how much he had aged. His tonal inflections had always reminded her of Yertle the Turtle, but now he even looked like that wrinkled cartoon character.

It wasn't a pleasant conversation that they had been having when Eddie got up to answer the kettle. Not to say that it had been unpleasant. The thing was, she had come hoping for some insight into the phage problem, but Eddie had steered the conversation around to Nick.

"Do you miss him?" he asked, depositing himself in a worn chair.

"Sometimes," she said as she poured for both of them.

"Bartlett," he said, switching to the heavier version of his Brooklyn accent, the one he used to emphasize that he was now speaking *ex cathedra*, in his official capacity as New York Jew. "I'm an old man sticking his nose where it don't belong, what else is new?"

"Nothing new about that," she smiled.

"Look at me. I am a scientist, a total rationalist. So why do I keep kosher, Bartlett? Is it because I fear the wrath of God, I should be turned into a pillar of salt?"

"No?" That was the word in her script.

"No. One keeps Kosher to remind oneself of one's ability to control one's appetites, to remind oneself that one has power over one's own actions. And to accept the covenant. Now forgive me Bartlett. I watched you being married to this man for years, long after you left my lab. I have eyes, I have ears; I watched you from a distance. So now you are separated. But you do not get divorced. A beautiful woman like yourself, you could have any man in the Commonwealth. But no, you sit at home. Why? Because you understand a covenant. Marriage is not right for everybody, I'm not stupid? But—speaking as your friend now I say this— you will never be unmarried, just as I will never be unJew."

"Sometimes things don't work out as you plan."

"You never had a desire for children? You're still young? What, not forty? Not thirty-five?"

She found herself answering, in spite of herself.

"Whenever I brought up the subject he would only say, 'enna booby.'"

"Annie Booby? What kind of answer is that?"

"It's in an African language he learned overseas. It means 'it's cold.'"

"What does that have to do with having children?"

"I never found that out."

Eddie, thank God, apparently was ready to let the matter drop. His face became more stern, and he waved his hand dismissively to show he was changing the subject.

"This phage stuff, let me speak frankly, to me it is not science. It is Jurassic Park mumbo jumbo science. Phage do not occur in people. The body gobbles them up."

"Do you think the proteins could have been produced by an artificial agent? Something that could resist the immune system, be invisible to the immune system?"

"What, 'artificial agent'? A machine?"

"Some kind of nanomachine?"

"Bartlett, listen to yourself. Nanomachines are a theoretical construct. The only place they exist is *Star Trek, Deep Space Nine.*"

"I heard a story on National Public Radio only yesterday. A lab in Australia has made a device smaller than the AIDS virus, that if you put one of them in Sidney Harbor it can detect a single molecule of benzene. A single molecule."

Eddie put his hands up.

"They don't exist. Not phage factories. No, Bartlett. There must have been a phage contaminant in your laboratory equipment."

He was ignoring one crucial fact: the T4 tail fibers were from a strain she had never used.

"Bacteriophage provide the best biological models for simple DNA-repair machines," she said. "If I were looking for primitive machines, I might start by looking for phage. It's a hunch."

"Like a hunch that aliens lurk behind comets. Jurassic Park Deep Space Nine."

"How would I prove you wrong? What would I look for?"

"You would be talking about a major research project. There is no easy way to detect something that does not exist and you don't know what it looks like if it does exist."

Eddie looked relieved when the phone rang.

"She is here," he said into the receiver. "Would you like to speak with her?"

Who could have called her here? She hadn't told anybody she was coming to Dr. Fessman's house. Eddie covered the mouthpiece with his hand as he handed her the receiver.

"Is it not as I said? You can never be unmarried. Forget nanomachines. Go to him."

If the classic American diner echoed the architectural lines of a railroad car, the

Duke Diner echoed the lines of a mobile home park after a tornado. He wondered that Bartlett would still deign to cross the threshold of this funky old place where they used to go for breakfast. He went in and soon he found himself again drinking coffee. It wasn't as if he needed more caffeine: his heart was thumping as if it wanted to crash through his sternum and land on the table.

He was still trying to rid his mind of the Aztec with the flint knife when Bartlett walked in. Her hair was in a bun and she wore a plain grey baggy sweatshirt. Her hair had the faintest hints of grey, and her slimmer face showed the smallest wrinkles at the corners of her eyes. She was the most beautiful woman he had ever seen.

She looked around for him but didn't see him. He had said to meet her inside, hadn't he, not in the lot? A greasy-haired tramp waved to her from a booth. The meek smile on his face seemed familiar. Could that be Nick? She walked over to his booth, still not certain that this was the man to whom she was married. She had never seen him looking worse.

As she approached he tried to interpret the look on her face. Was it annoyance or boredom? He had hoped for a more neutral reaction, but maybe that had been asking for too much.

She sat in the seat opposite him, trying to comprehend how he could have come to such a state. He was unshaven and wearing the most ridiculously tight shirt she had ever seen. Where did he think he was, *Beirut*? The short haircut looked preposterous on him, and the moustache made it worse. The bags under his eyes were black as coal—was that *mascara*?—and he smelled like stale wine and cheap cologne.

"Hello, Bartlett," he said. He had decided that he wasn't going to pester her with anything personal; he wasn't even going to say anything overly friendly. The look on her face was enough to tell him to keep his distance, to keep their conversation on business matters.

"Hello Nick. How are you?" She wasn't sure she wanted to hear his answer. Why had he followed her here? Clearly he was in distress. But his distress was his problem now, he would have to manage it without her help. It had taken her months—no, years—to summon the courage to do what had to be done. Yertle or no Yertle, marriage was *not* right for her.

Nick looked at her— imploringly, she thought—and said:

"I want to talk about brain research."

Somehow she had expected a different overture.

"Brain research?"

"Cognitive neuroscience. The structure and function of the human brain."

It was a rather broad question, as if she were to say to him, 'tell me about computers.'

"What do you want to know?" she said, tentatively.

How could he bring himself to ask her? He already knew the answer to his own question. The answer was that he was out of his mind.

"Is it possible to know what somebody's thinking by reading his EEG?" He asked, then cringed waiting for her reply. He knew that you couldn't use an electroencephalogram to tell what somebody was thinking. But he needed to hear it from her. She was the expert.

Why this sudden interest in neuroscience? Five years ago cognitive neuroscience had been as much *terra incognita* to her as it had been to him. She had learned. It was crucial to her attack on the Fitzgibbon parasite. Was Nick's out-of-the-blue question his clumsy way of showing that he still cared about what she cared about?

"EEGs are a fairly crude tool," she said. "They can show brain waves and identify the type and general location of some kinds of seizures."

"You can't tell anything else from brain waves?"

"They're relatively crude, not completely crude. Sometimes EEGs and PET scans are used together. PET stands for positron-emission tomography. It traces a radioactive isotope of oxygen, which shows where blood is flowing in the brain. Blood flow in the brain is a very accurate indicator of what sections of the brain are in use."

It *was* mascara. And it *was* cheap wine. Tending to vinegar.

"A PET scan is like a CT scan, right? A big, bulky machine? You couldn't be in a room with one and not know it, could you?"

"No. Well, I suppose you could construct a walk-in model. But why would you want to hide it in the first place?"

"It's not important, I'm just daydreaming. Why are the two methods used together?"

"PETs are more accurate in space, and the EEG is more accurate in time. EEGs can capture events on the scale of milliseconds, but they're only accurate to within centimeters. Scans are like slow motion, a thousand times slower—but they're accurate to the millionth of an inch. Plus EEGs are a lot cheaper and easier than CT scans or PET scans, and you can use them continuously on the same patient in a way that you can't with PETs and CTs. "

"Why's that?" he asked.

"Because the oxygen isotope used for PET scans has a half life of only about two minutes. Once the radioactivity fades your experiment is over. The CT scan also uses radioactivity, and you can only pump so much radioactivity into one subject. Unless you don't care what happens to his brain, of course."

Of course.

"Do they do any brain scans without radioactivity?"

That was one thing Bartlett had always liked about Nick: he loved to learn. He didn't care what he looked like or what he sounded like. When she thought about it that way, Nick's sitting here wearing mascara, cheap wine and body odor and asking her about neuroscience was in a sense a statement that nothing had changed between them. It was, in a way, quite touching.

How different Nick was from his brother. Unlike Nick, Paul obviously paid attention to how he looked. And why not? He looked great! She didn't care what anyone said: men who looked as good in a suit as Cary Grant did made her weak in the knees. Paul's conversation was subtle, flirtatious even. Which showed, at least, that he was interested in her. Nick was interested only in the topic at hand. Could two brothers be more different?

"MRI. Magnetic resonance imaging," she said. "You put the person into a giant magnetic field, and the atoms in the brain become little bar magnets. You record an image of that."

"Another of those giant machines?"

"All three kinds of scanners look the same: you lie on a bed-carriage that slides into a great metallic doughnut."

"Like Michael Jackson's hypobaric chamber," Nick said.

An odd analogy, she thought.

"Yes. So to answer your question, none of these techniques can actually read thoughts, but if you hooked all of them up together somehow you could have a pretty good general idea of what was going on inside somebody's skull. You could tell whether they were concentrating on a visual skill like recognizing a face, or doing math, or playing violin, or thinking up a joke, or having sex."

"You say 'general idea.' What would it take to have an exact idea?"

"An exact understanding of the human brain."

"And that's what you're working on."

"I'm a molecular biologist. I'm working on Fitzgibbon's Disease."

Nick didn't seem to pay much attention to her answers.

"You could find out a lot more about somebody's thought if you weren't fussy about ethical considerations. If you did to human subjects the kinds of things that they do to animals."

"Of course you could," she said. "But that's not done."

A sudden, horrible thought came to her. Did Nick have brain tumor? Was that were these questions were coming from?

"What kinds of things are done to animals but not to people?" he asked.

"That's not my field," she said. "I don't do animal studies."

"But your colleagues do, don't they?"

"Yes, some of them."

"What kinds of things do they do?"

"They use microelectrodes to stimulate and measure event-related potentials inside the brain instead of just passively reading them from the scalp, the way an EEG does. "

"Like honey," he said.

"Honey?"

"I mean, like Wilder Penfield."

"Yes, like Wilder Penfield. He was the first to use microelectrode stimulation."

"How do they do it in animals?" Nick asked.

"In animals they sometimes destroy part of the brain to see how the rest reacts."

"What do they do, shoot it in the back of the head?"

"I don't know how they do it. Sometimes they inject voltage-sensitive dyes to measure strength of electrical currents. They do video microscopy of blood vessels in the brain. All of these procedures are dangerous; that's why they don't use them on people."

"Because if they damage a brain, there's no way to fix it."

"Brain cells don't replicate. Nerve cells don't replicate."

"But there must be a gene that controls that."

"Nick. Our laboratory has been looking for that gene for five solid years."

"Yes, of course. I knew that. So you kill the animal and do the autopsy."

Bartlett couldn't remember ever having seen Nick so agitated.

A waitress came by with a pot of coffee. She looked no older than fifteen, Nick thought, but already she was completely adept at pouring refills over cluttered tables. She probably thinks she's seen it all, Nick thought. But she hasn't.

"You know I'm squeamish," Bartlett said. "I've never been to an autopsy. I've never even seen a brain—human or otherwise."

"You've never seen a brain?"

"I don't need to see it. It's a complex device made of cheap chemicals. I only care about how it works to the extent that I need to in order to find a cure for Fitzgibbon's."

"But animal experiments can't give you all the answers, can they? Monkeys aren't human. Their brains aren't human brains."

"Monkeys don't speak. They shriek, and shrieking is controlled by subcortical structures. Human speech is a cortical function. You can touch the cerebral cortex with a wire, like Wilder Penfield did, and the person can tell you what it makes them think of. You can't do that with monkeys. If language is our most human trait, then only human brains can tell us how we work."

"Is it possible then to insert a thought into somebody's brain?" he asked.

"Not without opening it up and sticking wires into it."

Bartlett didn't like these questions at all. Belief that others were inserting thoughts into your mind—or that you could control other people's thoughts—was a classic sign of schizophrenia. Every now and then you'd hear a story on the radio about somebody lining his house with aluminum foil to keep the evil microwaves out. But schizophrenia didn't just appear at age forty-two. It generally showed up in the teenage years. On the other hand, she had to consider the possibility that something was seriously wrong with Nick. *Just look at him, girl.*

"What would you perceive?" Nick said, with bewilderment in his racoon eyes. "How would the world appear to you if your thoughts were manipulated by electrodes?"

"It would probably be very hard to tell where you stopped and the rest of the world began. Schizophrenics hear voices that they have to obey. There's an inverse condition called the 'alien hand.' If you place a cup near the injured person's hand, it grabs the cup. The person cannot let go by simply willing to do so. But if somebody yells 'drop it' out loud, the hand obeys."

Nick could only imagine how nuts this conversation must seem to her—he himself could no longer could tell what was reasonable from what was insane. Maybe he should tell her why he was asking her all these crazy questions. Maybe he should tell her about Barlow's nanomachines, and Todd's Soyuz skull cap, about Corporate Fellows, True Patriots and secret laboratories in Basel. If anybody could help him figure out a logical explanation of all this weirdness, it was Bartlett. But had no right, anymore, to intrude his own world upon hers. He would have to clean up this mess himself.

"In other words," she continued, "under certain conditions the human brain cannot tell the difference between its own thoughts and outside stimuli."

"That's the holy grail of cognitive neuroscience, isn't it," he said. "A complete model of the mind—awareness, consciousness, thought—and how it arises from the activities in the brain."

There was only an indirect connection, Bartlett thought, between what she had said and Nick's response.

"And that's what the Neuro Group is working on," he continued.

"Yes."

"But isn't it creepy? Taking brains apart as if they were little wind-up toys?"

She thought of the photograph in the bookstore, the nerve cell grafted to a computer chip. Yes, she thought much neuroscience was creepy. She believed in it, but she was disturbed by it at the same time. She needed someone with whom she could share those feelings. Once upon a time that someone would have been Nick.

"Until we have that complete model of the brain," she said, "we won't cure Alzheimer's, we won't cure schizophrenia, we won't cure Fitzgibbon's. The model is creepy, and it's built by murdering monkeys. I don't care. I want the model."

"Does Hoff-Zeigy pharmaceuticals have an interest in the Neuro-Group model?" he asked.

"They might."

"Is that what you and Paul spoke about?"

How did Nick know she had met with Paul? Was he spying on her? Considering how Nick was behaving, she had to consider the possibility that he really had come off his hinges.

"My relationship with your brother does not concern you," she said.

"Bartlett, please. Just a few more questions. It's very important, but I can't tell you why. Have you heard from Paul since yesterday?"

"Yes," she said. "He called me from the airport. He's on his way back to Basel."

"He's gone back to *Basel*?"

"Sure, why not? He lives there."

"Why not? Because the Biodigital Forum doesn't start until tomorrow, and I was going to meet him there. Because Paul is terrified to go back to Basel, that's why not."

"He did not seem terrified to me. He seemed rather assured."

Oh Jesus, Nick thought. Why had Paul gone back? Because of who he had seen in California? Because of something Judith Knight had told him? Or because Nick had given him the diskette? If Paul had told Nick the truth at the Tied House, then it made no sense for him to go back to Basel. Nick needed to think, but his ability to reason was fading fast. Absentmindedly he picked up his cup and took a sip, trying to gather his thoughts. The coffee was awful.

"Enna boubi," he said. "It's cold."

It was the wrong thing to say. Bartlett fairly screamed.

"What does that mean? Why do you say that? Why? Why?"

Why did he say it? It was automatic. The words just came out, as if somebody had tickled his brain with a microelectrode. Sometimes, when he was lucky, he actually managed to forget where those words had come from. How could he explain? A memory so deep, a dream so real. . .

"I don't know why I say that," he said. Was he telling the truth? He didn't even know.

"Well maybe you better try to find out."

The look on her face was anger, sadness, fury, confusion. Tears formed in her eyes.

"Nicholas Aubrey. How I loved you. Oh, God, the night we met, how you danced. How you danced! Now look at you. Look at you! You have broken my heart!"

She stood up and pulled her gloves on. Tears were streaming down her face.

"You have broken my heart! You need help. Go get it."

She turned and walked away.

Nick reached out his hand.

"It was a little girl. . ." he said. But Bartlett neither saw nor heard.

The gorgeous woman, the white-smocked scientist, the Trojan Woman with the Big Tits who had lived in his soul for so long, walked out the door and was gone.

Chapter 38

The clearing in the beeches was just as it had been when he and Paul used to sleep out here. Nick made his campfire right where they had used to make theirs, and by the light of the fire he set up the tent. Tomorrow he would head back to California.

He had thought to find a hotel somewhere along Route 23. But as he was walking down Main Street he noticed that the Army/Navy store was still open, and he got an idea. The sleeping bag cost thirty dollars. The Korean War vintage pup tent cost fifteen. A coffee pot went for three-fifty. It was supposed to snow tonight, but he had built the fire in a sheltered spot and he should be plenty warm if he kept it going. The farm's new owners would never see him out in the beech copse beyond the bend in the stream. Not even the smoke would be visible from the house, and he would be gone within an hour after dawn. Two hours of sleep on the red-eye was all the rest he had had in the last three days. It was past dark, and snow was beginning to fall. It was time, at last, to close his eyes.

He had been getting used to the idea of living without Bartlett, but now the longing was back again, stronger than ever. It didn't matter what she said or how she said it. It only mattered that she existed. As long as she did he would want her.

The sound of snow falling, turning to rain: and with it came a memory of her sitting naked at the edge of their bed, with the dark morning rain lashing against the window —the last morning he had awakened with her; the last time he had seen her naked in natural light: the green-grey light of a distant sun reflected off the big spruce in their yard, through the raindrops and fire-red maple branches, into their room, onto their bed. She was leaving, she said. And then she kissed him, and was gone.

And then hell. Not one phone call. Not one letter. A daily hell, wondering if he would ever be with her again, ever see her again. It was still hell, today. He couldn't shake her. He didn't want her back: he knew that was impossible. All he wanted was relief from this addiction. To shake her out of his blood, to be clean of her. Christ, to be clean of her.

With no clear idea of what he wanted to say, he took out a pen and began to write in his spiral-bound notebook, by the light of a lantern:

The sun plays over the sound of the surf, I call to you, Bartlett, come waltzing with me.

I live in a void, my heart is black, as I strive ever to be more like you, my own Black Bart, to embrace your cunning array of stunts. Shall we dance our dance together, our dance of cruelty and forgetting? I miss you like the child misses her daddy, off to war, he has been taken out against the wall and shot, the mother feeds the child elaborate lies, unable to face the truth. Enna boubi, the child says. It is cold. Bartlett, without you in my life there is no blood in my veins, only a synthetic substitute of fluorocarbons and industrial emulsifiers.

You can call the dance, it needn't be a waltz. Let it be some kind of cowboy line dance, or that interlocking arm dance, what do they call it? Melissa's bat mitzvah, you wore that blue dress— silk? — I loved the way it rode your ass — I saw that night the true evil of your soul, the way you pretended not to know the effect you had on every man in that hotel ballroom, (klezmer band playing, wailing clarinet, the vests, the earlocks) as you sashayed with such grace, and that smile, such joyousness! It was hell-sent! Every cock you set to attention. Every one, I tell you, aged one month to Melissa's blind great-grandfather's —he felt your presence, I saw this happen— he covered his lap with a plastic top hat in his embarrassment. That ass, I repeat. John McLarin looked at me imploringly, 'that ass, may I touch it? my wife, my home, my money: all is yours, Nick, for one touch, one possession' 'it's not mine to give,' I replied. He was across the room from me, this conversation took place with our eyes, and I saw, I alone saw what you did to that man. You knew he was consuming your divine ass with his eyes, his blood pressure nearly zero over zero in his swoon, and yet you turned on your divine ankle and presented your luscious bosom to his unprepared eyes. He sleeps now in a cardboard box under the expressway.

Come back to me and be my love. For too long I have said it is cold. It is time to make it warm. Miracles come from strange places; Another miracle is waiting for us. I know it is.

He tore the page out, folded it and placed in the notebook, which he tossed to the far end of the tent. He would never send it. Some things were better left alone.

The stream made its continual gurgle, never changing. Lying in the tent, he could imagine the field on the other side—corn stalks cut and turned under with one pass of the harrow, waiting for spring. As a child he had dreamed of going to exotic places and teaching people what he knew about farming. Even as he went away to college and learned about French movies and Renaissance painting—even after he had been bitten by the computer bug and learned to think in FORTRAN instead of English— the dream had stayed intact. He had followed it to Africa and Brazil. Sometimes he had been sick or lonely, but always his soul had been at rest. He had come back to the states and begun a new life, and finding Bartlett had seemed more than fair compensation for the remote field stations he had left behind. From a modest start he had been promoted often, had found his way to the hottest company, then to the hottest projects, coming to take for granted the life of the high-tech manager. But somewhere along the way he had begun to lose his soul, and when his world came crashing down about him there was little left of it. But here, by the brook, with the crisp smells of cold February filling the air, something was whispering to him that he could have it back.

∞V∞

TEACHERS
& DISCIPLES

Chapter 39

"We've reserved a non-smoking Taurus for you, Mr. Aubrey. You're all set."

The yellow polyester jacket assaulted Nick's eyes. Shouldn't this kid be in school someplace? Which way to Burlingame High?

"What do you mean, non-smoking?" Nick said.

"For non-smokers like yourself, Mr. Aubrey, we have a fleet of cars that have never been smoked in."

"What makes you say I'm a non-smoker?"

"Right here in your profile," the helpful agent said, pointing to a screen Nick couldn't see.

"What profile? I've never rented from your company before. The only profile you have on me is my name and credit card number."

"Oh! I see your confusion. Our system builds profiles from the Sabre database. You rent non-smoking hotel rooms. You see? The system knows what you like! Your car is waiting for you. The bus leaves from the next level up, every five minutes."

"But I didn't ask for a non-smoking car. And I didn't authorize Sabre to release any information about me."

The kid gave a look that was much too patronizing for someone of his meager years.

"No need to be concerned, sir. The system doesn't release any private information, like your credit history. Just your profile."

"My profile isn't private?" Nick asked. "Who cares. Give me a car I can smoke in."

"Oh, so you've taken up smoking! But there's a non-smoking room reserved for you at the Saratoga Club. I'll change it for you," he said, and began to type.

"You will do no such thing. My accommodations at the Saratoga Club are not the business of the pimple-faced clerk at the car-rental company. Your job is to give me the car I reserved."

Nick Aubrey is an irascible bastard. Put *that* in your profile.

"So you would like a smoking mid-sized sedan," the child asked, somewhat more cautiously.

"Correct."

"It seems that we're out. How about full-size?"

"Fine."

It was thirty seconds of typing before the answer came back. Nick could hear sighs from the line forming behind him.

"We have no full-size smoking sedans. Would you like a compact?"

"I'm six feet three inches tall. I'll take the Taurus."

Forty minutes later Nick turned off 101 South at University Avenue in Palo Alto and headed for Mac's Tobacco. He parked in the little lot near the English Pub and crossed Emerson street to the shop, where he bought a six-dollar Dr. Grabow pipe and two ounces of a Latakia-heavy Balkan blend, as pungent as camel shit. He lit the first bowl and felt a particular satisfaction watching the stinky billows fill the interior of the car. The car didn't seem to mind. In fact Nick thought he detected a slightly more spritely response to the accelerator as he pulled out of the lot.

There were undoubtably faster ways to get to Saratoga than by going down El Camino. But for once in his life Nick was traveling with a little extra time built into his schedule. The Biodigital Forum didn't start until tomorrow, so there was no hurry to check in. He would read the Vannevar Bush article, work out at the gym, get a good night's rest. Tomorrow he would become James Bond, collecting specimens for Casey to use in cracking the Corporate Fellows' system.

Nick entertained these thoughts while traveling south, stoplight after stoplight, down El Camino. He passed drug stores, furniture stores, liquor stores, food stores, hardware stores, hotels, software stores, pornography stores, flower stores, clothing stores, restaurants, video stores, office equipment stores. El Camino, once a thoroughfare between San Jose and San Francisco, was no longer a highway to anywhere. It had become a thirty-mile long shopping mall of national chain franchises, the human interface to the global economy. Before the invention of the first integrated circuit, this region had been orchardland—as open as the farmland on the outskirts of Oneonta. And before that it had been grassland, as open as the Sahel. Soon, he supposed, it would become a wasteland, as shoppers forsook the quasi-human interaction of BlockBuster Video and The Gap for the onanistic delight of Internet shopping.

Through Santa Clara, Campbell, Los Gatos he drove, until he came to Saratoga. Here the crush of the Silicon Valley relented before the memory of its more rustic past. Around a corner from a school or church there would be a hidden steep valley covered with evergreens, or an old barn or orchard.

Following the directions Carl had given him, Nick came, at around four-thirty, to a modest driveway at the apparent end of a short valley. He followed the driveway around to the left underneath drooping branches, and suddenly before him there opened up a spectacular box canyon, the back end of which was a giant cliff. The modest sign on the guardhouse told him he had found the right place, and the uniformed, side-armed attendant—after checking Nick's identification— indicated where to park amid the Jaguars, Rolls Royces, Porches, and Lotuses.

The walls of the canyon sloped up quickly on either side, and here and there amid the trees he noticed little white cabins. The one thing he hadn't noticed was an obvious place to check in. Leaving his pipe and tobacco on the passenger seat, he opened his door and got out. Before he could get to the trunk to retrieve his luggage, a golf cart silently arrived and a uniformed attendant hopped out.

"I'll get your bags, Mr. Aubrey," the attendant said, taking the keys from Nick's hand.

With little choice in the matter, Nick got into the cart's passenger seat. Soon they were on their way, with Nick's bags on the back. In about two minutes they came to a low white California Rustic building that was not visible from the lot. The style, and probably the building itself, dated from around the time of the Gold Rush. The house had been perfectly maintained, and everything about the place bespoke wealth and taste.

"Register here, please," the man said. "I'll wait to give you a ride to your cabin."

Nick walked though the lobby doors and instantly felt the presence of something beautiful. Actually, he heard the presence before he felt it. The woman was reading something at the front desk, with her head down

"Pascale Pacheco. Yes, sank you, I'll be staying for the conference entire," she said, in the astonishingly sexual cadences of Catherine Deneuve.

The sound of the doors opening caused her to look up, and Nick found himself gazing into the eyes of a textbook French bombshell, right out of central casting, perhaps thirty years old: pouty Bridget Bardot lips glossed in pink, a slender nose, impossibly deep eyes under eyebrows furrowed in Gallic concentration, blonde hair pulled back in a very loose braid with casual ringlets framing her face. She wore gold hoop earrings, and there was even a sweater draped over her shoulders, with the sleeves loosely knotted around her neck. She wasn't merely beautiful, Nick thought: she was awe-inspiring.

She noticed his grin and looked at him quizzically, as if to say "should I know you?"

"*Bonjour, Mademoiselle,*" he said.

"*Bonjour, Monsieur,*" she answered, with half a smile, still trying to place him. He took out his credit card and placed it on the counter. The switchboard rang again, and two more calls came in while the clerk was handling the first one.

"*Je m'excuse, Monsieur. Vous êtes francais? Est-ce que je vous connais?*"

"No, I'm American, and you don't know me. My name's Aubrey, Nick Aubrey." He extended his hand, and she shook it.

"Pascale," she said. "*Je croyais que vous etiez Francais.*"

"*Enchanté* How very nice of you to say so."

She looked up at him, blankly, as if waiting for him to continue the conversation. But all he could think to do was to slide the credit card toward the clerk and say "Aubrey."

But no credit card was needed, the clerk informed him; the room was pre-paid. And also, Mr. Aubrey, there was a cellular telephone and an envelope that Mr. Swirsing had left for him.

"I'm here for the conference entire myself," Nick said to Pascale. "So maybe we'll meet again."

"I ope zo," she answered, glancing over her shoulder.

Nick's cart-taxi dropped him off at a little white-washed two-room cabin stocked with fruit, bread, cheese, juice, champagne, beer and wine. It was a place after his own heart: no television, very decent stereo.

He threw his suitcase and gym bag on the bed, tuned the radio to a grunge-megapop show on KFJC, prepared himself a snack and sat down to read. First he read as much of Maslow's Motivation and Personality as he could stomach, and then, again, the Atlantic article by Vannevar Bush that Casey had given him. The language was convoluted, but the ideas were astonishing, especially considering that the piece had been written in 1946. It was damn enervating, was what it was. Astounding. Metaphysical. Creepy:

"The inheritance from the master becomes, not only his additions to the world's record, but for his disciples the entire scaffolding by which they were erected."

"Okaaaay. . ." Nick said.

"Thus science may implement the ways in which man produces, stores, and consults the record of the race [. . .] All our steps in creating or absorbing material of the record proceed through one of the senses[. . .] Is it not possible that some day the path may be established more directly?"

Well Vannevar, if we had chips planted in our brains, and Ethernet drops or radio transmitters too. . . Until then we're kind of stuck.

"In the outside world, all forms of intelligence, whether of sound or sight, have been reduced to the form of varying currents in an electric circuit. Inside the human frame exactly the same sort of process occurs. Must we always transform to mechanical movements in order to proceed from one electrical phenomenon to another?"

So Vannevar *was* talking about direct brain-to-brain electrical communication. That was enough for Nick. *I can't sit still in here,* he thought. It was 7:30 PM, 10:30 Eastern, but Nick was now totally wired. He didn't need to be reading this stuff; he needed to be benching 350 on the decline press. Lifting heavy weights made it impossible to think about anything else. *Tomorrow* Nick would have time enough to worry about Vannevar Bush's Technotopia. Today was a day built for getting smelly. He tossed the article on the bed and put on his rancid workout clothes, which had been fermenting in his gym bag since the last time he had been in California. After consulting the Saratoga Club directory, he headed for the 'fitness center.'

The so-called fitness center. Fitness for croquet players, maybe: too many mirrors, and not nearly enough iron. The barbells were as thick as pencils, with little twirly things at the end, and the dumbbells stopped at forty pounds. The music being piped through the system—which should have been Black Flag or Breeders, or at a minimum, AC/DC—was Phil Collins.

Nick walked slowly around, trying not to think bad thoughts about spandex. Then, as if an answer to an unsaid prayer, he came upon a doorway that opened into a free-weight Mecca. The room was empty—which, to judge by the pristine condition of the equipment, was its usual condition. Nick did a few perfunctory stretches, threw a couple of 'quarter' plates on a barbell for warm-up, and lay back on a straight bench. The bar felt good in his hands, and at first he pushed up reps as if the bar were empty.

But when he tried to concentrate on the last rep he found himself imagining a quizzical look on an upturned face, a blush, a tentative smile, that astonishingly sexual accent. It was a miracle he didn't drop the bar and crush his windpipe.

He gave himself a little pep talk, to empty his mind: Pump iron, Nick. Don't think about nothing else. Actualize yourself.

An unfortunate choice of exhortation. Now Maslow-isms came flooding in:

"Self-actualizing people are occasionally capable of extraordinary and unexpected ruthlessness. It must be remembered that they are very strong people. This makes it possible for them to display a surgical coldness when this is called for, beyond the power of average people."

"Self-actualizing people are capable of more fusion, greater love, more perfect identification, more obliteration of the ego boundaries, than other people would consider possible."

Damn it, No. He was not going to lose his concentration. He would start with biceps and work his way back up to the bench—he was not going to allow himself to daydream. He slapped fifty pounds onto the E-Z bar and sat down at the preacher curl bench. He imagined himself a prizefighter, lacing up, waiting for the bell. When he flexed, the bar felt as light as a feather. Maslow? My ass. Bring it on, motherfucker. Let's rock and roll. Let's blast every muscle in my arms, legs and shoulders until I'm too week to lift a pencil. Chest, arms, legs, shoulders, gut, back. Bring it to me. Lat pull down. Rope pull. Seated row. Dumbbell row. Pull overs. Come on. Kickbacks. Crunches. More, I'm ready. Overhead press. Butterflies. Quad extenders. Fuck you. Toe raisers. Shrugs. Let's go. Not even the anemic Phil Collins could slow him down. Seated curl. Cheat curl. Arnold's press. Is that all you got? Straight bench. Incline bench. Decline bench. Chest press. And squats. God damn hell and death: Squats.

It was a heavier workout than he'd ever done, but the macho man in him wouldn't say quit yet. He put a hundred pounds on the bench press and lay under the bar. Two hours ago he had easily done thirty reps with this weight. His goal now was ten. But after the third rep he scaled back his ambition. Seven reps was a fine goal, he decided. After the fourth rep he re-scaled again. Five would be just fine. But he couldn't do it. His arms, chest, and legs were vibrating like Jello, and there was no way this bar was going an inch higher. He closed his eyes and strained for all he was worth, and felt the bar grow miraculously light, raising itself into its rest. Nick opened his eyes to see Pascale's two slender but very strong hands releasing the bar.

"I finish my work-out and come to hear what makes noise like an animal. Good thing for you!" she smiled.

"Thanks for the spot," he panted. As before, he could think of nothing else to say.

"In America," she called as she walked away from him, laughing, back into the mirrored work-out room, "eets important to have big muscles. In France it's more important to know how to use zem."

Half an hour later Nick was finishing up his last shoulder routine, after having tortured every muscle in his body three times over. He was going to do one more set on his biceps. He loaded the E-Z curl bar with five pounds, two and a half pounds on each side. He couldn't lift it. He was cooked.

But not quite: for good measure, the stair machine. He walked into the main room. The room was empty, mercifully. Nick clambered aboard the mechanical ladder to nowhere, his arms shaking from the exertion. It was only then that he noticed that the room was not empty, after all. Out of the corner of his eye he became aware that someone had emerged from the women's locker room. He could feel her eyes on him, watching him as one might watch a hamster on a treadmill.

He was climbing at level 2, more or less challenging for garden slugs, looking at CNN on the television, trying what, if anything, to say to the person next to him. There was a story on the tube about a husband and wife who had been doing research on Gulf War syndrome. Their names sounded familiar. . .Christian and Janine somebody or other. A car crash in Vermont, and some people were crying foul, saying they had been murdered. Christian and Janine. . . where did Nick know those names from? He missed a step and nearly fell off the machine, staggering backwards on the floor. He stopped when bumped into something soft. Slender arms helped him find his balance.

Pascale, freshly showered, dressed in khaki slacks and blue cotton shirt, looked at Nick intently. Was that fear on her face?

"Do you know them alzo?" she asked, nodding at the television.

"I can't place them," he said. "But I don't like the sound of this. Gulf War disease frightens me."

"Me too. Those two people write to me about my research," she said. "I think somebody use it to make weapons. I think somebody kill these people."

"What was your research?"

"Neek," she said. She glanced around her and placed her hand on his.

"We cannot talk here. Come on. I know someplace *Allons*."

"I think I should shower first," he said.

"I come with you."

Confused, scared, tired and aroused, accompanied by a living goddess, he retreated to his little bungalow room to shower. If Pascale had not been waiting for him just outside the bathroom door he would have stayed in the warm water for hours. Instead, he turned the shower off, grabbed a towel, a damned heavy towel, and began to dry himself in the chilly air. It wasn't clear to him whether he was shivering from cold, fear, or exhaustion. Only now did he notice that he hadn't brought a change of clothes with him into the shower. What was worse, he realized, was that the funky pair of slacks on the door hook was the only pair he had brought on this trip. He slipped into them, and wearing nothing else, he stepped out of the bathroom.

She was not in the bungalow's tiny parlor, but in the bedroom, going through his little bedside library. Instead of Balzac, the top book on the pile was now Sembene Ousmanne's *L'Aventure Ambigue*. Her hand was resting on it. She had uncorked a bottle of Chardonnay and poured two glasses which rested on the bed table, next to the books.

"Do you know it?" he asked, trying to act casual as he buttoned his one clean shirt. He grabbed a pair of socks, but decided to forgo the underwear. He hadn't been naked in front of a woman other than Bartlett since the dawn of time.

"Silly title," she pouted.

"How so?"

"It wouldn't be an adventure if it wasn't ambiguous. Bottoms up," she said, handing Nick the glass.

They got into his car and headed for San Jose. On the way, Pascale's mood changed. Yes, she said, she had corresponded, briefly, with Christian and Janine. Yes, she had a nagging fear—probably nothing more than paranoia—that her research had been misused. Some years ago she had been approached by a very nasty man who had some outlandish ideas about biological warfare. In fact this man was going to be at the conference tomorrow. But for now she was too exhausted, too jet-lagged, to talk about such things. All she wanted was to do was relax, and she knew just the place to do it. Nick drove, following her directions.

Max's, in San Jose, did not meet Nick's expectations for a gay bar. Nobody looked like the vain and muscular men of the magazines Casey had shown him. The average age of the patrons appeared to be about fifty, the average nationality something between Mexican and Japanese, the average occupation something between truck driver and newspaper reporter—a far cry from the yuppies at Gordon Biersch. Nick liked this place better. Clearly Pascale had been here before; she excused herself to go say hello to two men sitting in a corner. Nick talked for a few minutes with the guys sitting next to him, then turned to see if she were still talking with her friends. She was, and Nick got the distinct impression that three sets of eyes had been checking out his ass.

Cripes, she was blushing. This was so implausible that he assumed a practical joke was in progress. But she came and sat next to him, and as time went on it seemed less and less likely that it was a joke. She had one glass of wine, then another. She shouldn't drink any more, she said But she didn't care, she was going to have the glass of wine.

Their conversation rambled; he could hardly keep up with its twists and turns. Pascale, it seemed, was a person who got bored when a conversation stayed on one topic for more than five minutes. They talked about California, pinball, bocce ball, Kansas, Hegel, the Beatles, Johnny Holiday, Socrates, pederasty, structural anthropology, de Sade, and the Biodigital Forum.

He studied the gorgeous creature on the next stool. She was halfway through a thought about the relationship between the Vichy government and the wartime existentialists, when, in a flash, she turned her attention away from Nick, and now she was engaged in an animated conversation with the tank-topped bartender about the rules of Liar's Poker. Before Nick knew it, it was closing time, and Nick was just finding out where Pascale was from: the west part of France, near Basel, Switzerland.

"I have to go to Basel," Nick said.

"Basel?" she asked. *"Bâle, en Suisse?* You have gone there one time?"

"My brother lives there," he said. "I gave him a puzzle."

"A puzzle? *Neek, tu es fou, non?* You're not making sense. Here," she said, placing the Liar's Poker cup in Nick's hand. "Read the future. Tell me what will be."

He looked in the cup; there were five dice. "Five sixes," he said, and turned the cup over on the bar. It was four sixes and a single.

"Almost," he said.

"Mais non. You were right. The single is wild. It's fate." She looked into his eyes, for the moment completely serious. "Do you believe in fate? I do."

He said, "Of course I believe in fate. I'm a Puritan."

Three hundred and fifty years ago Pilgrims brought to Massachusetts a harsh theology based on the proposition that every man's fate was sealed. The Puritans held that you were predestined for heaven or hell, nothing you could do about it, and that the purpose of living was not to decide your fate but simply to find out what it was. Given the evidence, it was hard to make a counter-argument. Consider Nick's own case: he didn't want to be here, and a gay bar in San Jose at two in the morning the night before he was going to take on Monty Meekman. He wanted desperately to be in his little Condé Nast bungalow, sound asleep just like a rich person. Yet here he was, looking into her beautiful Socratic eyes, contemplating how her existential breast might feel to his hell-bound tongue.

She gathered the dice back into the cup and raised it to Nick's mouth.

"Blow," she said. "For luck."

He made a raspberry, *"thppt."*

"What? You spit on my dice? That is the same as to spit at me. How would you like it if I spit at you?" She smiled, put her hand on Nick's hand, touched her lips to his ear. "Because I would love to, you know. I would love to spit all over you."

Nick said, "Roll the dice."

"Ce n'est pas la peine," she said. "I already know what it is, fate for us. Let's go."

Once in the car, Pascale put her head on his shoulder. From time to time she lifted it and said "*Quelle idiote! J'ai trop bu.*" What an idiot. I drank too much.

Eventually he found his way back to the Saratoga club, and somehow they figured out which bungalow was hers. He hesitated at her door.

"Come on," she said. "*Tu viens?*"

How did he explain that he was married, and even though his wife had in fact left him a lifetime ago, he was still carrying a pathetic torch? That even though Bartlett hadn't had sex with him in about nine million six hundred thousand four hundred and twenty-two years three months nineteen days six hours and five seconds that he, Nick, didn't want to ravish the living daylights out of the most provocative creature that he had ever seen or heard tell about?

"*Viens, fait-moi l'amour,*" she said.

"Pascale," he said "it's been fun. I'm just going to use your bathroom and then I'm going back to my own room."

"Make love to me," she said, "Make love to me or you can't pee here. Go pee in the fooking bushes."

She put her arms up to block her doorway; he pushed them down, laughing, and strode past her. When he came out she put her arms around him. She licked his neck, bit his ear lobe. She raised her right thigh between his and rubbed. Then, standing there in the dark hallway, illuminated only slightly by a faint light from the kitchenette , with her arms still around his neck, she said, "you make love to me right now or I scream 'rape.'"

She put her head back and screamed "RAPE!" in her irresistible accent, and laughed.

He tried to say "I am too old for this."

He tried to say "If I have an affair with you, Pascale, my sanity, which is more fragile than the cigarette paper upon which the bumble-bees have urinated, will never survive."

He tried to say, "I'm tangled up in an intrigue of murder, industrial espionage, biological warfare, who-knows-what, and if you hang with me, mignone, you won't see your next birthday."

What he said was "OK."

She insisted, first, on feeding him, as if they were newlyweds. She put the brie on the bread, the bread in his mouth—from behind, standing while he sat, kissing his neck, hugging him, both arms in his shirt, pinching his nipples.

"Pascale, you are going to drive me out of my mind," he said.

"Oh shut up. Weight lifter. Macho man. You need to rebuild your strent. Drink. Idiot."

He drank a swig of champagne from the bottle.

"I swear to God," he said. "You are the sexiest woman in the world."

"*Ah Non,*" she said, walking to stand in front of him. "Look at me. No teets. No azz."

That did it, the force was beyond his control. He exploded out of the chair like a saber tooth tiger in a cartoon show. The first time was in the living room, with most of their clothes still on. There were bread crumbs, cheese and some spilled champagne to be cleaned up, but that was why one tipped housekeeping. The second time was in her bed, like normal people, naked.

The third time was back in the living room, on the chair, with her facing away from him. Then somehow they fell asleep.

He must have slept for about ten minutes. She was laying on his left arm; his body was half-on her mattress, which had somehow become separated from her bed and now lay on the floor. By the faint light coming in through the hallway he could see a picture hanging askew on the wall, the toppled-over champaign bottle, the upset chair, the books knocked off the shelf, the blankets strewn everywhere. He touched his knees. Ouch. There were rug burns on each, seeping. He tried to push himself up, his arms were not strong enough. He touched his right hand to his left ear. It was still bleeding, just a little.

At seven o'clock— about two hours and fifty yards from here and now—he would be at the coffee-and-pastry opening of the Biodigital Forum, where the techno-capitalists of the global village would be gathered to plot, spy, gossip, and preen, like Medicis and Borgias at a Papal ball. The place would be crawling with Corporate Fellows—ideal conditions for Nick to gather the biometrics he needed to crack the Lab's system. He needed, therefore, to awake, arise, and gird his loins for battle. But first he had to get this extremely beautiful naked French woman off of his arm.

"Pascale," he said, "I've got to go." He started to raise himself up; she pulled him back.

"*Non, reste là.*" Stay here. "*Je te ferrai des tendresses.*" I'll do sweet things to you.

"I'm sorry, I have to go. I have to work, I have to get ready."

With superhuman strength, he stood up.

Pascale called after him half-heartedly as he made his way down the hall.

"Make love to me again. *Encore! Sauvage!*" You beast.

He stumbled to the fateful bathroom, checked himself out in the mirror. What a mess. There was a hickey on his neck the size of a golf ball, a very clearly visible set of teeth marks on his ear, bags under his rheumy eyes. Good Christ. It was 5:39 AM.

He stayed in her shower for fifteen minutes, hoping for a miracle of rejuvenation. He would figure out some story about the band-aid on his ear. Visine would take care of the eyes. Five good strong cups of coffee would tighten up his facial muscles and moderate the bags. But the hickey, that was a problem. Age forty-two, man gets first hickey. This one was going to take a miracle.

He came out of the shower, his mind on business. He had one goal: get dressed and get out before she seduced him again.

The fourth time was back on the living room floor, missionary. This late in the day, after this kind of evening, at his age, nothing fancier was called for. Or possible. *Oh God,* he shuddered. He had never felt so completely sated in his life. "Whatever the opposite of horny is, I'm it," he said, looking down into her smiling thirty-year-old face.

"Oh, you air," she said. *"Pas mois.* Not me. Come on. *Je veux plus!"*

"You want more? Go find yourself a younger man." He went to get up, but she held him where he was.

"Well stay there anyway. You never know what might happen," she was saying, when his phone, the cellular that Carl Swirsing had left for him a the front desk, rang. It was on the couch; he just managed to reach it.

He hadn't heard Bartlett's voice on the phone in so long it was like a dream.

"Hey, Nick, how are you?"

"I'm fine Bartlett, how are you?"

"Good. Lonely. Good."

"Good."

He was keeping his weight up with one elbow. He was trying to get up, but Pascale had both arms around his back, securely locked, and she was starting to rock beneath him.

"I got your letter," Bartlett said.

"Oh."

"I'm glad to know you still like my ass, Nick. You always said you did."

"Yeah, well. . ."

"Remember how you always used to tell me you wanted me to wake you up with phone sex, Nick?"

"Sure I remember."

"I never did, did I?"

"Yeah, well. . ."

"Would that be an OK way for me to come back into your life after all this time?"

"Uh, sure."

"Tell me you like my ass, Nick."

"Huh?"

"Come on. Tell me you like my ass."

"It's been a long time, Bartlett."

"Not that long, Nick. Do you remember what my ass looks like? I'll describe it for you, if that helps you imagine it. Better than ever. A heart. . ."

"Oh."

"Come on Nick, tell me," Bartlett said. Pascale was licking his left nipple, both arms still around him.

"I like your ass," he said.

"Ah non!" Pascale said. *"Ce n'est pas ça.. "* She grabbed the phone from his hand.

"*Allo?* This is Pascale. Maybe he like your ass, but zis morning the only ass he is going to do belongs to me! Go away! *Au revoir!*" and with an enormous laugh, she threw the phone against the wall. It exploded into a billion pieces.

Chapter 40

Nick Aubrey sat staring at the digital clock as it turned from 6:02 to 6:03. He continued staring as it turned from 6:03 to 6:04, from 6:04 to 6:05. He might just stare all day. There had been no answer when he tried to call Bartlett in Boston, and for the life of him he couldn't recall the name of her friend the professor in Oneonta. He might just sit there all day, or until he could think of some way to get in touch with her. No, he told himself. Pull yourself together. You have a job to do, and work will free your mind. Besides, if you stay here you will surely go mad—and if that happens you'll never get her back.

He said good-bye to Pascale; she kissed his cheek. What was there to say? An apology, a thank you, a "Maybe I'll see you again some time. . .?"

At six fifteen he was driving down El Camino, forcing himself to think about how to hide his hickey so he wouldn't think about Bartlett. *It's no big deal*, he kept telling himself. It wasn't as if Scott Beckwith himself had never had to come to work with a hickey. But that was different: Scott was *of* the Temple; Nick was trying to *infiltrate* the temple. And the druids of the infotocracy smelled self-doubt the way a shark smelled blood. This hickey might be his undoing.

Out of the corner of his eye he saw the sign for Ross Dress For Less. *Saint Jude*, he said, swinging the car into the lot, *pray for us.* Wasn't that what the Catholics said, Saint Jude, the patron saint of hopeless causes? There was one other car there. Nick parked, went to the door, started tapping with his keys. *You're wasting your time. There's nobody here.* Then he saw the figure walking towards him down the darkened aisle.

"We're closed. Nine AM," the man said.

"Please," Nick said, hoping his voice would carry the depth of his sincerity through the plate glass. "I need a shirt." He pressed a hundred dollar bill against the door.

"Nine o'clock," the man said. "Sorry."

"Look," Nick said. He pulled his open collar back, and pointed to the hickey.

"OK you win," the guy said, reaching for his keys. "Man, you *are* in trouble, aren't you?"

Forty-five minutes later, wearing a large floral-print shirt buttoned at the neck in hip MTV fashion, Dorothy arrived at the witch's castle. She parked her camel-smelly Taurus in the upper lot by the practice croquet field, said "Sweet Jesus have mercy on a sinner," and got out, heading for the Papal Ball.

The first person Nick met was Carl Swirsing. He was at the pastry table on a terrace that overlooked the competition croquet lawn, talking with an earnest man-boy wearing Gatesian oversized glasses. All around there were small groups of people talking, dressed in the studied casualness of an Eddie Bauer catalog, wearing sweaters over khaki pants or hundred-dollar blue jeans. Nick was surprised at the number of women; they were about forty percent of the total. Carl was wearing tan pants, boating moccasins, and a cable-knit sweater. Nick, in his sore-thumb shirt, might be fighting the urge to run for his life, but Carl fit right in. Nick had never seen Carl look out of place, actually. What a chameleon he was, Nick thought. He could fit in anywhere.

Carl, having seen Nick, deftly excused himself from the conversation. He was a pro.

"Welcome to the Commission," Carl said. "You look like Joey Za-za."

"I feel like Lucco Brazia," Nick said. "When does the action start?"

"At Rachel's Forum there is action in non-action, like the dog that didn't bark in the night."

"Oh?" Nick said. "What dog isn't barking?"

"Gates is boycotting. He's very offended that Rachel would give over her event for a partisan deed like the unveiling of espresso *tone*. Of course, he never complained when she used her clout to convince the world that Windows was the Future."

"When do I get to see what she looks like?"

"As soon as you turn around. That's her talking with Scooter."

They turned and walked back to the pastry table. From there Nick was able to look upon Rachel Tryson talking to Scott Beckwith, with the magnificent backdrop of a cliff face rising several hundred feet straight up at the other side of the lawn. At the top of the cliff there was a tiny guardrail.

Rachel Tryson was a standard-issue white woman, neither pretty nor not pretty. Her shoulder-length hair was chestnut and shining; she appeared to be wearing conservative makeup and some kind of modest earrings. She was wearing Levis and a Gap sweatshirt, and her watch had a cloth band. She might have been a soccer mom on her way to pick the kids up from practice. Nick got the feeling that Rachel, unlike everyone around her who seemed to be affecting relaxation, was actually relaxed.

Beckwith was wearing the same outfit he had worn for his cover shoot for *Fortune* magazine; the only thing missing was the golf club. His smile was gigantic and brilliant. Those teeth: incredible. Scott could have made a living as the Energizer Bunny if he hadn't landed the gig as Chairman and CEO of Digital MicroSystems. The business magazines all focused on whether Beckwith had what it took to unseat the wealthiest man in the world. They missed the point. Scott Beckwith was a brilliant executive, but he couldn't assemble and lead the team that could build espresso. Only one man could do that. In the grand scheme of things, Beckwith was irrelevant. Dijjy-Mike versus Microsoft came down to Meekman vs. Gates.

Nick said, "Where is the old bastard? Is he here yet?" It was taking all his concentration to keep up this facade. All Nick could think of was how and where to call Bartlett. He had tried her home number: no answer. He had tried Professor Fessman's place in Oneonta: no answer. So how the hell was he going to reach her?

"Monty won't be here; not when Gates hasn't come," Carl said. "Reagan wouldn't have gone to Reykjavik if Gorbachev didn't go, and Monty won't come here without his counterpart."

"I thought he would come to orchestrate the unveiling of *espresso* and bask in the acclaim."

"You remember the broadcast from SCRI to the ACM? Engleton didn't go to San Francisco. He stayed in Mountain View and sent his acolytes up to the city."

"You think there will be a remote broadcast today?"

"There's going to be *something*. Jim Bates and the Corporate Fellows will ensure *espresso tone* makes a dramatic entrance, don't you worry."

"Are they here?"

"Keep your eyes open."

Nick looked up, and as if on cue several golf carts whizzed by, each carrying two young men wearing the purple tunics that Nick remembered from his visit to Pajaro Dunes. The Fellows were out in force, and nobody had bothered to tell them about the preppy dress code. Stepford Fellows. Well, at least that meant Nick wasn't the only one here who was dressed like a total dork. He turned again to Carl.

"What do you think: can espresso unseat Windows?"

"It's up to Rachel. There are three camps here: Microsoft, Dijjy-Mike, and neutral. Everybody who's here from a neutral camp will take their cue from her. When she makes hints about technology trends it's like when the Chairman of the Federal Reserve makes hints about interest rates. If she says espresso is dead in the water, it will sink like a stone. "

"And if she likes it?"

"Every company in the world will buy an evaluation copy, which will be enough to boost Dijjy-Mike's stock by ten bucks a share even if it eventually fails."

"And you hedge your advice to your clients based on her hints."

"I advise the timid. I make scads of money by reading the Forum tea leaves for Corporate America. I don't have to see the future years ahead of everybody else. A week is all it takes."

"And that's not enough for you?"

Carl gave Nick the kind of look Michael Corleone might give an underling who had stepped out of line.

"Nick," Carl answered, "prepare yourself for weirdness."

Prepare, himself, for, weirdness? Ach, du lieber.

"If it's anything weirder than what I've seen in the last two weeks," Nick said, " I'm going to jump off the bridge; I swear it. I'm going to jump off the Dumbarton Bridge head first at low tide."

"I can feel some weirdness approaching right now," Carl said.

Over Carl's shoulder Nick noticed another face he knew from somewhere— Mad Antonio's. The manchild VC Vulture. What was the guy's name? Whatever it was, he was heading this way.

"I gotta check out the men's lounge," Nick said.

Carl grabbed Nick's sleeve. He suddenly again looked as severe as Don Swirsing Corleone.

"Do you have that cellular phone I gave you?"

"It's broken. It got smashed. Anyway, I can't stand the idea of being always reachable."

When Carl spoke he sounded like a gunnery sergeant. In combat.

"Hey, Nick. I spotted you a plane ticket, a car; and I've given you a couple grand just for nosing around today. Don't blow me off, O.K.? Go the front desk and get another phone. Keep it with you."

What the hell, Nick thought. He could use a break, already.

By the time Nick had returned from retrieving the phone the terrace was deserted. Everybody was walking across the lawns towards the base of the cliff. There was a giant rockpile there where, over the eons, pieces of mountain had fallen to the earth. The cliff itself was concave; its chord length was about thirty yards. Within this hollow the rocks made a natural amphitheater, and scores of people were quickly filling it— scrambling over the stones, angling for a good vantage to see and hear—like disciples on the banks of the Galilee. Nick found a spot and sat. His eyes, like everyone's, naturally fixed on the focus of the arc. There Rachel Tryson sat on a table, cross-legged like a swami, waiting for her audience to ready itself.

Off beyond her, a hundred or so yards away, a small army of purple shirts appeared to be assembling some kind of stage. Giant speaker columns were going up on either side. Nerdstock?

The only sound was wind rustling through some nearby bushes, and even that quieted. Nick saw no microphone, but when Rachel spoke her voice was conversational, yet perfectly audible.

"Computation is future of biology; biology is the future of computation."

She allowed this profundity to sink in for a full minute, it seemed, before she continued.

"At the atomic and molecular scale, viruses and human-built molecular machinery perform similar functions, act on similar scales. A virus is a simple machine for manipulating strings of information; within the virus this information is encoded in the four nucleotides of DNA. Over the last decade we have made enormous strides in DNA-based technology. Genetic engineering, in the true sense of engineering, is commonplace. At the same time silicon and other types of computer chips have become ever smaller and faster, approaching biological scale. Computers manipulate strings of digitally encoded information. The difference between life and computers is that life works on a quaternary code and computers operate on a binary code. That is not a very significant difference. The union of these two technologies is immanent, as when two sides tunnel towards each other under a river. In laboratories, in fact, the two sides of the tunnel have met. It is only a matter of time before the tunnel is open to commercial traffic.

"On a macroscopic scale too, computation and biology converge. To the extent that people wear data gloves, or virtual reality visors, or electrodes in their skin to stimulate nerves in paralyzed legs or arms; to that extent the human information-processing system, which basically means the brain and nervous system, becomes part of the electronically mediated environment, which, at a first approximation, is the Internet. This integration will continue to accelerate.

"There is a third sense in which computation and biology will converge, and that is in the understanding of how the human perception of 'mind' arises from the brain. This understanding will be formalized in neural network models operating on traditional hardware. Thus in the near future, intelligences entirely akin to humans will reside in the Internet. These intelligences, not being physically limited, will merge and transform themselves in ways we cannot imagine. The idea of the discrete intelligence, such that I stop *here*, and you begin *there*, will disappear.

"These developments are profound and irreversible. The future belongs to those who are unafraid to look them in the eye, and who have to wisdom to think through their implications. I will draw your attention to one implication only. It has to do with the role of culture— culture in the anthropological sense of a large shared set of data filters.

"Because the human brain is bombarded with much more information than it can ever assimilate, it must devise filters. Amazonian Indians perceive thirty shades of green. You and I cannot perceive these differences. Even painters, artists— if they have been raised in North America—cannot see the differences. But it is possible to measure these wavelengths electronically, and the Yanamammo can see them. People are born with this ability, but unless the culture recognizes and re-enforces it, distinctions are filtered out and the ability atrophies.

"Until recently, cultures were formed at human speed, around human senses. Institutions and traditions emerged to act as custodians of culture. Institutions, hence culture, changed slowly. These institutions include, for example, families, religions, languages, and nations. These institutions are now obsolete. They cannot adapt fast enough to adapt to the information stream, and they will all whither away. What will replace them? Instantaneous cultures sold retail by transnational corporations. The transnational corporation will supplant families, religions, languages, and nations. In every way, culture will be designed by the transnational corporation, and around the ideas of impermanence and biodigital convergence.

"Traditionalists, whether they be Islamic militants, bombers of abortion clinics, or Unabombers, will selectively appropriate the tools of the transnational corporations to fight the transnational culture, fighting fire with fire. Thus Islamic fundamentalists will use the Internet, cellular telephones, biological warfare, whatever, with the aim of ultimately destroying the very civilization that produced these devices. But not only Islamic fundamentalists. Not only Islamic, and not only fundamentalists. Traditionalists of all kinds will fight to prevent the two ends of the tunnel from touching. Thus the fight is not between North and South, or between Islam and infidel. It is between the discrete and the continuous. It will be a fight to the death, and institutions that want it both ways—that is, that want the benefits of modern transnational commerce and at the same time want the benefits of traditional culture-preserving institutions— are houses divided against themselves, and they cannot stand. This class of divided houses includes most governments, and in particular, the government of the United States.

"The only significant geographical area that will retain traditional institutions at all will be Sub-Saharan Africa, and for a very simple reason: AIDS. This disease, and other, newer epidemics— designer diseases—will of course appear in every corner of the world. The difference is that unlike, say, Russia, Africa has not yet developed enough infrastructure to withstand a thirty-to-sixty percent child mortality rate. Whatever modern infrastructure that currently exists will soon collapse. And no person in his right mind will go to Africa to rebuild it. It will be too dangerous, in every way. Therefor Africa is likely to remain the last place on earth where human beings— although ill, desperately poor, and mired in constant anarchy and warfare—live as our species has lived for hundreds of millennia. For that they are to be pitied. Or envied."

She finished speaking and sat quietly. No one said anything for a long while. Nick could not think when, if ever, he had seen such a large group of people behave so quietly. It was as if Rachel Tryson's words had been a soothing balm to their souls.

She left her perch after introducing the next speaker, Jim Boerr. In an astonishingly athletic move, Boerr jumped up on the table. He talked much more quickly and energetically than Tryson had, but Nick still saw no evidence of amplification.

"I think we can draw some very important conclusions from what Rachel has just told us," he said. He was obviously used to speaking to large groups. He was poised, he enunciated clearly, and he moved as gracefully as a tiger.

"The most important conclusion, I think we'll all agree, is that there's a lot of money to be made when the two ends of the biodigital tunnel are opened up for traffic. Imagine the value of a complete simulation of the human brain! It would be worth hundreds of millions of dollars, for drug companies alone. New therapies could be tried out without the time and expense of experiments on human subjects. I'm sure you can think of a million other uses. A working model of the human brain is going to make somebody, or some group of somebodies, very very wealthy."

An appreciative chuckle went up from the crowd.

"Think for a minute about what Rachel said about the irrelevance of governments. Imagine, the pace of progress in brain research in the absence of legal restrictions once the United States has been privatized. China is already a lucrative source of kidneys and other organs; imagine the money to be made in brains once the market opens! No wonder Bill wanted so badly to get into China!"

Another chuckle went up from the crowd.

"In the absence of national governments, two things happen. First, so-called privacy rights cease to be a problem. Second, the need for private security service increases exponentially. How can we capitalize on this situation? Imagine a biometric database for every person in North America. Finger prints, DNA phenotype, iris scan, one or two other markers. That would enhance security, wouldn't it? Who would be foolish enough to attempt a crime when their apprehension was certain and justice was administered according to market prices? With today's technology it would not be difficult to compile such a database, and it's about to become much easier.

"With *espresso tone* the day of ubiquitous computing is truly here. Your challenge, your opportunity, is to imagine ways to combine the power of*espresso* with the breakthroughs in biocomputation that Rachel spoke of.

"Don't think this market window will stay open very long. Somebody in this audience is going to tap this opportunity, and the rest of your are going to be going 'd'oh!'. Biometrics will make it possible to know, at any time, the whereabouts of every single person who participates in the modern world. Homes will be wired to know who is in what room of the house doing what activities, and cars likewise will track the location of drivers and passengers. In public people will be tracked by cameras; in stores their biometrics will be recorded—and soon satellites will be able to detect DNA trails as easily as they now detect heat trails of ballistic missiles. Building such a database and tracking system will take a lot of capital. But once it's in place, we're talking return on equity here, *major* return on equity for this kind of information. . . "

Nick found himself thinking of another song on the great second album of Human Sexual Response, "In a Roman Mood." It was the story of a boy who jumped or fell or was pushed out the tenth floor dormitory window, but whose body was never found.

Everybody in the dormitory
Said they were real sorry
Everybody had a different story
How Andy fell down, Andy fell down.

Andy had evidently told his friends something about Bishop Pike. Nick tried to remember: Bishop Pike: was he the one who went by the name of 'Bo', and led his followers into the desert to meet a spaceship?

Across the way the purple-shirts were assembling the stage.

Nick didn't notice how long Boerr spoke, but before he knew it Rachel was back on the table announcing a break for lunch. The afternoon was open, she said; this evening there would be a plenary session and presentation at the stage, when Jim Bates, *espresso*'s lead designer, would introduce its newest incarnation, release 2.0.

Nick was in no mood for sitting down at a table and making small talk with the Jim Bateses and Mini-Gateses of the world. Instead he went back to his room, put on his ever-more putrid gym clothes, ran to the eentsy-teentsy antiseptic weight room with the half-size barbells and full sized mirrors, worked out for two hours, showered, put on the his pants and hickey shirt, and loaded up his car. He wanted to be ready in case there was a need for a quick getaway.

It was in while in the shower that Nick began to think seriously about the non-appearance of Pascale. The Biodigital Forum was a small-enough conference. If she had attended any of it, Nick would have seen her. But it was still only three o'clock, too early to jump to any conclusions. The plenary session didn't start until six; he would probably see her there. Maybe she was sleeping off her jet lag. Maybe she was simply being discrete. Maybe, on the other hand, she was long gone. Maybe she had been a plant—sent by the CIA, or by Carl, or by the True Patriots to give him a happy and get some information. Which he had obligingly done, he now realized. He had told her, more or less, where the diskette was. But this was paranoid thinking; undoubtably she was simply recovering from a long and exhausting evening. He rejoined the Forum, walking in a daze from one discussion group to another, speaking to nobody but trying not to stand out, until late afternoon.

Chapter 41

Shock, fear, regret and weariness. Or maybe the breakfast she had eaten at the Oneonta Airport before boarding the puddle-jumper for Boston. Whatever had caused it, she seemed to have lost her ability to think. She had been in Logan Airport for half an hour, and she was no closer to locating the Blue Line than she had been when the plane landed. What was worse, she knew that this conditions was preposterous, but she had literally no idea what to do about it.

From time to time, in the past, she had tried to imagine how the world presented itself to pre-scientific, non-scientific people. Nick would describe an experience from deep in the Senegalese Fouta or far up the Amazon River—where magic existed, and science didn't—and it would be literally incomprehensible to her. But if Nick were to suddenly appear and tell her those same stories now, she felt certain that she would understand. Because as she looked around Logan airport nothing made sense. The only explanation of why things held together at all was magic. It was magic that kept the planes from falling out of the sky, magic that held the ceiling up, magic that put the writing on the televisions that all the people looked at before scurrying down this corridor or that.

Bartlett had accepted Eddie's invitation to stay at his house in Oneonta for a few days. By magic Nick had found her there. She had met with him in the Duke Diner. There, despite his odd appearance and odder questions, she had felt the stirring of feelings for him that she had given up for dead. Uncertain, confused, she had spent the next day walking through the hills where she and Nick had used to go walking, and she had come back to Eddie's place to find a letter from Nick. It was not high literature, to be sure, but it was a letter which, by magic, dissolved the years of corrosion that had built up on her heart. She had decided that Eddie was right, after all: she could never be unmarried. It was time to go back to her husband. This morning she had gathered her courage and called him—from a closet in Eddie's guest room—and sat in mute horror as all her magic turned from good to bad.

"Allo? This is Pascale. Maybe he like your ass, but zis morning the only ass he is going to do belongs to me! Go away! Au revoir!" Bartlett could still hear Pascale's voice; the woman's laughter seemed to echo throughout Logan.

To avoid meeting Eddie at breakfast, Bartlett had remained in the guest room until ten. By noon, with much exertion of will, she had composed herself. She packed her things, then went to Eddie's campus office to say goodbye. When she arrived there, Eddie, looking pale and suddenly older, told her that Christian and Janine had been killed in a car crash in Vermont. 'Reckless, high-speed driving' was to blame, the preliminary report said. Dumbstruck, Bartlett had fled to the tiny Oneonta airport, and now she was here. Home, allegedly.

She needed to get to Downtown Crossing. She was going to go shopping. She needed to buy some clothes—a skirt and a blouse, perhaps. Nick always said she was sexy when she dressed in a skirt and blouse. She reminded him of a schoolgirl, he said. He was always telling her to buy saddle shoes too. Well, this time she would. As soon as she got to Boston she was going to buy a pair of saddle shoes. Then she would put on her new skirt and blouse ensemble and show up unannounced at their house in Newcastle. No, what was she thinking? Bartlett and Nick had sold their house. And she didn't need clothes to wear on a date, she needed clothes to wear to a *funeral*. A dark suit for dual funeral.

Christian, a reckless driver! Bartlett would sooner have believed that Eddie

Fessman, retired professor of Biochemistry, was running an international cocaine and prostitution ring from his SUNY study. How could she make sense of it all? How could a rational scientist like Bartlett McGovern Aubrey make sense of a world in which diskettes erased themselves, phage infected people, and the world's most cautious man drove eighty miles an hour down winding snowy roads?

"Pascale," at the Biodigital Forum. Could there be any doubt that Nick's new girlfriend was the same Pascale who had published the nonsensical articles about bacteriophage in 'monster cells?' The same woman who had written the Frankensteinian book in the Logan airport? To lose Nick through her own hard-headedness was one thing. But to *that* woman?

Bartlett was walking by the kinetic sculpture when her hard shell cracked, and she began to sob. The sculpture had incited a memory of Jackson—his loping gate, his tripping and falling, his diminishing sight, his increasing fears, his final weakness—which clashed in Bartlett's mind with the recollection of Pascale's mocking laughter. The shell did not go all at once, exactly, but neither was it a very thick shell, and it didn't take very long once it started. Sucking in her breath, clutching her notebook to her chest like a child with a rag doll, she ran to the nearest ladies' room and threw water on her increasingly red and puffy face.

She looked wild, she knew it. But her friends Christian and Janine had been murdered, and only Bartlett knew why: because they had found out that bacteriophage, the wet noodles of the viral world, caused Gulf War disease. And now it was up to Bartlett to make this fact known to the world, for which her career would be destroyed and she would be killed. If only she had Nick here. But she had given him the boot. And now he was with Pascale.

If only she had reached out to Nick when he had reached out to her. But no, she had let two little words ruin her life. Enna bouby. Why had she let those words stop her? Whenever she tried to discuss having children with Nick, he would, sooner or later, say those words—with a laugh, an evasion—and then he would shut down. But it had always been within *her* power to create life—it wasn't as if Nick had erectile dysfunction. *He* was the one who had needed her. She could have helped him find escape from whatever African demon it was that had plagued him, that made him so fear fatherhood. Why had she been so polite? She should have tossed her damn birth control pills in the garbage!

How different their lives would be now if they had a little three year old daughter or four year old son who needed their love and attention. Her grief over Jackson would have been tempered. They would have carried on with their lives, their marriage. There was nothing *wrong* with adoption. There was nothing *wrong* with having no children at all. For other people. But not for Bartlett and Nick. They had needed to make a child, and she had known it. Before today she had always blamed him. But now she knew the blame was hers.

Where would she go? What would she do? She couldn't go back to the lab, back to nosy Irwin and his little bits of tuna sandwich caught in his beard. She couldn't go back to her solitary apartment on Commonwealth Avenue—that was a life for college students. She couldn't go back to Nick; if there was one fantasy that crept up in Nick's fervid pillow talk more often than any other it was Nick-with-sexy-French-chick. Now that he had finally found one, what would she say, 'sorry about the breakup, never mind?"

The taxi let her off at Commonwealth. She ran up the stairs with her travel bag slipping off her shoulder. Her clothes were wrinkled like crumpled tinfoil. She was afraid that she herself would crumple right where she was. She began trotting towards her door as if trying to outrun flying devils with pitchforks.

She needed somebody to hold, somebody to hold her. She would have gone and pulled Nick from Pascale's arms if they were anywhere near, but they were in California. She was absolutely all alone in the world, and feared that she might kill herself once she got in the door.

And then she saw him. He was a vision. He was waiting for her at her door. He was holding some kind of package.

He turned to say "Hello Bartlett," and had got the words half-way out before her arms were around him and she was kissing all over his face. She felt his arms go around her, awkwardly. She was still carrying the notebooks and shoulder bag, which were getting heavy, but she couldn't lower her arms. She had to hold him. He was a life preserver floating by as the ship went down in the distance. Her mind was finally being allowed to rest; her instinct for self-preservation was taking over.

As if hearing someone else speak, some other lost soul in a dream, far away, she heard herself say, "Paul, take me inside, right now."

Chapter 42

The chill was back in the air as the crowd began to converge before the stage. The sun dipped behind the mountains and some of the famous fog started to cascade down the cliff. It was almost as if the fog were an alive being, crawling up over the ridge from the unseen Pacific side, and slithering down the bay side—sentient eddies and swirls that merged into each other and separated: a shifting, mutating, caressing, consuming heart of whiteness.

The conversations going on around him were more animated this evening than those he had heard in the morning. Many people held drinks. There was laughter. But when Rachel walked on the stage that same preternatural silence descended. Again she spoke without amplification.

"Tonight Jim will tell us about *espresso*. Then we have a little entertainment."

That was it? Evidently it was. She walked off the stage.

Jim Bates now walked on. His scraggy beard, unkempt hair and intense stare made him look like a cross between the early Bob Dylan and the later Albert Einstein. Next to Meekman, Bates was said to be the most brilliant engineer at the Labs, and Monty's alter ego. He lived on a mountaintop in Colorado and only came down on rare occasions, appearing to some, leaving behind him rumors and blurry photos, like Elvis.

"Good evening," Bates said. Nick almost expected him to spin his head in a circle. "Our friend Monty Meekman couldn't be here this evening," Bates said. "But he's with us in spirit."

As he said these words a giant holographic image of Monty appeared behind him. "Hello everybody," Monty chirped. "I'm with you in spirit." Then the holograph vanished.

Was *that* the dramatic introduction Carl had predicted? The cheesiest Las Vegas act was ten times more impressive than that. Along the edges of the crowd, the purple-shirts were passing out flyers. Eventually one was handed to Nick. What would it be, a free pass to Siegfried and Roy?

It was a glossy photo of Monty Meekman. Nick turned the photo over; on there reverse was a reproduction of a bronze plaque, the System Software Award of the ACM:

To Montaigne Meekman
in Recognition of his Pioneering and Brilliant Investigations of
Parallel Distributed Processing, Artificial Intelligence,
Neural Network Topologies, Self-Organizing Systems
and Countless other Domains of Computer Science
June, 1992

This was getting tackier and tackier. What were they going to do next, invoke Monty's blessing, like a rabbi at a football game? Nick didn't care what he had promised Carl, it was time to blow this pop stand. The only reason he had come here was to collect the biometric data that Casey needed to crack into the Labs' system. Nick was going to find a Corporate Fellow, take a glass from his hand and a few hairs from his head, and then he was going to split.

On the stage Bates was going on about *espresso tone*, an analogy to the dial tone of the telephone. The *espresso* protocol was going to be even more ubiquitous. Using *espresso*, not only would computers communicate with each other, but thermostats would communicate with televisions, cars would communicate with toasters, wristwatches would communicate with nuclear launch control centers. *Espresso* the language was software, but it could be put into a rom, incarnated in hardware. The Labs had created just such rom chips, and they were distributing them freely, starting tonight. Starting next week video stores would give *espresso* chips out with rentals, and the hamburger chains would be enclosing *espresso*-powered games with children's meals.

The sky had become more dark, and now when the holograph appeared it was more impressive than it had been earlier. It took the shape of a slowly spinning globe that showed the projected density of *espresso* devices over the next five, ten, twenty years. The globe became first like a golf ball with the skin stripped away: layer up on layer of rubber bands representing communications links. North America, Europe, Japan were heavily saturated, South America, Russia, China, India less so. Only Africa seemed devoid of the presence of *espresso*. Satellites filled the distance above the earth. As more and more devices and links were simulated, the golf ball shape became increasingly asymmetric. Folds were developing in the links, and folds within folds. The holograph now more clearly resembled a brain than the globe that it had started out as, with Africa a deep indentation, like a brain stem.

The fog was getting thicker and Nick was finding it harder and harder to concentrate. Bates announced a three-part collaboration among Hoff-Zeigy Pharmaceuticals, Digital MicroSystems, and the Neuro Group to develop a global simulated brain and decode the Human Genome faster than the federal Human Genome Project. When this effort succeeded, Bates said, Digital MicroSystems would have proprietary rights to the design of post-human beings.

The Fellows in matching outfits were everywhere. Bates was talking about teleomeres and the regeneration of nerve cells. On behalf of Monty Meekman, the Corporate Fellows were announcing today that the Labs had determined the structure and function of the genes that controlled the generation of brain cells. Full particulars, including the structure, function, and chromosomal location of the genes were spelled out microscopically in the inscription on the back of the cards that the Fellows had handed out. This was Monty's gift today to mankind: the power to heal damaged brains. And there was an extra special secret there for those who knew where to look.

The Microsoft man-boy with the large glasses walked up to the microphone that had been set up on the field before the stage.

"*Espresso* is a fine concept," he said. "But a lousy, lousy implementation. There is an implicit clock pulse at twelve point five milliseconds. This implies a forty hertz rate for handshakes, which is preposterously slow, and it cannot be fixed without changing the entire protocol. It's a killer bug. *espresso* is doomed, like Betamax. Like eight-track. Like vinyl."

The decorum that had prevailed until now suddenly disintegrated. All around Nick people began shouting about the virtues of *espresso* on one side, its design flaws on the other. Bates walked off the stage in the pandemonium, and what appeared to be a rock band appeared on the stage in the middle of the still-spinning brain-globe. More fog began to appear out of the towers. It was time for Nick to find a Corporate Fellow and do some James Bonding.

No problem. Here was Jim Bates, right in front of him, along with five or six Corporate Fellows. Something wasn't right. On this monumental occasions, surely there was somebody Bates would want to talk with more than Nick Aubrey, the has-been software manager.

"Nice to see you again Nick," Bates said. "I don't think I've seen you since Pajaro dunes."

"You were great," Nick answered. "Taking all that flack, like Gregory Peck in that movie Monty showed us at that retreat. Remember?"

"Twelve O'clock High," six voices said in unison.

"What do you think was the point of that movie, Nick? What was it about?"

Corporate fellows seemed to be materializing out of thin air, all happy to see him. He decided to use some live bait himself.

"The airmen wanted the commander to be their friend, but he has to be their leader, and a lot of the airmen don't understand the difference. His actions appear ruthless, but it's just doing the job. Like when Monty canceled the Kali project. Everybody was saying 'it's just a stupid off-by-one error. Todd will get that in the next pass.' Nobody would accept that a simple off-by-one error was reason to cancel the project. And all that talk about the nucleotide encoding."

It was a hunch.

"Who was talking about nucleotide encoding?" Bates said. "Who?"

Evidently a good hunch.

"I don't remember," Nick said. It was getting difficult to see more than a few yards away.

"Nucleotide encoding had nothing to do with Kali," Bates said. "Some people took Monty's ideas and developed chips that can electronically recognize pre-programmed segments of DNA."

"That's Monty's fate," Nick said. "People resent his superiority. That's why everybody was trying to reverse-engineer those Kali's, I guess. Trying to get back at him."

"What?"

"Oh, maybe you didn't know about that. After Kali got canceled some of the diagnostics guys were trying to parse the chip by brute force. Ridiculous: they only had the chip; no specs."

There was a moment of silence.

"There *were* no Kali chips," Bates said. "We collected all of them."

"Oh you're right, there were none in the Mill. But there were three or four of them out here in California, in, what, Building 19, the Bonehead Computer Museum?"

"What are you talking about?" three purple shirts said. "What Bonehead Museum?"

What had Casey said? *'All I want you to do is see if you can flush some bunnies out of the woods?'* Nick was pretty sure he had just seen a bunny.

"Hell I don't know," Nick said, trying to cover his tracks. "It was a West coast, hardware thing. I'm East coast, software. Is it important?"

"It's just that we promised Intel we would give them all the Kali chips."

Nick didn't believe that was all there was to it. It was time to go on the offensive again.

"It was nice of the ACM to give him this award," Nick said, holding up the picture of Monty. "Too bad they were too chicken to publish his article. It seems kind of hypocritical to me."

"What article?" Bates and several others said.

"That policy article, you know, the one they call the New Gospel."

"I'm not sure I know what article you're talking about, Nick," Bates said, in a way that made Nick think of movie prison-wardens.

"I probably got the story wrong," Nick said, folding the picture and putting it in his back pocket. "Where is Monty, by the way? Is he still in Basel?"

Bates looked very serious. How could Albert Einstein be so menacing?

"What makes you say Monty was in Basel?"

"Oh, my wife was there for a meeting at Hoff-Zeigy. She says she saw him there but he was with somebody else, so she didn't say hello."

Nick! You've just made Bartlett a possible witness to a murder. Oh, you idiot! Backtrack, quick!

"Monty isn't in Basel." Bates said. "She must have been mistaken. He's here."

"Oh, I'm sure she was mistaken," Nick said. "She's always mistaking people for somebody else. One time she thought this guy walking a baby around Central Park was Dustin Hoffman so she went up to him to say she liked his movies and the guy thought she was nuts."

"Where is she now, Nick? Where is your wife?"

"She's in Amsterdam." It was the first place that popped into his head. "She has family there, and she's never been to Europe before so she's kind of making a trip of it."

Nick didn't like the turn this conversation was taking. Too many bunnies.

"I'm just a little confused Nick, that's all," another Fellow said.

"I thought you went to Oneonta to see her."

"What the hell? How did you know I was in Oneonta?"

"What brought you there, Nick? You haven't been there in years, have you?"

"It was my mother's funeral, for the love of God."

Nick no longer had any idea what was going to come out of his own mouth. "Your mother died last week?"

"Yes."

"Do you remember the first time Dr. Meekman invited you to dinner?"

"You mean the first time he stood me up? Sure. What does that have to do with anything?"

"It was on February 26th, 1990 at *Chez Louis* in Palo Alto. You had *sole meuniere;*. Your white wine was an 86 Pouilly Fusee and you also had a glass of red, an 81 Mount St. Michael Cabernet. Do you remember?"

"Not as well as you do, evidently."

"Then perhaps you don't recall telling Monty, on the telephone, that your father died when you were in Africa and your mother died when you were in Brazil."

Shit! Bushwhacked! How could they possibly have known that?

He stammered for a minute. Saint Jude, how about twice in one day?

"For Christ's sake!" he said. Use the old indignation till something better comes along.

"We don't like being lied to. Not by somebody who's been calling us Stepford Fellows."

"I didn't lie to you," he lied. St. Jude was thinking over his request for help, apparently. But wait a second. Had Nick called these guys Stepford Fellows, or had he only thought that?

"Where did you *really* go last week, Nick? It was Utah, wasn't it?"

"Utah? What are you talking about? What makes you say I was in Utah?"

"Detective Ivan Marki was found shot dead in a Utah gully. Police say he was killed two or three days ago. While you say that you were in Oneonta at a funeral that never happened."

"Ivan Marki?"

"Come on Nick. You know who he is."

The band was playing an inept cover of the Velvet Underground, *White Light, White Heat.*

"What does his death have to do with me?" Nick said.

"He took a bullet in the head. Just like your friend Todd. Like your brother's friend Dieter."

"Oh fuck you," Nick said. "Fuck all of you."

With his right hand Nick snatched the glass from Bate's right hand, and with his left hand he grabbed a handful of hair and yanked Bates's face into his right knee.

He stuck the bloody wad of hair in the glass, and with his other hand grabbed the cell phone so it wouldn't fall out of his pocket. He turned in the direction of his car, so far as he could tell direction at all, and ran.

Chapter 43

Casey Montgomery walked down the hall, opened the door to her office, and knew immediately that she was hosed.

Oh God save me, it's him! she thought. She turned to run but it was too late—there was someone behind her. They must have staked out her office: one had been waiting inside the office while the other waited around the corner at the little coffee station.

Some corporate security, she thought, *these people both had weapons.* But who was Casey to complain about security at the Mill? She had been flaunting it for years. If there was any getting out of this predicament, which she doubted, she was going to have to do it by herself.

The man had a black gun in his hand. The barrel looked very long. Oh, a silencer. Tacky.

"I need the Kali chip," he said. "I understand that you have one in the bone-headed computer museum. Kindly take us there. Don't try to give me a substitute; I know what a real Kali looks like."

"Sorry. Museum's closed," she said. "Come back tomorrow."

"Don't fuck with me. Take me to your so-called museum."

"Why would I fuck with you?" she said. "You ugly."

She turned and looked over her shoulder at the person standing behind her. Person? Upon closer inspection it appeared to be a female alien from the cast of Star Trek: she was wearing not a mask, but expertly applied heavy makeup that completely distorted every feature of her face. There was no telling what she looked like underneath all that.

"Come on, I'll take you to the damn museum," Casey said.

She made a motion towards her desk, but he pointed the pistol right at her head and said,

"Stop, what are you doing?"

"'Stop, what am I doing,'" she mimicked. "I'm coming to give you a blow job. Unzip. You moron, I'm getting the key. The key, OK?"

He nodded OK.

She opened her desk drawer and pulled out a knotted loop of pink ribbon, about ten inches long, with a key on it. She picked it up and held it toward them by the knot; the key swung back and forth.

"The key? OK? The key?" she said. Then she started towards the hall way.

She could feel them both following her. She heard a rustle of clothing but she didn't look behind. What a cliché, she thought. They've probably both put on black leather jackets. "OK," she said, "museum this way."

She started walking with no clear idea of where she was heading. One thing for certain: she wasn't going towards the shrine until she had ditched these two heavies. Where could she do that?

She remembered an enormous room, about four floors and six buildings away from the shrine, that still contained manufacturing equipment from Newcastle Textile. If she could lure her pursuers there, maybe she could lose them amid the warps and woofs of the ancient looms. In any event the Mill was one very large place. Nobody knew it better than Casey did, and if you had told her to find a chip hidden in it she would have needed two thousand years. These goons could kill her if they wanted to, but she wasn't going to give them the Kali.

If memory served, this door on her left led to the loom room. She pushed the door open and immediately began to run. After about five seconds she could hear the bullets as they danced around her. Cripes, just like the movies, she thought.

As another bullet whizzed past, she ducked behind a large wooden bench. She raised her head above it, not knowing where they were, and called out, "Bet you can't tell I'm not wearing any underpants."

Two bullets answered. OK, *that's* where they were. She ran down a half flight of stairs, where, by an act of God, she found a shovel, relic from who-knew-what activity a century before. She picked it up and swung, never looking, only trusting somebody would be there. The shovel hit something soft. There was a muffled shriek and she heard a gun drop. She ran back up the short flight and back through the door that she had come through, reasonably confident that the uninjured one would leave his companion and continue chasing Casey alone. She was also reasonably confident that he would not shoot her in a main hallway. There was after all some security in the Mill.

The trick was going to be to get him to follow her to the Void without letting him catch her, and then to lose him. She clutched the key tightly. She didn't hear anybody following, so she turned around. He was at least fifteen yards behind. She stopped, turned, held up the key and said, "nyah-nyan-na-boo-boo" and took off at a trot.

Down Daniel Shays to Two, up the stairs, four flights. He was still behind her. Down Publick Alley 4754 to Building three, then right at Turners Falls. There was the door; she had made it as far as the Void. So far, so good.

She turned to make sure that he was still with her, and pushed the door to the Void. Now it was time to see if she could really run. *Come on,* she said to herself, *Come on, Rosie Ruiz. You can do it.* She ran harder than she had ever run in her life. Past the empty rows of cubicles, past the cubicles filled with cables, monitors, chairs, circuit boards, testers, boxes; past Nick's cube. Through the door that said, "DO NOT ENTER, ALARM WILL SOUND." Up, up. Would she have time? Only one was following her, right? But was that two sets of footsteps following behind? Up.

Up. Up. The key, the key, the key, up, up. The key fit. She opened the lock. Through the window miraculously open, slamming it behind her. Into the cold night air.

She heard the door swing open.

She heard it clang against the wall.

She heard silence.

She heard the sound of his body hitting the bridge five stories below. His skull, when it split, sounded remarkably like a cantaloupe.

She thought she heard the sound of his gun falling in the upper pond, but she couldn't be sure.

One down, one to go.

⊕

Damn, damn, *damn*, what had made Nick think he could tangle with those guys? Tonight's performance had been something right out of amateur hour: "In *this* corner, decent guy, weighing in at 'smart': *Nick Aubrey*. In *that* corner, weighing in at IQ three million and still counting: *Monty Meekman's Corporate Fellow Tag Team*." Indeed Nick's cover was blown for sure, and he had dragged Casey and Bartlett in along with him. How long until Monty murdered all of them?

Nick had driven his rental car down to San Antonio, in Palo Alto and followed that road to its end. He parked it near a dumpster in a lot that abutted the marshes of the South Bay. The dikes and levees were Nick's favorite place to think. He would have tens of square miles to himself, because nobody went there after dark. Nobody would find him here walking along the moonlit dike that ran through the marshes along the edge of the bay.

⊕

Casey waited. The other footsteps had been right behind the first pair, but they had stopped at the top of the stairs. Now she had a decision to make. She could continue to wait there outside the window and try to jump the woman when she climbed out onto the roof. Or, she could run. *Let's see, hmmm. . .Which will it be? Run for my life? Or stay here and engage Lady Terminator in hand to hand combat?* She ran. Her legs were much heavier than they had been a ten seconds ago.

If she could make it to the parapet, maybe she could time her jump just right. Maybe she could get this one to fall for the same trick, to jump where there was no ledge, to fall to her death. She could hear footsteps getting closer. Closer.

Now!

She jumped. But she was more tired than she had thought. She wasn't going to clear the distance. In the split second in the air, with the nothingness beneath her, a single thought went through her head.

No.

That was the thought. *No.*

You took my lover.

You took five years of my life.

You don't get me.

No.

She stretched her arms as far as they would go. Somehow they managed to reach the ledge, and she scrambled up. But Lady Terminator had seen the ruse, and Casey wasn't going to be able to get rid of her that way.

She scrambled in the window, down the halls. Her pursuer was only ten yards behind. There was no time for fancy strategy. Casey was never going to set foot in this dark satanic Mill again. She was going to have to go to the museum for the Kali. Now. She would figure out what to do about powerbitch when she got there.

Most of the Mill's corridors were lit up like a K-mart, but if she could make it to the museum maybe she could lose her in the dark. Down the hall, through the swinging doors. It was pitch black, thank God. She knew her way, her attacker didn't. With any luck she wouldn't find the light switch. If Casey could just make it into the cooler, grab the Kali, put it in her shirt pocket, then dash back out. . . Maybe later she could get a friend to bring the etch plot to her when things had settled down, in a day or two. For now the only important thing was the chip. She had to have the chip.

Breathing hard, quietly, with her lungs screaming for more air, she used her toes to slip off her shoes. The linoleum felt cold on her bare feet as she inched her way down the hall. Was there somebody else breathing there, behind her? She couldn't tell, the sound of her own heart was too loud. Foot by careful foot she made her way through the empty kitchen. Was she alone?

She put her hand on the handle of the cooler. She could see, in her mind's eye, four-armed impassive Kali floating above her. Kali, Goddess of death, destroyer of worlds. *Hope you're enjoying this,* she thought. The door made a loud click as it opened. Shit! But no response. Maybe somehow she had done it, gotten away. She stepped into the cooler.

Damn! What did you have to do that for? The pain to the back of her head was excruciating, and her cheek didn't feel too good either. Then the blinding light in her eyes. She knew she should get up, but her legs and arms had been replaced with silly string. Pistol whipped. This was a real education she was getting tonight, that was for sure.

The woman was wearing a black leather jacket. What a cliché. How tacky. But the bitch was good, Casey had to admit it. She couldn't move. Had she been tied up? No. Her body just wouldn't work. Then she saw the gun come out. With a silencer, just like the one funny boy had pointed at her in her office. So this was going to be it, after all. *'Chip designer found shot dead.' Deja vu all over again, Todd.* The alien woman aimed, fired.

The last remaining Kali chip was no more. A million bits of glass dust were floating in the air; Casey couldn't see them: a tiny invisible silent crashing. With this Kali went all hope of figuring out the mystery, all hope of solving Todd's murder, all hope of rectifying injustice. She might as well have taken the bullet in her head. Her life was over. Then she saw the Bic lighter come out. Tacky again. A classy assassin would have had a *gold* lighter. The etch map was glorious as the flames devoured it, the multicolored lines writhing in the flames like a map of hell. *If you can read this you're too damn close.* That's precisely my problem, Todd. I got too damn close.

She heard the door close. She heard the lock go on. What had she told Nick? *"You could kill somebody in here, but not by accident. You would have to lock it from the outside."*

Famous last words.

Chapter 44

Paul Aubrey sat at the café table, enjoying, if one could call it that, commingled sensations of warmth, coffee, bewilderment, fear, and a contentment at being, for the moment, home. Out the window and across the street he could see the little balcony of his apartment. He had taken most of his meals here, *Chez Jacques,* for nearly six years. Being in this café was the closest thing to being at his mother's place. Upon arrival at the airport, Paul's first stop had been at the Bank, for a short meeting with a managing director. Then he had gone home to his apartment long enough to take care of one or two important matters. It was natural that, having taken care of the things he had come back to Basel to take care of, Paul would come here next.

He was not really surprised when he saw the woman entering through the front door. She had watched him in France, he had seen her in Basel, he had seen her in Palo Alto and in Sunnyvale. At some point the furtiveness would have to end; they would have to meet face-to-face. Paul signaled to his friend Jacques, the café's owner; he arrived at Paul's table just before the woman did, in time to hear Paul's urgent request.

Ever the gentleman, Paul rose to welcome his guest and indicated her seat. They sat.

So, she said. They met at last.

Indeed, he said.

Had he guessed who she was? He had. She was his angel.

Well then, she said. He certainly also must have guessed what she wanted of him, and what she was prepared to offer to get it.

What she wanted, primarily, was the diskette, he guessed. What she was prepared to offer to Paul was a promotion to General Manager of the NanoSection, or something comparable.

A good guess, she said. Well, she said. What was his answer?

The answer, he said. Was no.

He had better be certain, she said. There would be no protracted negotiation.

He was certain, he said.

Jacques brought the telephone to the table; as Paul had requested, Jacques had already found and dialed the number for him.

Just a moment, Paul said, putting the phone to his ear. He could hear it ringing on the other end.

No, she said. No 'moment.'

The first time the steel pierced his heart, Paul felt a stabbing pain. He still held the phone to his ear. The second time he felt less pain; mostly he felt incredible weakness. Too weak to hold the phone he let it drop, but he could still hear it ringing on the other end. The third time the ice pick pierced his heart Paul felt only sadness that he was dying. He fell forward on the table. When the ice pick pierced his heart the fourth time, through his back, he felt nothing at all.

❁

Casey sat up slowly. Where was that faint light coming from? What time was it? How long had she been out? If only she wore a digital watch as befit the nerd she was, she might be able to tell. If only she wore any watch. She felt the swelling on the back of her head. This bruise will look great with my purple hair, she thought. I'll make a beautiful corpse. Unless of course they don't discover me until I've bloated three times my size. The air was already pretty stuffy. How long until the oxygen ran out? Or was it the CO_2 that would kill her? Not that it made any difference.

The dim light was coming in from the kitchen through a little lens the diameter of a pencil. Some kind of indicator light, perhaps? If she had a screwdriver maybe she could smash it. Then maybe she could fashion an air supply by punching a hole through to the other side. It would be like breathing through a straw. Within a day or two, or week, somebody was bound to wander close enough to hear her cries from deep within the thick, insulated cooler. Or within a month, maybe? A decade? The smell of the burned etch-plot filled the place. Who was she trying to kid? She was hosed, and she knew it.

OK, Casey. *Mission Impossible.* Let's think.

She stood. She could reach the lens. There was no bulb to unscrew; it was a built-in bit of plastic. It would be really hard to get *that* out, or to smash it, even if she had a screwdriver. And she didn't have a screwdriver, of course. What *did* she have?

She tried to recall the offerings of remembrance that lay on the floor in front of the plot. Even though her eyes were getting used to the light, it was still too dark. She would have to rely upon her memory. *Come on, Casey, remember. Is there anything useful there?* Let's see. Some incense, some candles, some matches. *Good.* What else? Some candlesticks, the *Uncle Meat* album and CD. *What else?* Sand. Cheech Wizard comics. *What else?* Drumsticks. *Think!* Toy cars. Jolt Cola.

That was all she could think of, although she was certain that there was more.

But the mere exertion of remembering had tired her out; she needed to rest, to conserve her breath. She would think of something later.

Hey Todd!

Yeah, you, ghost-boy!

Get your ectoplasmic ass over here and open the door.

⊕

Nick was half asleep when the vibration started. He had spent four hours walking on that dusty dike path, until the moon set and he fell in the mud. Too scared to go anywhere and too tired to think, he had sat to consider his options. Evidently he had dozed off, because he was waking now. What was that buzz, that clanging, that rudeness? He suddenly realized that it was the telephone in his shirt pocket, and tried to figure out how to answer it. As he fumbled with the answer button, he looked at the dashboard clock. It was 4:17 AM, twenty-two hours since he had last seen Pascale.

⊕

Sometimes, Casey, she scolded herself, your tendency to make a joke of everything can really get on my nerves. Dying in an unplugged refrigerator is bad. Dying without ever having told Nick that you have a big crush on him is worse. Dying without undoing Meekman is very, very bad; it means your life has been meaningless. But dying with the theme from *Mission: Impossible* playing through your head is too much, too goddamn much.

Smashing at the little lens with the candlestick had done nothing to help her. It had hurt her hand and bent the candlestick, but the lens was built of strong stuff and it wouldn't give. Her other escape ideas were hardly any better. Lighting the *Cheech Wizard* comic in an effort to get a sprinkler to go off had been world-class stupid: she should have remembered from the time she had lit some very smoky incense that the sprinkler didn't work. At that time she had prayed that it wouldn't go off. It hadn't then, so why would it go off now? And besides, that Cheech was a signed original, probably worth about a trillion bucks. The only quasi-intelligent thing she had done so far was to drink the Jolt Cola, but she was beginning to worry about the lack of toilet facilities.

⊕

By the time Nick figured out how to answer the phone, the caller had evidently gotten bored. Either that or it had been a crank call or wrong number all along. Nick said, "Hello? Hello?" four or five times. All he heard in response were confusing faint sounds, like a fox hunt heard from a distant valley. He hung up. It occurred to him, now, that Carl had been awfully insistent that Nick take this cell phone with him wherever he went. Why was that, Nick supposed? Nick didn't like the feel of it. It was fishy. He tossed the phone out the window, pulled the car back, and ran over it.

⊕

It was clear to Casey that she was going to die. She was really pissed at herself for never having removed the tough vinyl seal around the door. That's what was keeping the air out. Well, next time she would do it differently. She stood and went to the wall, feeling where the etch map had been. She could at least die with a piece of Kali next to her, and Kali was Todd. She found a piece about a foot square, charcoaled around an irregular edge, taped to the wall. She folded it into a little wad and put it in her brassiere.

She was sweating heavily. She had a headache. Her neck was wrenched. Her eyes smarted. She was very weak. The back of her head hurt. Her ribs were bruised. Her cheek was sore. She had to pee. Her left hand hurt from smashing the candlestick; her right hand was burned. Her period was going to start any minute. Why the hell were her knees killing her? Oh yeah, she probably had banged them when she was hanging from the ledge. She slumped against the wall and knocked something; she heard the sound of breaking glass as it hit the floor; it startled her, she fell, her hand hit the floor and she felt, vaguely, dully, the glass piercing her skin. What was that glass from, she wondered? The sampler? One of the Grand Prix photos? If only she had thought to break the glass and use it to cut the vinyl seal, she could have gotten air to breathe. But it was too late now, she was too tired. She lay back on the floor. She cupped her bleeding hand to her breast, where the Kali map was.

"Look, Todd," she whispered, "falsies."

His answer was so gentle, so loving, she hardly would have known it was him: Cold Todd; Silent Todd, Unsentimental Todd. But the voice was his, unmistakably. And then she saw him.

"You don't need falsies, Casey," he said "Your breasts are perfect. Joan of Arc had breasts like yours."

Chapter 45

The light was blinding, and the rush of cold air was like pure Antarctica released in Newcastle. Todd was standing at the open door to the cooler.

Todd, my love!

No, wait. Wait a minute.

You're not Todd.

"What are *you* doing here?" Casey said.

"We followed a trail of blood and we cut the lock to see if anybody was inside. Who are *you*?" the cop said.

"O.J. Simpson," Casey said, and passed out again.

She awoke in time to try to discharge herself from Newcastle Hospital before being admitted. She would have discharged herself from the ambulance, but they wouldn't stop to let her out. Funny thing about oxygen: it smells bad. Or maybe that was just a kinesthetic response, the sensation of something unpleasant on her face translated in to perception of foul smell. Whatever it was, she tore the mask off her face, which startled the hell out of the paramedic and the cop who were riding in the back with her. They had thought she was going to die before they made it to the emergency room. She asked if they would please just stop the vehicle wherever they were and let her out, but they declined. Having been so insistent about not being admitted, she felt a little sheepish when, in the middle of a mild tirade, she realized that her left hand still had glass in it. "OK, OK" she said. "Admit me. But can we take care of this hand soon please? There are things I need to see to."

The Newcastle police couldn't have agreed more. For starters, she had to see to answering some questions. Like, what in the hell had happened last night?

She answered police questions while doctors poked around in her hand. She could feel nothing in her left arm from the shoulder down, but she could answer questions just fine.

It seemed unlikely that the police believed her when she said she had no idea who the dead guy was, or why two people with guns and silencers had been chasing her all over the Mill. And really, did she have no idea how that door came to be opened at the top of the stairs? Really, she lied. How about the trail of blood that led them to the freezer, did she have any idea about that? Well, Casey said, that was easy: she had whomped the alien bitch with a shovel. So it was a woman? Casey didn't really know, she said. Before last night she hadn't had much experience with extraterrestrials. Why had the assailant shot a computer board in the bizarre room in the cooler? Hell, I guess she just missed me, Casey said.

It was all a mystery to her, she told them. After going home for dinner, she had gone back to work— yes, she should get a life, she was working on it—and these two people had started pointing guns at her, telling her to go with them. So she had run. Why had she ended up in the food locker? Because she figured it would be a good hiding place. Wasn't such a smart choice, was it? Now could she please go, she was very tired. The bandage on her left hand was the size of a football.

The police told her that her story contradicted the known facts in about a half a dozen places and let her go home. But, they informed her, she was a material witness in an investigation involving at least one dead body. She should not leave town. If she decided to skip they would find her, they would convict her of obstruction of justice, and she would be a very unhappy camper.

Thank God for modems. She had to get a message to Nick, real quick. She didn't trust her phone, of course. She was convinced that she was dealing with big-time trouble: not just slimy Meekman but a conspiracy of at least three people. She assumed that her files had all been read, that her phone was tapped, that her mail would be watched. "Security through obscurity" didn't work when you were up against world-class computer designers. She could hope, at least, that they didn't know about her account on the Internet Access Company server. She used it for her private life only, and it was under an assumed name.

Of course the chance of maintaining any of her old private life now were about as great as the chance of her sitting down at a piano and playing Ravel's Concerto for Left Hand. She was going to have to get a message to Nick. Then she was going have to start her life on the lam.

❀

Nick sat in the front seat of his car, unable to decide where to go. All he could do was try think of how to get in touch with Bartlett. He could send her E-mail— why hadn't he thought of it sooner? He had the laptop in the car with him, all he needed was a phone jack to plug his modem into. Where would he find one at five in the morning? He knew just the place. He put the car in gear and took off.

Ten minutes later he screamed into the Value Right 24-Hour Liquor store on El Camino. For a consideration the nice Korean lady let him disconnect her phone and plug in his machine. In his mind Nick was trying to concoct a letter. What could he possibly say now?

There was only one message in his mailbox. It was from an4444@anon.tippi.swed. Might that be Bartlett?

  `Subject: decrypt will's friend`

He pulled up the message. It read

```
kj09un09uve073,vj8äÆffHw!!BBB*;#fcsaÒ_[[Jhy5yeCGyu6e@
```
and on for thirty more lines, each one just as readable as the first one. He needed a password to decrypt it. What password? He didn't know who an4444 was, so they didn't have one. He looked again: Will's friend. *Duh.*

He typed in 'billy', and the message came up:

```
they're on to us last night they tried to kill me.
did yo mention the word bonehead. trust nobody.
some good news I killed michael jacskon. run fast
they mean business. I didnt recognize the woman.
checkboston globe. kisses, casey. PS RESCUE ME!!!
POLICE WATCHING! YOU HAVE 4 days. Candygirl 'larson.
```

Alright Nick, he said to himself, let's parse this one info-unit at a time: *they're on to us.* Well, that was thanks to Nick's ineptitude. He should just have hired out a full-page ad in the San Jose *Mercury News*; that would have been more subtle than his clever interview with Bates and the Corporate Fellows. But, at least, the bunnies had undeniably been flushed out of the woods. Actually they were turning out to be more like man-eating Bengal tigers than bunnies, but they were out of the woods.

Next point. *They had tried to kill Casey.* Casey was given to understatement, not overstatement. If she said that somebody had tried to kill her, then he was absolutely certain that somebody had tried to kill her.

Did you mention the word "bonehead." Unfortunately, yes. All that, and more. . .

Next: *some good news, last night I killed Michael Jackson.* He had to take this statement at face value. 'Michael Jackson.' That was her name for Pavel Isaacs. She had said that Pavel and Meekman together they were responsible for the failure of Kali. If Meekman was responsible for Todd's death, then Isaacs was implicated. And now he was dead.

Next: *Run fast they mean business.* No shit.

Next: *I didn't recognize the woman.* What woman? Good God, could it have been Pascale? Maybe Nick would understand after he had read the *Boston Globe.* Did she mean today's *Globe*? The one that would come out tomorrow?

Kisses, Casey. He would have to think about that later. *Rescue me, police watching, you have four days.* All pretty straightforward. What the hell did *Candygirl larson* mean? No time to figure it out now. He needed to clear out, fast. But where?

Chapter 46

Nick was taking no chances. He jogged to his car, hunched over, head down, carrying his laptop, and looking, he supposed, a little like a Marine at Hué. Or maybe like John Cleese of Monty Python doing the 'Minister of Silly Walks' skit. Sometimes it was better to take the risk of looking like a jackass. He opened the car door from a crouched position, threw his things in, and started the engine. He jammed the car into gear and cut across the parking lot—full speed, without looking—onto El Camino, heading north.

His plan was rudimentary: Buy a *Globe*. Head east.

He took the Central Expressway. Glancing left over the tracks at Castro Street he could see the back terrace of the Tied House, where he and Paul had toasted Dieter, their fallen comrade. The Expressway became Alma Street, soul street; he followed it to University.

Downtown Palo Alto was jammed with cars. He parked in front of Mac's, directly in front of the large "NO PARKING UNDER ANY CIRCUM-STANCES." He jumped out, trotted into the newsstand and began to look for the *Globe* among the thirty or so newspapers from around the world. He found the spot for the *Globe*, but it was empty. *Damn.*

Just outside the door a man of about thirty stepped out of a double-parked Porsche that now blocked in the front third of Nick's Taurus. Nick watched, irritated, as the man swaggered to the cigar counter. *Yuppies*, Nick thought. He was turning to leave when another man came in and deposited next to Nick a stack of the late AM San Jose *Mercury News*. Instinctively Nick checked out the headlines.

Something about Bosnia, something about O.J. Simpson, something about the 49ers, something about the Mayor. And in the upper right hand column, in a moderate-sized headline,

Man Falls to Death at Digital MicroSystems East Coast Facility

Police Hold Employee for Questioning

He threw a dollar on the counter, took a paper and began to read. Man fell, discovered 6:00 AM by arriving employees, circumstances unclear, bloody trail in hall-

way, police held woman for questioning, later released, Scott Beckwith issues statement cooperating with authorities, etc.

Nick was halfway through the third paragraph when he heard an insistent horn
and screaming voices coming from the corner of Emerson and University. He looked
up and saw a blue Lincoln barreling up the street. When the car was slightly beyond
the Porsche, the driver slammed on the brakes with a loud squeal. Just as he did, the
Porsche pulled out behind him.

Nick ran to the his car and jumped in. Ahead, the Lincoln was trying to back but
the Porsche was in the way and wouldn't back up to let the other car pass around him.
God bless the power yuppie, Nick thought as he backed down Emerson at full throttle, steering by rearview mirror. As he switched into drive and pulled onto University,
he caught a glimpse of the cigar-buying Porsche driver getting out of his car, standing
in the middle of the Street. Road rage to the rescue, thank God in Heaven.

Driving fast, but, he hoped, not fast enough to guarantee a police escort, Nick
headed down University towards Highway 101. Where now? He had no idea. What
was it that kids in the Magic Box used to say?

> *Criss-cross*
> *Applesauce*
> *Do me a favor*
> *Get lost*

Soon he was on the Dumbarton Bridge, heading east across the bay. What had
he told Carl? *If things get weirder than what I've seen in the last two weeks, I'm going
to jump off the Dumbarton Bridge head first at low tide.* But it wasn't low tide, so he
kept driving. When he arrived at the other end of the bridge he got off the highway
and started following back roads through the industrial fringes of suburban
Fremont. He still had no plan, but half an hour later he needed to go to the bathroom; he was hungry, too, and he needed to collect his thoughts. It was ten in the
morning. He pulled into a parking spot in front of *Runway 32 Pizza*, made his way
through the swarm of teenagers already congregating there.

As he crossed the threshold into near darkness, he figured out how to find Paul.
There had to be a number someplace for ARB, the Association for Responsible
Biotechnology. That woman, whatever he name was, would probably have some
idea where Nick might track down his brother. He headed for the back, where, due
to the intervention of Saint Jude, there was a telephone. Three minutes later he had
in hand Judith Knight's name and her Boulder phone number.

"Hello Dr. Knight. My name is Nicholas Aubrey. I believe you know my
brother Paul."

"Yes. Mr. Aubrey, my telephone may not be secure. Please give me a number
where you are—"

"No. Listen to me. I am coming to Boulder, and I am going to take you with me until I get answers to some questions. I will be there within thirty-six hours. Tell me where to meet you."

He had expected indignation, refusal, and perhaps a threat to call the police.

"Call me when you get to Boulder, day or night, and I will tell you where to pick me up," she said. "I will be ready for you. Be very careful. I will be at this number."

Nick left the phone booth and sat at the counter to order some pizza for breakfast. A television was tuned to news:

Salt Lake City Police had issued a statement about the man they had questioned about the death of Peter Barlow on Flight 44 last month. It was Nicholas Aubrey, of Newcastle Massachusetts. The police had reopened the investigation and Mr. Aubrey was a suspect in Barlow's death—now considered murder—and also in the murder of Detective Ivan Marki, of the Salt Lake City Airport Police.

He wolfed down three pepperoni slices and walked through the ever-growing throng of teenagers, most of whom were tattooed, nose-ringed, purple- or orange-haired and chain smoking, speaking the universal teenager tongue—

"And I was like, man, get for real, and he was like, no way. . ."

That was it!

Candygirl Larsen.

He went back to the phone booth, dialed directory assistance for the 508 area code: "In Newcastle. Do you have a number for Larsen, first name Kirsten?"

Kirsten, duh, was in school when Nick called, but now, at least, he had her number and therefor a way to communicate with Casey. Therefor all he had to do in order to rescue Casey was to cross the country alive. But before he could do that, he was going to have to get one of the more ferocious-looking smokers off the front fender of his car.

"Hey," Nick said, trying to decide whether he should be a nice guy or a hard-ass. That was when he got the idea.

"Like this car?" he asked.

"Sure," the kid said, making no move to get off the hood.

"I rented it. It's due back in a week. It won't be missing for a week. If somebody stole it they would have a week to make it real lost."

"So what?"

"How about I give it to you? All you gotta do is get somebody to permanently lend me some piece of shit car that they legally own.'

"I got a Chevy Eurosport with a hundred and forty thousand miles."

"Deal," Nick said. "Where is it?"

"Right over there, man," the kid said. "Are you serious?"

"Serious as all hell. Come with me to the bank machine and I'll give you some money."

In a minute Nick had withdrawn $350, his bank card limit, and incidentally his last penny. He still had two thousand dollars from Carl. What were the chances that it was somehow marked? Pretty good. He gave five hundred of it to the teenager.

"Here's some bucks, and my bank card," Nick said. "And my PIN." He wrote the number on the kid's hand.

"Drive to Portland, Oregon, and stop to check your balance every three hours. A day or two after you get to Portland there will be a couple hundred dollars in the account. It's yours."

Nick handed over the rental car keys and pocketed the keys that were handed to him.

"Tell me something," Nick said, as he transferred his worldly goods into his new car. "Where do you get that shit you use to make your hair green?"

The kid cocked his head to the side.

"Lucky's, man," the kid said. "Right there behind you. Fucking lime Jello. Lime Jello, man. Mix it in, let it sit for fifteen minutes. You can even eat the shit right out of your hair."

"Yummy," Nick said. "Drive safely."

More than fourteen hours later Nick was wending his way down the mountain, down and east. Suddenly the road was nowhere before him, and the sound of flying gravel startled him awake. He grabbed the wheel tightly and slowed down, somehow having found the road again. He pulled over, turned off the engine and the lights. It took him a few moments to remember that he was on Highway 50, "the loneliest highway in America," somewhere west of Ely, Nevada. It was past two AM; how far past he had no idea—he had been dozing, driving for some miles while nine-tenths asleep. He stepped out of the car, walked about ten paces over the sand, undid his zipper and stood peeing, dangerously looking straight up at the magnificent stars, as bright as any he had seen on the edge of the Sahara. How did that poem go? *And at night, the drear starry spaces. . .?'* Oh, forget it.

He walked back to the car, swept thirty spent Styrofoam cups from the back seat onto the floor, lay down and went to sleep. Or rather, he did something that vaguely approximated sleeping. For a six-foot-three-inch man lying in the back seat of much-battered smelly car—a man who furthermore was in fear for his life and whose blood-coffee level was nearly toxic—the concept of sleep needed to be interpreted very loosely.

⬡

"Ohmygod Casey I can't believe it. There was this cop in like scuba gear getting ready to go in the pond, right, and there's this helicopter up there, *budda budda budda budda* like Rambo—"

"Rambo?" said voice two. "What century are *you* in?"

"—and everybody's going 'is he looking for another body?' and everybody's like

'No, he's looking for a gun' and everybody's like 'A *gun?*' and he's pulling down his mask, right? when all of a sudden all the water disappears, like somebody pulled the plug or something and it was so funny. . ."

The throbbing in Casey's left hand was becoming increasingly bothersome, more or less equaling the sum of the throbbing in all the other parts of her body. And she had gotten her period. Of course. She generally felt as if she had been run over by a steam roller, and the girl's voices resonated in her head like jackhammers.

She loved these girls, but all Casey wanted now was for everything and everybody to go away. All of it: the girls, the cops, the person from the Mill; the cameras, the pain, the knowledge. She wanted it all to just go away. And she wanted Todd Griffith to come back down from wherever it was that he had spoken to her from. She wanted him to swoop back down on a beautiful ghostly white horse. She wanted him to fly back down like a powerful angel on a ghostly, heavenly horse and take her far, far away.

Given the circumstances, however, she would be willing to settle for Nick Aubrey in a beat-up Volvo.

❀

Nick took his longest break of the day at a little place ten feet on the Nevada side of the Utah line. He gassed the car, used the restroom, got something to eat, and spent five dollars in the slot machines. He was there for eleven minutes.

It was nine in the morning when he pulled into the short term parking lot at Salt Lake City International Airport. It was hot, and as he took the ticket from the machine and waited for the gate to lift he felt something warm and slimy trickle under his collar and down his back. The smell of limes filled the car. He found a parking spot amid well-polished Buicks, Cherokees, and Dodge pickups by a streetlight pylon marked J-18, and stepped out onto the warm asphalt. His hands were covered with road grime from the flat he had changed two hours ago, and there were green Jell-O splotches on his pants as well as on the ludicrous shirt he had bought yesterday.

The woman at the toll booth was the most clean-cut person he had ever seen. She looked no more than twenty, and was reading a blue book with the word "marketing" in the title.

"Excuse me," he said.

She gasped.

"Don't be alarmed, ma'am. I'm an undercover policeman. I need for you to call Jake Carelli, who works inside at the airport police. Tell him to meet me right away, alone, at the L22 pylon. I need to see him within eight minutes, alone, on foot. Can you tell him that for me please? He needs to come right now, walking, not running. Thank you. You're a model citizen."

"Sir? I don't know your name."

"Joe Hill," Nick said.

Nick had barely arrived back at the Chevy when he saw Carelli emerge from the terminal, walking rapidly.

"Anybody know you're here?" Nick asked.

"No."

"Good. Now, please, kindly tell me what is going on."

"Marki was murdered. Nine millimeter through the head. You're the prime suspect."

"Why me?"

"Because Marki was pursuing you for Barlow's murder."

"Barlow's death was suicide. Your own coroner said so."

"They exhumed the body and did a second autopsy. This time they found a needle mark in his thigh, and traces of a curare derivative that has a lot of the same breakdown products as cyanide in his blood. Barlow was dying even before he ate his poison, but it perfectly masked the effects of what really killed him. Any pathologist could have made the same mistake."

"Did Marki think I did it?"

"That's what you get for being a wise-ass."

"Jake, I need your help."

"Count me in."

"But if you do help me, you're probably going to wind up dead too."

"I'm in."

"Do you need to talk to your wife first?"

"She's filed for divorce. And for sole custody. On account of I've got 'unresolved issues' about the Gulf War. I'd rather leave with you and fight the CIA than stick around and fight her lawyers."

Nick told him about Casey's situation, and gave him the Larsen girl's phone number and a password. He told him that he was going to get Judith, in Boulder. And then he told him where Bartlett's apartment was.

"Pick up Casey," Nick instructed Carelli. "She'll tell you where to go next. You have two days."

"What do you want me to do with your wife?"

"Tell her what's up. She'll decide what she wants to do."

"I'll see you then," Carelli said. "Be cool."

"Hop out. I'm gone."

Carelli got out of the car, then leaned over and rested his hands on the passenger side door.

"Aubrey."

"What?"

"That green stuff in your hair is a fine disguise. You might want to get an earring or a nose ring and some shades, too. But for the love of God find a truck stop and take a shower. You stink so bad you're gonna have the environmental police after you on top of everything else."

❋

Nick got to Boulder shortly after 4:30 PM, and called Judith from the first phone booth inside boulder city limits, outside a gas station.

"Listen to me carefully," she said. "Assume that they're listening to this conversation. Do not tell me where you are. Head right now to Boulder airport. I'll meet you there. I've got a friend who can fly us. You can ask anybody for directions. Hurry. If they get there before you do we're dead." She hung up before he could say a word.

The kid at the Texaco station pointed the way to the airport. It was only a mile away, and within seconds Nick was peeling out of the station, squealing tires and spraying gravel behind him.

He never noticed the flashing lights: it was the siren that got his attention. For a few seconds he even considered trying to outrun the cop to the airport, and gunned it a little. Perhaps that gambit accounted for the extremely sour look that was now on the cop's dark face as she approached. There was no she could know that she had just pulled over the cop-killing terrorist wanted all over America, was there? And what was a plain-clothes cop doing in a cruiser? How the hell was he going to get out of this one? Nick had no idea where his license was, much less the registration.

"Hello Nick, I'm Judith Knight," the cop said. "I'm going to get in the front seat, and you are going to turn your car around and get us out of here in a big hurry."

"Are you a *police officer?*"

"No."

"But. . ."

"I've got a friend. It's a long story."

"I don't believe you."

"You gave your brother Paul a diskette containing Barlow's plans for a cure for Gulf War Syndrome. Your brother placed that diskette in his violin case. He is now dead, murdered in Basel."

"How do you know he's dead?"

"Do you want to stay there talking with me and die too, or do you want me to let me in, and live?"

"Get in," he said.

She did, pulling the door shut as Nick accelerated into a U-turn.

"Buckle up."

He fishtailed from the shoulder onto the pavement, sending gravel flying.

Chapter 47

Casey Montgomery stood at her living room window. She looked, she paced, she looked again. This hanging around doing nothing was going to kill her. But what else was she going to do? Anything that required concentration was impossible: not only was she too agitated, but she had taken five Tylenol 2's and washed them down with a shot of tequila at eight this morning, ten minutes ago. The throbbings were still there, if duller than before, but her ability to concentrate was considerably diminished. So, what to do? Sometime within the next day or two she was going to have to visit the bathroom, but that was not a pleasant prospect, so she was putting it off as long as possible. In the meantime she would keep pacing back and forth like a puppy whimpering after a squirrel on the other side of a picture window.

She had been informed that Detectives Susan Roy and Jim Myers of the Newcastle police would be there to question her at one PM. She should plan on spending the afternoon with them, she was told, from one until whenever, and she might want to have her lawyer handy.

She looked at the media mob outside, on First Street. It had considerably diminished since yesterday. There was one news truck, its antenna sticking 30 feet in the air. There were several cars with people sitting in them drinking coffee and doing crossword puzzles. She walked around to her kitchen, from which she could see her back yard. On the other side of a fence, in an ill-maintained playground another news crew awaited.

She returned to the front room, in time to see Kirsten and Danielle running towards her house from opposite directions. They were up her porch stairs before she had gotten to the door to open it.

"Ohmygod, did you hear?" Danielle said, addressing both of them.

"Hear what?" Kirsten said.

"About the finger?"

"What finger?"

"Didn't you hear? It was on the news. They found a finger! Casey! Isn't that cool!" Then she looked at Casey's enormous bandage. "Ohmygod I'm sorry, is it yours?"

"No," Casey said. "I have all my fingers."

"That's nothing," Kirsten said. "Wait till you hear this. Ohmygod. Wait, I have to get my breath." She breathed deeply several times.

"OK. About ten minutes ago, right? The phone rings at my house and my brother gets it and says its for me but he won't tell me who it is and I figure he's just being a jerk, right? And I say hello and this guy gets on, I swear I have never heard his voice before in my life, and he says that he has a very important message for Casey! First, his name is Billy, or something like that. Then he said that you are supposed to meet your driver in the game room at the Mall at two o'clock. You know, the arcade, with the video games? Then he said, this is very important, you were supposed to tell your driver to take you to the town that has the animal you are looking for and leave a message at the nearest house of colley. I had to write it down and I could not give the message to anybody else, only you. Can you believe it!"

"I can believe it." Casey said. "You just saved my life."

"Oh yeah. Also he said to bring all your green stuff."

At 10:10 that morning three more teenage girls and two teenage boys with skateboards walked into Casey's house to say hello. At 11:00, five teenage girls and three teenage boys (one of whom had a backwards baseball cap over his short purple hair) walked out. They were going to the Mall.

At 1:40 PM— after a little more than two hours of hanging out, eating pizza, playing video games — all but the boy with purple hair had left. He went to the Mall branch of Newcastle Savings and wrote a check payable to himself for nine thousand, nine hundred dollars. The signature was a little shaky because he had cut his hand, and the haircut was different from the one on his driver's license, but he was clearly the right person, and the check was cashed. Evidently the teller didn't spend a lot of time watching the news, or she would have known that the boy was notorious. The boy left the arcade with a man at 2 PM, exactly.

That was clever, Nick, Casey thought. The animal I am looking for: that would be a Trojan horse. Where do Trojan horses live? In Troy, of course. 'House of Kali' would be a shrine. Two minutes with the yellow pages was all it took to start the thread; five minutes and two calls later she was on the phone with Shriners International headquarters, in Fort Lauderdale. They were more than happy to give her the address of the Shrine in Troy, New York. "Green stuff" had taken no thought at all.

⊕

Nick and Judith were averaging close to seventy-five miles an hour, including rest stops. Nick knew that it wouldn't take a rocket scientist to figure out that they were heading east, although the Portland ruse might have thrown Monty off the scent. Anybody who knew Nick—and Monty clearly fell into that category—would figure that he was heading to Boston; more precisely, to Newcastle. Nick was counting on that. Outside Cincinnati they stopped to shop. Fifteen minutes later they emerged with sleeping bags, rice, coffee, beans, pots, pans, toilet paper, salt, pepper, canned soup, can openers, paper plates and cups, potatoes, onions, towels, cooking oil, soap, flashlights, batteries, radio.

Then they got back into the Eurosport and drove.

At 7:45 PM the next day Nick pulled into the outskirts of Troy, New York, having just completed a drive across virtually all of the United States of America in something around two and one-half days. He called the police to get directions to the local Shriner's Lodge.

It turned out to be a dignified white Greek Revival, with a colonnaded portico, that resembled the White House—or perhaps a funeral home. It was locked up tight when Nick and Judith arrived there, but there was a sealed envelope taped next to the door. The single-word address was NICK, and the note inside gave the location of the hotel where Casey and Jake were staying.

They didn't have much time, Nick explained when the four had united. They needed to get to Raquette Lake, up in the Adirondack Preserve, before the bars closed. So, he suggested, why didn't they just keep the same traveling arrangements: Nick and Judith in one car; Casey and Jake in the other. It was agreed and they left, with Jake following Nick in a weather-beaten Jeep Wagoneer. Before getting back in the car, Casey gave Nick a thick envelope.

They got lost several times. It wasn't until 10:49 that, after driving along the winding roads in the vicinity of Tupper Lake, that they came upon what Nick considered a suitable bar, the Park Street Tavern. In the lot there were nine Harley-Davidson motorcycles, three pickup trucks with very big wheels, and one rather weary-looking black Monte Carlo with a Harley decal in the rear window next to the decal of a kid pissing on a Ford logo.

Nick pulled the van into the lot and Jake followed in his Wagoneer, and they all got out. Nick said, "After Jake and I go in, you guys can come on in and get a drink; whatever you want. Just let me and this guy do the talking."

He put his arm on Jake's shoulder, and continued speaking.

"We're trying to find the baddest guy in here, and they traditionally have less enlightened views on equality of the sexes. Jake, back me up, OK?

"You got it, Cap."

"OK let's go," Nick said.

Nick and Jake walked in the bar, followed by the two women. Everybody in the room turned around when they walked in, and the conversation stopped. The jukebox played the last notes of "Tied to the Whipping Post," then fell silent. There were, by Nick's instant calculation, about fifteen men and eight women in the place. The attire of the men tended to leather, Nick noticed, and they evinced a fondness for tattoos. The women appeared to have similar tastes.

Nick made a big wave with his right hand, took a giant step forward and said, "My name's Shepp Hall, from North Caldwell, New Jersey, and I'm lookin' to find the meanest motherfucking asshole in this dump."

Nick noticed the bartender reach for something under the bar. Nick couldn't tell what it was, but it took two hands to hold it. Otherwise there was no movement in the entire room. Nick was glad that he hadn't shaved or showered since Salt Lake, and that his hair looked like some dog had peed on it.

Finally, an answer. A big booming voice from the bar said,

"Well you found him, Dickface, so now why don't you get outta here."

Nick stepped forward, extending his hand. He was glad to see, out of the corner of his eye, that Jake was stepping along with him.

"Pleased to meet you," Nick said. "What's your name?"

"Fuck you," the man answered. He was classic Harley material, Nick thought. He was older than Nick, but not by too much. His grey hair— thinning, greasy— was over his shoulders. He had obviously once been very muscular. It was also obvious that he had spent a lot of time in places like the Park Street Tavern since his muscular heyday.

"Hey," Nick said "Not looking for trouble. I just got a business proposition for you."

"Start talking," the tattooed biker said.

"Do you know the lake?"

"Which one. I know all the lakes," he said.

"Raquette Lake," Nick said. "You know that cove out beyond Marcy Point?"

"Yeah,"

"Used to be some church buildings out there. They still there?"

"Last time I looked."

"Anybody been out there lately?"

"You're doin' a lot of talkin' but I'm not hearing a lot of business," the tattooed guy said.

Nick took out his wallet, pulled a twenty dollar bill from it and put it on the bar. The guy nodded.

"Anybody been out there lately?" Nick said again.

"Not in five, six, seven years, I don't think."

"Is the lake passable? Is there ice?"

"Where you been? It all melted last week."

"Well," Nick said, waving his hand towards the two women behind him, "I would like to introduce you to the Prospect Hill Christian Fellowship. And I am pleased to inform you that the Prospect Hill Christian Fellowship has recently completed the purchase of the aforementioned property from the now defunct Second Swedish Baptist Church of Oneonta, New York. And we would like to take possession of said property. Preferably within the hour. So we need a couple of boats pronto to ferry ourselves and a lot of shit out there. And some big flashlights. And a guy to help us."

"You already used up your twenty bucks," the biker said.

"How's three hundred sound?"

"Sounds interesting."

"And also," Nick said "Since the world hates a Christian, there are those who might want to do us ill. So it would be better if nobody knew we were out there. Also, it would be better if our vehicles were kept safely out of sight but available to us at a moment's notice."

"That's rent money you're talking about now."

"OK. Fifty dollars a month."

"Deal."

Nick leaned forward, looked the guy in they eye.

"Now, people are eventually going to notice us, and see smoke coming from the old place," he said. "And when the subject comes up, you're going to tell everybody you know how you ferried a nice group of Christians over there one Sunday afternoon by pre-arrangement, and how we sang hosannas to praise Jesus till the sun went down."

"Whatever you say. You're paying."

Nick grabbed the guy's vest with both hands and pulled himself closer to him. "And if you ever tell anybody anything different, motherfucker, I'll come back here and rip your tongue out."

The big guy knocked both hands off with one motion.

"Don't fuck with me, small fry," he said. "I was in Nam. Most of us here was in Nam. We're not given to taking a lot of shit."

Now Jake stepped forward, displacing Nick.

"Don't give us this 'Nam' shit," he said. "I was in Desert Storm. Third ACR, Seventh Corps. Battle of Seventy-three Easting, we ate the Tawakalna Division Republican Guards for breakfast. We're younger, smarter, stronger, than all you Nam guys," he paused, looking the guy in the eye from two inches away, *"and we won."*

There was a long pause; Nick distinctly heard at least two bottles break, and thought he saw a pool cue raised wrong side up out of the corner of his eye.

"But tell me something," Jake continued. "You were in 'Nam, what was your outfit?"

"Seventh Cav," the guy said.

"Seventh Cav? What year?"

"Sixty five."

"Seventh Cav, sixty-five. That was Ia Drang, wasn't it?

"Fuckin' A."

"Holy shit. Ia Drang, Landing Zone X-Ray, you were there?"

"Damn fuckin' straight," he said. "LZ Xray. Colonel Moore and his merry men."

Jake stood up straighter and made a brief military salute.

"Gary Owen, motherfucker," he said.

"Gary Owen," the guy said.

"Well, Shepp," Jake said. "You wanted a bad motherfucker, you found one. Ia Drang. Holy shit. Shepp, you better reach in your wallet, and you better pull out a C-note. You better buy a round for this man and his friends. You better say 'Gary Owen.'"

"Gary Owen," Nick said. There were a couple of answering faint cheers in the bar as Nick reached in his wallet and pulled out a hundred dollar bill with red marking on it.

"This ones's on Carl," he said.

Small talk was starting to pick up again, and pool cues resumed their proper attitude.

"Ia Drang," Jake continued. "Four companies tore a new asshole for a whole NVA regiment."

"You got that right," the guy said.

"How about you finish your beer and give us a hand then," Jake said.

"I'm with you in five minutes," the guy said.

Out of earshot, Nick turned to Jake and said "Who the hell is Gary Owen?"

"It's a song," Jake said. "Seventh Cav anthem. You want to survive eight years with the infantry, it helps to know your regimental history."

It was nearly four AM before they had unloaded, by moonlight and flashlight, the last canoe's worth of supplies at the cove beyond Marcy Point, five miles up the lake. The stars were impossibly bright; the air was impossibly clear. It was about thirty-five degrees out. Brooms had materialized from nowhere, and somebody — maybe it was everybody— organized the sweeping out of the meeting room in the dilapidated big house. The supplies were all in one corner, the sleeping bags were stretched out. There was a fire in a fireplace that by some fluke was not clogged with debris or old nests.

Nick walked with Jake down to the three canoes as the tattooed work brigade prepared to shove off. He had been consuming Budweiser 16 oz cans all evening, tossing his empties into the lake. "Listen," Nick said, "our fellowship made a little miscalculation. We're kind of shy one boat. Think you could lend us one?"

"OK," the guy said. "But if you don't bring it back I'm gonna come back here and rip your tongue out."

"OK motherfucker," Nick said. "Gary Owen."

"Gary Owen," the big guy said, as he tipsily situated himself in the middle of the other canoe. "Christian women, Damn. That's some fine brown sugar. I'm thinking of goin' to church."

Nick was the last one into the room. By the light of the fire, he could tell that everybody was still awake, as if waiting for his blessing before going to sleep.

"Listen," he said. "Tomorrow let's sleep as late as we can. We should be safe here. I've got bread, coffee, and cheese for breakfast. We can fix up the place during the light, and then tomorrow night we can talk and try to figure out what the hell is going on. I'm sure Dr. Knight will have a lot of the answers."

"I will," she said. "And all I can say is, I hope we have a good fire to sit around. Because the story I have to tell you is going to turn your blood to ice."

Chapter 48

Nick Aubrey awoke on his back, looking at rafters high above him. He was in a sleeping bag; his body was warm but his face was cold. What place was this? He puffed and saw his breath. In a moment it came back to him: he was in an abandoned building at the edge of a lake, in the woods. It was a place he had once known well.

The room was about fifteen feet by thirty, with a dusty wooden floor and a peaked plank ceiling supported by rough-hewn timbers. Along one long wall there was a large divided window that looked out over a meadow to a lake, where fog still hung low on the water. Along a shorter perpendicular wall there was an enormous stone fireplace. In it were ashes and charred logs, but no hint of fire. To the right of the fireplace there was an opening. Nick got up and walked toward it, the cold coming up through the dirt-black soles of his once-white socks.

The room behind the fireplace was a dirty and cobwebbed kitchen that had an eight-burner cast-iron wood stove as its centerpiece. There was a large deep soapstone sink with a drain board tilting into it. Nick didn't even try the porcelain faucet, which he supposed dated from the early nineteen hundreds: the water here had been turned off for twenty years.

A large coffee pot still wrapped in its plastic packaging was sitting on a counter, with a three-pound tin of coffee next to it. Nick couldn't find a can opener, but there was an old heavy knife. He took the knife, the coffee and pot, a tin cup and some matches from the hearth. With his sleeping bag wrapped around him, he tiptoed out the door.

At 11:20 there was still no sign of life from the others. Nick sat on his haunches sipping coffee, remembering those mornings on the edge of the Sahara, drinking coffee at dawn with shepherds and farmers. The men there always squatted, they never sat on the ground. The hell with it: Nick was American, not African, and squatting was an unnatural contortion best left in the weight room. He moved to a boulder and sat. Now here came an woman walking towards him, wearing a nightshirt to her knees and a scarf around her head, oblivious to the cold. She approached wordlessly and sat next to him.

"Hello Nick," she said. "You look good. I like the hair."

"Yeah," he said, glancing at her bandaged hand and polychromatic face. "You too."

Jake Carelli wasn't far behind Casey. He was wearing blue jeans and a flannel jacket, carrying an empty cup in one hand and a small picnic cooler in the other. He placed the cooler behind the rock that Nick sat on, away from the fire.

"Morning," he said.

"I guess," Nick answered.

Carelli bent over the fire, grabbed the pot and poured himself some coffee.

"Your wife gave me that to give to you," he said, nodding toward the cooler.

"A picnic lunch?"

Jake paused.

"You really don't know?"

"I really don't know."

"Your brother's blood. Seven test-tubes of it. It was frozen when I left Boston. Cold now, but not frozen. Your brother left it with her on his way to Basel. Something about his laboratory. She had it in her freezer."

Basel, Nick thought. Damn Basel! Why had Paul gone back? Nick felt his own blood turn a few degrees colder as he remembered telling Pascale that he had to go to Basel to retrieve from his brother a puzzle on a diskette. Her last words haunted him: "Maybe I see you sometime at Fasnacht."

Maybe you will, he now thought, recalling his pledge to his brother: *If anything happens to me, you've got to go to that secret lab in Basel and find out what the hell is going on there,* Paul had said.

"You're on," Nick now whispered to his brother, as tears filled his eyes, then he asked Jake, "She gave you nothing else?"

"No. She said 'good luck.'"

What, exactly, had Nick expected?

Carelli continued, "I told her it was up to her whether she came with me or not. She asked if you were alone. When I told her you were going to pick up a woman in Boulder, she decided not to come. She said to give you her best."

Damn it, Nick thought. Why did you tell her that? But it wasn't Jake's fault; Nick knew that. It was nobody's fault. Things fall apart. Shit happens. Sometimes you lose your brother and your wife on the same frigid morning, and all you get for a souvenir is seven vials of frozen blood.

Judith appeared, and all four members of the Prospect Hill Christian Fellowship now stood around the fire like druids about to begin a ceremony. Nick, lead pagan, gathered his courage.

"We're on Raquette Lake, in the Adirondack Preserve," he said, "the largest protected space in the lower forty-eight states. Behind us there's fifteen miles of woods, no roads; so anybody coming here after us will come by water. Or air. This site really does belong to the Second Swedish Baptist Church, of Oneonta, New York. I was a member of that church, before it shriveled up and died. We used to come up here for Bible camp. So a Christian group fixing up this place will make perfect sense to the locals. Especially since I came up here every summer when I was a kid.

"We need to get to work on winterizing the place a little in case the weather changes. There's a hole in the ceiling that needs fixing and I think we might be able to get the pump working so we can have some indoor plumbing, too. Fortunately Swedish Baptists were pretty methodical people. There're tools here, and some dry lumber.

"I desperately need ice for my blood." His eyes smarted; he swallowed and corrected himself: "I mean my brother's blood, that Jake brought from Boston. There's a general store not far from the Park Street Tavern, where we were last night. It's two hours to paddle there and two hours back, so whoever's going to go should get going."

"I'll go," Judith said.

"I'll go with you," Casey said. "It's not like I'm too handy right now."

"Remember our cover story," Nick said. "A Christian fellowship."

"That will be easy for me," Judith answered. "I am a Christian, and we are a fellowship."

Judith's words sounded so hopeful and confident that to Nick it was as if they were spoken by an angel in a dream. As he watched the women pick up their paddles and dip them into the tranquil lake, he felt no such hope and confidence. Jake turned back to the lodge to begin work on a makeshift ladder, but Nick stood motionless, watching. He stayed motionless a quarter of an hour, until the canoe rounded Marcy Point. It took all the strength he had to restrain himself from swimming out into the ice-cold water after it, until his surrender might be accepted.

Chapter 49

Illuminated only by flickering yellow firelight, Judith's face blended into the darkness.

"Perfect weather for a ghost story, isn't it?" she began.

It would be nicer, Nick thought, if there weren't so much real death involved. But he had to agree that the rain gusting on the roof and rattling the windows added a certain atmosphere.

"My tale is more of a Frankenstein story than a ghost story. But they're really the same thing—stories of lost souls. But what is a ghost?" Judith continued. "Some say that it is a soul that walks the earth, refusing to accept that it no longer has a body. So what, then, is a soul? Catholic dogma holds that a soul is a living being, without a body, having reason and free will. I am a Catholic, and this is what I believe. Among biologists this belief makes me an oddity. Neurophysiologists have no need for souls. According to them, *reason* exists in harmonic oscillations of cortical layers four and six, mediated by the thalamus. *Free will* is an illusion caused the brain's forward planning functions. Francis Crick thinks free will is located in a region of the brain called the anterior cingulate sulcus; others think it resides elsewhere in the brain—anywhere but in the soul.

"In September 1959, Abraham Angevine, the bright sixteen-year-old son of a minor actress and a mathematician who had worked on the hydrogen bomb, began his freshman year at Stanford. There he met Thomas Engleton—and discovered computers. Now, Engleton is a revolutionary figure in the history of computers. While engineers at IBM were thinking of how to make machines *bigger and faster*, Engleton was thinking about how to make them smaller, easier to use, portable—even embedded into human brains. Engleton's work remains central to computer technology today. The young Abraham Angevine was a present witness to Engleton's greatest work. Angevine became Engleton's understudy—and, some say, his muse.

"Abraham Angevine was a gifted, original thinker, and the Santa Clara Research Institute produced non-stop innovation while he and Engleton worked there together. Memory, CPUs, compilers, theories of computation, neural networks, operating systems, disk storage systems, ergonomics—hardware or software, Angevine excelled at all of it. Meanwhile, elsewhere within the same think-tank scientists were developing biological warfare strategies for the Navy.

"Although brilliant, Abraham Angevine was odd and disagreeable. Not to put too fine a point on it, he was an obnoxious, smug little creep, and nobody other than his mentor Engleton could stand to be near him for more than a few minutes at a time. Nevertheless, within two years of joining Engleton at SCRI—and while still an undergraduate at Stanford—Angevine had made himself a star. He completed his B.S. degree in two years, and his Ph.D. in two more.

"Upon graduation he was hired by Stanford as a research associate in computer science, and his reputation continued to grow. At the same time—and perhaps influenced by the germ warfare work at SCRI, which was theoretically top secret—he was began to study biology. He wrote papers that propounded information-theoretical analyses of life processes, and he attended symposia on molecular genetics. It was at such a symposium that he and I met."

At this point in her story, Judith paused and poured half an inch of bourbon into the tin cup in front of her as Casey put another log on the fire.

"I met Abraham Angevine at the Asilomar Conference on Recombinant DNA Molecules, which took place at the Asilomar retreat on Monterey Peninsula in 1975," Judith said. "I was a seventeen-year-old black schoolgirl, and naturally enough I received a lot of unwanted attention at Asilomar. It was all very unpleasant until Angevine took me under his wing. He was a thirty-two year old a Stanford professor who already had an international reputation.

"I don't know whether it's more accurate to say that I was protected by him or that I was kidnaped by him. He escorted me to meetings, sat next to me at meals, told me where to go and what to do. He never once acted kindly; — it was more as if he had purchased me at auction. I did not like him. But somehow—through sheer repulsiveness, I suppose—he kept the gawkers at bay, and I was grateful for the swath that cleared for me.

"My own family history is not very dramatic. I don't know who my father was. My mother, Rose Wayne, was a very angry woman. She had grown up in the South under Jim Crow, and had suffered grievously from racism. She named me Blackpride and left me alone—she was hardly present at all during my childhood. Her cherished grandfather —Rosingnol Wayne, who had lovingly raised her despite terrible poverty—had been a subject in the notorious Tuskeegee syphilis study. My great-grandfather, who was derisively called Mad Anthony by the white doctors of the Public Health, spent the last twenty years of his life going in and out of syphilitic dementia. To the extent that my mother taught me anything, she taught me that white people were obsessed by a cult of science. She taught me that scientists worshiped curiosity as their only God. This scientific curiosity might be gussied up with fancy names, she said, but in truth it was only a lust like any other lust. There were no limits the depredations that people would commit in the name of science. That is what my bitter, hate-filled mother taught me.

"But Aunt Rachel was the one who raised me; Rachel Knight. Aunt Rachel was a religious person, a Catholic, and she was as kind-hearted as my mother was bitter. After my mother died, Rachel adopted me. At the same time I became baptized a Catholic, and later was confirmed. Judith is my confirmation name. Despite my mother's warning—or maybe because of it, because I so resented the way she had neglected me—I became a scientist myself.

"An article I wrote appeared in Science in January of 1980. Shortly thereafter I got a letter from Abraham Angevine in which he invited me to come to California for what he called a 'family reunion.' He included some money and an airplane ticket. Remembering Asilomar, I didn't really want to see him again. But I was intrigued, so I went.

"He met me at the airport and we drove to a remote cabin in the Sierras. During the whole drive, several hours, he hardly said a thing. It was very odd. I was no longer a teenager, but I was still in many ways just a kid. I re-experienced that same feeling of being kidnaped— of his taking an attitude of ownership of me. At the 'reunion' there were about twenty young people, mostly men, but including a few women. We were all in our teens and early twenties. Everybody there was brilliant, but there was a creepiness about the event that I cannot put into words. It was as if Angevine were a spiritual master, and these others were disciples. Among these disciples there was one who was clearly Angevine's favorite: another black kid like me— Pavel Isaacs. It was clear that Isaacs and Angevine had already formed some special kind of bond.

"By this time, 1980, Angevine, at 37, was a full professor at Stanford. His specialty was artificial intelligence. He had come to believe that computers could be made to have minds, not just simulate them— minds that could be combined and amplified. He synthesized his ideas in a paper that has become an underground classic of computer science. It was called simply "Overmind," and it was to be published in the *Communications of the Association for Computing Machinery* in 1978, when he was invited to be guest editor."

"The New Gospel," Casey said.

"Some people call it the New Gospel," Judith said. "I prefer to call it 'Overmind.' It contained hundreds of brilliant ideas, all sharing the theme of electronically harnessing together human minds and computers. If individual processing units—people, in other words—could be made to let go of their built-in but no longer necessary senses of self-direction and self preservation, then all minds could be united in a simple computer architecture. The result, he claimed, would be an 'Overmind,' as fully conscious and self-aware as any human mind, only infinitely more intelligent.

"This marriage of hardware, software and 'wetware' —human brains—was the next obvious evolutionary step, Angevine said. Overmind was inevitable. Superstition could delay its arrival, but nothing could stop it. The computer science he expounded was brilliant, but the ethical ideas were outlandish, and at the last minute the ACM canceled publication and cobbled together a substitute. After the ACM demurred he realized his blunder and tried to suppress any copies that had been made, like an actor trying buying up copies of a porno film made early in his career.

"Pavel and the others at the 'reunion', however, were quite familiar with the Overmind article, and didn't find it outlandish at all. The article circulated freely among them and Monty had no reservations about showing it to me either. Other than myself, nobody at that Sierra retreat thought that the Overmind article was immoral or insane. I myself thought it was both. Meanwhile, things were turning creepier. At the close of the second day, Angevine spoke of his superior genetic endowment. He said that we who were there were all his children. Then he said he said he was the new Christ, and that a great destiny awaited us, his first apostles."

"You mean he really thought he was *God*?" Jake said.

"In an Emersonian or Whiteheadian sense, perhaps," Judith answered. "His goal was to become God, if you think of God as an evolutionary concept more or less synonymous with intelligence. Soon ways would be invented for direct brain-to-brain communication, he said. We would accrete into Overmind just as single cells accrete into jellyfish. And Angevine would be at its center."

"How so?" Nick asked. "A distributed architecture has no center."

"Correct, but just as every hive has but one queen around whom all activities center, the Overmind would be set up with one brain, Angevine's, 'more equal' than the others. Every computer and every person on earth would become just an extension of his brain, and he would experience a rapidly growing consciousness, as when a child grows into adulthood.

"'It's all in your Gospel,' he said, singling me out. He did this because I was the only one there who had religious faith. 'The Sermon on the Mount: 'Blessed are the meek, for they shall inherit the earth.' He then said that the meek, indeed, were going to inherit the earth. And that from now on he was to be their leader. He announced his intention to change his name."

"To Monty Meekman," Nick said.

"Yes," Judith said. "Abraham Angevine now goes by the name of Montaigne Meekman. Upon changing his name he set out to rewrite history, expunging the name Abraham Angevine from wherever it appeared."

"Successfully," Nick said. "I've never heard that name before today."

"I have observed," Judith said, "That people are willing to accept invented biographies. It worked for Ronald Reagan, it worked for Kurt Waldheim, and it worked for Monty Meekman."

"What did 'Overmind' say?" Casey asked. "*How* were we all to be joined in Monty?"

"Neurophysiologists associate conscious thought with an harmonic oscillation between the fourth and sixth cortical layers of the brain," Judith said. "The pulse from the thalamus which unifies brain processes and gives rise to the perception of consciousness—that pulse is the same for everybody, one pulse every twelve point five milliseconds."

"The implicit clock rate of *espresso*," Nick said.

"Yes. Monty proposed to create the Overmind by synchronizing these oscillations, just as you can make a laser from ordinary light by harmonizing the light waves. So Step One in the process would be to establish the Internet everywhere; to make ubiquitous computing possible.

"Now, in the early years of the Internet, computing units would use different operating systems, languages and protocols. It would be an electronic Tower of Babel, and too inefficient to support the Overmind that Monty envisioned. Therefor Step Two would be to standardize the Internet on a common language, *espresso*, and to 'architect' the *espresso* language in such a way that every *espresso* device would act as a data acquisition and control processor. The final step, Step Three, would be to re-engineer human brains to act as *espresso* devices."

"So there were to be two lines of development," Nick said. "Like two sides digging a tunnel. On the digital side, the Internet had to be developed to the point that it could directly interact with human brains. This involved governing its throughput rate; deliberately slowing itself down to accommodate the slower clock of biological systems. And on the biological side, human brains had to be developed to the point that they could directly interact with the Internet. But in order to accomplish that, people would have to give up their autonomy, their free will."

"That's right," Judith said. "*espresso* slows down the net, and brains must be modified in order to interact with it. But the result is, once *espresso* was deployed, it would be literally impossible to escape it. Your brain would not be yours to control; it would be at the disposition of the Overmind. Thus all human experience would be brought together in a single consciousness by a uniform thought process, just as the sensations from the millions of nerve endings in your eyes, ears, hands and hearts unify in the experience that is your own mind. Monty's thought would be the operating system of this inconceivably vast new meta-computer. The system would start out crudely, of course, but it would rapidly evolve once every person and computer in the world was directed to the one goal of knitting ourselves together."

"But I don't *want to be an espresso device*," Casey said, in the voice of Kirsten or Danielle. "I'm like, *hello?* I like it better just being human? Are we OK with this?"

"*Nobody* wants to give up their soul, whatever they may call it," Judith said. "Not even atheists. This resistance is what Monty calls a superstitious preference for the illusion of free will and autonomy. But change the DNA that builds the free-will function into our souls, and the problem goes away. So the first task of the human re-engineering would be to disable human free will, while leaving intact all other aspects of human mental working."

"Human re-engineering?" Jake asked. "I don't like the sound of that."

"Todd Griffith doesn't like the sound of it either," Nick said. Then added, for Judith's benefit, "Todd was the co-designer of the Kali chip. Monty shot him in the head and then hooked his brain up to a Masscomp data acquisition and control processor, a DA/CP."

"It doesn't surprise me," Judith said. "The Overmind article called for precisely that kind of 'experimental platform' for debugging the 'wetware' implementation of *espresso*. But it would be impractical, obviously, to surgically enhance every person in the world. The only reasonable way to proceed would be by gene therapy, the genetic re-engineering of living people.

"Before devices could be designed to re-engineer living people, Monty needed a much greater understanding of the human immune system. He needed this knowledge in order to devise machines that could escape destruction within the body while they went about their business of rearranging genes."

"Don't tell me," Nick said. "He proposed a massive study of the Tuskeegee variety, to direct the world medical research community's attention to this one problem, understanding immunity."

"I'm afraid he did exactly that," Judith said. "May God have mercy me."

"I don't get it," Jake said. "What do you mean?"

"AIDS," Casey whispered.

"I didn't believe it at the time," Judith said. "But I believe it now."

"Sounds like they were taking an enormous chance," Jake said. "Weren't they afraid that somebody might catch them creating these diseases?"

"Whenever anybody came close to figuring out the connection to Monty, they were killed. Like Christian and Janine Garbougian, who found evidence of nanomachines in Gulf War veterans. They were found dead last week."

This answer did not sit well with Jake.

"When you discovered these things, why didn't you just go public?"

"I had no proof. I was afraid people would say that I was crazy. That was wrong, of course; I should have done something. But I had convinced myself that my theory about AIDS was simply paranoia. It does sound crazy, doesn't it? And the rest of my theories were even more far out than that one. Until Paul Aubrey visited my company last December, I truly thought it would be a century before Monty's ideas could pose any danger to the world. Then I met with Dieter, and knew that the future had arrived ahead of schedule. I was trying to figure out what to do next when Dieter was murdered and things spun out of control. And now it's too late."

She sipped again from her whiskey, and continued.

"Within days of leaving that cabin in the Sierras, Abraham Angevine had legally changed his name to Montaigne Meekman. To him his new name signifies that he is the new Christ, come down from the *montaigne*, the mountain. But of course 'Montaigne' is his mother's name, too."

"This is insanity," Nick said. "It is all insanity."

"It gets more insane," Judith said. "Much more."

Chapter 50

"When I arrived back home I felt as if I had miraculously escaped from a horror movie," Judith continued, "and tried to forget the whole weird escapade. But years later I couldn't get what had happened out of my mind. I founded the Association for Responsible Biotechnology to guard against nightmarish visions like Monty's."

"That's why Monty took so much interest in the Neuro Group," Nick said. "If his ultimate goal is to use nanomachines to rearrange the living brains of each person on earth, the Neuro Group's software simulation of the brain is exactly what he needs perfect his plan."

"Precisely," Judith said. "But we're getting ahead of ourselves. I lost track of Pavel when he moved to Switzerland. For six years I had no news of him, until Paul

Aubrey approached my company last December on behalf of Hoff-Zeigy. Paul told me that Dieter Steffen and Pavel Isaacs had invented a rudimentary nanomachine that could rearrange DNA into any arbitrary sequence programmed into it.

"I went to Basel to speak with Dieter Steffen, and at my urging he built a weakness into the Feynman machines. Dieter sent me e-mail—which he encrypted—to tell me how he had weakened the machines: they cannot withstand carbon dioxide. Exposed to air, they disintegrate. I got his messages and decrypted them. Nobody besides Dieter and myself knew about this vulnerability.

"Pavel tried the nanomachines in an experiment on mice, and they worked—after a fashion. That is to say, the devices changed lots of DNA. The mice grew all out of kilter, developed tumors and died within a few hours. Dieter Steffen, a technician named Kurt Adler and Paul Aubrey witnessed the experiment. All three are now dead."

"So now we know the secret of the Kali, anyway," Nick said. "It holds genetic information, which is transferred into nanomachines that cut and splice DNA according to the Kali pattern."

"Yes," Judith said. "There must be a way to make different versions of the chip with different DNA sequences. Some might be programmed with the gene to turn mice into dwarfs, others with the gene to turn off human volition."

"'The gene to turn off human volition,'" Nick repeated. "In other words, the gene that acts like a skeleton key to give Monty access to your mind."

"To your *soul*," Judith corrected. "Over time, you would certainly lose it to him. Even if your mind—that is, your ability to think independently—remained intact."

" That's some fancy footwork—making a cache-controller do double-duty as a PROM," Casey said. "No wonder Pavel couldn't quite pull it off."

"But Pavel and Dieter are dead," Nick said. " And they were the only two people who knew how their machine worked. Doesn't that put a monkey wrench in the plans?"

"There's no shortage of brilliant people who would die for the chance to complete them," Judith said. "This is the most intellectually intoxicating work in the history of mankind. All over the world, in every multinational drug company, in every graduate school, in every bio-warfare group of every army, ambitious scientists are working on technology to manipulate the human genome."

"Meanwhile," Nick said, "every computer company is working on chemical computers that work like living cells. Overmind is simply the biodigital convergence that Rachel Tryson and Wall Street are masturbating over. But when you put Monty in charge, however, it becomes an Obedient Remote Servo-Organic Network: ORSON."

"But it sounds so *silly*," Jake Carelli said. "The people of the world responding to this guy Monty's whim? What are we going to do, walk around like zombies with our arms outstretched in front of us? How could anyone believe it's the next stage in human evolution?"

"When you think of the Overmind, don't think of zombies," Judith said. "

Think of a swarm of bees, instantly communicating, sharing the same thought. Think of the best of the Guarneri String Quartet, when four musicians magically become one. Think of the person who knows what you're thinking without asking, whose thoughts you share. In other words, think of love. From the dawn of time, holy people have sought Holy Union. And the Overmind *is* union—real, physical, chemical, electrical union. All it will cost you is your soul."

Soul, schmole. Nick didn't want to talk about metaphysics. He wanted first to completely understand the ORSON jigsaw puzzle— he still had some pieces in his hand, and he needed to make them fit. After that, the only thing he wanted to discuss was what to do with Monty: should they throw him off a cliff, or should they push him in front of a Basel trolley?

"Let me see if I have it," Nick said. "The Kali chip contains the genome; the genome is transferred from the chip into Dieter's nanomachines; the nanomachines rearrange DNA in our brains, which mutate until we're all linked in Monty's Overmind."

"That's it," Judith said. "You've got it."

"Well what the hell does any of this have to do with the Gulf War Syndrome? These machines didn't even exist in 1989, or 1990, when Saddam was building his stockpile. There *can't* be any nanomachines floating around in Gulf War veterans."

"You're right," Judith said, "There are no nanomachines in Gulf War veterans."

"Then what the hell was Barlow talking about? What evidence did the Garbougians find?"

"Yeah," Jake said. "What's turning my cheeks so red?"

"The abstract from Pavel's 1990 MIT dissertation described building a prototype pseudo- nanomachine based on T4 bacteriophage," Judith said. "I obtained the abstract from the MIT library. The dissertation itself is missing."

"You think that Saddam used Pavel's prototype during the Gulf War?" Casey asked.

"If you were to inspect an Iraqi missile warhead," Judith said. "I'll bet you would find that it contained a Kali-chip and a 'monster-cell' full of T4 bacteriophage somehow reprogrammed with snippets of the human genome, probably Monty's genotype."

"I give up," Casey said. "Why would Saddam be interested in throwing T4 bacteriophage altered with Monty's genotype at soldiers on a battlefield? It doesn't kill them, but five years later they get headaches and skin rashes. That's hardly a weapon to strike fear in the hearts of his foes."

"Remember Irangate?" Jake said. "The CIA acting like a loose conglomeration of individuals, corporations, and crime rings? Maybe some Ollie North figure was willing to trade prototype weapons for cash and some test results. He might have thought it was a 'neat idea.'"

"Don't forget Monty's Naval connections from SCRI," Judith said.

"Are you trying to tell me," asked Nick, "that at the behest of Montaigne Meekman, the Gulf War was engineered by the CIA to test DNA-active weapons on

American soldiers?"

"As Barlow proved," Judith said, "it wouldn't be the first time that American soldiers were used as guinea pigs for the benefit of a third party. I doubt that anyone but Monty knew the truth about his 'weapon.' My guess is that Monty himself swindled the CIA, and they in turn duped Hussein Kamel, Saddam's son-in-law—the one who ran the Iraqi biological weapons program. Kamel probably told Saddam that his SCUDs would turn American soldiers in to the kind of obedient zombies that Jake asked about. Saddam may have attacked Kuwait in the hope of getting the 82nd Airborne under his telepathic command."

"Subedai," Nick said. "What would you do if you had a biological weapon that would put America's armies under your control? I'll bet Saddam was pissed when it didn't work."

"No wonder Kamel defected to Jordan," Casey said.

"No wonder Saddam killed him when he went back to Iraq," Jake added.

With this comment they all fell silent for a moment, as if exhausted. The wind whistling in the eaves sounded like a freight train passing.

Casey was the first to resume speaking.

"So Monty is building nanomachines right now at Hoff-Zeigy?" she asked.

"Actually the machines are built at Digital MicroSystems Laboratories, in Basel," Judith said. "Kurt Adler sent the Association for Responsible Biotechnology a note to that effect, posthumously. The machines are used at Hoff-Zeigy." Then she added, distractedly, "Corporations. Hitler never could have built his ovens so efficiently without them."

"But your company works on the Human Genome Project too," Casey said. "Aren't you taking part, in a way, in the same undertaking?"

Judith answered slowly.

"Human Potential will develop very specific drugs, tools that can used for one purpose only, not a general-purpose tool like Dieter built. They're working on a set of box wrenches, not an adjustable wrench. But this is hair-splitting, as I've come too late to understand. Accordingly, I have resigned from Human Potential, Incorporated."

Jake had been pacing for the last few minutes, and now he exploded.

"That's it?" he shouted at Judith. "You've resigned? You stand by and do nothing as this madman and his group of madmen infect millions of us; you sit there and tell us how the whole human race is under assault, and that's all you're going to do? Resign your job? Well Thank You. That's very big of you."

He walked over and leaned, with his face near hers, a boot-camp sergeant dressing down a green recruit, and raised his voice another few decibels.

"Let's get for real, Judith: You're smart. You're the smartest one here. Hell, if I had half your brains I wouldn't be an airport cop, I'd be the president of a fucking airline."

"Jake!" Nick said, jumping up and pushing Carelli back. "Give her a break.

She's done all anybody could have done."

"No," Judith said. "Jake is right; I should have done more. But I never said I wouldn't be part of the counterattack."

This seemed to mollify Jake. He walked a few steps closer to the fire.

"Counter attack?" Casey said. "What's the point? Even if we stop Meekman, what kind of lives can we ever hope to have in this world they are making? How are we supposed to go on living, knowing what we know?"

There was a long silence.

"Sorry I blew up," Jake said, finally. "Us good guys better stick together. There ain't many of us."

Jake now walked to the door and opened it. The wind nearly took it off its hinges as he stepped into the night. Nick stepped outside too, closing the door behind him. He walked alongside Jake into the meadow, where they stopped, standing in water up to their ankles. The rain was coming down as hard as Nick had ever seen rain come down; almost instantly he was soaked to the bone. The only light came from the window behind them; all around them was darkness.

Jake spoke without looking at Nick.

"Where's the Seventh Cavalry when you really need them?" he said.

"Gary Owen, motherfucker," Nick answered.

Five minutes later Nick restarted the conversation as the steam rose from his clothes. Somebody had attended to the fire, and it was roaring now.

"If Monty needed a computer chip to contain his genetic pattern," Nick asked, "why didn't he just build his own chip from scratch? Why bury the design in Kali?"

Casey had the answer.

"Monty needs to accomplish things by deception, to prove to himself that he's the most clever. It's what keeps him going. Besides," she said, "Kali was a cache controller, designed to hold large amounts of regular information that it flushed very quickly. It's the perfect chip to hide DNA in. Todd's goal was to load, unload, and rearrange patterns as quickly as possible, like one of those puzzles that you slide the letters around. He didn't care what the patterns were, only that he could move them fast. Whenever the Kali was done doing its real job, it reset itself to the Monty pattern. The only problem was, Pavel's *reset* logic kept messing up Todd's *shuffle* logic. That's how Todd discovered the trick."

"But Todd's chip was canceled. They never built it," Nick said.

"It was canceled after they had built the prototypes," Casey said. "Probably about five hundred of them. But that doesn't matter. What matters is the design, which they now have. They can give a tape to any silicon foundry and have a chip in their hands four days later."

Nick's skin was chafing against his wet clothes, and his face felt absolutely on fire. As he moved back from the heat he noticed that the redness in Jake's cheeks had grown brighter, too.

"What would happen," Nick asked, "if you had these machines inside you? Is there any antidote for someone who's been infected?"

"I suppose that the body would destroy the machines eventually," Judith said. "After all, there's CO2 in blood. These are only first-generation machines; fragile, unreliable. But I can't think of any way to undo the damage."

"I can," Casey said.

The other three looked at her, and waited. Over in a back corner, there was a tap tap tap from a leak in the roof.

"First we would have to know how an original DNA sequence was packed into the chip," she said. "DNA has four nucleotides: cytosine, adenine, somethingel-seiforgetanine, guanine. CATG. Let's say you're tiling the floor of your house with DNA. C is a red tile, A is blue, T is green, G is white. When you know the sequence, it's like you have a stack of tiles in the exact right order. A Kali chip is like a house already tiled. If you can figure out how your stack of tiles was laid out to create the pattern in your house, then you know the packing algorithm. Once you know that, you can substitute any stack for the original one, and make a new chip. With that new chip you program new nanomachines. Voila, antidote.

"Let's say Judith has been infected with nanomachines that are changing her DNA to Overmind DNA. We just reinfect her with machines that change *that* DNA back to Judith DNA. End of problem. Of course," she added, "once we've all been infected, we'll have to repeat this procedure six billion times, with six billion individually-cus-tomized antidote chips. Assuming everyone's not dead already, like those mice."

"As you say, hardly practical," Judith said. "To get back to my story: I did a fool-ish thing when I got back from visiting Dieter. We had agreed upon a certain pass-word to encrypt our correspondence. Dieter wrote that password on one of his busi-ness cards, and I left it in my daily missel, the book I take to mass to follow the litur-gy. The day after Dieter died, my office was rifled and the card was taken. So I assume that all my messages to and from Dieter have been decoded."

Over in the back corner, the *tap tap tap* from the leak in the roof echoed, resounded, reverberated, thundered. . .

It was like a nagging mosquito: irritating all out of proportion to its size.

Funny, wasn't it, how such a little thing could have such large consequences?

A little thing, like a little moisture in the air? A little moisture, falling from sky to earth?

Nick said, "They've already made machines programmed with human genes, haven't they?"

The rain seemed to have grown suddenly quieter. The leak tapped, but more slowly.

"Yes," Judith said, finally, looking right at Nick. "They have made human-acting machines."

"And released them," he said.

"Yes."

"In an oily matrix," Nick said, "to protect the machines from carbon dioxide."

"Yes. Protected by an oily fog, nanomachines programmed with human genes were released by the Corporate Fellows at the Biodigital Forum."

In the firelight Nick considered in turn the faces of the other three members of the Prospect Hill Christian Fellowship. Casey looked stunned, punchy from this latest blow. Jake looked angry and confused, ready to beat the snot out of a phantom he couldn't see. But Judith looked sad, infinitely sad.

"My mother was right," she said. "My bitter, hate-filled mother was right. This scientific curiosity that we celebrate, this 'noble quest to understand our universe.' . . It's a lie. It's just a fancy name for lust. And for pride. There is no limit to the depravity that mankind will commit in the name of 'progress.' And why? Because we feel like it. That's it. No other reason. Because we feel like it. It amuses us."

"I've been wondering," Nick said. "How is the Church of Monty structured? Clearly there's some kind of ecclesiastical hierarchy. You've got your Corporate Fellows, you've got those kids you met up on the mountaintop; Barlow mentioned the EMVERK alumni society. Are these all different names for the same thing? And where will I fit in?"

"I don't know," Judith said.

"Are there different orders, like Jesuits and Franciscans? Different ranks, like Cardinals and Monseigneurs?"

"I don't know."

"Different essences, like cherubim and seraphim, thrones and dominations?"

"I don't know, Nick," she said. "I'm sorry."

"I've got some Sunday school to catch up on before my first communion," he said.

"And so we reach the climax of this ghost story," Judith said quietly. "This tale of a lost soul. A soul not lost yet, but doomed to be lost. Here is the Frankenstein I promised. It's Nick."

She reached over and placed a loving hand on his. "Nick is the monster, is becoming the monster."

"How can you be so sure?" Jake said. "How do you know that Nick's been infected? You weren't even there!"

"Because," Judith said. "Monty proved it to me."

Chapter 51

"Monty called me a few days ago, just before you did, Nick," Judith said. "He told me about the release of nanomachines at the Biodigital Forum. He predicted that you would call me. Moments later you did call."

"Of course I did," Nick said. Monty was right: the world was what it was. Events were predictable. People were predictable. What was Nick but a walking Markov process?

"To make sure he had my attention, he e-mailed me a video clip of Paul's murder," Judith said. "Monty said that you would know how to get in touch with him when the time came. He said that you would feel his call, and that you would be ready—eager—for the second dose."

"How do you know the sick bastard wasn't bluffing?" Jake asked.

"He may have been bluffing about the machines," Judith said. "But he wasn't bluffing about having decoded Dieter's and my correspondence—he told me what was in it."

Casey said, impatiently, "Did he tell you anything about the nanomachines? Like whether they used an improved model, or just the same old shoddy types they used on the mice? Did he say what genes they might be altering?"

Casey was questioning Judith as aggressively as Jake Carelli had once interrogated Nick.

"What does it matter?" Nick said.

"What does it *matter*?" Casey asked, incredulously. "What does it *matter*?"

"What's the point?" Nick said. "They've infected me. I am becoming a Corporate Fellow. I am filled with nanomachines that are busily changing me, right now, into something lacking reason and free will, a drone in Monty's hive. And there's not a damn thing I can do about it."

"Listen, honey," Casey said. "There are billions of cells in the brain, and no easy pathway for machines to get to them all. No gene therapy has *ever* worked—and people have tried scads of them. So don't you go conceding the game yet. We must act on the premise that the attack, even if it is real, is weak. Jake's right: We have to mount a counterattack. We have to fight the machines, real or imaginary, in your brain. Monty himself said you need at least one more dose to complete the job."

"I wish I could share your optimism. But I've seen too much of what he can do."

"Nick, ask yourself," Casey said. "If the machines are foolproof, then why did Monty go out of his way to recruit you? Why did he try to seduce you into the fellowship if he could just take over your brain by remote control?"

"For the same reason that the serpent tempted Eve: he likes a challenge."

"Maybe," Casey said. "But I don't think he's confident in his machines. And I also think that whatever Mr. Barlow had on his diskette scared him. He's not omnipotent. We can beat him."

"I 'ope zo," Nick sighed.

"But only if we restore you to yourself before you succumb to that next dose. And then we have to destroy Monty Meekman and his foul Orson. You can't go mope-a-dope on us now."

"She's right, Nick," Jake said. "The only way you're going to wind up like your friend Todd is if you let it happen. And we're not going to let you let it happen."

"Believe me, I'm on your side. But please explain to me how we're going to do this counterattack? And while you're at it, could you show me how to spin straw into gold?"

"Let's work backwards," Casey said, ignoring Nick's pessimism. "So we don't let obstacles psyche us out. What's the last thing we need to do in order to bring Nick back to his initial condition?"

"Administer the antidote," Judith said.

"O.K.," Casey said. "And that has to be done at Hoff-Zeigy, because it's the only place we can do it. We don't have that matrix that the Corporate Fellows used to protect the nanomachines from carbon dioxide, and Hoff-Zeigy *does* have some kind of facility for just that purpose."

"My brother told me about it," Nick said. "To get in you have to get past a lock that sucks your blood to verify that you're authorized. That's why Paul sent me his blood: we're brothers, so if I had his blood running in my veins, a mixture might fool the scanner and open the door."

"You'll die before you cross the threshold," Judith said.

"What makes you say that?" Nick asked. "People get transfusions all the time."

"But the blood must be properly prepared," Judith said. "This blood wasn't spun down or anything. The cells are all ruptured. Transfusion shock will kill you before you get in the door."

"It's a chance I'm going to have to take. If we're really serious about this we can't let little things like that derail us. So. What's the step immediately before that?"

"Even if you were to get in, what would you do?" Judith persisted. "There would be so much to find out, so much to destroy. You would have to find all the files, all the plans, all the prototypes. . . It would take months."

"One problem at a time, Judith," Casey said. "First we fix his brain. Then we figure out how to stop Monty. So, working backwards, the immediate prior step is: we make the antidote nanomachines. We do that at Dijjy-Mike Labs, Basel."

"Not so fast," Jake said. "We haven't finished with the Hoff-Zeigy laboratory yet. Meekman said Nick would know where to find him for the second dose. Evidently this lab in Switzerland must be the place?"

"Monty wasn't explicit," Judith said. "But I think that's a plausible surmise."

"Then why does Nick need to go through the dumb-show with the blood? Why doesn't he just knock on the door and say 'I'm here!'?"

"No way," Nick said. "If I go in under my own steam, there's always the hope that I can self-administer the antidote before anybody can stop me. If I go in on their terms, who knows what they'll do to me? I'd rather risk dying from bad blood."

"Settled, then," Casey said. "He goes in by transfusion."

"Right," Nick said. "So the immediately prior step is manufacturing the nanomachines, which I do at the Labs by substituting the Nick-Kali chip for whatever chip they're using now in the manufacturing process. Before we can do that, we have to get into Dijjy-Mike Basel."

"That's a non-problem," Casey said. "I'll get you in. Fucking-up Dijjy-Mike corporate security is my speciality. The next prior step is to make the 'Nick-Kali,' the chip that contains your genetic information. Actually, I won't make a Kali, instead I'll make a PROM that works like a Kali, a much simpler job."

"Where are you going to make a chip?" Jake asked.

"Making it isn't the problem; I know where to make it. The problem is designing it. I need two things in order to do that: Nick's genotype, and the packing algorithm."

Casey turned to Judith.

"If you can get me the genetic information, I'll work out the packing."

"I know how to sequence DNA," Judith said. "So in theory I could provide the genetic information, the restorative sequence Nick needs. I just don't see how it's possible, now."

"Why not?" Casey said. "Why not, why not?"

"First, I need a sample of DNA from Nick before he was infected. . ."

"No problem," Nick said. The sample he had in mind was funky, but it would work.

"I still need to know what I'm looking for and where to start looking," Judith said. " I need to know where the gene resides: at what marker on which chromosome. The human genome has more than eighty thousand genes."

"You have no idea where to start?" Casey asked.

"Monty said he had spelled it all out," Judith said. "But I have no idea what he meant."

"I do," Nick said.

He reached into his back pocket and withdrew the photo of Monty that the Fellows had distributed at the Forum. As the other three looked at and passed around the flyer, Nick explained Monty's 'gift to Mankind,' the genetic sequence written in microdots.

"The genes to allow regrowth of nerve cells are explicated here. But that's only one set of genes. You need a second gene suite that actually determines what structures the nerve cells will grow into; you get that information in a shifted reading frame, by using the text itself as a decoder ring on the first set. Like a double-crosstic puzzle."

"Trojan genes," Judith said. "Two genes for the price of one."

Jake was having a hard time following this line.

"You mean he actually tells you on that piece of paper exactly what these nanomachine things are doing?"

"He couldn't resist gloating over his brilliant Subedai move," Nick said. "Luring all the top information-soldiers to an ambush in a box canyon, then converting them to soldiers in his own army. But by showing them the genes he's not only taunting everybody, he's also giving them the information that they can use in turn on other victims once they've been won over to his side."

"He must be very confident that the things work," Casey said, "to tip his cards like that."

"His arrogance may be his undoing," Judith said. "Presumably, everybody else needs second doses too, just like Nick does. I wonder if Monty's really expecting them all to show up for their inoculations? People who get invitations to Rachel Tryson events are not weak-willed."

"Let's not worry about them," Nick said. "We have enough problems of our own. So where were we?"

"My biggest problem: I don't have a laboratory."

"But . . . " Jake said.

"I don't dare go back to Human Potential. I'm sure it's being watched."

"You must have friends, other facilities. . ."

"Let me guess," Nick said. "Monty has started some rumor on the Internet that will make people very curious when you show up asking to borrow access to a DNA-sequencing lab."

"You're starting to know him as well as he knows you," Judith said.

"Well screw it," Nick said. "I know somebody with her own molecular genetics laboratory. As a matter of fact, I'm married to somebody who has her own molecular genetics laboratory. And if we ask her the right way, I'll bet we can get her to discretely help us."

Nick hoped she would help, anyway. After their discussion at the Duke Diner, Bartlett was equally likely to send for the men in the white coats when Nick called.

"She's probably being watched too," Jake said. "I would stake her out if I were Meekman."

"In that case we'll just have to be careful," Nick said. "Let's assume that it all works, and that Judith had just divined the nucleotide base-pair sequence that needs to go into Casey's PROM. How do we learn the packing order?"

"We reverse engineer a Kali chip," Casey said. "Using Todd's work diaries and a clever test-bed, we tease the structure out of her."

The silence that followed this remark was long, excruciatingly long.

Finally Nick asked, "If the machines are working, how long do I have?"

"If Monty's right," Judith said. "It's probably about two weeks. One fortnight until 'Nick Aubrey' is completely gone, and a new member of the Overmind walks the earth."

"I guess you'll know soon enough," Jake said.

No, and that was the rub. That was the bite in the ass.

"I'll never know. Either the machines aren't working, and are in fact harmless, or they are working perfectly, and it is only a matter of time until my thought becomes meshed with Monty Meekman's. If they are working, how will I know? I will no more feel myself losing my free will than I felt myself growing taller when I was a child. Everything Monty says will seem to make more and more sense to me, until I have completely given myself over to him."

Nick put some wood on the fire, poured another taste of whiskey.

Casey muffled a sob. She got up and walked about now, unable to look at Nick.

"What's everybody walking around for?" Jake asked. "Let's draw up the rest of the plan."

"There is no 'rest of the plan,' you jackass," Casey said. "We're fucked. Without a Kali chip there is no plan. And, unfortunately, we have no Kali chip."

"Get one."

"The chip that was destroyed in the Bonehead Museum was the last Kali we'll ever see. There are no more. Monty has them all."

"So all we lack, then, is a Kali chip?" Jake said "Is that the only problem?"

"Yes Jake," Casey said, with manifest irritation. "That's the only problem. But it's a very big problem."

"I'll have a chip for you in seven days," Jake said. "March seventh."

The room was even more quiet now. The tap from the leak had ceased.

"There's Kali chips on Iraqi SCUDs, right?"

"That's my hypothesis," Judith said.

"I know a secret," Jake said.

"We're like Ross Perot," Nick said. "All ears."

"The CIA has a SCUD, and I know where it is."

"Keep talking."

"A good buddy of mine is in Tech Int, technical intelligence, the group in the Army that's in charge of analyzing captured enemy weapons. He works at the SCIF. That's the Secret Compartmentalized Information Facility, at the Army chemical warfare center in Maryland. You, know, the 'hot zone' place. They've been trying to get their hands on a SCUD warhead for four years now."

"And what are you saying?" Nick said. "They have one now?"

"They wish they did."

"Jake, is this a guessing game?"

"A SCUD warhead fell intact over Dahrain. This is court-martial stuff if it ever gets out that he told me."

"Where is it?" Nick said. "Where is the fucking warhead?"

"Fort Devens, Massachusetts. "

Damn! So close, so tantalizingly close! And yet infinitely far away.

"I might have useta been at Devens," Nick said. "But it ain't there no more. They closed that place down after the Gulf War, after you mustered out of the Army."

"Listen, it's at Devens, and I'll tell you how I know. Over in Saudi, Technical Intelligence had the warhead. They were packing it up for shipment back to the States when these spooks came out of nowhere and pulled rank. They said they were from Tech Int senior staff, and they had orders to prove it. They took the warhead and left on a flight bound for Devens. Of course, they weren't *really* Tech Int. They were black intelligence. They were all from USAISD."

"What's that?"

"U.S. Army Intelligence School, Devens. Everybody who ever trained in Military Intelligence went to school there at some point. I did eighteen months, myself. And everybody at Devens knew that there was a contingent at USAISD that wasn't kosher."

"Not kosher? How?" Nick said.

"Not Army. They were CIA or National Security Agency or something. They were using the base as a cover. They're still there, some of them. Devens is ninety-nine percent shut down. But there's still a spook crew at the old school, USAISD. You can see their cars in the parking lot. They're not with the Army. There's only one real Army group left at Devens, and it ain't them. It's a reserve group that's a Tech Int counterpart of the Hot Zone guys, which is how I know this. Nobody knows who these spooks at USAISD really are or what they really do. Nobody goes near them. You gotta be afraid of that kind of people."

"I *am* afraid of them," Nick said.

"Well buck yourself up, Nick, because you and me, we're going to go take that SCUD away from them."

Nothing further was said until dawn. Nick tried to sleep, but it was hopeless. He knew that the others were awake as well, because from time to time each of the other three got up to put wood on the fire. It was a good thing, too, that the Swedish Baptists had left behind a large supply of dry logs. Because outside the lodge the furious wind still howled, and the snow had drifted to the edge of the window.

Chapter 52

Bartlett Aubrey poured more whiskey in her glass and drank. It wasn't working. It was only making her drunk, a condition she had never liked and consequently grown unused to. But how else could she make the pain go away, the anguish, the confusion of her own motives, the loneliness, the fear? She poured again and drank again. This is stupid, Bartlett, she told herself. This is really stupid.

Remorse was a useless emotion, but the only one her heart now knew. She looked around her miserable darkened apartment. The wretched dying plants. The generic I-have-no-taste-why-don't-you-just-choose-something-for-me prints on the wall. Baseball magazines! Who was she kidding? Next to her bed. Upon which she had practically raped her bewildered brother-in-law.

She couldn't bear to remember. Her cheeks burned and she thought of Nick.

It was at Thanksgiving time, the night she met him. She had gone to a feast, a quasi-hippie vegetarian affair with lots of flowing dresses, barefoot children, blue-grass music and contra-dancing. Her *Science* article had come out. Her prelims had been passed. She was ready to dance.

Nick was tall, Gary Cooper. He knew virtually nothing about molecular biology. He had studied farming and computers, and had just come back from years overseas in Africa and Brazil. He and she danced: he told her stories, she told him stories, he recited 'Letter from Birmingham Jail,' she recited the atomic weights of sixty-seven elements. He loved children and hated injustice. She loved Red Sox and hated Mets. She lost her heart. She tumbled like a brick falling into a well.

Atomic weights and valences. . . Funny, she hadn't done much organic synthesis since leaving grad school. At one time she could have taught that course in her sleep. She wondered if she could still remember how to synthesize cyanide without looking at a textbook.

She poured one more bit of whiskey and drank it. She took a look around her apartment.

She grabbed her coat and hat, and left. . .

At the suspension bridge, Bartlett remembers. In the Dark. In the Snow. Mr. And Mrs. Mallard. Where are they this winter? Make way! Make Way! Why make way for Ducklings? Ducklings are ducks. Ducks are birds. Their shit falls every-where, on the living and the dead.

How did we decide to start our married life in Boston? I don't recall. There were other offers. I could have worked at NIH or CDC, or Stanford, or Chicago. Something about Boston and New England caught us. It was so different from the

coal hills of southern Illinois, where my grandfather was a hellfire Baptist preacher and
credentialed mining engineer. Credentialed? He could read. And he knew how to
work in a deep shaft without blowing it up. Grandpa quoted Scripture: *"I will make
all my beauty pass before you, and in your presence I will pronounce my name. But my face
you cannot see, for no man sees me and still lives."* But Bartlett was not man. *She* would
look upon the secret of life, she would find the face of God in messenger RNA. And
rearrange it with restriction enzymes. And blow up a deep shaft.

The red-faced man Nick's friend wanted me to go with him.

There was danger, he said.

But how could I face Nick? He whom I deserted? And his new girlfriend the
monster-maker?

I gave him Paul's blood.

The face of God in messenger RNA? No man sees it and still lives.

So goodbye to this stupid bridge. I will never come here again. . .

She drank again and started walking. . . and a monster walked up behind her.

A monstrous secret.

I never told Nick that I had met his precious Monty.

A one-minute meeting. To my laboratory at MIT he came. He had read my
Trojan Gene; he knew of my letter to Nature about Fitzgibbon's Disease. He was an
oily, ugly snake. Would I come to join his team? No, I said. Very well, he said He
would never trouble me again, on one condition: I should not tell Nick that we had
spoken, he said. It would not be prudent. A month later his photo was in the newspaper: a meeting with the governor of Massachusetts. 'No layoffs' was Monty's
promise, according to the *Globe*. A week later the merger of Stanford MicroSystems
Digital Data and was approved, abetted by generous tax concessions. Nick's pay-
checks had a new name on them, and were drawn on a bank in California. The layoffs started a month later, but the angel of death passed by Nick's house.

A secret like this is a monster in a marriage. Kill it Bartlett, kill it!

Too late.

Could it be? Could it possibly be? That Stanford MicroSystems had acquired Digital
Data in order that Monty could get his hands on Nick, and thus get his hands on me?

Gravitus: The weight of the world. On my Nick, so that he would give Monty
the Neuro Group Model. Thought made tangible. Thought in Software.
Monstrosity! My poor Nicholas!

God forgive me, I should have talked to Irwin. I should have talked to Eddie. I
should have strangled the Neuro Group in its crib. Instead I strangled my marriage.

I never told Nick. It wouldn't have been prudent.

Jumping from the Prudential Center. Would that be Prudent?

Would I feel, as I fell, that my heart had become a billion pounds of lead?

Would I feel, as I fell, as if I were falling into a well, in love?

∞·VI·∞

ST. MATTHEW'S PASSION

Chapter 53

Casey Montgomery, herself, didn't care one rat's ass about God or religion. She didn't care about Holy Water or the Torah or the Sabbath or eating fish on Friday or the yarmulkes or the no shoes in the mosque or the veil or fasting or crossing fingers when she drove by a graveyard. She didn't care about genuflecting in front of the altar, keeping kosher, honoring the Prophet, sacred mountains, the Dalai Lama, Toni Morrison, extreme unction, spiritual awakening, ritual cleansing, Hopi dancing, or touching a teammate's hands between foul shots. She didn't care about any of that crap, superstition or religion. The next bumper sticker she put on her car would be the one that said

GUNS DON'T KILL PEOPLE
RELIGIONS KILL PEOPLE

She didn't care about any of that stuff. But she had spent a lot of time lately wondering if there was anyway to get back in touch with Todd, short of hiring somebody to lock her in a freezer and stab her with shards of glass.

Her longing for him was of two well-defined natures. The first nature was her longing for him to come as he had come to her in the shrine in the Mill, to unify his soul with hers; to make her whole, hale, complete. Her sure knowledge that that experience would never be repeated was not enough to make her stop wanting it. The second nature of her longing was in the aspect of Deus Ex Machina. *Get your ectoplasmic ass over here and open the door*, she had commanded. And he had obeyed. Ever since then she had been commanding him to reappear and explain his Kali work notebooks, but so far he was keeping mum.

For a Mill rat such as herself, sneaking back into the Mill hadn't been such a big deal. The fact that there was a five-state manhunt out for her, however, had put a little excitement into the proposition. But she had made it in, she was safe; she had equipped a tiny hardware-lab-slash-living quarters, replete with sleeping bag, chamber pot, potable water, and hardware testbed. She had jury-rigged a motion sensor that would alert her if anybody happened to come her way. But this particular neck of the Mill, she knew from years of prowling, was lucky if it saw more than five people a year. As a consequence of which, well, yes, it was filthy. But Mission

Impossible heroes and heroines get used to that. They can shower up after they have once again made the world safe.

Her goal was to have the test suite written by the time the Nick showed up with the Kali chip. If everything went according to plan, that would be in about a week. Not a lot of time to rig up a lab and engineer a test suite. On the other hand, what else was she going to do with her time? She was a fugitive, for Christ's sake. Was she supposed to go hang out at the Newcastle Diner? Once a day, around 3 AM, she would take the long route, the *very* long route, down to the cafeteria, where she would steal the next day's food. She would use a real toilet, wash up in the sink, then go shopping—stealing whatever supplies she needed from wherever she needed to steal them—and then head back up to the Alpha Annex's store-room's closet's back hall, to write code furiously and solder circuit boards.

She thought of Kali as a padlock. Her test suite would try keys against the lock. If the program found the key, that meant they had found the packing algorithm—and that would allow them to create a Kali packed with Nick's genotype instead of Monty's. Her program would test about one route per millisecond, a thousand a second. That would make sixty thousand a minute, a couple of million an hour. In other words, nothing. It would be like looking for the Titanic one bucket of water at a time.

The charred bit of the Kali plot was taped to the wall of her tiny lab; otherwise the walls were bare. If she had been able to bring it, she would have loved to have put up the photo of the guy with the pencil moustache from *Mandate* magazine that she had used as a model when cutting Nick's hair. But since she didn't have it, the plot was going to have to be the only decoration.

She had hoped that somehow that bit of charred paper would prove to be her Rosetta Stone, the fragment that would lead to the deciphering of the entire chip. So far no good, but she could hope. She had traced every line on the paper until it either met a pin-out or disappeared into carbon on a burned edge. The Kali had thirty-two pin-outs per side, a hundred and twenty eight total. The portion of paper that she had salvaged contained a single chip edge; there were seven pin-outs on it and she could only follow them a tiny portion of the way into the chip. Some Rosetta Stone. Rosetta Pebble was more like it.

Realistically, of course, she was hosed—unless she figured out some way to decipher the notebooks. Which meant that Nick was hosed. And that would mean that perhaps many many other people were hosed as well.

Perhaps everybody.

⊕

Nick turned off the television and walked over to the window. On O'Heany Street four floors below him some of the less prosperous citizens of Albany, New

York, stood huddled in an alleyway. Six days ago Jake had rented this room at the Henry Hudson Hotel. While Nick sat outside in the 'borrowed' pickup truck with the stolen New York plates, Jake had gone inside to pay for a week in advance. Then he opened a side door, let Nick in (with his bag of groceries), and, after asking Nick what size shoe he wore, he left to park the truck in an even worse section of town.

Nick's rental car had been found in Portland, Oregon, with a seventeen year old behind the wheel who had been very willing to talk. So hopping back into the Eurosport with the California plates didn't look like such a hot idea anymore. Instead Jake had helped a tourist with Colorado plates to donate use of his new shiny truck with the big wheels and chrome roll bar.

Even after Nick's hair had been dyed black, it was too dangerous for him to accompany Jake as he assembled the supplies. Nick was going to have to stay in this flea-bag until they were ready to move. He had brought along eight magazines, a Tom Clancy book and one by Michael Crichton. He had finished the magazines by five PM the first day, and soon thereafter discovered that he didn't care for thrillers. TV was unwatchable. He had already done two hundred and fifty pushups. If he ate another baloney sandwich he would hurl. So what was he to do now?

He knew, of course. He would follow the only course of action consistent with prudence and common sense. He would wait. If all went well, the real fun would begin tomorrow.

⊕

By the light of the four computer screens in the back hall of the Alpha Annex closet, Casey Montgomery read, for the thousandth time, the snow-melt-smudged page 99 of Todd's *Kali log # 4*:

> 'Ive got a timing bogon on chevy39, I think it is the
> master reset bogon. That would give me the off-by-
> one. It should go clear to the air, but vectors off at
> king kong one. Funny boy's bist is toying with
> carucha. No reason to. ''

A "bogon" was obviously a bogus entity, something that was there but shouldn't be. So, Todd had detected a timing glitch that gave rise to an off-by-one error. The bist was the built-in-system-test, part of the logic that Pavel had taken over from Casey. So Pavel's system test was disturbing Todd's logic somehow. That much was easy to understand. But what about Chevy39, the air, king kong one, carucha? It was nonsense. She tossed the book on the floor and went back to work on the testbed.

⊕

Somewhere east of Athol Nick lost the signal.

He had picked up the Umass-Amherst radio station half an hour ago, when they were near the intersection where Route 2 met 91 north and all the cars with ski racks got off to head to Vermont, leaving the highway to working stiffs like Nick and Jake. It was the Afro-Pop show, and the feature today had been *Bambara Jazz Nationale*, the pioneering band of the Afro-Cuban style. At a Thanksgiving party during a sandstorm a lifetime ago he had listened to one of their albums over and over, watching the African guests gracefully dancing, their sandals grinding sand into the tile floor with a *ch-ch, ch-ch,* in time to the music.

"I fear these things," Nick said, switching off the radio as static took over.

Jake, half asleep, looked over at him curiously, and said nothing.

Three hours ago Jake collected Nick from the Henry Hudson. This time their car was quasi-legitimate: a dented Chrysler Le Baron that he had bought off a lot for twelve hundred dollars. It was only quasi-legitimate because it was registered to a fictitious person. They were making a good dent in Casey's money, and Nick didn't want to ask how much the diamond-encrusted rotary bone saw or the false passports and licenses had cost. At least the used golf clubs looked cheap.

They hadn't spoken much during the hour and a half that it had taken them to reach this far after leaving the McDonald's just outside of Albany. Jake hadn't had much time to sleep in the last few days, and Nick had had time for little else, so he drove. They crested the hill, rounded the gentle bend and saw before them a grand vista: the factory chimneys of Gardner jutted skyward, and away beyond them the church tower of the village of Hubardston poked out of the woods.

"How far to Devens?" Nick asked.

"Half an hour, maybe."

"What then?"

"We drive in and look around. I know that place like the back of my hand, but you should get a feel for it in case we have to bolt in the dark."

"You can do that, just drive in there?"

"They've go a sign up that says 'official business only' but nobody cares. People who are real die-hard even use the golf course this time of year. In the summer it's more restricted."

"It's not patrolled? How big is it?"

"The base is a couple thousand acres, but most of that is woods that they used to use for training. The actual base, where there's buildings and stuff, is a couple hundred acres. The cops from the town of Ayer patrol it but they won't bother you unless you're dealing dope or vandalizing the place. There's no official security 'til ten PM. Then there's a private company that checks for IDs. Tonight we'll be breaking into the USAISD buildings. There's four of them on a quadrangle about thirty meters by two hundred meters, and they're all connected by tunnels underground.

"There might be a whole army of spooks in there or some kind of secret laboratory, like James Bond or something, but my bet is that there's just a bunch of low-level losers with not much to do, like in The Falcon and the Snowman. There's a bunker room down there off one of the corridors; that's where the SCUD will be."

"How do you know?" Nick said.

"Because it has to be there."

"What if it isn't?"

"We'll have to kidnap somebody and get him to tell us where it is. We'll go in after dark tonight, before ten. I'll put the boys to sleep, blow the locks; you go in and get the chip out of the warhead, then we get in our car and drive away. We'll stash our things someplace off the base, collect them later. After we get the chip and safely away, it's happy trails until we meet again."

"Sounds like a plan," Nick said.

⊕

The test bed was ready, waiting for a Kali chip like a bassinet waiting for the baby. Once Jake and Nick got back with the chip she would plug it in and start the test. But it would be a shot in the dark. Unless she found a way to constrain the search, it would be an absolute shot in the dark.

"Damn you, Todd," she said. "Why won't you tell me what these notebooks mean?"

⊕

"What's all this?" Nick said. "I thought the base was shut down."

"That must be the new federal prison. I didn't know that they had started construction yet."

All along the right side of the Devens road there were bulldozers, mounds of earth, pickup trucks, trailers, stacks of girders. In a minute they were past the site, and a golf course appeared on either side of the road. A lone golfer wearing a light windbreaker was addressing a ball. The crazy bastard: Nick remembered hearing on the radio that the expected high temperature today was forty degrees. The road continued down a long gentle hill and eventually reached a T. There was a large open field on his right and a baseball field on his left.

"See that cannon?" Jake said. "One night before a parade drill we filled it with golf balls, and when they set it off the next morning the balls went through the base commandant's windows."

"Oh you funny soldiers," Nick said.

They saw no other cars as they drove through a ghost village of vacant old and tired buildings amid acres of lawns leaf-covered and brown under majestic bare trees.

He tried to imagine what this place must have looked like in the summer of 1990. For months Route 2 east and west had funneled convoy after convoy of forest-camouflaged trucks, jeeps and artillery into the base, and desert-camouflaged convoys out, heading for Westover Air Force Base. This empty base was the emblem of a passing era. How long before Monty's way of warfare became the norm, and tanks, planes, rifles and bullets became as obsolete as bows and arrows?

"Park here," Jake said, handing a pair of cleats to Nick. "Let's go play some golf."

Chapter 54

At 9:00 PM Eastern Nick turned off his headlights and cautiously pulled the convertible behind a mound of earth next to a bulldozer. Nobody would see it here unless they were looking for it. By the rising three-quarter moon he could make out the profile of Jake Carelli in the passenger seat. As Jake applied the black grease paint to his face, he seemed to melt into the night.

"Listen," Jake said. "Be careful on that golf course. A buddy of mine broke his ankle on a sand trap."

"Yeah, I got that. I'm more concerned about the hand grenades."

"Don't worry about them. Last resort. I'm going to use the tranquilizer darts. Failing that, I'll shoot 'em with plastic bullets."

"I hope we don't have to kill anybody."

Jake handed Nick the grease paint. Nick applied the goo to his face as Jake rechecked his weapons.

"Let me tell you something. In the Army they've got this book, see, FM 34-54 Battlefield Technical Intelligence Procedures. It spells out in more detail than you ever want to know what to do when you capture enemy materiel, and who does what to whom once the shit comes Stateside. There's no CIA or NSA listed anywhere in FM 34-54. So if anybody other than the Army is holding onto captured weapons that have been used against the Army. . . Let's say I've got a problem with that. The CIA can't legally operate on a military base on US soil; these guys are running open loop. That pisses me off. Three quarters of a million soldiers might be helped by understanding that warhead. But these anti-constitutional Gordon Liddies are holding out on us. And why are they holding out on us? Because they're embarrassed that they fucked up yet again? Because they want to clone the technology and sell it to the highest bidder? Because Hussein Kamel never really died?

Because they want to take over? Who knows? Fuck 'em. You ever shoot a gun?"

"I'm a farm boy. All farm boys are shooters."

"OK. Worse comes to worst, we'll shoot em with real ammo. Only if we are totally screwed—"

"In Massachusetts we say 'scrod.'"

"— Only if we are totally *scrod* will I think about using the hand grenades. Main thing is, you get the chip and board, and you get your ass the hell out. You're a damn Peace Corps Volunteer and I'm a damn commando. So you let me worry about this stuff, OK?"

"I am not a Peace Corps Volunteer. I worked for OXFAM. Oxford Famine Relief."

"Same difference."

"And you're no commando, neither. You're a repairman and jeep driver."

"I'm a damn site closer to being a commando than you are. Here, put this stuff on the back of your hands too."

"I will agree that you're the lead commando. But only if you agree that I am a very *macho* famine relief worker. I want that in the record."

"I'll grant you that much. You are a very macho famine relief worker. Do you know how to work the safety?"

"We've been over this, Jake."

"We've been over it in the Army too, and we still manage to fuck it up from time to time."

"I know how to work the safety. Like this."

"Good. You know the plan?"

"Across the golf course and parade ground, past the infirmary to the USAISD quadrangle. We throw the rope up and pull ourselves up to the third floor balcony in the north building. I wait there while you find and tranquilize anybody who's around. Then you come back for me, we go to the basement, blow the lock to the throne room. The warhead will be in there. I cut open the skin with the bone-saw. I remove the Kali and monster cell. Assuming that they're in there."

"They will be."

"Then we get the fuck out of Dodge."

"Sounds like you got it. Ready?"

"Ready."

"Good. Me too."

"Jake?"

"Yeah?"

"Are we going to pull this off?"

"Nick, these spooks are nerds. If the day ever comes when a US Army jeep driver and a Peace Corps Volunteer can't handle a dozen of them, you better sell all your stock short."

"What do you know about stock?"

"I saw it on television. Let's go."

"Let's go."

They set off at loping gait across the fields and Jake's military training was very apparent. It was amazing how quickly Nick could lose him in the darkness. They quickly crossed the fields and skirted the vacant infirmary. Jake's military training was also obvious by the speed with which he placed the grappling iron over the balcony and scurried up. Nick scrambled up behind him.

"Stay here. I'll be back after I've put the children to bed," Jake said, and vanished. He was back within five minutes.

"Hurry before they wake up. You've got a baby to deliver, doctor."

The SCUD was right where Jake said it would be. With the smell of the explosive they had used to blow the door still in his nose, Nick began to work. Cutting through the skin of the warhead proved easy: the bone-saw went right through it. He cut a small square, removed it, and peered into the nose of the SCUD. He wouldn't have believed it if he hadn't seen it with his own eyes.

It was Kali, a sure as he was born, sitting right there on a circuit board at the very tip of the rocket. He recognized it as he would an old friend, despite the crazy contraption that hung off its side like a leech. On a conventionally-mounted Kali he would have expected to find, on each of its four sides, thirty-two little gold wires—nearly microscopic, like the finest gossamer—connecting the chip to the surrounding ceramic mount. The SCUD Kali was different. Three of the four sides were normally mounted: the gold gossamer joined the surrounding ceramic as he would have expected. But the thirty-two leads out of the fourth side were fused not into the ceramic, but into a glass tube that was mounted on the board. It looked like a small test tube that had been melted shut at either end. There was a green liquid in it that reminded Nick of a plastic tubes of frozen fruit punch.

"Jesus God in heaven, Judith was right," Nick said. "Saddam's revenge. It's a Kali chip, with a God-damned monster cell full of $T4$ bacteriophage. Holy shit."

"Can you get it out?"

"Hope so," Nick said. "I'm going to try to take the whole board instead of the chip."

He removed the board and held it above his head like a trophy, feeling flushed and giddy. Success! But suddenly he felt Jake's hand in an iron grip around his left wrist.

"Company," Jake said. Nick could hear the agitated voices coming down the stairwell. Two voices, maybe three. The nature of the echo made it hard for Nick to tell how far away they were.

"Is there another way out?"

"It's a maze; I'd get us lost. We'll go out this way; wait till I call you."

Before Nick could say a word, Jake was running up the stairs. Nick switched the board from his right hand to his left, and with his right withdrew the pistol and ran after Jake.

An eruption of sound and smell: gunfire, explosions.

"Nick," he heard Jake calling, after the noise stopped, "Come on. Come on."

He ran up the stairs and darted his head through the doorway, looking left. No one.

"Nick, here."

He turned to his right and saw Jake. He was leaning against the wall, bleeding heavily from his right shoulder and obviously in pain, fussing with the two hand grenades on his belt. "Right through that door," Jake said. "Take the car. Good luck."

"Oh Christ, Jake. Oh Christ," he said. "Come on, we've got to get you out of here."

There were shouts coming down the hallway.

"I'm done, Nick. Get going."

"Jake, come on."

"Nick," Jake said. "Remember what you told me at Raquette Lake?'

"What?"

"You told me to back you up. Now go. Get your ass out of here. If that chip doesn't make it, I'm dying for nothing."

Nick could see a pair of headlights rapidly approaching. Already?

"Go!" Jake said.

Oh good Christ, Nick thought. But he knew what he had to do.

"Gary Owen, brother," Nick said.

"Gary Owen," Jake said, as he pulled the pin from a grenade and threw it past Nick, down the hall.

Nick pushed at the door and it swung open. He took two steps out into the night. Suddenly there was noise and bright light all around. He was in the air, doing a flip off the high dive at Oneonta Swim Club.

⊕

From the opposite side of the laboratory bench, Bartlett Aubrey considered her new friend Judith. Bartlett was a laboratory adept herself, but Judith, performing procedures, had a natural grace unlike any Bartlett had ever seen. Her slender fingers seemed to caress the glassware, as a violinist's might caress a fingerboard. She had a graceful way of speaking, too: they had only met four days ago, but already Bartlett felt that Judith was someone to help her sort out the confusion in her addled noggin.

Lord knew Bartlett's attempts to sort it out on her own had been a pathetic fiasco: five days ago she had awakened under the suspension bridge in the Public Garden at four AM, nearly frozen. Only now was the hangover fully abated. Arriving back at her apartment a few hours later, still drunk, but now full of Kenmore Square coffee too, she had found a message from her baseball and tuna-loving boss Irwin Goldberg on her answering machine. It was an urgent-sounding invitation to coffee at Temple Beth Israel on the following day. Odd that Irwin should have called her at home; that was a first. Odder still that the message had come at two-thirty in the morning. It was noggin-addling in the extreme.

She had gone to the synagogue, of course, after an hour-long shower. Irwin had met her at the door and welcomed her inside. She had barely said 'hello' before she was taken into a side room by some very serious women, who immediately gave her a rather radical haircut, dressed her in a simple black dress, tied a scarf over her head and hustled her out a side door into a waiting limousine with darkened windows, which trundled her to Logan airport. Evidently a simple phone call from Judith Knight to Irwin Goldberg requesting help in thwarting Iraqi biological warfare carried a lot of weight. So now here were Bartlett and Judith, with full rein of the most advanced genetics laboratory in Tel Aviv, purifying and refining DNA samples from Nick Aubrey's jock strap.

Their conversation had just taken a natural turn from orphan diseases to nineteenth century literature. A natural turn for Judith, anyway. Bartlett wasn't too deep into the American Renaissance, but Judith clearly knew her Emerson and Melville. Bartlett had told her of her work on Fitzgibbon's disease, coming more quickly in the telling to the loss of young Jackson than she usually did. Judith had tactfully steered the conversation to her own firm's particular adopted modern plague.

Human Potential, Inc, had identified the mechanism of action of Ousman's anemia, another new disease like AIDS. Like sickle-cell anemia, Ousman's was hundreds of times more prevalent in African people than in Caucasian.

"It's actually related to genetic factors that cause skin coloration," she said. "Those genes are pretty well understood. The sickness is not an off-or-on thing. There's a degree of anemia that's directly proportional to the amount of melanin in a person's skin. So if you took a person who had the anemia and altered their genes to make them white, as each new layer of skin grew, in the natural process of replacing shedding cells, they would become stronger."

"Like adjusting a rheostat," Bartlett said. "Up a little darker, down a little lighter."

"Nathaniel Hawthorne wrote a story about a scientist whose beautiful wife had a single blemish—a tiny birthmark on her cheek in the shape of a hand. He worked for years to find the potion that would eradicate the birthmark. At last he succeeded. She consumed the potion, the birthmark faded to invisibility, and she died. I sometimes wonder if Pavel Isaacs had Ousman's anemia. I have wondered whether his first human experiments were on himself."

"The operation was a success but the patient died."

"If you're white, you're alright," Judith said. "Unless you fall out a fifth floor door."

"I suppose that it's an occupational hazard for those in our field. Self experimentation."

Judith put down the pipette she had been using and took off her gloves.

"I used to think I knew how I felt about human genetics," she said. "I had a carefully reasoned, well-buttressed argument that allowed for exactly *this*, but not for *that*. I had it all worked out."

"I take it you don't feel that way any more," Bartlett said.

"I know less now than I did when I was seventeen. I say that I no longer believe in adjusting people's genetic endowments, yet here I am determining a sequence for us to insert into Nick, whoever he has become."

"I never thought I'd be doing genetic experiments on my own husband," Bartlett said. "I guess this is my final gift to him."

"So you never expect to see him again?"

How many times did Bartlett have to face this fact? It was like a newsreel that would never stop running.

"No," she said. "I don't. How could I, now?"

"Look inside yourself, Bartlett. I think you'll find a way."

⊕

He must not have been out long; when he awoke the lights were still approaching. He found the board almost immediately, and miraculously the Kali chip was intact. The cell, however, was gone. It must have slipped off when the concussion catapulted him out of the building. He didn't need the cell; all he needed was the chip—and he wasn't about to take the time to go on a scavenger hunt. He glanced towards the street lamp and saw the light glinting off the metal of the gun he had dropped; he picked it up at a run. There was no time for a fancy evasion strategy: he would sprint for the car, straight across the open field and golf course.

He had only gone a hundred yards or so when his chest began to ache from the cold air. Why hadn't he built more aerobic exercise into his weight training? Breathing heavily through his open mouth, he ran past the parade-ground cannon under some evergreen trees that appeared as negative shapes against the stars and onto the golf course. He knew that if he stopped to rest he would never be able to start up again. It seemed like an eternity before he came upon the edge of the construction site. His car had to be about two hundred yards away. But what would he do if he got there? Already more headlights were rapidly coming down the entrance road from Route 2. One set, now another. More would come, certainly. And they would notice a car speeding in the other direction. There was hardly any point at all in reaching the Le Baron. But he couldn't think, he could only run, his lungs on fire, his legs made of lead. Now he was among the piles of construction supplies; a   trailer on his left; beyond that three port-o-lets and a large new bulldozer, shiny in the moonlight.

He tripped and found himself flying again, but this time he was conscious of himself in the air. He dropped the gun mid-flight to have a hand free to break his fall, as with his right hand he cradled the board to his chest.

His landing was soft—soft and muddy. Nick's heart was trying to beat its way out of his chest. Just as he was about to stand he saw headlights sweeping the golf course behind him. Somebody was driving right over the fairways.

Oh hell.

The headlights momentarily rose up in the sky as the car went up an incline. *Now, Nick!* He grabbed the gun, jumped up and ran to the nearest port-o-let, tore the door open, entered and pulled the door shut. Less than two seconds later the headlights leveled, and they stayed fixed as the car drew closer. Finally the car stopped and he heard a door slam. The headlights stayed on. Their light, entering the outhouse through ventilation slits, reflected off the back plastic wall and glinted off the pistol in Nick's trembling fist.

Chapter 55

Two o'clock in the morning and Casey Montgomery was sequestered in the Mill reading Internet newsgoups. Nothing new in that. But the appearance of a care package of pure information just for her was kind of exciting. Prissy net fetishists took great offense when binary nonsense clogged up space on a discussion group, but on the Internet nobody knows if you're a dog and you can post binaries anywhere you want.

It was the sequence, from Judith. Everything had evidently gone according to plan, because already Casey had snarfed and decrypted the binaries from alt.comics.pogo, nucleotide by nucleotide, megabyte upon megabyte listing the Monty blueprint and the Nick blueprint for their *anterior cingulate sulcuses,* or whatever the hell it was.

So, she had both stacks of tiles. All she needed now was the tiled house, the Kali.

That was to say, all she needed now was a Kali chip and a miracle. Built into the Kali, hidden among its nearly three hundred thousand AND gates, OR gates, NANDs and NORs, was the secret recipe for making the chip upon which Nick's soul and life depended. There were hundreds of billions of possible ways to distribute the tiles throughout the house. She would never be able to do it by chance; she needed Todd's recipe. But to read the recipe Casey needed to decode Todd's notebooks. And that was going to take a miracle.

The response from the State Police had been amazingly rapid, Nick thought. They had come from everywhere. Then he realized: he had seen no blue lights. Heard no sirens. There had been no cackle of car radios or walkie-talkie. It had been a stealth response. He had no doubt now, if he had any before, that he was dealing with the CIA or something worse.

The next three hours were absolutely the most wretched of his life. Trying to remain motionless, holding his breath, expecting any instant to hear the call to come out with his hands up, he listened as the men inspected his car. The smell from the open shit-tank was not nearly as bad as the fright he felt every time someone walked close by. But eventually, to Nick's utter amazed relief, the cars all left. He guessed that it must be about three in the morning now. He waited for what he felt had to be half an hour, counting the seconds out in his head. Then he slowly opened the door and stepped out into the frigid moonlight on legs so cramped that he could barely stand. When he was sure there was nobody about, he tossed the pistol into the toilet.

It took him half an hour to walk the quarter of a mile or so though the woods, swamp, and bracken towards the sound of the cars that passed at a rate of one every five minutes or so down Route 2. With the Kali board uncomfortably tucked under his shirt, he scaled the twelve foot tall chain link fence at the highway. Then, after wiping the black greasepaint off his face, he walked six dark miles to the Searstown Mall—certain, every time a car approached behind him, that he would be run down. He spent two hours drinking a pot of coffee at Denny's before catching a bus to Fitchburg center and walking up the hill to the Fitchburg State College library.

Half an hour after the library opened he walked in as if he belonged there and, from a public Internet account, he made a simple posting to alt.comix.pogo: *Albert requests a guide through the swamp. 2 AM.* Then he climbed the stairs to the stacks, where he retrieved the counterfeit driver's license and passport that he had placed in pages of the *1967 Journal of Forensic Pathology.*

Standing there amid the dusky stacks he became aware of a rank smell, and realized it was coming from him. Despite the scrubbing he had given himself in the Denny's rest room, the stench of the place where he had spent the night was still on him, almost as if an unclean spirit had somehow passed into him.

He waited in the stacks until closing time, then walked to the Unitarian Church at the west end of the town green. As he had guessed, the trusting and parsimonious Unitarians had not upgraded their front door lock in the one hundred and more years since the edifice had been constructed, and it took him less than ten seconds to smash it apart with a heavy rock and a piece of re-bar that he found on the side of the road. He stayed there until around midnight, when the freight trains passed half a mile away; he hopped one as it slowed to a walk near the overpass by

Maryann's Donuts and jumped off at Newcastle, suffering a twisted ankle and skinned elbow.

At two AM Casey met him at a door at the bottom of a leaf-strewn stairwell by the lower pond. Fifteen minutes after that they were in the annex, carefully installing the Kali chip in the waiting test bed. She didn't mention the obvious fact that he was alone.

Now he watched as Casey wrapped a crude anti-static bracelet of naked copper wire around her left wrist and wrapped the other end around an exposed pipe near the floor. Then quickly, deliberately she detached each lead from the Kali chip to the SCUD board, and, with an amazing deftness she instantly inserted the chip into her home-made pattern-tester.

"Let's kick this pig," she said, and touched a switch.

A tiny light on the test board lit. Messages began to scroll on monitors.

"And?" Nick said.

"We wait."

"How long?"

"We wait until we find a packing pattern that fits," she said, testily. "You don't have anywhere to go do you?"

"How long? How long until you find it?"

"How do I know? My program will test about one key per millisecond. There are about ten-to-the-thirtieth ways to pack that genotype in here. There hasn't been enough time since the big goddamn bang to try them all. If we get lucky we'll find it. If we're not lucky, we won't. So climb off my back, why don't you? I haven't slept ten hours since I started making this test bed. You ought be saying 'thank you.'"

He sat on the dusty floor and leaned against the wall. His mind was completely empty.

He liked it better that way.

"Here, amuse yourself," she said, and threw a notebook in his lap.

He thumbed the pages slowly, looking at the logic diagrams, the margin notes, the dated entries. Half an hour later he was still silently reading, and she was silently staring at the hypnotic messages scrolling off the screens: reports of one failed lock after another, a thousand a second.

He was on his sixth notebook when one entry seemed to prevent him from turning the page.

> 'Ive got a timing bogon on chevy39, I think it is the
> master reset bogon. That would give me the off-by-
> one. It should go clear to the air, but vectors off at
> king kong one. Funny boy's bist is toying with
> carucha. No reason to. ''

It was tantalizing. Something was nearly there, on the tip of his tongue. It was almost painful, as if he had a violent itch in the middle of his back.

"Casey," he said. "This carucha, chevy thirty-nine, king kong stuff. It's familiar. Where's it from?"

"I don't know. It's familiar to me too," she said. "But I can't think where I know it from."

"It must be some kind of private language of his. But it's not totally private; it's something you and I know vaguely, but something Todd knew intimately. What did Todd know that you and I know? Some movie? A Dr. Seuss book? An episode of Star Trek? Cheech Wizard? What?"

"I don't know Nick, I told you that. I've been thinking about these notebooks for weeks."

"I don't care if you've been thinking about them since the big goddamn bang. Think harder. What did Todd know intimately?"

She thought for only a few seconds,

"Music," she said. "Rock 'n roll."

"Good. What kind of rock 'n roll?"

"Loud rock 'n roll." Her ironic smile had come back. "Very loud."

"Good, good. What else? Drumming. He was a drummer. He loved drumming."

"Not just drumming," Casey said. "Percussion."

"Percussion. . . Percussion. . . . Zappa!"

"Zappa!" she said. "*Uncle Meat!* There's a copy in the shrine, unless the cops took it." She was already running down the hall.

"Wait up." He jumped up and began to sprint after her.

"You'll get us caught," she called without slowing down. "You don't know the route and you won't fit through some of the places I have to fit through. Stay here."

It was the longest ten minutes of his life. She came back silently, flush-faced and drenched in perspiration. In her right hand was the CD, with eight sets of teeth in bad need of orthodontia on the cover.

"I've got it," she said. "The chip structure."

"Are you serious?"

"Absolutely. Kali is *Uncle Meat.* It's all through the notebooks; I don't know how I missed it. Cruddy teeth. Suzy Creamcheese. *Louie Louie* on the pipe organ at the Royal Albert Hall. Todd listened to it all the time. It's the album where Frank says, 'They like it *loud,* you know.' That's what Todd always said when he put in his earplugs and turned up the mikes on his drum kit."

"I remember," Nick said. "But how is Uncle Meat the Kali chip?"

As she took the small disk out of its case and inserted it into the computer's CD drive, Casey cleared her throat and began to sing:

Prima mi carucha Chevy-Thirty-Nine

Going to El Monte Legion Stadium
Pick up on my Weesa, she is so divine
Helps me stealing hubcaps, wasted all the time

"Oh good God," Nick said. "You're right. But what does it mean?"

"There are one hundred and twenty-eight leads going into the chip," she said. "Every one has a name. The first one, of course, is *Prima*. Starting with Prima, all the leads are named according to the words on the record. *Mi* is the second lead, carucha is the third, and so forth."

"There's more," she said, as she sat down and began to type at the keyboard. "Every major logic section of the chip is named after a song on the album. Like, *King Kong* is one area, *The Air* is another, *Dog Breath in the Year of the Plague* is another."

"A little cryptic," Nick said, weakly. He didn't know how he could have missed it either. Simply by virtue of being Todd's friend, Nick must have heard this album thirty times.

"Listen to *The Air*," she said.

In a moment he heard the Mothers of Invention singing the words, sweet and clear, the final verse coming from the tiny, tinny stolen speakers that Casey had attached to her hand-built computer:

"Eye Eye Eyee -I
Got busted
Coming through customs
With a suitcase
Full of tapes
It was a special
Tape recording
And they nabbed me
While I was boarding
Oh they nabbed me, and they beat me, and they told me
They don't like me. . ."

"A special tape recording," she said, her eyes filling with tears. "He took a copy of the tape-out. The tape that they use to make the mask! He made a copy of the tape." She sat down, lowered her head, and hugged her legs. "But where is it?" she said. "Where is the tape he made?"

"Here," Nick said, handing a notebook back to her. "Read the last entry in book seven. It was the last thing he wrote."

Casey found the page and read aloud. "It was a special tape recording. I put it with my Mommy and Daddy."

"Do you know now?" he asked her. "Do you remember?"

"Yes," she said, and whispered, "I love you, Todd."

And then, with the light of the four flickering monitors reflected from her weary face, her exhausted, sharply angled and beautiful face limned with purple hair with strawberry blonde roots, she looked up at him, typed a few keystrokes to change the track, and, as if repeating an ancient sacred liturgy, sang, along with the Mothers and Nick:

"It's the middle of the night
And your Mommy and your Daddy are sleeping
Mom and Dad are sleeping
Sleeping
Sleeping in a jar.
The jar is under the bed."

"I need to find a telephone," she said, in her lilting, tear-choked voice. "*Will* has just received a transmission from the other dimension, and it would be *inhuman* to wait until *morning* to let John and Richard know."

Chapter 56

Casey Montgomery was tired, tired to death. It had been three hard days since she and Nick had broken the skylight and rappelled into the Klingon fabrication line. There they had shaved, showered, and put on the bunny suits—hoping that the dirt they had already cascaded into the far end of the line hadn't hopelessly contaminated the near end, where the particular steppers that they needed for their new version of the Kali chip were located.

She remembered being naked before him, him naked too, as they raced to get the stupid clean-room garb on. As she bent to adjust her pants leg, she had let her left nipple brush, ever so lightly, the hair of his right forearm, and she had been gratified to notice the response. But, she knew, that was only reflex. If she had been fully clothed, weighed four hundred pounds and brushed his forearm with a tire iron instead of her breast she probably would have seen his penis flinch in exactly the same way. It was clear as day that he felt absolutely no attraction to her.

And what had she been thinking about anyway? They had had to get in and start making the chip immediately, before the wafer-steppers had cooled down. They were going to do the nearly impossible: force an eleven-layer chip while the lab was empty over the weekend: less than three days to do what the laws of physics said should take four or five. It would have been only marginally impossible if Nick had known anything about the process, and he didn't know Jack Shit. All she could expect him to do was try to stay alert, and when she told him to do something, do it. The chip was entirely up to her.

"Basically we're making a glass trinket; you understand that," she had said. "We can fool around with the layout, but once we commit to it we've got to be perfect. We can't fuck up the radicals. We only get one chance. The radicals are everything."

"'Radical'?" Nick had asked, with, it seemed to her, a suddenly chilly tone.

"Radical; you know," she said. "Each glass layer of the chip is called a radical."

It was amazing what these software boys did not know. But in any event they had done it, somehow. Nick was off and running with the four good chips they had made from the single wafer. Less than twenty hours from now—if he didn't fall asleep at the wheel, and the police didn't nab him at the airport—he would be in Basel, one man on a mission to save the human species.

His last words to her still burned.

"I'll be off on a few errands now, dear. Call me if you need a ride."

Call you if I need a ride? Nick, my precious, if you only knew.

As for her part, Casey had made the pre-arranged anonymous posting to the Pogo newsgroup, her signal to the void that Nick was on the way: "I'm leaving, on a jet-plane. . ."

And now she was going home. Alone. More alone than she had ever been in her life.

She was walking across her porch with her key in her hand when she heard the voice—she hadn't even reached the door yet. Didn't the Newcastle police have *any-thing* better to do than stake out her apartment?

"Casey Montgomery?"

"Yes."

"Please stay where you are and put your hands up. I am placing you under arrest for obstruction of justice and interstate flight. You have the right. . ."

"Let's not fuck around with each other, officer. You don't want me. You want Nick Aubrey. Let me have a nap and get me a lawyer. I'll give you your Nick Aubrey."

Chapter 57

Streaking over the Atlantic at five hundred miles an hour, Nick tried to understand what it meant for one person to become transformed into another. He professed to believe that Judith had been wrong; that Monty had been bluffing, that there were no nanomachines inside his skull at this very instant, changing, rearranging. But what if she had been right? He tried to think of the transformations that might be taking place inside himself as a series of organ transplants, one cell transplanted at a time. After all the transplants were done, would he still be Nick?

Of course he would still be Nick, he reassured himself. For that's what life was: transformation. The infant becomes the child, the child becomes the adult—each instant bringing infinitesimal changes that somehow add up. After all, what did it mean to say that the man having these thoughts was the same Nick Aubrey who had done flips off the high-dive at the Oneonta Swim Club? It didn't mean much, he concluded. The only thing that *this* Nick Aubrey had in common with some of those earlier versions of Nick Aubrey was the name—and the DNA, of course. But this Nick didn't really even have his name any more: there was a manhunt on, so he had relinquished the rights to it and was traveling on the passport of one imaginary Daniel Quinn. So all Nick had in common with his earlier selves was the DNA. But what if his DNA were changing too? Who would he be then?

What if, tomorrow, he woke up thinking that Monty was kind of an intriguing fellow after all? What if he woke up thinking that maybe this Overmind idea was pretty cool? Who would it be who was having those thoughts? Would it be Nick? Would it be Monty?

Under the seat in front of him, in a cheap nylon carry-on bag, there was a little Styrofoam case that contained five test tubes of blood and a plastic pillbox with five compartments. Each of those five compartments contained a dip-mounted chip that had been cut from the single wafer he and Casey had made. Blood and silicon: his brother's DNA in red, his own in silver. Identity, mind, matter. He ordered a whiskey from the passing flight attendant, determined to steer his thought down a different channel.

On his lap there was a photo-essay book on Fasnacht, Basil's answer to Carnival and Mardi Gras. He flipped through the pages, barely registering the pictures of eerie masks. He concentrated instead on the sensation of the whiskey. In all likelihood he was going to die tomorrow. This might be the last time he would ever taste it.

And what if he didn't die; what if his half-baked James Bond plan miraculously worked, and Nick successfully eliminated Monty? What would that accomplish? Hundreds of Corporate Fellows, apostles of the New Christ, stood ready to build Monty's cybertopia. Monty's death would no more slow them than the death of the original Christ had slowed down the first Christians.

Speaking of Christians, tomorrow was the beginning of *Fasnacht*, Basil's Lenten-Pagan communal happening. Starting at about four AM the streets would be filled with masked people. Moorgestreich was the official start, the silent march of ghostly apparitions right before dawn. Later the drums and fifes would fill the air. According to the book, that was the thing about Basel Fasnacht: it was unpredictable. There was no pre-set route. Of its own free will it went where it wanted to go, more mysterious than joyous. Faces came and went, whole platoons of Harlequins or Old Aunts could disappear into the fog, leaving spectators to wonder whether they had ever actually been there at all.

Nick was reading Trachsler and Roberts' *Basler Fasnacht: for Insiders and Outsiders*, which he had stolen from the Fitchburg State College library. *"The Basler Fasnacht defies explanation: it undergoes a constant process of renewal;"* they wrote, *"it is always a novel, individual experience subject to personal interpretation. There can be no exact, scientific explanation."*

"Exact, scientific explanation," Nick said, and gulped the last of his whiskey. "Who needs that shit."

He would stay at Paul's apartment. The diskette would be there, in his brother's violin case. It was too late to try to crack it, but Nick could at least send it along to Casey—who had a better chance of flapping her wings and flying to Pluto than she did of cracking it—whether he survived the day or not. On that happy thought he closed his eyes.

He awoke as the plane landed. He quickly cleared customs, and took a taxi directly to the address he had for his brother's apartment. The key turned easily in the lock, and Nick found himself face to face with small man whose head, nearly two feet tall, was distinguished by an enormous leering smile, very poor oral hygiene, a bulbous red nose the size of a grapefruit with black hair protruding from the nostrils, and orange hair that erupted sideways, like Bozo's. He looked like a farmer from Ken Kesey's Kommune, where the main crop is LSD.

It took Nick a moment to realize that there was no man there. It was only a paper maché mask. He recognized the type from the Fasnacht book: it was a *Wagis*, the bumpkin, mounted at face height on the vestibule wall directly behind the door that opened to the hallway.

Leaving the lights off, Nick entered the room.

By the faint light coming through the windows, he was able to make out a low table in front of a couch. He placed the suitcase and travel bag on it and walked slowly around the apartment — bedroom, sitting room, kitchen, bath; all small by American standards— checking out the alabaster outline of a dozen masks: jesters, burghers, women with watering cans for hats; clowns, waifs, and horned devils. All the masks in the apartment were creepy, but the *Wagis* at the door was the creepiest.

He went to the bedroom and opened the closet, and there, just as Paul had said, he found the violin case. After putting the case on the bed, and flicking the clasps, he removed the nearly weightless instrument and placed it on the bed. There was a little compartment in the neck of the case. This was where he expected to find the diskette. He drew in his breath and pulled the little tab. There were two little blocks of rosin, each twice the size of an eraser; nothing else. He removed them and furiously worked his fingers around the empty space. The hinged lid to the case—maybe there was a compartment there? No, only a pair of featherweight bows. Nick tossed them on the bed, with panic welling up inside him. Where could Paul have put the damn thing? Had he been joking about putting it in the case? Then why had he sent the key?

"Fuck!" Nick said, half shouting, half whispering. He lifted the case up over his head and threw it on the floor with all his might. It broke in pieces, yielding, to his utter astonishment, a small flat square object, three and a half inches on each side: Barlow's diskette. He stared for a long time, not wanting to believe that it was really there. When he picked it up his hands were shaking.

Now that he had it he could think about rest. He was tired beyond exhaustion.

Overwhelmed with sleepiness, he placed the diskette on the small table next to his brother's bed. There was only one more thing he needed to do before he could collapse. In the half-dark sitting room he fumbled until he found the thermos, which he took into the kitchen. There were seven test tubes of blood packed in dry ice in it; he needed to let them thaw. He placed the test tubes in a bowl and put the bowl in the sink. The dry ice had evaporated but the blood was still frozen; he turned on the water and let it run until the bowl was full. Then he walked back into the sitting room to lock the door, went back to the bedroom, kicked off his shoes and lay down, facing the ceiling.

He tried to plan his day, but the thoughts wouldn't hold. He considered looking for an alarm clock, but the task seemed too daunting. Unless somebody killed him in the night, he would sleep until he woke up. *That's enough for now*, he told himself, as words from somewhere deep in his memory lulled him to oblivion.

> *Matthew, Mark, Luke, John*
> *Bless the bed that I lay on*
> *If I should die before I wake*
> *I pray the Lord my soul to take*

Chapter 58

A rocking. . .

Deep in Amazonia, Nick lies face up in the canoe, terrified. He can feel the invisible people there along the riverbank. He can see them without looking. Feathers, color. Color in darkness? An arrow splashes near him. Another thunks into the gunwale. Of its own volition, the canoe moves upstream against the current. Nick is lying in the mud. Invisible people are visible now, corporal fellows. One of them takes a green gooey glob from his mouth and places it on Nick's upper lip. The fellows gather around their shaman, chanting, "Sig-eye, pig-stye." The shaman's body is painted blue and white, his hair plastered with mud. Feathers pierce his skin. The invisible people pass a long wooden tube to the shaman, the end of it is placed before Nick's nose. Nick struggles to escape, but he his held too tightly. "I notice you filed a bug on the espresso release," the shaman says. The shaman fills his cheeks with air and blows. The green goo goes up Nick's nose, into his brain, into his soul. It possesses him. He floats in the air. . .he dies. . .

St. Matthew floats in the air beside him. "Nine three two three three," St. Matthew says. "Chapter nine, verses thirty-two and thirty-three. . . "

Nick sat up, gasping, drenched in sweat, and looked around him. Amazonia? Moonlight reflected off the pale white jester's mask above his head, mocking him. Oh. Basel. But St. Matthew's words were still with him. Nine three two three three. Would Paul have a Bible? Nick switched on the light. There, on a bookshelf on the opposite side of the room, was a green-bound Gideon's. Thank you. Nick got it and turned to the verse:

"As they went out behold they brought to him a dumb man possessed with a devil. And when the devil was cast out, the dumb spake: and the multitudes marvelled, saying, It was never so seen in Israel. . ."

Nick knew without counting that there would be one hundred and sixty characters, exactly. He had done it: he had cracked Barlow's diskette. Vividly he could recall Crazy Peter's pronouncement to the startled passengers of Flight 44: *"Gulf War Syndrome is only the beginning. I have left proof and a plan for the cure on a diskette with a friend in California."* And now, by God, with this password, Nick was going to read all about it.

He stumbled into the hall, then down it; tried to get his bearings in the kitchen. By the dim light coming from the street the room looked sad—so small, white, and tidy. He could see that there was nothing on the counters, nothing on the table. He opened a cabinet to reach for a class. But as he did he noticed, in the corner of his eye, that there appeared to be something affixed to the refrigerator. Something small, flat, square; three inches on a side, with a hand-written label. Held there with a giant U-shaped magnet that had not been there yesterday. *No, don't tell me. Please, no.*

Yes. There was no mistaking the diskette: the word MATTHEW in Barlow's handwriting was unique, and Nick had stared at it a thousand times. And there was no mistaking what information that diskette now held: zilch, zippo, nada, hy-darra; the null set.

Nick barely made it to the water closet in time, as heave after heave shook his body. After an eternity he sat back and rested against the wall. The edges of his eyes perspired as if he had just eaten a jalapeno, and his arms quivered as if he was going into hypothermia. For a moment he thought, again, that he was going to die. Then he took a deep breath, stood, found the bathroom sink, filled it, and plunged his face into the ice-cold water.

Back in the kitchen, he took the diskette tossed it on the table, feeling nothing. He had tried not to invest too much hope in finding out what was on the diskette. Without realizing it, however, he had come to equate deciphering the diskette with getting his life back. He had come to accept that he would never see Todd again, nor his brother. But if he could have found out what was on that diskette perhaps it would have given some meaning to their deaths; perhaps he could have had some hope of a new life after this was all over. But now he saw with complete clarity that it was all pointless.

That was when he noticed something else on the table, a piece of paper: a note. He walked to the window, where there was more light.

Block letters, in heavy ballpoint:

Nick. Go away. You cannot win. Run while you can. Look under your pillow. Leave right now.

Shit, Nick suddenly thought. *Where's the blood? Where's Paul's blood?*

He jumped up and ran to the sink. The bowl was there, exactly as he had left it, with the cold test tubes still in it. Whoever had visited him in the night didn't know about the blood, or didn't care. Or maybe they had switched vials.

He read the note again. *Look under the pillow.* He ran into the bedroom and reached under the pillow; there were papers there and some kind of booklet. He took them back into the kitchen where the light was better. Outside, dawn was breaking over the city. By its rosy-fingered light he inspected a United States passport, with an airline ticket inserted between the last pages. He opened the cover and read the name Isaac Angevine next to the photo of himself. It took a while to make out the writing on the ticket, but soon it was clear: one-way, by way of London and Miami, from Basel to Mexico City.

"Fuck you," Nick said, softly. "Fuck you." He tore the tickets easily. The passport required a little more strength.

But what was that sound? A whispering; a muffled stampede. It was coming from outside on the far end of the apartment. Quietly Nick went to the window and looked down into the street. Good God, he had died. He was in Hades: there was an army of apparitions walking by, wraiths of Subedai coming for him. . .

No, he realized, as he resumed breathing: Fasnacht had begun. He looked with mixed awe and dread at the costumed figures with oversized heads—porcelain-faced harlequins, brooding *alte dantes,* the "old aunts;" leering *Wagis,* corpulent magistrates, and *Pierrots* with pillbox hats and eyes as blank as death: *Moorgesreich,* march of the ghosts. There was not a light on anywhere in the entire city. Across the street, above the café, he could dimly make out the form of a woman looking down from her window at the silent parade.

He went again to the kitchen sink. The test tubes were cold to the touch, but not frozen. He went into the bedroom to retrieve his travel bag, stripping off his shirt as he went. Sitting on the edge of the bed, he opened the bag and withdrew the US Army field blood-transfusion kit, along with several syringes and a roll of white tape. Quickly, methodically, he used a syringe to transfer the blood into the transfusion kit. It filled halfway: eight ounces of liquid Paul.

Awkwardly, he ran the tape several times around his torso, securing the kit to his rib cage. Then he put on a loose-fitting shirt and put the container that held the chips in the shirt pocket. He put his counterfeit Dijjy-mike badge in his pants pocket, and walked towards the door. What was he forgetting? Oh, yeah. Paul told him he had purchased a gun. Where would that be? The hell with it, he decided. Whoever had cracked the diskette had probably already taken it. If Nick had to kill anybody today he would do it with his bare hands. He picked up the diskette and put it in his pocket. He had risked his life several times for this damn thing, if he lived it would make a nice souvenir of his quaint adventure.

"Here I come, brother," he said.

He took a deep breath and opened the door. He walked into the hall way, down the stairs and prepared to enter the silent crowd on the street. He opened the door.

A pale dead face with hints of bronze in the coloring; large sad eyes with dead black pupils; a black pill-box hat with a peacock feather sticking straight up from it: *Pierrot le Fou,* Crazy Peter, staring straight at Nick—with a recorder poised like a blow gun at his lips.

Nick felt his heart stop.

I loved you, Bartlett.

The Pierrot played a trill on his recorder and walked on.

It was five AM.

By seven AM Nick realized that there was no more putting it off. He had stopped for coffee several times, consulted his dog-eared little map of Basel countless times. He had so memorized the street names that he hardly needed it at all; the map was more like a security blanket.

He would walk down this street, cross the bridge, go up the other street; the Digital MicroSystems lab would be right there. He would watch the people going in, choose a likely group and walk in behind him, just as he had walked into the Mill at thousand times at the tail end bunch of employees. As simple as that, just like Lion, Tin Man and Scarecrow entering the witch's castle. He took one last sip of his coffee, then reached in his pocket for some change for a tip, feeling the Dijjy-Mike badge. He had no idea what any of the coins in his hand were worth, so he threw them all on the table. It wasn't bloody likely that he would ever need money again, in any event. He kept the badge in his hand, nervously turning it as he stood.

That was when he saw the *Pierrot* again, the one that had been waiting for him. He knew that many of the masks looked alike; that many of them were in fact identical, made from the same mold. The costumes were identical too. There was no way to tell one *Pierrot* from another. But this was the one that had met him at his door this morning. He knew it.

He left, trying not to run.

He found himself wondering about Carl Swirsing, and whether the model Porsche he drove was the same as the one that had blocked his way on Emerson Street. He wondered about Pascale. *Maybe I see you in Fasnacht* she had said. Well, maybe.

Two blocks later he looked over his shoulder. The *Pierrot* was still there.

Nick needed to stay calm. Down this street, then over one. He could lose the tail by cutting through the Theatre tram stop. The street he was on would be *Ausgrabben*. When he looked around this corner to the left he should see the Basel Civic Opera, and across from that a large tram stop. He got to the corner, turned left. There was no Opera house, no tram stop. Instead he found some kind of school or something, with two ghostly jesters walking in front of it. He looked up; there were no signs. How had he managed to get lost so quickly?

Don't panic, Nick.

But he *was* panicking. He saw the Pierrot again, running towards him. There was something in its right hand. And Nick became aware that he had dropped the badge; where, he had no idea.

He started to run. He glanced over his shoulder. He was not imagining things: the *Pierrot* was there, running towards him. Nick sprinted, turned right down a narrow street. It was a cobble-stoned cul-de-sac. *Damn my luck.* He stopped, trapped. Then he saw a narrow passageway leading to another street. It was wide enough for two people to pass abreast. Nick would have to turn on the afterburners now, outrace this masked assassin. How fast could somebody run while wearing a two foot high mask, for Pete's sake? Then he heard his name called, and even though he knew he should keep running he stopped. He knew that voice. Who was it? He turned. *Pierrot* was gone.

"*Maceo?*" Nick said. His pulse was pounding; he was so full of fright that he could barely stand. What was *Maceo* doing here?

"*Jesus Christ*, Maceo," Nick said. "You scared the living fuck out of me. What are you doing here?"

"Hey, I live here now," he said. "I took a job at the Labs. I know, I know, I was going to quit when they shit-canned Docudisc. But this real interesting assignment came up; they said they would pay to relocate me here. Hey, who wouldn't like to live in Europe? Where the hell have you been? Last time I heard from you, you were sprinting across the country. You disappear from planet Earth for weeks, next thing

I know you're running down a Basel street as if Beelzebub was on your ass. . ."

Nick was hardly listening. He was still catching his breath when he noticed the Pierrot approaching Maceo's back.

"Get ready to run, Maceo, when I tell you," Nick said. "Don't turn around."

But Maceo did turn, just in time to see the Pierrot leveling a gun at his chest. Before Nick realized what was happening three loud shots had been fired in the alleyway. Two had hit Maceo, one had hit a wall, sending fragments of masonry into Nick's hair.

At first Nick thought he had been shot, but in a moment he realized that he was untouched. He turned his gaze to the costumed figure. With a visibly trembling hand it was pointing the gun towards the ground, where Maceo was lying on his back, looking up at Nick. Nick could see that Maceo was still breathing, barely.

What a way to go, Nick thought. *Damnation.*

Slowly, the *Pierrot* put down the pistol and removed its head.

"You?" Nick said. "I never thought I'd see you again."

Chapter 59

Jake Carelli dropped the Pierrot mask on the ground.

"Look," he said, and kicked Maceo's hand. A black gun, with a silencer, fell out of Maceo's loosening grip. "He was going to shoot you down, Nick. He's been following you all morning." Jake's speech was halting. He was out of breath.

"You're lying," Nick said.

"Look," Jake said, "The Mill. Casey." He kicked Maceo's other hand. Nick looked down and saw: Maceo's left hand was missing the ring and pinky fingers. The wound was still pink.

Maceo had locked Casey in the cooler? Nick dropped to the ground, breathing hard.

"Maceo," Nick said. "What's up man, what's up?"

"You should have left, Nick. I got you the ticket. They would have left you alone."

"Oh God, Maceo. Why? Why you?"

Had his best friend really planned to shoot him in the name of a crackpot never-never land?

"You could have come with us, Nick," Maceo said. "Cybertopia. No more suffering. No more injustice. Level above human, behind the next comet."

"Maceo, you crazy white motherfucker," Nick said, as tears welled up in his eyes.

"Blood for oil. We're all yuppies now." That was all Maceo could say, and Nick could tell he was dead without taking a pulse. He crawled backwards and sat against the wall..

He looked up to see Jake sliding down the opposite wall, a dazed look on his face.

"I thought I lost you at Devens," Nick said.

"That was nothing," Jake said, softly. "But this is bad." He weekly touched his hand to his belly, where for the first time Nick noticed blood seeping through the costume. Then Jake seemed to hiccup, and blood poured from his mouth.

Nick jumped up and ran to him.

"Mercy. Hell. Hell." He had no idea what to do. He was frozen.

"Nick," Jake whispered through red foam. "You go ahead. I've got your back." Then he shook once more, and his eyes sprang wide open.

Nick felt as if a spell had been broken, as if he were Merlin stepping out of thralldom in solid rock. Monty Meekman had taken every friend Nick had ever had; here, in this alley, he had taken two at once. Now, at last, Nick knew what Monty had been talking about on that hilltop above Los Altos. He understood what Abraham Maslow had meant by that ability of self-actualized people to bring *all* their passion and talents to bear on a single goal. Nick was finally, ruthlessly, self-actualized. He was ready to play rule the roost. From this moment on, until he saw Monty dead, anything and anybody that got in his way was in for a whole lot of trouble.

He stepped over to Maceo's body and patted his pockets until he found the Digital MicroSystems employee badge with Maceo's photo on the front and a magnetic stripe on the reverse. *Bingo.*

He took the pistol from Jake's hand, then reached over for the gun that lay in the alley near Maceo. Nick took that and began to trot down the alley with a pistol in each hand. At the far end, before walking out into the street, he stopped to tuck the guns into his pants. He turned left and ran. Within minutes he had ended up at the bank of the river, no longer lost. He knew exactly where he was; he knew exactly where he was going. And *this* time no quahog from Corporate Security was going to turn him away.

Nick slid Maceo's card through the card reader and heard the click of the lock opening. As simple as that, he was in. Now to find the Feynman machinery. Nick looked at his watch. 8:30 AM. *Alright.* He turned left down a hallway that exited off the lobby, with no idea where he was going. It was all ad-lib from here on.

The first person he saw could have been right out of the Mill or the California offices. It was a man of about forty, a little overweight and very unathletic, with a greying beard and black hair in a long ponytail.

Nick approached him.

"Hi, how ya doin'," he said.

The fellow nodded, didn't say anything.

"Don't tell me," Nick said. "You're one of those Corporate Fellows!"

"No," he said. "But I know Monty very well. I have reason to expect—"

Nick didn't have time for this loser's bullshit.

"Listen," he said. "I'm just in from the States, never been here, I've gotta find Monty's lab. Can you tell us where it is?"

"Which lab?" he said, in a dry, superior tone. "He works in several."

"Oh you know," Nick said "The nanolab."

"You won't get in," he said. "You're not on the project. I don't know you."

"Oh, are you on that project?" Nick said.

A nearly imperceptible nod.

"Great! You can let me in."

"I'm afraid I can't," he said.

"Really, you have to," Nick said. "It's a matter of some urgency. Monty won't object, and if he does you can say I made you do it."

"You should leave your pressure tactics in the States," Mr. Ponytail said. "Here they're considered in very poor taste."

Nick grabbed his shirt.

"You haven't seen a pressure tactic yet and you don't want to. Let me in the lab, or I am going to take my gun and shoot off your left big toe."

"Where do you work, the Mill?" the guy said. "I bet you're a Miller, one of those hard-core Digital Data guys."

"Oh God dammit," Nick said.

He took Maceo's gun from the waistband of his pants, placed it against the man's shoe where the big toe would be and pulled the trigger. He felt the kick but heard no sound except a shout of pain. A pink mist settled to the floor.

"Now listen, Stock Option," Nick said. "You get me into the nanolab before you leave too much blood around here, or I'm going to show you a real pressure tactic."

It was two doors down. The pony-tailed man pressed some numbers on a key-pad and the door swung open.

"Give me your shirt," Nick said. While pointing the gun at the man's chest, he ran back and cleaned what she could of the blood trail, leaving it barely visible.

"OK," Nick said. "Now then. I am going to take off your shoe and bandage your foot with your shirt while I ask a few questions. You will answer them, or I promise you on my brother's grave that I will put a bullet through your head. OK?"

"OK," he said. Nick could see the fear on the man's face, which was rapidly blanching. It would be too bad if the guy died from shock or blood loss, but Nick couldn't worry about that now.

"Simple answers. Is this where they program the Feynman nanomachines?"

"Yes," he panted, clearly in pain.

"How many programming machines are there here?"

"Ten."

"My lucky day. I have four chips that I want you to substitute for the Kali chip. Do you know how to do that?"

"Yes."

"How long will it take?"

"Five minutes."

"How long will it take to make me one million Feynman machines with the new chips?"

"Half an hour."

"What do you put them in?"

"A pressurized tank. I really don't feel very well," he said.

"I'm not feeling so hot myself," Nick said. "Work with me, quickly, and I'll make sure you don't bleed to death. Here," Nick said, reaching into his shirt pocket for the plastic case that contained the chips.

Nick kept the gun trained on the man's chest as he stood up and began to work on the gleaming metal devices.

Nick hardly noticed what the man was doing. His mind was racing but covering no ground. Throughout the lab there were machines, lasers, glass tubes; it was a blur. He should have tried to watch and understand what Stock Option was doing, but his mind could not handle any more data. It only processed one thought: "Hurry."

After an eternity the man handed him a canister the size of can of shaving cream. His face was white, his hands were shaking. Nick looked to the man's foot. There was a lot of blood, but not as much as there might have been. He would make it.

"Tell me something," Nick said. "What do you do with all these things?"

"I don't know what the Fellows do with them. I'm only a technician. A lab rat."

"Do they use them on human beings?"

"Not here," he said.

"At Hoff-Zeigy do they?"

A shrug.

"I guess so."

Nick thought about shooting off his other big toe but decided against it.

"You're going to give me one hour, Stock Option, or you are going to experience pressure tactics that Amnesty International never even heard of. Lie down and put your foot in the air, you'll be fine. One hour."

He ran out the lab door, down the hall to the left, where found an exit on the opposite side of the building and burst onto a sidewalk, canister in hand. Somehow he found a taxi.

"Hoff-Zeigy," he said. "Building Two. Very quickly."

"Oaf," the driver said, in heavily accented English "Fasnacht. Not fast. Many people. Slow."

"Listen," Nick said. "Three hundred dollars American." He waved a handful of dollars in front of the driver's eyes. "Slow, I pay you the meter. Fast, I pay you this."

"OK, fast," he said. In a moment they were hurtling over cobblestone streets, horn honking, as costumed figures and crowds of watchers jumped back out of the way. It took twelve minutes. The taxi pulled up before the door, and the driver turned to Nick with a broad smile.

"Fast," he said.

"Is this Two?" Nick said, as he handed the bills. The driver nodded.

Nick got out and ran into the building and up as fast as he could. At the landing of the second floor he stopped. He ripped off his shirt, tore off the tape, and placed the pack between the handrail and the wall as he sat on the stair, using the banister as a makeshift I-V caddy from which the long clear plastic tube dangled down. He took the rubber cover off the two-inch stainless steel needle and placed it against a vein in his forearm.

"Here goes nuttin," he said, and he pushed it in.

Whoa, Nellie Bellie. Painful to feel, obscene to contemplate, nauseating to look at, Nick's brother's dead cells filled his veins. He pressed against the bag to speed the transfer, a process that took only a minute. After squeezing the last drops through the long clear plastic tube and into his arm, Nick withdrew the needle and let it drop. It swung, a graceless pendulum, and slapped against the stairs, leaving a red splatter. He remained sitting for just a moment, wondering if he would feel it coming. Transfusion shock could happen under the best of conditions, and the conditions under which he had just transfused Paul's blood into himself were hardly ideal. The liquid that he had just put into his own veins could hardly even be considered blood anymore —it had been frozen, thawed, refrozen, re-thawed until it was a nameless reddish glop. He didn't want to think about what damage it might be doing inside him right now.

He stood up, already light headed, nauseated. But he had done the hard part. He patted the handles of the guns protruding from his waistband.

"Gary Owen, motherfucker," he announced to the empty stairwell.

He ran up the steps two at a time. Just as Judith had said, the door to the lab was on his left as soon as he exited the stairs. He knew it was the right door by the device mounted chest-high on the wall next to it. It was the size of a submarine sandwich, and had five holes in it, positioned so a person could put fingers in it, like a five-holed bowling ball.

"Bisim' Allah," he said, and stuck the thumb and fingers of his right hand into the holes. Something locked around them like and he could feel suction, as if he had just been attacked by a squid. It stayed like that for what seemed an eternity. He was getting more light-headed by the minute. He was on the point of collapse when the his fingers were released and the door swung open.

Chapter 60

A large window reflected his image back to him; beneath the window there was a control panel. There was a single four-legged stool with shiny metal legs. The other three walls were packed with electrical equipment— VCRs, patch cords, dials, sliders, indicator lights and meters—and a whole lot of stuff he didn't recognize. In the wall on the left, amid the equipment, there was a door.

"Bravo!" Nick heard the tinny voice of Monty Meekman say. It took him an instant to realize that Meekman was not in the room with him, that the voice was coming through a speaker.

"Put down your popgun, Nick," he said. "This isn't cops and robbers we're playing, it's chess. And I was a Grand Master when I was eight years old. The only worthy opponent for me is Deep Blue, and soon I will know its secrets from the inside out."

Suddenly the lights dimmed in the control room and came on in the room behind the mirror. Nick saw his reflection give way to a darkened view of the room behind the glass, as if he were looking through amber sunglasses. This sudden change in lighting nearly caused him to lose his balance again. In the room beyond he saw gleaming stainless steel machines along with track-mounted cameras in the ceiling. There was a shelf along one wall that appeared to contain a row of canisters like the one in his pocket. He also saw what appeared to be an operating table.

In the middle of the room was a large transparent box. Nick remembered Paul's description of chambers used for the experiment on the mice; here was a person-sized version of the same thing. Nick's knees started to buckle. His palms were sweaty, his vision was blurring. Was it fear, or the middle stage of anaphylactic shock, his body rejecting the massive invasion of something not its own?

Jake's gun was in Nick's right hand; with his left hand he took the second out of his waistband and placed it on the control panel. He tried to raise his right hand. It weighed about a million pounds. He placed his left hand under his right wrist and tried again. This time he succeeded, more or less, in aiming through the glass at Meekman.

"I'm no good at chess. I'm more of a barroom poker guy," Nick said, and pulled the trigger.

His arm felt like it had been torn off; his entire body was pushed back and twisted to the right; the ringing in his ears was painful. The window was still there. Like an afterthought, a piece of something dislodged by the ricochet landed on his foot. *I'll be lucky if I don't kill myself,* he thought. He raised his right hand and fired five more times, until he heard the "click" of an empty chamber. The gun now weighed about two million pounds and he let it drop from his hand.

Monty was saying something, but Nick couldn't make out the words. He picked up Maceo's silenced gun with his left hand and shot until it was empty, as ricochets tore apart the wall behind him. Was this doing any good at all?

Monty was still saying something, but Nick didn't want to hear it. "Shut up," he said, as he staggered forward. "That's not my model."

The glass was still there. But he could see hairline cracks feathering out from eight or ten places. The room was filled with acrid smoke. Bullets had destroyed equipment on two side walls and the wall behind him. The floor was littered with debris, and there was a fizzling sound of an electrical fire coming from someplace. The window was still there, and beyond it, Monty. But the glass was weakened, it had to be. He looked around the room. *What the hell would break that glass?*

The stool.

Monty was saying something incomprehensible, the room was white but somehow filled with color, the walls were dull but shiny, he felt like death, nothing made sense. He was in the Amazon jungle, floating in the air with a head full of some kind of jungle hallucinogen, and somehow the words of the *Encyclopedia of Modern Bodybuilding* had come into his head.

"Let us recite the scriptures," Nick said, picking up the stool and setting it upside down on the floor. "From the book of Arnold:

"*'The body is amazingly adaptable and can accustom itself to workloads that would fell a horse,'*" he grabbed two of the legs. "*'However, if you always put the same kind of stress on the body, in the same way, it gets used to this and even very intense training will yield less response than you expected.'*"

He raised the stool over his head and swung it at the window. It bounced back, vibrating in his hands. He was vaguely aware of Monty laughing. Nick kept talking as he adjusted his hold.

"*The way to avoid this is by surprising the body with new workouts, unusual exercises, or exercises performed in a different way or order.'*"

He raised the chair above his head and stepped backwards about five steps. He stopped there, with the stool held high, for the space of three deep breaths. Then he ran three steps towards the glass and swung the stool with all the effort he had in him. The window shattered; the stool carried into the next room and clanged to the floor. Immediately, without realizing what he was doing, he found himself hurtling after it like a fullback jumping over the goal line from three yards out. He landed on the floor in a pile of glass—no sound; no pain from the fall. It didn't take long to see the blood streaming from a hundred small cuts. Feeling more asleep than awake, and weaker than a kitten, he sat at Monty's feet.

Chapter 61

There was sound coming from somewhere, faint music. What was that tune? Lilting reggae. Bob Marley and the Wailers: *Get up, Stand up.* He stood.

"Aubrey," Monty said.

"Here I am."

"Take off your shoes. You are standing on sacred ground."

"I'm not going to take off my shoes until you speak from a burning bush," Nick said, gingerly dusting broken glass from his hands.

"Take off your shoes, Nick. I've been waiting for you. In fact, if you had stopped shooting long enough to listen to me, son, you would have learned that the door was open. We're going to have a little talk, you and I."

Nick observed his hands untying the laces. As he tossed his second shoe aside, he realized that that was just what he was looking forward to—a little talk with Meekman.

"So who are we today?" Nick asked. "Monty Meekman? Abraham Angevine? Vannevar Engleton?"

"I am; that is who I am," Monty said, and chirped his schoolboy laugh.

"That's God's line," Nick said. "God is the supreme being, infinitely perfect, who made all things and keeps them in existence. You are Monty Meekman, corporate dweeb."

Nick found it hard to follow his own thoughts in the hot white noise of this laboratory. White light, white heat: God, or the Big Bang? Or Lou Reed shooting speed? White people. They gave him hives. *White light. . .* No, not Velvet Underground: Bob Marley singing, *Get up, stand up.* Which reminded Nick of nothing so much as. . . As what? As his being white. White boy menaced by black-man poet in a drunken sandstorm. White walls of the room around him. The white floors of Todd's hardware lab. White lab smock that Bartlett had worn, her alabaster white-bread shiksa skin. *Stand up for you right, Nicky.* But Monty's voice was stronger.

Meekman said, "The Baltimore Catechism. You're regressing. Next you'll be telling me that God requires a goat sacrifice every time there's an eclipse. It's time for you to come beyond such superstition: God is nothing but a consciousness higher than your own. Complex systems give rise to consciousness as day follows night. Cow is God to grass, man to cow, Meekman to man."

"Then who is God to Meekman?"

"That is an impertinence, Nick. You can no more understand my God than a neuron can understand the brain or a bee can understand the hive. But you can *participate* in that thought."

"What a brilliant theology," Nick said, woozily. "Maybe for *this* you'll get the Turing Award."

*Get up, stand up. . .*He was standing, but why couldn't he will himself to move? He had come here to throttle the man, but found himself unable to initiate any action other than talk. Didn't volition count for anything around here? This wasn't alien *hand* syndrome, it was alien *Nick* syndrome.

"That would really annoy Hussein," Monty said. "He could not abide to see me reckoned a theologian. Theology is the Arab strong suit, you know. Be seated Nick, you look tired."

"There is no God but God," Nick said, as he clumsily sat, overwhelmed by fatigue. "And Monty is his prophet."

He hoped he was being sarcastic, but he hardly knew what he was saying anymore.

"Saddam didn't trust me, at first," Monty said, ignoring him. "It was my challenge to him to restore the primacy of the Baghdad caliphate that won him over. If he didn't act, I said, Godless materialism would vanquish Islam. 'There's the Moslem world and there's the infidel world,' I told him, 'and Earth isn't big enough for both of them any more. It's a war of the worlds.' Thanks to me, when Saddam says 'jihad' he really means it!"

"War of the Worlds," Nick said. "Very funny."

"How is it funny, Nick?"

Was this a test? Monty knew why Nick had said that.

"Orson Welles had *The War of the Worlds*; your hoax was Desert Storm."

"So you did get the joke, " Monty said. "The name was a *dry* touch, don't you think?"

"You mean the quasi-oxymoron of 'Desert Storm?' About as dry as a gorilla in season."

"I meant, Orson, wells: the Baghdad oil man and the Texas oil man using a servo-organic network to fight over petroleum reserves!"

Monty was beaming as he had beamed after the earthquake.

"It's a lot of work for not very much joke," Nick said.

"It was no work at all. The Americans gave me a billion dollars, the Iraqis gave me a billion dollars. Then they marched their armies into the desert! Lights, camera, action! And they call *Orson Welles* a genius. His war was imaginary, and so were his robots." Monty laughed.

There was an acrid smell coming from somewhere, as if Nick were downwind of an oil fire. There was a snap-crackle-pop sound over it, too. White light, white heat. Still Nick was enthralled, like Merlin in solid rock. Again.

"Your war was real enough," Nick said. "I'm not convinced about the robots."

"Look inside your soul and tell me that my robots aren't real," Monty said. "Do you want to go back to your freedom, your autonomy, your bleak exhaustion? That is the life you had without me. Or do you want, *in me*, any pleasure your heart desires?"

"Let me think about it."

"When you partake of me, simulation is reality. When you are in me, to think about a thing makes it real."

"I'll pass," Nick said.

"Too late, my son. You have joined me. Look at her: is she real? And don't you want her?"

When had Pascale shown up? She certainly looked real. This time there was a different sweater draped over her shoulders, but other than that she looked pretty much exactly as she had looked when he first met her at the Saratoga Club.

"I told you maybe we meet at Fasnacht," she said, and melted away. Monty giggled.

If anything was going to break Nick's paralysis, it would be that laugh. As for the discovery that his own soul was nothing but the object of a silly game, a pawn in a contest between Monty Meekman, Bill Gates and Saddam Hussein—them, and their ilk; the Self-Actualized—along with their hired liars and bumsuckers, the *Forbes* readers—Nick could tolerate that. It was Monty's laugh he couldn't take.

But was Pascale really there in the laboratory with him and Monty, or wasn't she? Assume she wasn't there, and that Nick had seen her anyway. OK, why had he seen her? Was it because Monty was inserting thoughts into his mind? Label that hypothesis 'Explanation A..' Or was it because Nick was full of LSD and MK-Ultra from his brother's blood? Call that hypothesis 'Explanation B.' He could go on. . . Whatever the reason, having Pascale show up certainly wasn't a *good* development. Even so Nick felt, whether from the blood transfusion, or the music, or the tiredness, or the machines in his brain, or from this, or from that: a languor, a pleasing gooseflesh. Casey was cutting his hair, massaging his scalp, showing him a photo of the man with the pencil moustache, his cock erect to his belly button: 'Now darling, *that's* technology,' Casey said.

Get up, stand up, Bobby Marley told him. *Time to rearrange some poetry.* Nick couldn't move. But he was determined, for this one instant, to resist.

"You used the word 'Orson,' in nineteen seventy-eight," Nick said. "Did you know about the Gulf War twelve years in advance?"

"As simple as predicting an earthquake. Selling an oil war is easier than selling soap."

Somehow Nick knew that Monty was bluffing. He saw the man behind the curtain.

"I don't believe you," Nick said, feeling stronger. "*Overmind* never said anything about a desert war. This is tabloid Nostradamus, reading present fact into past vagueness, *post hoc, ergo prompter hic.*"

"Simple Markov chains," Monty said. "Oil wars no less than earthquakes."

"You remain full of shit," Nick said.

That's telling him, Nicky, he told himself. On the other hand, his strength seemed to have faded again, and Monty's logic was starting to make sense. He tried to will himself not to believe that Monty caused the Gulf War, but he could not. Yet still. . . could Monty *really* have single-handedly worked two worlds into such a frenzy that they would send their sons and daughters to die for his amusement in the Saudi sandbox? Jesus, have mercy on us.

"Jesus wrote in the sand too," Monty said.

"Monty Meekman, Jesus Christ: It's still not very much joke," Nick said.

The lingering trace of the smile left Monty's face, which seemed to be obscured by a haze.

"I am no joke."

Monty was right about that much, anyway. He was no joke.

Consider Nick: his past was wreckage and his future was black. Moreover, he was a bloody mess, and his arm hurt. All in all he could sure use a damn beer right about now, but there was no hope of even that. Why? Because he had dared to tell Monty to take his job and shove it. In the ceiling above Monty, a video camera turned. Big Brother, Overmind, Orson. . .

"I fear these things," Nick said. Let that be his epitaph.

"There's nothing to fear," Monty said. "You surely will not die."

This last phrase had a textbook ring: the very words of the serpent to Eve. Nick was too tired for any more of this metaphysical hoe-down, this spiritualists' ball.

"Overmind isn't spirituality, Nick; it's physics," Monty said. "Orson will become; it is becoming. All consciousness is mine. You can't stop it. I rule the roost."

Not yet you don't, Nick almost said. But his inner voice was quieting— no words: thoughts melting into sensation: dark-haired beautiful women of the Tied House; Pascale calling, 'sauvage.'

"Talk to any school child; *they* know," Monty said. "They demand *espresso* in every classroom, every kitchen, every car, every store. They will not be constrained. They know self-will for what it is: impediment to participation in the level above human."

"Children should play outside," Nick dreamed. *" Turn off the television, turn off the computer. Go play outside!"*

"There is no more inside and outside. I am everywhere. I am the new protocol. In the beginning was the Word. In the end is the Word. My protocol, my language, my Word. In me there is no lost bit."

"But to join you, their souls must die."

"Not die, knot into."

Of course, whatever. Nick no longer felt like wrestling angels. He was bored with cosmic battle. Monty wanted to rule the roost? Let him. Just wrap me in my burial shroud, white as snow. Lou Reed and Bob Marley kept sonically morphing into each other: very distracting. And what was the deal with that camera on the ceiling?

"How many children must die for your higher consciousness?" Nick wondered.

"You yourself kill thousands of your brain cells every time you drink—and you drink a lot."

"So that's the end point of human spiritual evolution? A perpetual dwelling in the drunken wonderfulness of Monty Meekman?"

"'For this communication is an influx of the Divine mind into our mind. In these communications the power to see is not separated from the will to do, but the insight proceeds from obedience, and the obedience proceeds from a joyful perception.'"

"Vannevar Bush?"

"Ralph Waldo Emerson. Now Nick, it is time for you to join us completely. One more inhalation of the Holy Spirit, the breath of your new life."

"Guess again," Nick said.

Plain dying was one thing. No problem: Nick was ready to die. But fuck cosmic union with this bozo. Nick stood up.

"You want death," Monty said. "I offer you life. In fact I choose life for you," Monty said, suddenly switching to the menacing tone Nick remembered from their talk atop Skyline Drive.

It was so damn hot. Who had turned up the thermostat?

Monty was five feet away. Surely Nick could surprise him.

"To surprise me you would have to outsmart me," Monty said. "And that's impossible. It's simply not in my model."

"Tell me when," a Voice said. "Speak but the word and my soul shall be healed."

But it was hard for Nick to understand those sweet words over the noise of the fire that was raging in the control room behind him.

"So you're one of the Meek, too?" Nick asked the Voice. "Have you come to inherit the earth?"

"You know what the Scripture says, Nick," said the Voice. " The Book of Matthew, chapter five, verse six."

"Blessed are the meek, for they shall inherit the earth," Monty said.

Nick looked to where the video camera was pointing.

"Yes," Nick said. "I do know the scripture."

He had learned it well, whole portions by heart, at the summer camp out beyond Marcy Point. But he could think about Matthew, Mark, Luke and John later. Right now he was meditating once again on the sacred words of Arnold Schwarzenegger. *If you want large muscles,* Arnold had written in the <u>Encyclopedia of Modern Bodybuilding</u>, *there simply is no substitute for heavy squats.* It was a miracle, Nick thought, as he felt his whole body tensing: the squats were finally going to pay off for something.

"Step into the tabernacle," Meekman said.

"You first," Nick said, and lunged. When he hit Monty it was like hitting a scarecrow; there was no resistance to slow them down as they both flew straight back, nearly to the empty chamber.

Nick picked Monty up— he was as light as a doll—and dragged him to the Snow White glass coffin. He kicked the lever on the side with his right foot and the door sprang open; then he threw Meekman in with his full force, causing the back of Monty's head to smack against the back wall. As the door slammed shut he heard the lock and vacuum seal automatically engaging.

"It's not possible," Monty said, in shock. "It's not in my model."

"You had an off-by one error," Nick panted. "Matthew, five-*five* says the meek shall inherit the earth. Five-*six* says, 'Blessed are they who hunger and thirst after righteousness, for they shall be filled."

Nick was unable to think what to do next. Alien soul syndrome. A whispering, whirring overhead. A shelf that held a row of canisters like the one Nick had in his pocket. The arm grabbed one. Feynman 9. *Feynman Nine.* The version with the mouse gene in it? There was a valve built into the chamber wall that clearly matched the nozzle on the canister in his hand; within seconds the arm had mated the nanomachine container to its dock. Whose arm? Nick's arm. No. Yes. Reset.

A Voice, familiar but distorted; transformed. Like Hendrix at Woodstock.

"If you're God," the Voice said, "then I must be Nietzsche. . ."

Almost immediately there was a short, barely perceptible pneumatic sound, *fvt*, like the sound of an air hose being applied to a tire. A colorlessness, an essence of pure whiteness, more invisible than nothingness itself, filled the chamber. It was the white soul of the universe.

". . . because I'm declaring you dead," the Voice said.

Monty was straining at the door, trying to find a handle where there was none. Nick's ears were ringing, and this time when he lost his balance he knew that he would not be able to get up. He slid against the glass wall like a drunk sliding down a lamppost.

Inside the chamber, Monty had fallen as well. He now half-stood in a contorted posture; there was not room for him to fall to a prone position. His left arm began to writhe as if it were a snake shedding its skin, and suddenly a bloody bone broke through the skin above his wrist. He was gasping for air. His face was only inches from Nick's, and Nick could see sharp little teeth growing right in the middle his forehead, where a second mouth was forming. Meekman's human lips twitched and Nick strained to listen, but Monty's voice was weak and muffled by the glass, and Nick could not make out the words.

Blood began to weep from Monty's left eye; a little splotch of brown hair appeared on his chin. He was breathing shallow breaths with his mouth open and his tongue protruding like a rodent's. Nick turned away, resting his back against the wall of the chamber. Nick barely had the strength to keep his eyes open. He felt the chamber vibrate once, then again. And then nothing, only silence.

And from the ceiling speaker: "I fear these things—a mine, a mind, mindless faces, snow, snowpeas, and at night, the drear, starry spaces."

"That was my first draft," Nick said. "Give me a break."

What do you say to that, Todd? Nick couldn't tell. He was too tired. This time I mean it.

He reached into his pocket for the canister, as the room spun around him. She took it.

'Come," she said. "You have to make it to the other chamber. I have medicine for you too."

Oh no, he thought. But he, Nick, wasn't going into any damn glass coffin. Let her kill him where he sat.

"I die here," he said.

"No, you don't. Hurry, I hear sirens." And then more urgently. "If you will live, you must transform yourself from the inside out. Will you do it?"

"Yes," Nick said. "I will."

∞VII∞

CONVERSION

Chapter 62

Nick Aubrey sat in the back pew of the tiny half-empty church, letting his mind wander as the coal-black priest in extravagantly ornamented vestments delivered his sermon—something about the Holy Spirit—in Wolof-inflected French. Nick's own embroidered gown was pulled up over his shoulders to allow a holy breeze to pass over his naked torso. Not that Nick had come to any great spiritual reckoning. He wasn't expecting the paraclete to invest him from the lively air; he was simply hot.

Last week Nick had received a letter from Judith—it was slid to him under the door— saying she would arrive today. If her schedule still held, her plane would have arrived at Dakar six hours ago, and by now she would be somewhere north of Thies, scrunched into a Peugeot *taxi brousse*. She would be arriving in St. Louis, N'Darr, in about an hour. Nick had a lot of questions for her when she got here.

He was curious, for example, about how he had gotten out of Switzerland and safely to Senegal. Never mind Switzerland: Nick was curious about how he had escaped from Monty's laboratory. There must have been policemen and firemen all over the place when Building Two burned down. How had Nick evaded them? Could his transformation have begun that quickly?

He remembered, sketchily, the showdown with Monty in the O.K. Corral. He *distinctly* remembered Monty's definitive answer to the "Are you a man or a mouse?" question. Nick thought— but he wasn't certain—that he remembered an angel coming to him as Monty morphed into King Rodent. After that, the next thing Nick remembered was waking up in his African apartment.

It was a simple room: A table, a chair, an armoire, a bed; tiled floor, cement walls. One day he was just there, poof! on the bed, under a white muslin mosquito tent. He awoke under the gaze of ebony masks—the spiritual inverse of his brother's wagis and harlequin—mounted on the wall above him. He got out of bed and went to the window. He pushed open the weathered green wooden shutters and stepped out onto a narrow balcony. The drumming, the smell of *chebbu jenn* cooked over charcoal, the snippets of spoken Wolof rising up to his nose and ears gave him know—even before he had seen anybody in the sandy street four storeys below— that he was in Senegal.

Some children noticed him looking down from the balcony, but now no-one called toubab, white man, the way they used to do twenty years ago. The people in the street just kept on about their business. Some sat in doorways; some walked by. Some were dressed in flowing robes, some wore skin-tight pants and shirts that threatened to pop five buttons at once. Color was everywhere. There were blue turbans, red fezzes and black Chicago Bulls baseball caps. There were Mercedes sedans and donkey carts. In one direction a man walked by with ten open cardboard trays of eggs stacked on his head, three dozen eggs to the tray. In the other direction two young girls ran playing tag, like Jesus and Judas, one balancing a quart of cooking oil on her head, the other balancing a bag of flour.

Gradually Nick became aware of another scent, another very faint sound: sea salt and waves breaking. He knew then that he was near the ocean; it could be no more than a few blocks away. A quick glance up and down the quasi-New Orleans road led him to suspect that he was in St. Louis. Then he raised his eyes up, looked over the rooftops and across the river to the 'Blocks' on the Corniche—the apartment buildings where he had spent Thanksgiving long ago—and he knew. Returning to his room he noticed a mirror hanging near a corner. He consulted it and, seeing himself, understood: he was home.

He soon discovered that he was also a prisoner.

Djennaba, the landlady's shy teen age daughter, brought him his meals. She explained to him in French—her mother had no frasay, and Nick's Wolof was too rusty—that he was convalescing, forbidden to leave this top floor, under orders of the black *Americaine*, until he was well. The sunlight would hurt les machines. Uncles and brothers on floors below were prepared to enforce this injunction. But Nick had no inclination to test their resolve: walking to the balcony and back was all the exertion he could stand. That had been weeks ago; this visit to the church today was his first venture beyond his room. He was feeling much stronger, but still weak: healing comes slowly, he figured, when your brain—not to mention your body and soul—is being mechanically reassembled from piece-parts.

Or was the emotional strain of being back here, of seeing her, this French-speaking Djenneba, that made Nick so weak? He could not see her without getting his mind racing about his own daughter. How old would she be? She would be about Djennaba's age. Where would she be? Here. Or gone. *Oh Bartlett*, Nick thought. *I failed you. I'm sorry.* Why hadn't he ever told Bartlett about the child? What cowardice had prevented him from telling his own dear wife, his heart's soul, of a child left behind, of a little girl's pleading call, "enna boubi," it's cold?

He had tried to erase the memory, the guilt, with drink and work. Could a human being possibly have been more stupid than Nick had been? No, Nick sadly concluded. It was not conceivable. If he ever had the chance, he solemnly swore in the direction of the crucified Christ hanging over the priest's head, he *would* tell Bartlett. The whole story. It would take weeks, perhaps, to tell her. But tell her, he would. Maybe then he would find the peace he had sought for more than a decade.

He knew, of course, that that peace would never be his. He was never again going to see Bartlett. His life now was one of permanent exile. It wasn't only that he was still wanted by the Utah Police for the murders of Peter Barlow and Ivan Marki. He was probably also wanted by the Basel police for the murders of Montaigne Meekman, Maceo Burr and Jake Carelli. The True Patriots of the Natural Law were certainly still on his trail. The military-industrial-pharmaceutical-entertainment complex, for that matter—yea, the Overmind itself—was probably scanning the infosphere at this very instant for any trace of his phosphorescent datatracks. *And* Nick had left an unpaid bill at the Newcastle Hotel. No, he could never go back. Africa, now and forever, was home.

"Go in peace, the Mass has ended," said the priest.

Nick left. From the church he walked around the Governor's Mansion through warm streets filled with sounds of wedding drums. Ten long minutes later he arrived at the little sidewalk café at the Hotel de la Poste, site of many a beer-filled afternoon long ago, and ordered a lemonade. He sat, looking at the bridge from the island to the corniche, thinking of nothing. His glass was still half-full when Judith arrived. She was beautiful.

"Let's go on a picnic," she said. "I've hired a canoe."

The city of N'Darr was build around an island in the Senegal river several miles upstream from where its waters entered the Atlantic. Between the island and the sea there was a narrow sandy barrier, a pristine ten-mile white sand beach.

"The peninsula?" Nick asked.

"No," she said. "*Up* river. Hurry while the tide is still going our way."

They walked to the quay; it was near. There Judith handed bags to a young man in a lateen-sailed dugout. She had prepared a modest feast: bread and jams, butter, cheeses, apples, mangoes, oranges, bananas, bottles of water and jars of fruit juice. They clambered in after the provisions and headed upstream. With the tide mounting they hardly needed the sail, but they set it anyway, for the effect. Judith sat in the back, trailing her hands in the water. Nick sat facing her, with his back resting against the mast and his bare feet stretched out before him, touching hers. The only sounds came from the water, wind, birds, and ever-present drums. Time passed. They passed through the Makanna Djamma wildlife preserve, they sailed past villages along the river further inland, up the river, home, into a vast, loving, heart of darkness.

The tide had slackened and the wind had died. The boat's movement on the river had slowed to a standstill; soon the tide would flow downstream. The boatman took up his paddle and began to stroke.

Judith selected an orange. As she peeled it, she began to speak.

"Rolf Steffen, the Vice-chairman and chief stockholder of Hoff-Zeigy Pharmaceuticals, died in an alpine crash of a small jet," she said. "His niece Pascale Pacheco inherited a majority share of Hoff-Zeigy shares. She was elected chairman and CEO by the board of Directors, and almost immediately she and Scott Beckwith announced plans to combine Digital MicroSystems and Hoff-Zeigy. The

Security and Exchanges Commission is expected to approve the merger this week. The Neuro Group was already acquired by Hoff-Zeigy in a separate transaction.

"Together, Digital MicroSystems and Hoff-Zeigy are working around the clock to decode and patent the human genome; they've already contracted with several prison corporations to use the Neuro Group's model to predict inmate behavior—in return for which the Labs have obtained rights to the brains of all prisoners killed by lethal injection—a major coup. Phenotypes for strong, beautiful and hyper-intelligent babies will be on the market by the end of the decade. The Department of the Army and Department of the Navy have signed contracts for the development off brain-implant weapons systems. Wall Street has bid Dijjy-Mike and Hoff-Zeigy stocks through the roof."

"I wonder if shareholders would care that their CEO is an ice-pick murderer?"

"Nick, be serious. With her track record? In the short time since she took over for her Uncle Rolf, Hoff-Zeigy's market capitalization has nearly doubled. Frankly, I think her having a few murders on her resume adds to her mystique, her sexy allure. *Forbes* and *Fortune* love her; the *Wall Street Journal* is arguing for her canonization. So no, I don't think anybody cares. But I wrote up the whole story anyway, of course," Judith said. "I wrote practically a whole dissertation that spelled out everything I had learned about Meekman, doctored bacteriophage, monster cells, nanomachines, Corporate Fellows, souls in thraldom."

"What happened to it?"

"I sent it to the Centers for Disease Control, to the Pentagon, to my Senators and to the New York Times."

"What was the response?"

"Nothing from the CDC. The *Times* and my Senators thanked me with polite notes."

"And the Defense Department?"

"There was no official response. But soon the Pentagon began 'admitting' that soldiers had been exposed to Sarin nerve gas at Kasimiyah, and also changed its story on the PB anthrax vacination. A version of my memorandum, rewritten to make it sound even more crazy—if that's possible—showed up on conspiracy news groups. Photos of me began to appear on the cover of *Weekly World News*, with headlines like *Top Scientist* says '*Monster Viruses' Cause Phantom Illness.*"

"You're famous," Nick said.

"I'm a laughing stock," she answered. "It's just as well I've retired from science."

"And what about my fellow experimental subjects who were befogged with me at the Biodigital Forum? Do they now resonate on *espresso's* frequency? Have they lost their souls?"

"That depends on how you interpret the evidence," she said. "Even though the Forum was only a few months ago already you can see evidence, if you're inclined to see it, that Monty triumphed, that he won his game of Rule the Roost—even if he didn't live to see it. In fact, I tend to wonder whether the infection hasn't spread much further. There's pretty strong evidence that Monty's Subedai manoeuver at the Biodigital Forum was so effective that that first crop of Overmind converts has already turn around and infected most, if not all, of the developed world. Europe, all of North and most of South America, vast regions of Asia. . . They may all be infected."

"What kind of evidence?"

"Television commercials are the most obvious signs. Everywhere you look the Overmind is celebrated; the Internet itself is worshiped as a Deity, and all other notions of God or spirituality are mocked and ridiculed. I don't think you can even say that people are responsible anymore; the technology itself produces, schedules, broadcasts the message, the Overmind enlists people in its cause instead of the other way around. School teachers do ads for software monopolies. School boards sell access rights to children's minds. Rock stars prostrate themselves before the new God. Some have become Corporate Fellows of Digital MicroSystems; others work for Microsoft or Apple or any of a million Dijjy-Mike wannabes. Corporations and governments trample on privacy in ways that once would have sparked riots, sparked revolutions. In America, few people care. Some anachronistic dreamers, like me, try to make the case for going slowly. We say that our moral, ethical, legal, cultural systems are unprepared, not up to the assault. We suggest taking the time to think through our options, taking care that we don't destroy what may be our last chance to remain human. It's a losing cause. America—and the rest of the world under American cultural hegemony—has truly has come to love Big Brother. To question the wisdom of surrendering our autonomy to the Telescreen is literally enough to get you declared insane and locked up for life without a due process, without a trial. You can get away with just about anything in America, *except* challenging the hegemony of technology. Do that, and they'll lock you up and throw away the key."

"But are all these developments proof of contagion by nanomachines, or are they just signs of the times?"

"I don't know," Judith said. "But you are living proof that Pavel and Dieter's nanomachines do, in fact, work."

"There's no denying that," Nick said. "You administered them to me in Monty's lab."

"No," she said. "Somebody else, or some*thing* else, did that for you. By the time I found you the transformation was already underway—but yes, to answer your question, Bartlett and I did put the additional information necessary for your cure into the genome that we sent to Casey. We had to decide for you. There was no way that we could consult you."

"You made the right choice," Nick said.

"I administered the machines to myself, then took you by taxi to a hotel room—you looked like a Fasnacht drunk. Your recovery took much longer than— well, it took a long time—probably because you had so much further to go. Only one day after leaving Hoff-Zeigy I hired a jet to fly us to Dakar, and an ambulance from Dakar to here. And that's the end of my cloak-and-dagger days. I'm retired."

"*You hired a jet?*"

"I'll explain later."

"If you're retired, am I to understand that there's no more Association for Responsible Biotechnology?"

"A guy named Lazarus Gilmore has taken over as executive director. He's this fellow with a ponytail and a limp from the Basel Dijjy-Mike labs who recently had a life-changing experience. He's one of the few people on earth with the know-how to create an antidote program. I'm a client. Casey too."

"I'm glad I decided not to shoot his other toe off."

Nick looked at his bare feet touching Judith's.

"So, there it is: proof that nanotechnology works. Pavel and Dieter were an extraordinary team."

"Unknown giants. Fausts," she said.

"I guess it was early versions of the machines, prototypes, that Pavel used to change himself from black to white?"

"No, I don't see how that's possible," Judith said. "No early prototype had remotely enough capability to do that. I don't know how Pavel changed his pigmentation—changed himself— from black to white, or why. Perhaps it was surgery, or illness, or some kind of bleach that so dramatically changed his appearance. But we'll never know; he remains a cipher. I don't expect to ever learn where he came from—who his parents were, or how he came to be Monty's special altar boy. A black kid with a Caucasian name—the name Pavel comes from the Caucasus region, you know—who rejected soul, embraced a heartless science. . . I don't know if he chose the name Isaacs after meeting Abraham, of if that was another coincidence. Sometimes I wonder if Pavel was Monty's literal creation, not just his figurative one. What motivated Pavel Isaacs? Maybe science had inflamed his passion, as it once inflamed mine. Maybe he set out to win a Nobel Prize and became corrupted along the way. Or maybe he was already corrupt by the time I met him. Maybe it was just his fate. Maybe he was doomed from the day he was born."

"Speaking of life-changing experience, what news of Casey?"

"State's evidence. She's in Sao Paulo, helping Interpol track Nick Aubrey."

"Why Sao Paulo?"

"I guess because she's always wanted to go Brazil. You can read all about her adventures on the True Patriots' home page."

"She's leading *them* on a wild goose chase too?"

"The wildest. She cracked their system some time ago, Nick. So now we know why Barlow was so terrified of you on that red-eye flight. Do you remember Kurt Alder, the laboratory technician who was killed in Basel?"

"What, was he a True Patriot?"

"It turns out that he was. The Patriots already had their eye on your brother, and then they discovered that you worked with Monty. Barlow jumped to the wrong conclusion."

Judith smiled and continued, "Casey has teamed up with 'Frightened@TIAC.net' the guy who claims he saw you murder Barlow. Together they have confirmed several sightings of you consorting with the moneyed German community of Brazil, the Nazi next generation."

The only sad part of the story was that the few people who could appreciate the irony in Casey's turned-down smile would never see that smile again.

"I hope some day she'll get over Todd."

"Don't worry about her. She's having fun. When she's not actively derailing the manhunt for you she's off exploring the sensual extremes of Rio. You can read about her adventures on other newsgroups."

"And what of Judith Knight?" Nick asked. "What adventures lie in store for her?"

"Judith Knight has not been seen for a while. Sister Marie Grace, a young woman who once resembled Judith, has taken her first vows in a contemplative order. She is traveling in Africa now, on personal business, before taking her final vows and completely retreating from the World to become a bride of Christ."

He was afraid to ask the next question, but he had to.

"Any news of Bartlett?" he said.

"Look at me," she said.

He looked up an into her eyes. The water lapped behind her.

"Bartlett is pregnant," she said. "With your brother's child."

Tears flooded Nick's eyes.

"Nick," Judith said. "Paul's body lay in the Basel morgue until last week, when I made arrangements. Your brother loved you; he gave his life for you. I tried to dissuade him from returning to Basel. But he knew that trouble lay in store for you. He didn't know what trouble, exactly—none of us could have foreseen it. But he knew you would need money, and he knew where to get it: from Pascale Pacheco. She was the 'Angel' that Monty used to transfer money secretly and illegally, from Digital MicroSystems to Hoff-Zeigy. When Paul finally unraveled all the dummy corporations that Monty and Pascale had used to finance the NanoSection he redirected the funds to Swiss bank accounts established in your name. That was the real reason Paul went back to Basel. He was murdered there, but not before taking care of you. He loved you; you must try to forgive him Nick. You must forgive him and Bartlett their trespass."

"What trespass?"

Judith smiled, but she didn't seem surprised by his answer. Something else surprised both of them, however: the wind had picked up, cresting little wavelets on the river's surface, and a gust nearly capsized them.

"I am a trustee of your account, by they way, Nick, and I have spent some of your fortune."

"For my. . . convalescent care. For my transformation into what I am."

"Yes. And for your farm."

Not an answer he had expected.

"My farm? We sold the place in Oneonta years ago."

"Not Oneonta. Here. I bribed some people, Nick. Don't feel guilty, your circumstances are unique. You now have legal claim to two acres in this wildlife area, this national park. Your house is nearly complete: you can see it there, by those neem trees."

Nick look where she was pointing. Not far from the edge of the river, several workmen were lowering a skylight into the roof of an adobe house. It was no more than a double-wide trailer made out of mud block, but by the standards of villages along the Senegal river, it was quite grand.

"Skylights," Judith said. "You'll be able to see the stars at night."

"Ah."

"As well as the three hundred satellites that Microsoft will be launching for their network, and the four hundred that Dijjy-mike have announced for theirs."

"Surveillance satellites?"

"They'll never admit it."

"How long before they find me, do you suppose?"

"They may never. I expect they won't waste their batteries on Africa. Or maybe they will, who knows? Their plans will never be divulged; no government is strong enough to make them even answer a question. But even if you escape them, Nick, your idyll here is likely to be short-lived. Famine, drought, pestilence. . . they're all just over the horizon."

"I saw them all when I was here with OXFAM."

"That was a trickle. I'm talking about a flood. Your house is stocked with a year's food, and you have millions of dollars in a Swiss account. But if it goes to hell around here, and it may, there will be no protection for you."

"In the meantime I'll enjoy myself," Nick said. "I always liked it here."

"Your house of course has no electricity."

"I don't want any."

"You have gravity-fed running water from your own well. There's some marsh, some dunes, an irrigated plot for rice and wheat. There's an orchard, too. This used to be a mini agricultural experiment station."

"I remember," Nick said, with a numbing, overwhelming sensation of nostalgia. "A French guy from Catholic Relief Services lived here."

"Yes," she said. "You own his Peugeot pickup truck; it's been locked away for fifteen years. From your house to the paved road is four kilometers, and from there to N'Darr is only twenty minutes."

"They must have been working very fast," Nick said, trying, for some vestigial macho reason, to keep his emotions under control. He could see that improvements to the old experiment station had been made everywhere, and he wanted to cry, but couldn't.

"There is a very competent foreman in charge, even if she doesn't know the language."

"You," Nick said, as his heart swelled with gratitude.

"No. Not me. There she is, look. Do you recognize her?"

Bartlett was wearing a long African indigo dress, and her hair was braided close to her head, but yes, he recognized her.

"She's been to see Lazarus Gilmore too," Nick said, amazed. "She's taken a nanomachine regime, just like me."

"She wanted to be with you. There was no other way."

The canoe nestled the shore, and as Nick and Judith stepped out the breezed stiffened, and a cloud of sand assaulted their eyes. The wind had been getting worse for some while, and Nick as Nick looked towards the horizon he saw a large dust devil nearing. It might pass, or it might turn into a monster sandstorm.

"Hello Nicholas," Bartlett said. "Have you come to see the wildlife?"

"I've read that the birds are very beautiful here," he said.

"Listen to their songs. Did you ever hear anything so sweet?"

The birdsongs did sound sweet, but it was getting harder to hear them over the wind.

He glanced around the farm. "You're hired," he said, and kissed his wife.

"Not a chance," she said. "*You* work for *me*. You're my lifeguard. And you're on duty."

"And you, Matilda, are my Black Bart."

Indeed he noticed, as her arms reached out to embrace him amid the swirling sand, that her smooth skin was nearly as black as his own.

Acknowledgments

Grace, Jakob and Jainaba kept me alive. Betty kept them alive. Keith Thompson's original Bonehead Computer Museum (contents of which are in a box in my storage bus) provided the seed. Peter and Grace Sundman lent me an awful lot of money. All my other brothers and sisters (and spouses) and parents too. And Jo and Gene Burton. Joe Regal taught me how to write. (This took more than four years.) Certain friends & the grace of God helped keep me sober. Tim O'Reilly and Andy Oram cut me a lot of slack. Carol Baroudi and John Levine cut me a lot of slack. SGT. Mark Lange USA(ret), forgive me if I've misspelled that last name, I can't find my notes, shared with me his experiences in Desert Shield and Storm. This is really embarrassing, Mark's wife, I can't find my notes, a captain in the US Army, taught me a lot about how captured enemy technology is analyzed. Skod was good for target practice, and for explaining about steppers. Tom Athanasiou, you should read his book Divided Planet, cut me a lot of slack. The PR officer (lost notes) at Salt Lake City Airport police was very helpful and gracious. The guys at the State Police Barracks on Martha's Vineyard explained extradition and governor's warrants. Thanks to Chris Fried, Pam Carelli, Sue and Dave Roy for acts of family-saving generosity. Glynis Asu of the Hamilton College Library Staff did yeoman research, always on no notice. Joan Fitzgibbon gave me a tour of the labs at Nexagen. Jim Young lent me money. Brudda Paulie led the cheering section. If I've forgotten you let met know, I'll revise this at next printing. Bob Dixon stuck his neck out for me, and more than once. I love you, Bob.